AYL

BOMBERS
FIRST AND LAST

BOMBERS
FIRST AND LAST
GORDON THORBURN

ROBSON

First published in the United Kingdom in 2006 by
Robson Books
151 Freston Road
London
W10 6TH

An imprint of Anova Books Company Ltd

Front cover image: F/O Albert Manning and crew, home after Stettin, 5 January 1944, in W4964 WS/J, her 41st Op. From left: navigator F/O James Hearn, Manning, rear gunner F/Sgt 'Pinky' Hayler, mid-upper gunner Sgt John Zammit, flight engineer Sgt Bill Burkitt, w/op F/Lt A G Newbound standing in for F/Sgt G T M Caines. Just visible behind Manning is Canadian bomb aimer F/Sgt Peter Warywoda. The skipper and most of this crew, near the end of their tour, fell at Frankfurt on 22 March 1944.

Image courtesy of RAF Marham 9 Squadron Museum.

ISBN 1 86105 946 9

A CIP catalogue record for this book is available from the British Library.

10 9 8 7 6 5 4 3 2 1

Typeset by SX Composing DTP, Rayleigh, Essex.
Printed and bound by Creative Print & Design, Ebbw Vale, Wales.

Contents

Dedication

To the memory of my friend, the late Squadron Leader Dougie Melrose DFC and Bar.

Acknowledgements

These must, above all, go to those Number 9 Squadron personnel who fought World War Two and who allowed the author into their homes to record their memories or, where circumstances did not permit, corresponded freely and lengthily, and all for the squadron's sake.

Aircrew

W Frank Belben DFM, Jim Brookbank, Ken Chamberlain DFC, Rupert Cooling, Ken Dagnall DFM, Russell Gradwell, Sam Hall, Ray Harris DFC, Harry J Irons DFC, B A 'Jimmy' James, Bob Lasham DFC and Bar, Alan G D Mackay, George McRiner DFC, Dennis Nolan, H F C 'Jim' Parsons DFC, Vincent Peace, Jim Pinning, Norman F Wells, Graham T Welsh, Harry 'Tug' Wilson, Bob Woolf.

Groundcrew

Mrs P Brimson (Pip Beck), Mrs Aileen Glossop (Walker), Mrs Nancy Harrison (Bower), John H 'Mick' Maguire MBE, Ken J McClure.

The author has been given unstinting help also by enthusiasts, historians and others who share the belief that we, alive today, should praise, admire and never forget.

A particular and exceptional thank you is to Jim Shortland, whose generosity made much of the research possible and whose passion for the cause was infectious, and all the more remarkable considering he is a 617 Squadron man. Special thanks also to John Larder, Terry Linton, and to Mrs Doreen Melrose and Jim Melrose.

Thanks likewise to Sq/Ldr Dick James and F/O Tom Partrick of today's No. 9 Squadron at RAF Marham, Denise Ball, Bob Baxter, Eric Brothe, Anthony Bunker, David Fell, Wally Fydenchuk, Mark Haycock, Peter Johnson, Errol Martyn, Rod Mackenzie, Ross McNeill, Heinz Orlowski (*Luftwaffe*), Sarah Quinn (CWGC), Steve Smith, John Sugg, Mike Varley, Kevin Walford.

Apologies to anyone mistakenly left out.

Secret 9 Squadron Combat Report

Date: 24 March 1944 *Time:* 00.47 *Height:* 24,000 ft *Target:* Berlin
Lancaster: LL845 WS/L *Captain:* Flight Sergeant W R Horne

On leaving the target the Navigator was using broadcast winds that took the aircraft 60–70 miles off track, which eventually brought our aircraft into the Ruhr. Ten minutes previous to striking the Ruhr the Rear Gunner had gone unconscious due to lack of oxygen, cause unknown. The rear turret was unserviceable also, possibly due to frozen hydraulics.

On entering the Ruhr, a master beam picked us up and the aircraft was immediately coned by approx. 30 searchlights and fired on by very accurate heavy flak for 40 minutes, which holed the starboard mainplane, bomb aimer's position, pilot's windscreen, port mainplane, bomb doors and port fin. During all this period the Pilot was wounded and blind, the Bomb Aimer had flak in his leg and the Rear Gunner was unconscious on the rest bed. Through alteration of course and height and diving turns, our aircraft escaped the searchlights and flak.

The Mid Upper Gunner and Engineer were searching and our aircraft was almost at once attacked from the port beam at a range of approx. 200 yards by an unidentified enemy aircraft, which fired a two- or three-second burst and broke away starboard quarter down, where we lost him. The burst damaged the MU perspex. MU Gunner did not see him on account of his searching the starboard beam. RG Sergeant Parkes fired 0 rounds. MU Sergeant Morton fired 300 rounds.

On that night of 24 March 1944 more than eight hundred RAF bomber crews attacked Berlin. Of the 577 crews in Lancasters, 44 were shot down. No. 9 Squadron had lost eleven Lancasters on previous Berlin raids but all came home from this one, even LL845, a lucky Lanc called Lonesome Lola. F/Sgt Horne and crew were on their third trip together; they were back on Ops two weeks later.

Shooting the line

This elderly expression derived from a habit of certain actors who over-glorified their lines to make themselves more noticeable; hence anyone exaggerating or boasting was shooting a line. By extension, a 'line' became any small utterance requiring extra effort in belief. In the officers' mess at No. 9 Squadron there was an official hardback Line Book, in which such utterances were recorded. Extracts from the book are reproduced thus:

> 'No, I am not keeping a diary
> but I save the press cuttings of my flights'
> P/O Arnold

1

FROM BOX KITE TO WAR MACHINE, TO WAR

Standing by in case the September 1938 meeting between Hitler and Prime Minister Chamberlain failed to bring peace in our time, the crews of No. 9 Squadron RAF Bomber Command were briefed to attack targets in the Ruhr, knowing their aircraft could not fly far enough to get back. They were issued with passports, money and maps and told they would have to bale out over Holland.

Their aircraft was the Handley Page Heyford, a weird, long-nosed, sad-looking creature, a cumbersome biplane with open cockpit and massive fixed undercarriage that could do 140mph, provided it wasn't carrying any bombs. Things were about to change, due to the ideas of a design engineer called Barnes Wallis who worked for Vickers. He came up with the Wellington. It doubled the Heyford's performance being a modern, monoplane aircraft with great manoeuvrability; it was smaller, cheaper but equally as capable as the American B17 Flying Fortress, and it had a quality that made it uniquely suitable for a dangerous job. Its geodetic frame, a rigid aluminium network covered in fabric, could take enormous punishment and still stay in the air.

31 January 1939, Operations Record Book (ORB): 'Squadron took possession of its first Wellington aircraft'. A crew was six, seven or eight: pilot, second pilot, observer (combined navigator and bomb aimer) and two wireless-op/air-gunners with an optional extra gunner and one or two homing pigeons. The birds were the observer's responsibility and were to be released with positional details, should the aircraft crash in enemy territory.

War was coming. 6 March, ORB: '187 starlings were killed by Wing Commander H P Lloyd MC, DFC (CO of No. 9 Squadron) while taking off from Stradishall aerodrome. 178 were counted on the aerodrome itself and nine were removed from the engines on landing at Mildenhall.'

9 July: 9 Squadron took part in a Sunday flying display in Brussels, along with *Luftwaffe* pilots in trainer aircraft, Belgians in Bristol Gladiator biplanes and French in a trainer called the Parasol. No. 9 Squadron flew their Wellingtons in formation and a Hurricane fighter did a few tricks. The subsequent guest night at a nearby château was . . .

1

. . . aided by the presence of a great deal of beauty in the form of the girlfriends of Belgian officers. It has been rumoured that English officers, unable to speak a word of French at 20.00 hours were, by the small hours, conversing fluently in that language.

Universally known as 'The Wimpy', the Wellington was named after J Wellington Wimpy, the character in the 'Popeye' cartoons, who continuously ate hamburgers and said, 'I'll gladly pay you Tuesday'.

15 July: the squadron moved from Stradishall (between Bury St Edmunds and Haverhill) to Honington, another Suffolk grass airfield, off the Ixworth/Thetford road and very slightly nearer Germany.

1 September: 'Squadron mobilisation ordered. Aircraft despatched to dispersal points.' On this day, not counting Bristol Blenheim and Fairey Battle light bombers, Bomber Command had about one hundred and sixty serviceable aircraft with crews ready to operate from UK bases while the *Luftwaffe* was attacking Poland with nine hundred. No. 9 Squadron could put ten Wellingtons in the air, as could five other squadrons. The rest had the Whitley and the Hampden – better than the Heyford, but not much.

President Roosevelt had made it clear he would help Britain and France keep the peace against Germany and Italy. With home anti-war opinion to cope with, he told the RAF and the *Luftwaffe*: 'No civilian targets'. Obviously the British would respect this for perfectly practical, American-pleasing reasons, and the Germans too. They didn't want to tilt the apple cart any further towards the enemy. So, where were the RAF's targets with no possibility of civilian casualties? Only the German Navy seemed a legitimate aiming point but to have a good chance of finding a warship and hitting it, a raid would have to be in daylight. It would also need to be without fighter escorts because the RAF did not have fighters capable of staying in the air long enough.

On the morning of Sunday, 3 September at 11 a.m. on the BBC, war was publicly declared by Prime Minister Chamberlain. An hour later an attempt was made to carry the fight to the enemy by the only means possible. The offensive against the Third Reich began with a single Bristol Blenheim of 139 Squadron, which was sent Wilhelmshaven way to reconnoitre for ship movements. The crew saw a large contingent of the German Navy steaming north towards Heligoland and sent back a wireless message, but, because of a fault in the set, this was not understood at home. By the time the Blenheim landed and the message could be given without the aid of technology, it was mid-afternoon. Nevertheless, eighteen Hampdens of 49, 83 and 144 Squadrons set off to bomb the ships.

It was all too late and some were made even later by confusion over the type of bomb to use. Before they were anywhere near, darkness fell and the chance to attack was gone and so they turned for home. Instead of being made to tremble in their boots, a few of the enemy had seen or heard one small aircraft on a scouting mission.

On that night of 3 September, with the war only a few hours old, the strength of 58 Squadron, ten Whitleys at Linton-on-Ouse, was briefed to head for Bremen, or they could choose Hamburg or any one of a handful of industrial cities in the Ruhr. Later in the war, hundreds of aircraft would arrive together at one target and reduce it to nothing in half an hour of precise attack. For now the Air Marshals preferred not to be too overbearing in the matter of night target selection.

With no navigation equipment beyond a map and a compass, the Whitleys found their own routes to somewhere near, or not so near, where they were supposed to be and in their own time hit the enemy in several different places. They didn't do much damage; all they dropped were bundles of leaflets. To complete the sorry picture three homeward bound pilots had to crash-land in France; one, narrowly missing the River Marne, wrote his kite off in a cabbage field.

Day Two, World War Two, 4 September 1939 was another day of firsts, this time replacing embarrassment with shock, fear, blood and death. Another failed wireless message from a morning recce meant that, appointed to represent the airborne might of Great Britain, 9 Squadron could not take off for Germany in their six of the Wellington Mark I until the afternoon. With them were eight other Wellingtons and fifteen Blenheims from several squadrons.

Far more potent than the Blenheims, the Wellingtons approached Brunsbüttel, a small harbour town of Schleswig-Holstein near the Danish border with a population of around seven thousand. The population was safe but this was an important naval base on the Elbe estuary, the western terminus of the Kiel Canal, sixty miles downstream from Hamburg. With fourteen aircraft such a raid seems a small thing, minuscule compared to the massive raids that were to come later. To the crews in those Wellingtons, as in the Blenheims, it was extremely serious business.

> 'We can't bomb Wilhelmshaven.
> It's a prohibited area'
> Sq/Ldr Lamb

For 9 Squadron, L4268 piloted by Flight Sergeant Ian Borley and L4275 piloted by F/Sgt John Turner were the wingmen in Squadron Leader Lamb's section of three. Flight Lieutenant Grant led the other section with another Turner, Flying Officer Bob Turner beside him as second pilot. Sgt Tom Purdy and Sgt Charles Bowen were Grant's wingmen. These were mostly Heyford graduates, pilots brought up on biplanes and the old ways. They were married men, RAF regulars. Now they were going to a modern war, on their first Operation in their country's only modern bomber.

The ORB shows Grant's section taking off at 15.40. He reported:

The bombs were dropped at 18.12 hrs at a Battleship* which was at a point about seven eighths of a mile due south of the entrance to Kiel. Height 6,000 feet. Immediately after the release we were forced to pull up into the cloud owing to the very high concentration of anti-aircraft fire and turned for home without waiting to see the results. The shore batteries had three or four guns that were firing with far less accuracy than the ships. Six or eight cruisers were firing at us, as well as the battleship. We were hit three times.
*Gneisenau and Scharnhorst were both there.

Lamb's section was up later, at 16.05. By the time they arrived at Brunsbüttel the local *Staffel* (Squadron) of Messerschmitt 109s had scrambled and was stooging about, waiting. Nine very fast, very agile, heavily armed German fighters flew at Lamb's men and the ensuing display of flying to the death must have struck awe into everyone watching. Lamb's account is the usual RAF officer understatement:

I was ordered to carry out a bombing raid on warships inside Brunsbüttel Harbour. Towards the end of a fighter attack carried out by nine German fighters at approx. 18.35 I jettisoned my three bombs 'live and in stick' at 400 feet on the south side of the harbour. At the moment of bombing I felt sure there was no shipping in the vicinity but, having pressed the bomb release, I saw a merchant ship, approx. 7,000 tons (which was hit and set on fire by the bombs). I climbed rapidly, still being attacked by fighters, and succeeded in reaching cloud cover. It was necessary for the safety of my crew that these bombs were jettisoned as the decreased load enabled the machine to successfully evade the attack.

The squadron leader, while mindful of instructions about not wasting bombs and not hitting civilians, even maritime ones, failed to mention that his second pilot, F/O Torkington-Leech, with all hands to the guns, shot down one of the fighters.

The machines of Lamb's two wingmen, Sgt Borley and F/Sgt Turner, with or without decreased load, did not successfully evade the attack. In economical style the ORB reports the deaths of eleven airmen: 'Nos. 2 and 3 of No. 1 Section did not return to base. First Squadron to draw blood.'

True, 9 Squadron was the first RAF unit to score against the Germans in World War Two, claiming an Me109 down and a ship on fire, but the day was an emphatic home win. Of the fifteen Blenheims, five had got lost and given up. Five of 110 Squadron attacked the *Admiral Scheer* and, with the advantage of surprise, lost only one to flak (anti-aircraft artillery, abbreviated from *Fliegerabwehrkanonen* – flyer defence gun) and hit the ship with several bombs, all of which were duds. The five Blenheims of 107 Squadron ran right into a barrage of fully alerted gunnery and lost four. So the score was one German pilot and a fighter against five Blenheims, two Wellingtons; twenty-six aircrew dead and two prisoners. No bodies were found from Borley's aircraft and from the other Wellington only three were recovered by the Germans and buried.

Back home, Sq/Ldr Lamb had the normal service operational debrief, called the interrogation, followed by a non-standard one at Buckingham Palace, where he was commanded to appear so he could tell the story of the first air battle of the war to King George VI. While he was doing that, some more of his 9 Squadron colleagues were dying, this time flying into trees.

ORB: During air firing practice at Berners Heath an accident occurred to aircraft L4320. The following lost their lives: Pilot Officer Rosofsky, P/O Clifford-Jones, Aircraftman First Class McGreery, AC1 Purdie.

It was not thought appropriate to mention the death also of Aircraftman Second Class Hilsdon because he was on secondment from 215 Squadron and it was McGreevy, not McGreery. Either way, while most Wellingtons in the RAF had yet to go on an Op, 9 Squadron was showing the way by losing the first three of the war.

> 'If I am given a medal
> I will return it to the nation
> to be melted down for shells'
> F/O Turner

Air firing and bombing practice were not pursued as assiduously as they might have been during this period of the phoney war but they continued to be dangerous. In the scramble to find and train aircrew, more were lost in accidents than on Ops. Sq/Ldr Lamb, New Zealander, regal interviewee and the first notable flyer in these hostilities, was in a formation-practice accident on 30 October when his Wellington collided with Flying Officer Chandler's. Everyone was killed, including the first man to shoot down a German aircraft in World War Two, the South African F/O Peter Torkington-Leech, and two more of Lamb's crew on that Brunsbüttel day,

Sgt Cyril Bryant and LAC Stanley Hawkins. All the families were offered funerals with full Royal Air Force honours at Honington Church. Some said yes, some said no.

While two other Squadrons had crashed a Wellington, each with only one aircrew death, 9 Squadron had now lost five with 24 dead. Ops restarted on 9 November with armed reconnaissances, sweep searches for hostile ships in the North Sea. On the first of these six Wellingtons saw only some fishing vessels off Yarmouth. From this time until the ban was lifted against bombing enemy territory, sweeps would go on and on, each one usually about five hours, searching the grey ocean and almost always finding nothing. Every Wellington carried 250 or 500lb bombs but rarely dropped any.

Three aircraft (F/Lt Grant, Sgt Purdy, Sgt Ramshaw) co-ordinated with 37 Squadron on a sweep of the North Sea from the east coast to Terschelling Island thence along the Dutch coast. Apart from one neutral merchantman, no shipping was sighted and the sweep was carried out without opposition.

Everyone knew that eventually German territory would be attacked and the bombers would be allowed to do the job for which they were designed. Realisation had also come about, well after the war had begun, that such a job had never been done and no one knew quite how to do it. Bomber aircraft had been designed and built, crews had learned to fly them, and the assumption was that they would go out there and, well, bomb.

The RAF had never sent bombers in numbers to attack, say, an armaments factory in a well-defended, populated area, so they sent 9 Squadron to lead a formation on a dummy run to Rhyl, on 28 November 1939. Six Wellingtons took off at 08.45, kept a rendezvous over Upper Heyford with three more 3 Group squadrons, Nos. 37, 38 and 115 with six Wellingtons apiece, and 'formed a Wing in five minutes'. They were to fly over the Welsh hills and make a mock daylight attack on a target of opportunity while mock defences fired blanks at them. Almost four months into the war the idea was to see if it was practicable to mount what was then imagined to be an air raid.

The exercise was most useful and many points of instructional value were learned.
1. A force of 24 aircraft could put in a co-ordinated attack. First squadron to attack: 9 Squadron. Time over target 12.00 hours. Last squadron to attack: 115 Squadron. Time over target 12.15 hours. This time could be reduced under more favourable weather conditions.

In late 1939, the powers that ruled the air force asked 9 Squadron to prove that two dozen Wellingtons could attack a target in daylight in a quarter of an hour. A year later, four hours would be allowed for one hundred aircraft. On a night in August 1943, three targets at Peenemünde would be attacked by three waves of two hundred bombers, each wave bombing in ten minutes.

2. Rendezvous of squadrons can be carried out successfully provided care is taken in co-ordination prior to exercise and if squadrons are not rushed.

3. Get away. It will appear at the moment that we shall have to accept the fact that a Wing is unable to form up again quickly after an attack. Flights of six will have to keep together for support after the attack. On completion of attack, No. 9 Squadron turned quickly off target and when clear of A-A fire reduced to 140mph and continued for 30 minutes at that speed but still remaining squadrons did not close up.

4. The most difficult aspect of the whole exercise under trying weather conditions was the selecting of a target and passing the order to attack it to the Wing. Unless good weather conditions prevail, one is on top of the target before any definite action can be taken so the passing of an order selecting the target becomes a nearly impossible task.

A choice had to be made between bombing on clear, sunny days only, or selecting the target beforehand.

5. It is considered essential that good field or sea glasses should be provided for this type of commitment. No. 37 flew in pairs and the other squadrons in 'Vic'. It is considered that one type of formation should be adopted.

This was the state of the art of bombing in Britain at the end of 1939. Men of undoubted skill and limitless courage, but no training or direction from above, would fly in pairs or a 'V' and look for their targets with binoculars.

'The force on the pull-out was so great that
all the zip fasteners on my flying suit were undone by it'
P/O Bamford (in dive-bombing practice)

18 December: another armed reconnaissance, except this one would be different. This one would turn into the war's first decisive air action. At around 09.00, nine Wellingtons of 9 Squadron took off, their sea sweep

with 250lb bombs to include photographing the docks at Wilhelmshaven where lay the battlecruisers *Scharnhorst* and *Gneisenau* and many other warships. The nine of 9 were joined over Kings Lynn by six of 37 Squadron and nine of 149 Squadron. Until they were about ten miles from the German coast they flew in cloud and therefore in secret, it being universally understood that only the British had radar for air defence.

German navy operators, watching on their three recently delivered *Freya* radar sets had been near incredulous when, from about seventy miles away, their newfangled machines showed them a tight formation of aircraft. The local *Luftwaffe* had been less believing still, partly because it was Navy gen and partly because they could see only a cloudless sky. The Tommies would not come to Germany on such a beautiful day.

The Tommies in question broke out of their cloud into a fine winter afternoon. Many thousands of feet below in the Heligoland Bight, the Wellington crews saw Bremerhaven and a group of enemy destroyers. They also saw a lot of anti-aircraft fire, from the ground and the navy vessels, but it didn't interfere unduly and they were able to finish their triangular photographic sweep of the estuary and Wilhelmshaven. The Germans wondered why no bombs had fallen. The RAF thought, jolly good, duty carried out.

By now, the fighters were in the air. The *Freya* operators could see the bombers had divided into two groups, one staying along the Frisian coast, the other heading out to sea. With *Freya*, interception was easy. The fighters, Me109s and 110s, included those of *10 Staffel* of *Jagdgeschwader* (fighter group) *26* led by *Staffelkapitän* Macki Steinhoff, who would become a famous ace in the Battle of Britain. Other future top scorers there that day were Gordon Gollob, who would retire from the air with one hundred and fifty claimed kills, and Helmut Lent, destined to be one of the two most successful German nightfighter pilots.

In this, the biggest air battle any of the participants had yet seen or heard about, the Germans faced an enemy who had bravery, instincts and common sense but no training in how to fight a smaller, faster, better-armed and more acrobatic foe. The 110s had 20mm cannon effective at six hundred yards, beyond the range of the Wellington's machine guns. The fighter pilots knew that if they dived in from the side those machine guns couldn't get to them anyway.

The Wellington pilots had no real tactic other than hiding in the clouds, but the clouds had gone. As recommended after the Rhyl exercise, the aircraft kept together for support but four out of 9 Squadron's nine were shot down there and then, with all hands killed and only two bodies ever found. Of the 24 Wellingtons that went on the Operation, twelve were lost altogether, including five out of 37 Squadron's six, and 9 Squadron's total soon reached five as well.

In Sergeant Jack Ramshaw's crew was wireless operator/air gunner LAC Walter Lilley, a lad of 21 from Kippax in Yorkshire. The crew later claimed that in a truly outstanding feat of gunnery Walter Lilley shot down two Messerschmitt Me110s before being hit himself. With all claims added up later, six 110s and six 109s were reported downed. In fact, nine 110s were hit of which two were force-landed, and two 109s were destroyed and one force-landed. The Germans claimed 34 Wellingtons, later reduced to 27. Considering only 24 went out, that was very good shooting, but this was the excitement and adrenaline of the first big showdown of the air war. Neither side had been involved in anything like it.

Also in Ramshaw's Wimpy was AC1 Charlie Driver, an 18-year-old fitter/rigger from the Squadron's ground crew, who now found himself acting as temporary substitute air gunner. He was in the front turret and watched in horror as half of it was shot away, his guns were rendered u/s (unserviceable – no good at all) and a fire broke out behind him. Driver beat out the fire and went to help his mate at the back, Walter Lilley who, alas, was mortally wounded. Driver laid him on the aircraft floor and went to the pilot's aid. Petrol was leaking, the pumps weren't working properly and the second pilot, Sgt Bob Hewitt, had a gunshot wound in his right arm. As Ramshaw headed for home Driver began pumping petrol by hand. They lost height steadily and, by the time they saw the English coast, were almost in the sea. Driver kept pumping while Ramshaw ditched as close as he could to a trawler he'd spotted.

Trawler skipper Sinclair took the observer LAC Conolly and Ramshaw aboard his ship *Erillas* without difficulty. Hewitt fell in the December waves, Driver pulled him out and they too boarded the trawler and set off for the shore and Grimsby Hospital. LAC Walter Lilley had fought his heart out and went down with his aircraft.

For the rest of 9 Squadron, F/Lt Grant and Sgt Purdy were the only two pilots to land at Honington base. With two crew wounded, Sgt Petts force-landed at Sutton Bridge, his starboard wing badly shot up and having been on fire, the starboard side of the fuselage 'freely peppered' (as they called it then). F/O Macrae force-landed at North Coates with patterns of holes in the wings and tail section, plus a holed fuel tank and the fuselage peppered. That both were not downed was a matter of luck; the total could easily have been seven lost out of nine.

AC1 Charles Driver was recommended for the Distinguished Flying Medal, as was Ramshaw. Back on ground crew duties, Driver received his medal on Boxing Day 1939, another notable for 9 Squadron being the first DFM of the war. Ramshaw would have to wait until May of the following year for his. Macrae, being an officer, received the Distinguished Flying Cross, while Sgt Petts and LAC Conolly were mentioned in dispatches.

In his Book the Recorder of Operations noted: 'Complete crews of N2872, N2941, N2939, N2940 reported on Casualty Signal as missing.'

He did not note that Sq/Ldr Archibald Guthrie's Wimpy was seen going into the sea on fire, or that F/O John Challes's was literally shot to pieces in midair by Me110s, or that F/O Douglas Allison's was last sighted heading for home with an engine in flames. He could not have made a note about Pilot Officer Eric Lines and his four crew; no one will ever be able to do that.

The men left from this calamitous effort were interviewed by the RAF's commander-in-chief, Air Chief Marshal Sir Edgar R Ludlow-Hewitt KCB, CMG, DSO, MC. Afterwards, not knowing about the *Freya* radar, it was decided that losses had been mainly due to straggling.

For the time being, if any German ships were spotted out at sea, Squadrons Nos. 38 and 115 would have to deal with them as a consequence of operational losses suffered by other squadrons. In that matter, 9 was top of the chart.

1940

Into 1940 the leaflet raids carried on, causing aircrew to ask why they were supplying the enemy with so much free lavatory paper, and so did the sea sweeps. Not lavatory paper, but butter, sugar and bacon were rationed in Britain and Sq/Ldr Peacock arrived to lead a flight. Already a brilliant pilot with the DFC, before the war he had been with the Fleet Air Arm when it was run by the RAF.

13 February. 10.30. Telephonic communication from Group confirmed Routine Sweep to be carried out at Station Commander's discretion. 11.06, three aircraft took off for Routine Sweep. 14.15 all aircraft returned.

For the umpteenth time, they never saw a thing. The new CO, Sq/Ldr McKee, known as 'Square' McKee being about five foot five in both directions, introduced the novel idea of practising aerial combat. It was then called 'Fighter Co-operation' and they tried it, once.

There were some night attacks on naval targets that did about the same amount of damage as the sweeps and the leaflets, but war was about to break out. Two of the veterans of Wilhelmshaven would not live to see it.

8 March 1940. Flying accident at Vickers Armstrong, Weybridge. Wellington 1A aircraft N3017 was returning to squadron after undergoing modification to fuel tank armour plating. Aircraft took off at

14.35 hours and was seen to crash shortly afterwards. The aircraft was totally destroyed by fire and all occupants were killed instantaneously. Court of Enquiry was held and found the accident to be due to an error of judgement.

Occupants included the Canadian F/O Bill Macrae DFC and his 20-year-old observer from County Cork, Sgt Cornelius Murphy.

The last raids of the phoney war were coming up. 13 March: Sq/Ldr Marwood-Elton did one of his occasionals, a sea sweep. Marwood-Elton was, of course, a regular officer from before the war, a former flight commander at 149 Squadron. Later in the year he would join No. 20 Operational Training Unit and be forced to ditch his Wimpy in Loch Ness. Later still, as Group Captain Marwood-Elton of the Operations section of Bomber Command HQ, he would argue hard against the 617 (Dambusters) Squadron raid on the Dortmund-Ems canal in September 1943. He would lose the argument and 617 would lose six Lancasters and crews out of nine. Another lost argument for the Group Captain would be his own with the Germans in March 1944.

But this was March 1940 and Sq/Ldr Jarman, with Jack Ramshaw (now his permanent second pilot) and six other crews were sent on reconnaissance to Petershaven and Nimden. They were recalled but Sgt Buckley didn't get the message and flew on over Petershagen and Minden, which was almost certainly what he was meant to do. Rivett-Carnac and Heathcote went to Nienburg for a look with leaflets and that, gentlemen, was it. The bell had rung.

> 'I don't know why the Hell they bother
> us fighting men with such trivialities'
> F/O Bamford (warned of the necessity of carrying a gas mask)

Britain had become increasingly furious with neutral Norway. Thousands of tons of (neutral) Swedish iron ore were shipped from the Norwegian port of Narvik to Germany and thence down the ship-canal system to the industrial heartland, the Ruhr. For some time the possibility of Britain invading Scandinavia had been put about the German High Command.

1/2 April: 9 Squadron moved to Lossiemouth to form an advanced bomber wing with 115 Squadron, twelve Wellingtons each, termed 'a striking force against naval forces in northern waters'.

7 April: the wing took off to attack a cruiser and six destroyers said to be sixty miles off the Danish coast. 'No contact was made. A listening watch was to be kept on 18 Group frequency but w/ops had to leave sets

to load guns and man turrets so information was not reliably passed in the air.'

Also on 7 April the Royal Navy laid mines inside Norwegian territorial waters in an attempt to stop the traffic. The Norwegian Government issued a heated protest, threatening to declare war on Britain.

9 April: to the said government's astonishment, Germany simultaneously invaded Norway and Denmark. Apart from minor bits and pieces, it was all over in a few days. This incident, the conquering of two European countries by another as if it were no more than a char-à-banc trip from Leeds to Scarborough, was described in miniature by the actions and reports of 9 Squadron. 'Owing to invasion of Norway and Denmark, the squadron was allotted reconnaissance duties.'

In the morning of 9 April five sorties (individual aircraft missions) were flown and much enemy activity reported on sea, land and in the air. Reconnaissance duties were unallocated at 15.10 when orders were received to attack enemy cruisers at anchor in Bergen harbour. They took off at 15.40. 'The targets were located and bombs were dropped. No hits were observed' but they did shoot down a Dornier 18. 10 April: 'Order received at 14.52. All available aircraft to attack cruiser and battleship at anchor near Christiansand.' At 15.20 eleven aircraft took off – they didn't find anything.

11 April: five of 9 Squadron's Wellingtons joined 87 other Wellingtons, Blenheims and Hampdens on a shipping attack. 9 Squadron were looking for a troopship – the *Levante* – north of Bergen. They didn't find it, nor did they see any of the action that brought down ten of the other aircraft.

12 April: while trying to find two battle cruisers and a cruiser in ten tenths cloud down to six hundred feet, horizontal visibility one mile in rain and sleet, Wellington P2520, captain Sgt Charles Bowen, veteran of the Squadron's first Op, was lost with all hands. His was one of ten aircraft lost off the Norwegian coast that day, mostly to fighters. Those in charge of Bomber Command were finally convinced that night time was the right time. 14 April: squadron went home to Honington.

The Germans had what they wanted. They were secure against attack through Scandinavia, they had ports like Bergen that they could use for their U-boats against the American aid coming across the North Atlantic, they had fjords they could hide their battleships in and they had their iron ore. The Germans had also humiliated the opposition. With the utmost speed and efficiency they had invaded and taken two countries with the very minimum of losses, meanwhile exposing the British and French as unable to do the slightest thing about it. The British Government was shaken to its core. If the Germans could conquer Poland, Norway and Denmark without any trouble at all, who was next? It seemed that in her present state of spirit and preparedness the United Kingdom would not be much of a problem to them either.

Certainly the UK's air force wasn't exactly frightening the horses. On 21 April, equipped with nothing more than bravery, the crews of six Wellingtons of 9 Squadron went to their first target on land: Stavanger aerodrome. Attempts to locate the objective were largely foiled by low cloud although South African skipper 'Tintack' Rivett-Carnac located and bombed, which was no less than he would have expected. He looked as if he should have played flanker for the Springboks and he was a natural leader. People felt that if they stuck with him, they'd be all right.

> 'I cut two days off my last leave
> because I was ambitious and
> wanted to see how the squadron worked'
> F/Lt Rivett-Carnac

30 April: six went to Stavanger again. It was a long way so they only had one 250lb bomb each, five of which were delayed action. 'Each captain claims to have actually hit the aerodrome with the one bomb that was seen to burst. It is assumed that the remaining delayed action bombs were dropped on the aerodrome.'

Aircrew might have believed they'd had a hit but at night, unless they really saw it happen, they were doing well to get anywhere near aiming points. It is perhaps indicative that in a Wellington crew bomb aiming was not a specialised trade. The observer did it, leaving his navigator's table as the target approached to clamber into the nose, or the second pilot did it. Later, in some crews, the jobs of front gunner and bomb aimer were combined.

7 May: AC1 Settle (F G) was killed by a revolving airscrew whilst engaged in starting up Wellington aircraft N2987. An investigation was held and found the accident to be purely accidental.
9 May: Air Vice Marshal J E A Baldwin CB, DSO visited the station and presented the DFM to Sgt Ramshaw.

10 May: Neville Chamberlain resigned as Prime Minister in favour of Winston Churchill. Germany launched the Blitzkrieg against Holland and Belgium, British troops crossed the Belgian border from France to meet the Germans and some *Luftwaffe* Heinkel He111s got lost on their way to a French target and bombed one of their own cities, Freiburg, by mistake, killing about sixty people. In the heat of all the Blitzkrieg success and excitement, as the German army and air force began its sweep through

Western Europe, Hitler still found time to charge the British with the 'inhuman cruelty' of bombing the innocent citizens of Freiburg.

Also on this day a new boy went on his first Op. Six Wellingtons of 9 Squadron set off to attack Waalhaven aerodrome near Rotterdam, which had fallen to German paratroopers. Peacock, Kirby-Green and Smalley, experienced men all, flew together. F/Lt James R T Smalley, sometimes known as Tom, came across as a bit of a stickler, snooty even. The flak wouldn't dare hit him and no one had the courage to question the right of his enormous Afghan hound to accompany him to briefings and everywhere else. Any aircraftman given hound and leash at dispersal before Smalley climbed aboard would never question his duty to walk the animal back to the officers' mess, which was the only occasion on which this dog would deign to mix with non-commissioned ranks. One day Smalley would be shot down flying a Spitfire and would end up a POW, a fate worse than death for the man.

The other three aircraft followed along on their own on the Waalhaven trip. One was Kit Kitson's, on his first as skipper, and one Sergeant Douglas in L7777/U-Uncle on his first skippering. His second pilot was the new boy, Sgt Rupert Cooling, 20 years old, just arrived from training school and known as 'Tiny' because he was six foot seven.

Cooling: The phoney war was over and everywhere was bustle and confusion. The spectre of December 18 hovered over the airfield and for us freshmen, thrown together with some experienced fellows and told that we were now a crew, it was bewildering and ominous. After a few false starts we eventually had a briefing. We were to crater Waalhaven airfield and soften up the German army there, in support of a Dutch counter attack.

Navigator Sgt Jock Gilmour worked out his course and captain Douglas decided to stay low over the sea, climb on seeing the coast and make a bombing run east to west in line with the route home.

As we climbed above the shore, the setting sun glinted on windows and narrow waterways, and up ahead there was another set of lights, in a curtain, rising from the ground with smoke behind. It was my job to shut the wireless operator into the front turret, then I was ordered into the astrodome to watch for fighters although we weren't really expecting any. As we went into our bombing run routine, the curtain of lights, which was flak, was dead ahead, rising balls of pink, green, white, slowly ascending towards us, then hurtling past. Then three things happened at once. The flak curtain seemed to part and let us through, there was the bucking bronco effect of dropping our bombs, and I heard a smacking sound like hands clapping. I looked, and we had a hole in our wing. 'Pilot from second pilot,' I said. 'We've been hit outboard of the starboard engine.' I was quite surprised to hear myself on the intercom. I sounded rather nonchalant.

Cooling flew the aircraft over the sea while Douglas checked the damage – the damage that he could see.

The skipper took over for the landing, and we were down, and then we tugged viciously to the right and ended up square across the flarepath. The flak had punctured our starboard tyre, we had a self-sealing fuel tank bulging out like a huge hæmorrhoid dripping and ready to burst, and we had holes punctured all over the starboard engine. After the interrogation, where they gave you sweet milky tea and as many cigarettes as you could smoke, Sgt Douglas bought me a pint. So, that was it. My first trip. It was good to be home. And I'd learned that it was possible to go out and come back.

Everyone else was home too, reporting to the intelligence officer. 'All bombs were dropped and every captain claims to have dropped them on the aerodrome.'

This was the last time that 9 Squadron aircrew flew with a rank below Sergeant. The Air Ministry directive was not issued until 1 June 1940 but it seems that some squadrons were ahead of it. For example, in Sq/Ldr Peacock's crew that night were LAC Griffiths and AC Murton. Next time out they would be sergeants, likewise LAC Oliver, Douglas's wireless operator. This was all much to the shocked disgust of long-serving RAF regular sergeants who had taken ten or fifteen years to get those tapes on their arms. Now every Tom, Dick and Harry, no matter how wet behind the ears, was a sergeant if he was aircrew. Whether their promotion would be of long term benefit to Griffiths and Murton remained to be seen.

'I had a very good batman at FTS.
He pressed my tunic so much that it eventually split in half'
P/O Arnold

11 May: the barrel-like figure of Sq/Ldr Monypenny arrived, looking as if he was about to burst out of his uniform. With his extremely neat little ginger moustache curling up at the ends, he took over A Flight. Also coming on strength were P/Os Webster, McDiarmid, James and Maude-Roxby. All were destined for colourful careers, some more colourful than

others. P/O James: 'Maude-Roxby was a Canadian, well connected with family and society in England. He was, shall we say, quite a wild young man.' Tiny Cooling: 'Maude-Roxby was a mad bugger.'

P/O James, christened Bertram but, like so many Jameses of the time, called Jimmy after the famous comedian, was not so tame himself. Three years hence he would find his description posted all over Germany and the Occupied Countries and broadcast over national radio as part of a *Grossfahndung* (national alert): 'JAMES Bertram Arthur. Born 17.4.1915 in Assam, India. Height: 170cm. Dark brown hair, oval face, blue grey eyes, small narrow nose. Has all his teeth. Small figure. Healthy complexion.' The eye colour, the Gestapo might have noted later, was actually brown.

Hitler was going to bomb Rotterdam anyway to force the Dutch capitulation but if he needed an excuse to make the first all-out area raid on a city, the Freiburg mistake gave him it. On 14 May some eight hundred of the ordinary folk of Rotterdam were killed by German bombers and the Dutch army gave up. On the same day, while Ju87 Stuka dive-bombers created unopposed havoc among French artillery positions, the Germans shot down 47 of the British aircraft sent against them, 46 of them at Sedan where they valiantly tried in vain to stop the enemy crossing the River Meuse.

15 May: the British butter ration was halved to four ounces per person per week, Rommel smashed up the French tank regiments and full authority to bomb Germany was at last given to the RAF. They sent one hundred aircraft – Wellingtons, Hampdens and Whitleys – to half a dozen targets in the Ruhr. Six Wellingtons of No. 9 went, aiming for Bottrop, skippered by Sq/Ldr Monypenny, F/Lt Rivett-Carnac, P/O Walsh and Sergeants Douglas, Kitson and Bull. ORB: 'Six aircraft proceeded singly, taking off at irregular intervals between 20.50 and 22.35. At between 5,000 and 11,000 feet, the first four aircraft found a cloudless sky (over the target area) but very hazy. The last two aircraft arriving at approximately 00.45 and 01.15 encountered eight tenths cloud at 10,000 feet.'

Nobody knew if the Ruhr had felt the blow or not and 9 Squadron got lost. Tiny Cooling: 'We got to the Ruhr all right – God knows if we got to Bottrop.' There was further uncertainty to come. The Squadron's individuals flew through powerful electrical storms on the way home which rendered wireless sets u/s. Tintack Rivett-Carnac, out of petrol, crash-landed near Epping. Some of the others cruised unknowingly up and down the south coast, setting off the air raid sirens in Hastings. Tiny Cooling was one such:

We saw St Elmo's Fire for the first time, which turned the props into blue disks and there was a flickering lilac rainbow arc between the two

front guns. Our wireless had gone for a loop and Dougie said the compass was drifting idly around and around, and we flew along with absolutely no idea where we were or where we might be going. It was a kind of limbo – eerie really – and then somebody said, 'Maybe we're over England', so we came down through the cloud and saw we were over land but we didn't know which land. We signalled SOS with the downward recognition light and a flare path lit up. Of course, the Germans knew SOS as well as we did, and I was standing by with the Very pistol ready to fire the aircraft. But it was the strip of a private aero club at Shoreham-by-Sea, which, like a lot of south coast landing fields, had been alerted because of the expected escape of the Belgian royal family, following the Dutch a few days before. We weren't quite that important so we were offered sofas and chairs to kip down on in the clubhouse.

I don't know if our w/op Sgt Oliver had been practising his French in Morse or if he was perfecting his knowledge of Q codes.* Maybe nobody had told him that we were landing. Anyway, he hadn't wound in his trailing aerial and we lost it on the roof of Lancing College. They rang up next day and said they'd got 60 feet of copper wire with some lead balls on the end and did it belong to us? So Oliver was in for a half-crown fine for losing his aerial.

*Q codes were Morse abbreviations: QAA – airborne at (hrs); QBG – I am above cloud; QBH – I am below cloud; QBF – I am in cloud or, more popularly, I am a bloody fool; etc. Q code plus IMI became interrogative: QAH IMI – what is your height? Many w/ops prided themselves on their encyclopaedic knowledge and lightning use of Q codes.

At that time skippers of bombers were told the targets for the night, the weather forecast and the opposition they were likely to meet. They were given a general take-off time and a point at which to cross the English coast, but after that it was up to them. The navigator would work out where to enter enemy territory and the rest of the route. On a dark or cloudy night, with no possibility of matching the terrain below to the map on his table, the navigator had to work on dead reckoning. It didn't need much of a side wind to knock an aircraft ten, twenty or fifty miles off course and the initial navigational aim was to get somewhere near, say, within twenty miles. The aircraft would then cruise around trying to spot a landmark or an architectural feature which, of course, would not be there if they were too far off. If it was there, the navigator had to switch into the role of bomb aimer then he'd switch back again after bombing to try and get them home. It was unrealistic, if not out of the question at this time of the war, to expect bombers in bad weather to hit a specified area of a city, or a specified city at all.

> 'I was coming back from a sweep and flying low
> over the water and, do you know, the slipstream
> from our airscrews left quite a wake in the sea'
> Sq/Ldr Jarman

16 May: the oil refineries at Gelsenkirchen. Two came straight back from the attack, three more got lost but eventually found home and Smalley ran out of petrol and ditched in shallow French water not far from the Mont St Michel. No one was hurt; Smalley and his ditchers were back on Ops in a week. Good show, but neither was the adversary noticeably weakened, distressed, or indeed bothered.

18 May, Cologne. Six Wellingtons of 9 Squadron constituted the entire air raid aimed at the railway yards. Cooling was there with Douglas: 'We got dead on Cologne but we couldn't see our target so we bombed the alternative and started some nice fires.' That night Jimmy James went to Duisburg on his first Op as second pilot to Sq/Ldr Peacock with American gunner P/O Webster and an otherwise experienced crew ticked by the gods for adventure. Jimmy James: 'We circled the area for at least fifteen minutes at 10,000 feet in bright moonlight. Never a shot was fired although a searchlight turned on to us. Bill fired down the beam and it went out.'

Sedgwick Whiteley Webster, known as Bill, was a very rare bird indeed. He was a gunner and an officer, when most gunners had been ranks below sergeant, he was new into the RAF yet aged 36, and an American advertising executive from Litchfield County, Connecticut. Even with these qualifications, he would become rarer still.

Unlike the ferociously efficient anti-aircraft defences of the *Wehrmacht* and their swarms of supporting fighters, the Fatherland's urban equivalent, believed by the Germans until recently to be more or less unnecessary, was inadequate and scrambling about for a co-ordinated system which would work.

Cooling: As a force we were grotesquely undertrained, but so were the Germans. They didn't know what to do about it either and on this trip seemingly they were trying something fresh. Flying searchlights. We were picked up by a light so we flew up into some cloud and above it, and so did the searchlight. We couldn't get the cloud between us and the light – it was a highly disconcerting experience.

As the Blitzkrieg gathered pace, bombing German cities was not the first priority and 9 Squadron switched to supporting the British Army as it was pushed back towards the Channel. The air marshals had two main ideas: set fire to woods where Germans were hiding, or go out there and if you saw something, hit it. Finding the right wood on a dark night was nigh impossible and the German army had probably moved on anyway.

20 May: 9 Squadron was over the battle area: Le Cateau, Arras, Cambrai.

Cooling: It was that peculiar time in the war when nobody was sure about what to do. We've got this force, we'd better use it, but how? We were showing the flag more than anything; roaming the countryside in the moonlight. We didn't question the strategy. They told us that if we saw anything worth bombing, bomb it. I was second pilot as bomb aimer, staring down at the patterns of hedges and fields, and if we saw a likely looking crossroads or a railway line we'd drop a 250lb bomb on it. It was like shooting pigeons with a blindfold on. Kept a lot of people awake, though.

Jimmy James: We were bombing and machine-gunning their transport, roads and railways. It was armed reconnaissance basically, at low level. We had the Group Navigation Officer with us on this one, Sq/Ldr Graham, and he got us lost for a while. Somebody was chased by a fighter but we didn't see one. Two nights later we went with one other Wimpy from the squadron to a river bridge at Namur (over the River Meuse, near Charleroi, Belgium). We had a very hot reception from light flak. George (Peacock) set us up at about two thousand feet then went into a shallow dive, the flak whizzing past us. On these low-level jobs we'd bomb at about five-hundred-feet, when George would pull us up and we'd get a five-hundred-foot boost when our bombs exploded.

24 May: nine went looking in Belgium. Such targets were generally either a Semo or a Mopa: Self Evident Military Objective or Military Objective Previously Attacked. The nine of 9 fired 7,400 machine-gun bullets and dropped bombs on convoys. ORB: 'The intention was to interfere with the enemy movements and to prevent both rest and activity of troops in and about the target area throughout the hours of darkness.'

26 May: almost midnight and four went again to Belgium, to the aerodrome at Jumet, near Charleroi.

ORB: Three aircraft found and bombed the target. The fourth aircraft was unable – due to darkness – to locate the target. Two aircraft carried out high level bombing, one at ten thousand feet, one at seven thousand feet. The third aircraft carried out a gliding approach attack from ten thousand to five thousand feet. This type of attack proved very successful as very little opposition was met from AA guns. The bombs were dropped in sticks; two or three runs being made by each aircraft.

When 'Bungee' Fordham came home, he found an unexploded cannon shell in his tailfin. Such descriptions of an air raid make it sound like a leisurely gentleman's pursuit – two or three runs, gliding in, very little opposition equating to success. Whether to bomb this way or that was a decision made by the captain. Some favoured a low-level run, others a diving run; some a gliding run with the engines throttled back so the enemy would not be so aware of their approach, others an orthodox high-level run (high at that time would be considered low later on). Great claims were made by government statisticians concerning reductions in German industrial production based on the assumption that the workers were not getting a proper night's sleep.

27 May: on a raid against three road and rail targets at Brussels, Tournai and Courtrai, 9 Squadron pilots stated, 'the night was very dark, making it difficult to locate objectives', and these were not all novices. Making his debut as a captain pilot was Ramshaw's second, the post-Wilhelmshaven swimmer Bob Hewitt, but among the ten were some experienced men, like Kirby-Green, Rivett-Carnac, McDiarmid, Sq/Ldr Peacock, and Sq/Ldr Monypenny with Maude-Roxby as second pilot, the man whose party trick it was to eat the beer glass he'd just emptied.

Jimmy James: Tom Kirby-Green was a Flying Officer and so a bit loftier than mere Pilot Officers like me and Sergeants like Conk Canton, who'd just arrived on squadron. Kirby-Green used to read *The Times* from cover to cover in the mess. Maude-Roxby and I bought motor-bikes. He had a 500cc Norton and mine was a 250cc New Imperial. We used to tear around the country on them, mostly at night. Maude-Roxby sometimes careered around the station on his and everybody said that he would kill himself on it if he didn't get the chop on Ops.

James, Webster, Kirby-Green and Canton, plus Sgt Bull and a pilot from 1941, James Long, would reconvene in circumstances where loftiness and *The Times* didn't figure: POW camp, Stalag Luft III.

29 May, Honington: 'AC2 W E Middleton was accidentally shot and died of his injuries.' 31 May: Tom Purdy returned to the squadron and, with Monypenny, Douglas, Rivett-Carnac and the full available squadron strength, went to France. Cooling: 'Took off 21.40, back 00.30, bed 01.30. Bombed Soest, south of Dunkirk. Place all in flames. Terrible sight.' ORB:

'The night was very dark and all aircraft had to use parachute flares to locate their objective.'

'I wish I'd had a camera to take a picture of that Me110 I shot down'
F/O Smalley

With the evacuation from Dunkirk almost complete, attention switched back to Germany with another one hundred-plus raid while a few Wellingtons headed for German positions in a last desperate attempt to buy the retreating soldiers some time.

Tiny Cooling, 3 June: As we crossed the Suffolk coast near Southwold we could see two sunsets. One was the fires at Dunkirk. There were several other Wellingtons near us and it was one of the times I really felt I was doing something. Dougie had put me as first pilot on this sortie and I joined in a small formation with some other aircraft. Each was flying along, rising up and down on its own individual air currents, and I felt quite a surge of emotion.

The Wimpys went their separate ways and when we got to Dunkirk we made our approach high and to the south, avoiding the Royal Navy whose aircraft recognition wasn't so hot at that time. The sea was like a new sheet of beaten copper with movement frozen by our height and the thousands of waves reflecting the glow of the blaze all about. We had sixteen two-fifty bombs that we dropped, one at a time, hoping that we'd keep a few German heads down so that another boatload of our boys could get away.

5 June: Some of the squadron went to the Somme and some went to Duisburg including Jimmy James with Peacock on a repeat of his first Op.

James: Square McKee always went to the control tower to say a last word to the crews flying on Operations. We took off and Square came over on the radio saying 'Good luck' as ever. George Peacock's normal reply was, 'So long, sir' but tonight he said, 'Goodbye'. McKee said, 'Come off it, George – we never say goodbye' but George said nothing more.

An hour later, crossing the Dutch coast, they were caught in searchlights at ten thousand feet.

Four flak batteries opened up on us and the port engine caught fire. The skipper gave the order to bale out. Hargrave, Griffiths and I left by the front hatch but Ronnie Hargrave's parachute caught fire and he fell all the way and was killed. Murton left from the centre, Webster from the rear turret. We saw our aircraft blow up and go in. The skipper had no chance to get out himself.

Jimmy James would become a famous tunnel digger, taking part in twelve escape attempts including the most famous one of all. His first port of call and his first escape attempt would be at Stalag Luft I where he went with Sedgwick Whiteley Webster, who thus represented more 9 Squadron firsts: the first American to be shot down with Bomber Command and the first American airman taken prisoner in Europe.

10 June: Italy declared war. ORB: 'Nothing of operational importance occurred.'

Cooling: Frank Butler's navigator, Charlie Naylor, was a very unusual chap for aircrew. He didn't drink except in extreme moderation, he didn't smoke, he didn't chase women and he didn't swear. He was like the Son of the Manse. Unnatural, almost. Yet everybody liked him. He played chess all the time with a sergeant from the ack-ack unit. Anyway, he roomed over the corridor from me. We had our own rooms in the mess in those early days. One morning he knocked on my door and woke me up. We'd come back in the early hours from another raid on northern France, La Capelle, near the Belgian border. He came in with this anguished look on his face. 'Bob Hewitt's missing,' he said. 'His wife's expecting a baby.' He stood still in his shock – he was a big pal of Hewitt's. Then he collapsed onto his knees and buried his face in my bedding. He was sobbing his heart out, distraught, like a little girl. I was very embarrassed and had no idea what to say or do. Eventually he stopped. 'Sorry,' he said, 'I had to talk to someone.' I mumbled a few comforting words and put my arm around his shoulder. He just said, 'Thanks,' and went.

Back on squadron after recovering from his wounds and his dip in the sea with Ramshaw, Hewitt had lasted less than three weeks in his new role as skipper. He and all his crew were placed in a village churchyard near the French coast by Doudeville.

19 June: coastal radar picked up a distress signal from WS/P-Peter coming back from Germany, tracked it and lost it. The signal had been too weak to do much more than identify the aircraft but at 05.30 Square McKee was up with the stand-by crew, heading out to sea to search for Frank Butler. After only a couple of hours' sleep, Jock Gilmour woke Tiny Cooling to tell him he was a captain today. They would take off at 09.30 and go and help find Butler.

We began our sweeps fifty miles out, halfway to Holland. While the gunners searched the sea for a little yellow dot of a dinghy and the sky for a little black dot of a fighter I flew at six hundred feet in ever increasing rectangles making ninety-degree turns and lengthening the line each time until we'd drawn a straight-sided Catherine wheel and were twenty miles off the enemy coast. Then I flew to another starting point and did it over again.

If we found them, we'd have to circle over them with the telegraph key pressed down, so the rescue people could get a good bearing. This would alert the Germans too and we could expect interference from them by sea and air. But we didn't find anything. We got excited about a yellow oil drum, but that's all it was. Nobody found anything. They were down there on the sea bottom: Butler and his men, and the Son of the Manse, Charlie Naylor.

Others were searching too: 'Aircraft L7789 (WS/Y), P/O Nicholson, was conducting a search for the crew of Wellington N2897 (WS/P, P/O Butler), which had force-landed in the North Sea in the early morning, when the starboard engine caught fire. The aircraft was obliged to land in a field at Grange Farm, Hesgrave but no injury was sustained by any member of the crew.'

Life with new skipper Nicholson continued in similarly exciting vein. If he couldn't find someone else who had ditched, he could at least try the water for himself, when eight of 9 Squadron set off for the Focke-Wulf factory at Bremen which, unsurprisingly, was well defended. Nicholson, with Conk Canton as second, suffered two bursts of heavy flak very close, holing both wings.

ORB, 21 June: Aircraft L7807 (WS-J, a new Wellington on her first Op) experienced heavy AA fire over the target and the pilot took such avoiding action that subsequently on his journey home he unconsciously flew considerably north of his return route. A first class fix* which was given from Heston was interrupted and not fully received by the aircraft. Subsequently the wireless receiver appears to have become unserviceable and the pilot, then completely lost and having nearly run out of petrol, made a forced landing in the North Sea close to a convoy of four ships. The crew were picked up by a trawler and landed at Great Yarmouth. The crew were uninjured with the exception of Sgt Rayne (w/op), who received superficial cuts and abrasions on his face and hand.

*First class fix: three ground stations bounced a radio signal off the aircraft and, receiving a strong signal back, found their intersecting point. The position was calculated, probably within a mile, and *transmitted to the aircraft. Lesser degrees of confidence, due to weakness of signal or fewer ground stations receiving, produced second and third class fixes. As bad weather interfered with the process, poorer quality fixes had to be given when precision was most needed.*

Ditching warranted a little more sympathy than a crash on dry land with an engine on fire, so they gave Nicholson a couple of weeks off before supplying him with another new Wellington, T2458 WS/M and, consciously or unconsciously, he brought this one back.

There were few confirmed ditchings but many aircraft which failed to return for unknown reasons were searched for, if some sort of fix had indicated a possible sea crash, and until navigation improved greatly, there would be plenty of those. Sometimes the whole squadron, back from Germany, would take to the air again to scour the ocean for a lost comrade, sometimes close to the enemy coast. While this may have done wonders for squadron morale and team spirit, it clearly became less and less of a good idea as German fighters increased in numbers and skill. The practice was eventually stopped.

22 June: 'France signed armistice. Weather fair becoming cloudy with light rain after dark. Nothing of operational importance occurred.'

Britain was alone. Tiny Cooling flew to Düsseldorf and the Black Forest but it didn't stop the Germans taking the Channel Islands on 1 July. Invasion of mainland UK looked imminent and the emphasis in the RAF switched rapidly to defence and fighters. Even so, Churchill kept his far-sighted view: 'Fighters are our salvation, but the bombers alone provide the means of victory.'

In practical terms for 9 Squadron that meant the shipyards at Hamburg, 5 July. P/O McDiarmid was last home by two full hours, with good reason. Returning over the Dutch coast, second pilot Bob Murgatroyd, a big, hefty chap, was in the bomb aimer's position looking for a pinpoint to give the navigator. The flak opened up and he took a shell in the chest. Had he not been there the shell could have burst in the cockpit and killed both him and McDiarmid and, consequently, the rest of them. As it was, only Sgt Robert Beattie Murgatroyd was buried at Honington Churchyard and Wellington L7786 WS/X could have the hole mended and carry on for a while longer.

9 July: While it was definitely the case that tea went on the ration, it has since been decided that the Battle of Britain began the next day, perhaps because the air-to-air score was 8–1* to RAF Fighter Command, when on the two previous days it had been 7–4 and 5–6.

This is not counting the five Blenheims of Bomber Command lost on the same day attacking a French airfield.

The Germans had huge superiority in bomber numbers, the use of airfields just across the water and better technology for guiding their crews. They had *Knickebein* (crooked leg), which used radio beams to help navigators decide where they were. Luckily for the British Isles and the rest of the civilised world, they also had a commander in *Reichsmarschall* Hermann Göring who was hugely overconfident and still thought air war was simply a matter of shooting down more aircraft than the other fellow. This belief was born of his own experience and character: he was a sportsman, an outstanding shot and rider and a famous World War One air ace. Göring had succeeded Baron von Richtofen as master of the circus, having learned to fly after his legs were shattered in the trenches. He was the up-and-at-'em type. Fatally, his airborne cavalry let him down and he didn't really understand anything else.

While everyone watched the Spitfires and Hurricanes wheeling over England in mortal combat, 9 Squadron and the other bombers carried on trying to take the war to Germany. Bremen was the target for 13 July and Tiny Cooling was with Tom Smalley for his last trip as a second pilot. He was also bomb aimer of the day: 'Quite a few crews liked the second pilot to do it (bomb aiming) because that meant that the observer, the navigator, stayed at his table and they were that bit less likely to get lost.'

Sq/Ldr Monypenny, like all the senior officers in 1940, was a long-serving RAF regular in a stiff and starchy service, whose class structure was based in the early days of the Royal Flying Corps as a special branch of the army. Without realising that Wellington the aircraft and her sergeant crews signalled a revolution, officers looked back to Wellington, the Duke. It wasn't going to happen quite yet although Monypenny at least was somewhat different. An amiable chap who did not conform to the standard expectations of a squadron leader, he was not the stiff and starchy demigod. Monypenny always looked slightly lost, as if he'd turned up for the party but forgotten whose birthday it was. He was lost, finally, on a July raid to Wismar, up Rostock way, he and his crew, the youngest 20, the oldest 32, the Squadron's first total loss since Butler.

Stepping into the flight commander's shoes was Sq/Ldr Hinks, who would fare little better. Most of his experience had been in biplanes, doing daylight patrols on the North West Frontier. Making up the skipper numbers was Tiny Cooling:

Square McKee came bouncing up to me and did his usual trick of backing up to the briefing table, where there was a block the navigators used to stand on so they could lean over and peer at their maps. He stood on this block, which brought him somewhere near level with me. 'Can you be a captain?' he said. I said, I thought so, but he wasn't

interested in what I thought. 'Can you, or can't you? Damn it!' was his attitude. So I said I could and Square told me to pick up with the next new crew that came in. Jock Gilmour stayed with me and we were joined by Frank Bevan, who was the second pilot, and bomb aimer, Curly Jones the w/op, centre gunner young Rossiter and rear gunner Mac, John McKenzie McLean.

As far as I knew, the centre gunner was a leftover from the Mark IA Wellington that had the dustbin, the belly turret. They removed that for the Mark IC but we kept the crew member. He was supposed to fire the two beam guns, which poked out of the sides through two of the bits of basketwork near the Elsan, but we never carried those guns so Rossiter spent all his time searching in the astrodome and pumping oil when required.

After crewing up, a little night flying was required for new skippers. 'You'd do three circuits and landings, with a minimum crew on board, which was you, the second pilot and the w/op. I was made up to captain at the same time as P/O Wanklyn and we were on for our practice on the same night.'

Pilot Officer P R B Wanklyn was not, as might have been expected, the son of the 1916 CO of No. 9 Squadron RFC, Major J A Wanklyn, who survived his war.

Wanklyn said he was going to something in the mess, would I take first turn, so I did, and finished about half past nine. Wanklyn was in the crew room. He said, 'Aircraft all right?' and I said it was fine as far as I was concerned. He took off, and I was making my way back when there was a god almighty thump, the typical ball of flame that you learned to recognise with the black smoke, and it was Wanklyn going in. He might have been on the downwind part of his circuit – I don't know – but pilot error, I would say. When I walked into the mess some of my crew were there, looking like ghosts. 'Thank Christ!' they said. 'We thought that was you.'

Cooling was adjudged to have had sufficient practice in the dark and they were on Ops the very next night.

Our first was to that bloody oil refinery at Gelsenkirchen. Again. It had been my first with Sgt Douglas as well. Nobody ever seemed to hit it. Then we went to Eschweger, or rather set off for it, because we had engine trouble, bombed Schipol aerodrome instead and came home early.

In a month of German Ops with no losses there were some important arrivals, including a new CO, Wingco Tim Healy taking over from Square McKee who was bound for higher things, a new flight commander in Sq/Ldr Prichard and a shiny new Wellington for Tiny Cooling, T2468 WS/Y-Yorker. On the way home from Göttingen, Cooling found a new hazard.

We were off track, needless to say, when there was a yelp from the rear turret and Mac said, 'I can see a balloon.' I said, 'A balloon?' and he said, 'Yes, it's slightly to port and above us.' I looked and there were four barrage balloons that I could see so I don't know how many I couldn't. Jock thought we were somewhere near Hamm so we'd blundered into the Ruhr and right into a balloon barrage, and the flak hadn't opened up yet. So I did a quick 180-degree turn, back into a slightly less unfriendly part of Germany, and we found our way around the balloons.

Lunch on 19 August seemed no different to any other day. There was a queue outside the airmen's mess, the sergeants were tucking in and the officers finishing up. Tiny Cooling was in the sergeants' mess.

We heard the whistle of a stick of bombs coming down and immediately the dining room took on the look of the Marie Celeste. Plates of food steamed gently and not a soul in sight. We were under the tables. One bomb hit the parade ground and killed a number of airmen and WAAFs in that lunch queue, about a dozen. Another hit the barrack block and blew it to bits, and another blew in the window of my quarters. When the racket died down, most of us sat back at the table and finished our lunch. We would find out what happened later.

Part of what happened later were thoughts at HQ that this, and similar raids, might be a prelude to Herr Hitler's Operation *Seelöwe* (sea lion), the proposed and fully expected invasion of mainland UK. Orders were issued for invasion stand-by around the aerodromes.

Conk Canton had spent the summer as a second pilot with Wally Walsh, also assessing and reassessing the qualities of the pubs in Bury St Edmunds with Jimmy James. Norman Edward Canton, dark-haired, beetle-browed, had great organisational abilities, which would come in handy one day. Now he embarked on what amounted almost to a second tour, as a P/O captain. He'd already done a score of Ops with Walsh, mostly in Wellington L7799 WS/D, as reliable and lucky an aircraft as could be. She would end up as most of them did, but not Canton.

'Hell, no. I taught Bungee all he knows'
P/O Walsh (when asked if he'd been Sq/Ldr Fordham's second pilot)

24 August: German bombs fell in error on Croydon aerodrome. In the middle of a *Luftwaffe* campaign against Fighter Command airfields, Croydon was mistaken for Kenley; not very far away but Croydon was London's airport. Bombing the capital was contrary to Hitler's orders although it would no doubt have happened sooner or later. Albert Speer, architect to the Nazi Party and later armaments minister, reported Hitler speaking at a dinner in the Chancellery in 1940.

Have you ever seen a map of London? It is so densely built that one fire alone would be enough to destroy the whole city, just as it did hundreds of years ago. Göring will start fires all over London, fires everywhere, with countless incendiary bombs of an entirely new type – thousands of fires. They will unite in one huge blaze over the whole area. Göring has the right idea: high explosives don't work, but we can do it with incendiaries; we can destroy London completely. What will their firemen be able to do once it's really burning?

So began the London Blitz; but the truth of Hitler's vision would not be realised until Hamburg, July 1943.

Although he didn't know it precisely, Cooling's tour was coming to a close. In 1940 the definition of a tour was inexact. Initially, there had been no concept of a tour in Bomber Command and in the *Luftwaffe* there never would be. To the more caring RAF it seemed clear that aircrew could not be expected to go on indefinitely but no one knew how much they could take. A measure of two hundred operational hours was applied but its calculation was not the only factor in determining if a tour was over. Signs of stress in a pilot or crew member, for instance, might decide the CO to 'screen' him (declare him 'tour expired') a little earlier. The opposite kind of signs, overconfidence or cockiness, might produce the same result.

Anxious to gain some confidence was a new observer from New Zealand, P/O H R Sam Hall, the first officer observer on the squadron:

When I arrived, I found a much older chap in the mess hallway, waiting for me. This was Squadron Leader Pretty, pilot from the Great War, who was President of the Mess Committee. 'You're rather late,' he said. 'Sorry, sir, the train was . . .' 'Never mind that,' he replied. 'I mean, you're late for lunch and there isn't much left. Will a little cold pheasant do you?'

F/O Morgan, prewar regular and a new captain to 9 Squadron, would have had a similar reception, but the new sergeant pilots like Parkes, Willis and Harrison, whatever their background in civilian life, would be counted as somewhat inferior off-duty. When it came to flying aircraft in anger, surviving or being killed, sergeants and officers were in it together and these four would share the usual variety of fates.

Sgt Cooling went to the forests on the Hartz mountainsides that were supposed to contain ammunition dumps: 'We bombed the trees and machine-gunned them. Weren't we the brave ones?' Another forest trip, 7 September, turned out unexpectedly.

Cooling: It had been one of those days when everything went wrong. I was reserve pilot, expecting a nice day off, when another pilot went sick. We had faults with the aircraft, mag drops on both engines and a false start, and then, finally we were taxiing when a roll of barbed wire, blown by somebody's slipstream, tangled itself around our port wheel. So we had to scrub and, as we were coming down the ladder, Curly Jones (w/op) said that the way things had been going, if we had managed to fly we would never have got back again.

Hall: Our captain Bob Whitehead was reassigned to another crew so we were given a new leader, Bertie Barnard. We went to Calais for the barges and I got down into the bomb aimer's spot, issuing instructions to the pilot, who took no notice at all and veered away to starboard. I said, 'There's the target, away to the left, can't you see it?' Bertie, who usually stuttered, said very firmly, 'Are you flying this aircraft, or am I?' He waited until another Wimpy was coned by the searchlights, then turned in and followed my directions while the enemy was otherwise engaged.

Tiny Cooling's next Op almost became his last, as well as his shortest. Six were set for Hamm at 19.30.

We took off, reached the coast and there was something seriously wrong with the aircraft, although we couldn't tell what. We couldn't get her above what felt like about 85 knots, although we couldn't tell that either because the airspeed indicator was u/s. So I turned round and came back with a full fuel load and a full bomb load. We came in to land grossly overweight, with the airspeed showing as zero and the crew showing every sign of full confidence in me, such as tightly clenched arse cheeks and badly bitten lips. Anyway, we got down somehow by the seat of my pants, transferred to the standby aircraft WS/W and took off again. We had a pretty fair trip, crystal-clear skies and bombed Hamm, as ordered. We found out later that somebody in the ground crew had put de-icing paste over the pitot head which, on the Wellington, was on the starboard wing leading edge. They used to smear that paste all over to stop you icing up and they'd blocked the head, which works on air pressure, so the instruments were u/s. I was back at 20.10 the first time, and 02.30 the second time.

Sam and Bertie also went to Hamm, or somewhere.

Hall: This time it was quite different. We found cloud and nothing below seemed recognisable. Bertie kept saying, 'Can you see the target?' and I kept saying no, until he finally burst out, 'For Christ's sake, bomb something! I want to get home for breakfast.' I persuaded myself that what I was looking at was the Hamm marshalling yards, but I knew we should need some better methods and equipment before our bombing could be called accurate. Our main fear was getting lost and we relied almost entirely on a carefully prepared flight plan and Eyeball Mk I, that is, map reading. Astro-navigation wasn't used, at least, we weren't trained in it, and the fixes and signals we could get were all to do with finding home, not the target.

The date of victory in the Battle of Britain is usually set at 15 September, although the biggest London raid occurred on that date and there were many raids after, by day, but increasingly by night. In the three months that it took Fighter Command to win the Battle at the expense of over nine hundred aircraft, Bomber Command lost far more aircrew, but to rather less purpose. The fighters had claimed the air but there remained a threat from the sea, and 9 Squadron was one of many concentrating most of its attention on 'Blackpool Front', the invasion barges building up at the Channel ports, ready for Sealion. The barges were attractive targets, big and fat in the moonlight, and many were destroyed.

Hall: We were on an Op and I arrived at the aircraft with my usual armfuls of charts and kit, but with my cap still on and helmet hanging round my neck. I said, of course I intended to carry my cap on Ops in case we were shot down so I could enter a POW camp properly dressed. The cap became our good luck after that and I wasn't permitted to enter the aircraft without it.

The Germans claimed the RAF was dropping Colorado beetles on their potato fields. Back in the real war and in the middle of the Blackpool Front phase of 9 Squadron life, a raid to Berlin was announced. The squadron hadn't been on the first one when the only damage done was to a garden shed. Nine went this time, while four more went back to the barges, making thirteen sorties on one night, the greatest effort made by the squadron thus far. The nine were part of a large force – one hundred and thirty or so – and, in an extremely rare burst of tactical common sense, they were all sent to the same town rather than to the usual six or ten different towns.

We went to Berlin, September 23, with clear skies, good visibility and a particular target, the Siemens-Schukert works. I was reasonably sure that we'd found it, Bertie did his run, we dropped our bombs and the rear gunner saw them explode. Can't say more than that. There was plenty of flak but, as with us bombers, there was not much co-ordination.

Between them, the bombers had been given a dozen-and-a-half aiming points, all with military value, but whether the scattered fires they started were anywhere near the targets was extremely doubtful. The day after, the C-in-C of Bomber Command, Air Marshal Sir Richard Pierse, came to inspect Honington and No. 9 Squadron. Sam Hall was in the line.

Wingco Healy: This is Pilot Officer Hall, sir.
C-in-C: Ah, Hall, and when did you last operate?
Hall: Last night, sir.
C-in-C: Ah, good, good. And where did you go?
Hall (doesn't he know? He sent me): Berlin, sir.
C-in-C: Good, good. What did you think of it?
Hall (not the right time to say I was scared out of my wits): Very interesting, sir.
C-in-C: Good, good, and how many trips have you done?
Hall (with pride): Four, sir.
C-in-C (turns on heel, speaks to Wingco): And now I'd like to talk to someone with experience.

In among the standard barge raids on Calais, Le Havre and so on, the planners borrowed from Sir Francis Drake and his singeing of the Spanish King's beard at Cadíz and set up a hush-hush Op. The Royal Navy would send fire ships into Boulogne while the RAF bombed the docks. Sgt Thomas Purdy, back again a year after going to Brunsbüttel on the second day of the war, was without a second pilot for the three-hour trip. Cooling stepped in:

It was a highly specialised raid and desperately secret. We were to say

nothing about it, even if it was scrubbed. I had no worries about going anywhere with Tom Purdy. He was one of the very best and Boulogne was a great trip – good results, lots of flak, late back, bed 06.20. And then they decided I was to be screened, along with a tremendous lot of others. They shifted out the old lags and brought in a lot of new boys. It wasn't 200 hours or a number of Ops; they just decided, and that was that. I'd done 27 Ops, actually, and they sent me a short while later to Training Command. Kirby-Green went around the same time, and Bull, and Maude-Roxby.

Later, Maude-Roxby would eat one beer glass too many and die from peritonitis.

P/O Thomas Gresham Kirby-Green, posted to 311 Squadron, would be shot down as a squadron leader of 40 Squadron, and captured, on the night of 16 October 1941. Sgt Leslie George Bull was posted as pilot officer to 109 Squadron, a hush-hush outfit testing and developing the Boscombe Down boffins' secret radio kit. He would parachute into France when his starboard propeller fell off, Bonfire Night 1941. In 1944 these 9 Squadron old boys would meet a unique fate, unique in that it happened only once in the European war although fifty men shared it.

Cooling's crew disbanded in various directions. The skipper would fly Avro Ansons for two years before being rediscovered and sent out with Wellington squadron No. 142 to North Africa to do another 37 Ops. Of the six comrades, three would complete second tours and survive the war; three would not.

For the Kiwi Sam Hall life seemed to be getting better and better:

I had my own room in the mess and, for the first few weeks anyway, exclusive use of a batman. He was a rare example of the right man for the job, having left service as a butler to the managing director of Henley's Motors. He was only an AC2 but he was efficiency personified. He folded my clothes so that I could have dressed with my eyes closed. On his first morning I couldn't find my tie because, instead of it being crumpled up somewhere, it was pressed and on the dressing table. Second morning, I was aware of a cup of tea being placed beside me, but he didn't leave. Instead, in a voice of severe disapproval, he said, 'This morning, sir, I think we should have a clean shirt.'

He was also a brilliant therapist. He'd prompt me into telling him about last night's raid and I'd get all the stress and emotion off my chest while he said, 'No, goodness me, sir. Really? Oh, too bad, sir' and then he would come up with tea and toast at the moment he judged to be the right one. I didn't know how to show my appreciation. Money would have been a vulgarity, I was sure, so I gave him the fruity pound cakes my mother sent me from New Zealand.

ORB: 7 October. Nothing of operational importance occurred. Sgt J D Cross, LAC Painter and LAC K G Wheeler were killed in a flying accident when a Wellington aircraft of No. 149 Squadron attempted to land. This aircraft was returning from an operational flight and was damaged by enemy action. When landing it struck the Chance light, crashed and caught fire, killing the above three airmen who were on duty at the time on the flare path.

The Chance light was a floodlight mounted on top of a three-ton truck, so called because the manufacturers of the glass were Messrs Chance. It shone brightly, long enough for each aircraft to take off and land. As the pilot came in he would have been expecting to see green showing from an Aldis lamp, held by an airman leaning against the side of the little van containing the Chance light battery. The men in the truck would watch the incoming aircraft's navigation and identification lights to gauge when to switch on the Chance light and would switch it off when he was safely down. But not this time.

As the danger of invasion receded, defence turned into attack but for 9 Squadron losses were not unduly heavy as autumn turned to winter: eight Wellingtons from 1 October to the year end and four of those without loss of life, but some were especially keenly felt. It was still the custom, when either of the two flight commanders went down or completed a tour, to post in someone of squadron leader rank to replace him. Such luxuries would not be kept up when business became more intense, but when Sq/Ldr John Olding Hinks, prewar regular officer aged 29, Cambridge research fellow in aeronautics, failed to return on 14 October from a raid to Magdeburg, just two days went by before Sq/Ldr Wasse was posted in from an OTU.

ORB, 28 October: 535929 AC1 Snell T A killed and 536093 AC1 Hatton R seriously injured by hostile air action.

Sam Hall: We had quite a few intruder attacks and on one such the enemy was shot down right in front of a hangar. Apparently, as the aircraft started its bombing run, an airman manning a Lewis gun had jerked the barrel to vertical and, without waiting for orders, opened fire. The German flew right through the stream of bullets and went straight in. We looked at the crashed aircraft and the dead bodies, and thought, there but for the grace of God.

There were so many of these attacks that they moved us and the

NCOs to a stately home to sleep, Ampton Hall, about ten miles from Honington. All the furniture had been cleared out and we used our camp kits instead of normal beds, which entitled us to two shillings a day hard-lying allowance. They picked us up in station vehicles to take us in for breakfast and the thriving wildlife of the countryside was soon noticed. Several chaps produced shotguns and ordered the drivers to stop every time we flushed a pheasant or a partridge as we drove by. The journey certainly took a lot longer but the braces of game birds hanging from our headlights made up for it with the promising thoughts of dinners to come.

After the Berlin raid of 14 November Sq/Ldr Prichard and his crew parachuted into occupied Holland. Days later Sq/Ldr Batchelor was behind his desk. Sgt R A Akerman was w/op with Prichard:

We took off at 19.30 into a crystal-clear, cold night. We were by now quite an experienced crew and our terrified fears of earlier Operations had hardened. Our trip out to Berlin was much as we expected: heavy flak crossing the Dutch coast, sporadic flak all the way to the capital, very heavy flak over Berlin itself. We bombed our target and left for home. We experienced more flak somewhere around Bremen but there was no undue concern until we were coming up to the Dutch coast at about midnight when our captain expressed concern over our fuel. (It became obvious that) we were not going to fly back to England and he said that, rather than perish in the North Sea, we must bale out over enemy territory. I was last except for the skipper and after an age hit the ground in a field full of cows. The only way out was to wade through the dyke that surrounded the field and onto a road, which was straight for miles with no hiding place. I wandered, very tired, along this road until a motorcycle and sidecar with two Germans came along and took me prisoner. I was taken to Alkmaan, to the German HQ, and there were the rest of my crew, all alive.

New on squadron was an 18-year-old observer from Biggar, Sgt George McRiner. He went to Antwerp with P/O Berry. McRiner: 'Berry had just about had it by then. He had a very bad case of 'The Twitch'. Not so inspiring for your first trip.' The Twitch was a recognised phenomenon caused by too many bad Ops in too short a space of time. It was often a facial spasm, such as a vibrating lip, a jumping eyebrow or an irrepressible wink but it could be in the hands, too. Sometimes it had a parallel symptom, which was to laugh almost hysterically at something that wasn't, when analysed, funny at all.

'Hello, Bill,' said one. 'How's your twitch?'

'Not so bad today, Jim,' said the other. 'But you should have seen the bastard yesterday!'

George McRiner might have been excused for developing The Twitch very early in his flying career.

We were coming back from Düsseldorf and Berry made a complete hash of the landing. We spun off the flare path and caught fire. You had to get out quick because the Wellington's fabric went up in almost instant flames. We did all get out and I thought that was enough for Berry, but it wasn't. He never said a word about that landing and come November 11, I was off with him again to Gelsenkirchen, and a few days later I was with him again to Berlin, which was the kind of place that imprinted itself on your mind. That was a long trip too, eight hours and more, and navigating was hard. It was all dead reckoning, from height and airspeed, wind speed, and the best assessment you could make of your ground speed backed up by sightings of features on the ground. We often flew in very good weather. On those nights we could see Germany and the Germans could see us.

It was still the practice for navigators to decide on the route. Some captains wanted to know; some left it to the experts.

Sam Hall: Bertie left it to me but, being a Kiwi, I had some trouble with the pronunciation of English place names. At one briefing, Wingco Healy said we should avoid Harwich because there was now a balloon barrage there. I wrote this down as Harridge and never did find it on the map. I wasn't too bothered. I had my route worked out.

Barrage balloons used to give out a warning from radio transmitters, called squeakers, which our pilots could hear in their headphones, and on our way home across the sea Bertie said, 'I think I can hear squeakers. Are we on track?' 'Definitely,' I said. I'd got a good pinpoint on the enemy coast. 'They're getting louder,' he said. 'Make another check.' So I did, and we were right on track. 'Well, they're getting worse. Where are you heading for, anyway?' 'Harr-Witch,' I said, whereupon the aircraft was stood on one wingtip and flown swiftly in the opposite direction.

I had to give him a new course for Honington and then endure a continuous diatribe of incisive remarks connected with the inadvisability of being navigated by ill-educated, dim-witted, obscurely bred specimens of subhuman life from the colonies.

As with any group of professional people some pilots were better than others. That Bertie Barnard was a good one was never in doubt, but 'professional' was a word he would have hated.

The main thing in Bertie's life seemed to be the gathering around the messroom fire with drinks, in his case, pints of Guinness. If the chat and the beer were flowing he wouldn't bother about the regular dinner and would end up scrounging around the kitchen. One night all he could find was a loaf of bread. There was a slicer there, so he decided to operate it but was careless with the positioning of his left hand. The slicer took off the top joints of two fingers but did nothing for his stutter. 'C-c-c-c-Christ!' he bellowed. 'I've c-c-c-cut my b-b-b-bloody f-f-f-fingers off!' We ran to the kitchen. He was ferreting through the slices of bread. 'I've f-f-f-found them,' he said, holding up two little red things with white breadcrumbs sticking to them. He rinsed them under the cold tap and set off for Sq/Ldr McCarty's quarters. Aiden McCarty was the MO and greatly admired by all of us. He sewed the bits back on and Bertie was excused duties for three weeks.

Sam Hall had an exciting experience with a different pilot, and in Tiny Cooling's old Wimpy, T2468 Y-Yorker.

The Squadron was on a stand-down day and so some of the officers decided to pop over to Feltwell for tea with 75 Squadron. Our revered flight commander decided to pilot the aircraft and we didn't bother with parachutes as it was such a short hop. As we took off there was a distinctly heavy bump, which turned out to be due to the pilot retracting the undercart too early. The right leg was good, the left leg was broken and dangling uselessly. It was decided to forego tea and we circled our own field for half an hour to burn off fuel so we'd be a little lighter. In we came with a slight cant to starboard but the time had to come when the aircraft would be level and sure enough, the port leg collapsed, the port wing went in and we did a violent spin turn. Our pilot made his own entry in the log, which should have been in the Line Book really: 'Port u/c damaged on take off. Some damage to port wingtip and propeller after perfect one wheel landing.'

The RAF was settling into the deciding long game, Bombers -v- Germany in the dark, when the *Luftwaffe* hit Coventry, 14 November. Although that raid was mainly aimed at industrial resources, it also destroyed something like a hundred acres of the city, but it was a one-off. What might have been the consequences to national morale if the raiders had come again the next night, and the next, and razed all of Coventry to the ground? Instead, they switched back to London, to Bristol, to Southampton, scattering their effort and in the process ensuring that Britain's industry and commerce would never be more than injured.

Area bombing wrecked houses, fractured water mains, crippled transport and cut electricity and gas supplies. These seemed to do more damage to industrial production than trying to hit factories directly. The mistake the Germans made was in not concentrating their air war. They could have done it. At this time the RAF's nightfighters were pathetic. It took six hundred radar-guided fighter sorties to make four kills. The Germans were losing a single per cent of their aircraft flying at night over Britain and they could find their targets with their navaids, never having to fly far from the coast. At the time the damage and the civilian casualties in British cities seemed appalling, but bearable. Britain was not going to give in because of it. The Germans did not have heavy bombers, nor a heavy bombing policy, so they could do no more than wound the nation.

'I believe we are over a town of some sort'
P/O Nicholson (on finding himself
in the middle of the London balloon barrage)

Sam Hall: I was in the flight commander's office one day when I spied a modest little leaflet with the title 'Radio Aids to Navigation'. Nobody had thought fit to circulate this information but I studied it and found that the wireless operator could get fixes from a master station, which calculated our position from bearings taken from three other stations. This was news to me and I sought out our w/op and asked him if he could do this wonderful thing. He said he could, but it was rather a nuisance since he had to change the coils in his set.

Wonderful indeed except these fixes were still only of use when coming home and the master station could only handle one aircraft at a time. What was needed was a universal, automatic system that could pinpoint any aircraft's position on the way to the target. Such a system was in development and it would make a huge difference. Meanwhile, the old ways had to do.

Sgt Joseph Anderson, w/op: We went to Hamburg and circled the target for half an hour trying to see through cloud. There was very heavy flak, flares, flaming onions* and batteries of searchlights. No results observed. We got lost over England with the wireless u/s and no QDM†

or fixes, and when I got it repaired after cruising around at 500 feet for an hour, we found ourselves over Gloucester. Needless to say we were the last ones home.

Flaming onion – an early type of flak shell that was thus named from the way it exploded.

†*QDM – a bearing; magnetic course to the transmitter.*

The RAF was now using night cameras regularly. One aircraft would be nominated, given the camera and told to fly over the target last. A photoflash bomb was released with the load and a short time before it was due to go off, the camera shutter opened automatically. The flash exposed the film but fires, flak and other lights also showed up as streaks and squirls.

No. 9 Squadron took a camera to Cologne, 27 November, a night when half the force of sixty couldn't find the city at all, but Sam Hall was convinced he was on target. 'I had the new camera but got very little on my picture. They identified some woods that made us seven miles away from where we should have been.'

Next time out: to Düsseldorf. P/O Hall produced a photograph only two thousand yards from the aiming point. This was an outstanding result but it showed the parlous state of bombing despite captains' repeated claims that all bombs had been dropped on, or near the target, that fires were seen, explosions seen, bombs seen to burst. They thought that's what happened when they went out each night, but the camera proved otherwise.

'When force landing due to engine failure,
I had to guide my aircraft between the chimneys
of the Officers' Mess to the ploughed field beyond.
On disembarking from a perfect landing,
my crew complained about the muddy state of the airfield'
F/O Harman

21 December: Sgt Harrison, a veteran of three months' Ops as captain, was away at 20.15 for Venice, followed at 20.20 by P/O Hemmings, who force-landed at Bexhill on the return journey due to shortage of petrol. None of the crew was injured. Joe Anderson was his w/op:

We'd had headwinds all the way there and came straight back over the Alps with no oxygen. Dawn broke, we were over Germany, and then two hundred miles from the French coast with only forty gallons of petrol left on the gauges. We were ready to bale out, but somehow the engines kept going over the French coast and we prepared for ditching.

We saw a Spitfire, then the English coast and the engines cut. After force landing at a small village near Hastings we were given hot tea, breakfast at an hotel, then the train to London. I went home for the night and met the crew again at Liverpool Street next morning and we all arrived at Honington at about half past one to find the windows of the mess filled with smiling faces.

A new pilot in that sergeants' mess was Alan Mackay:

An ancient custom was with the non-return from an operation of a friend or roommate, and we were all one or the other. A share-out would be made of the best of his uniform and whatever was left of parcels from home. We did it in an atmosphere of 'it might be me next'. Gordon Heaysman, Hemmings's second pilot, who was a fresher like me, was reported shot down, as was another Wellington that night, with all lost. Next day we heard Hemmings, Heaysman and crew were all right so there was a mad scurry to return those things that had been reallocated. To the eternal credit of their friends, whom they may have otherwise thought a right bunch of gannets, it all went back, apart from the Christmas cake Heaysman's mother had made him.

The report about the second Wellington, the one Walsh and Conk Canton had found so reliable, was more accurate. 'Aircraft L7799 (Sgt Harrison and crew) on return to base crashed at Alfreston near Beachy Head. All the crew were killed but the cause of the accident is obscure.' For 'obscure', read 'running out of petrol after getting lost'.

McRiner: We went to Bordeaux with Batchelor, who was a very pleasant chap, to bomb the Condor base there. It was further than Berlin, nine hours twenty, but we had to try and stop these long-range reconnaissance aircraft, which looked for our convoys and guided in the U-boats. Of course with all that petrol aboard, we couldn't carry much in the way of bombs.

Bombs were constantly expected at Honington and every airbase.

Mackay: In the sergeants' mess someone had provided a record for the wind-up gramophone, set just inside the door, of Deanna Durbin singing 'One Fine Day'. The first notes sounded like the air-raid siren. Quite a few of the older aircrew fell for it and dived flat on the floor. They got accustomed eventually because we brash new boys kept requesting the record.

2

BLOOD-RED BLOSSOM, HEARTS OF FIRE: 1941

The year of 1940 had been one of blistering astonishment and furious combat. There were many serious questions to be asked and answered, such as, 'Would the 9 Squadron adjutant ever learn to salute?' F/Lt Robert Boothby MP – protegé of Winston Churchill – had left his job as PPS to the Minister of Food to join the RAF. He was a cheery, friendly character with no idea of military bearing. If saluted, he would wave in return.

Germany had seemed unstoppable until the gradual realisation that there had been a Battle of Britain and Britain had won it. Still, the enemy had occupied all of Europe that he appeared to want. How would he ever be displaced? In the New Year of 1941, ten of 9 Squadron went to Bremen.

Alan Mackay: I was joined up as second pilot with Batchelor, who had come from towing drogues in Fairey Battles. I think I had more hours on Wellingtons than he had, but he was a squadron leader and a regular officer, so he was the boss. He did the take-off and landing. I did some in the middle and searched through the astrodome, so that was my first sight of searchlights and so on, through the astrodome. And frightening it was. You saw the lines of tracer snaking up, waving, trying to seek you out.

On the way to Bremen and to his own and his crew's great satisfaction, P/O McIntosh proved something. As he was flying into enemy territory, one engine conked out, so he jettisoned his bombs and showed that the Wimpy could come home on just one engine. Joe Anderson: 'Bremen was a very cold trip. The temperature was off the clock, minus 35°C (minus 31°F), and three of us had frostbite because the heating system froze up.' On this, the first of three successive nights, Bremen took quite a lot of punishment. Focke-Wulf, working on the new FW190 fighter, was hit as was an army depot and several apartment buildings. The fire brigade had to call in help from out of town.

Mackay: As well as our bombs we often had leaflets, called nickels* for some reason, in largish bundles. We were supposed to undo the bundles and shove them down the flare chute. Sometimes, especially if the Germans were firing at us, we said, 'To hell with it' and let them go tied up in their bundles, hoping they might hit somebody.
*Nickel was a code word possibly chosen because in German the word implies a small mischief-causer.

9 January, Gelsenkirchen: sixty Wimpys and seventy-five assorted others went and less than half reported bombing the oil. It wasn't even as good as that: 'We had a report later that the Germans had built a dummy refinery out in the country and everybody had bombed it. We all volunteered to mount a daylight on Gelsenkirchen so we could see the real thing and bomb it properly. Our masters declined the offer, fortunately for us.' One oil-refinery person was killed in Gelsenkirchen while nine Hampden aircrew died, with one injured.

11 January: 9 Squadron sent six to the Royal Arsenal at Turin and five to Wilhelmshaven, including Alan Mackay on his last as second pilot. 'Nobody had told us about area bombing. It was still a gentleman's war as far as we knew and we were told to bomb shipping only and to keep well away from the houses.' Everyone came home except Sgt Parkes, skipper for almost two months, who was in the Turin contingent. F/Sgt Lionel Willis was the second pilot. He'd previously been with Morgan but didn't get on because the officer would never let the sergeant fly the aircraft. Parkes was always happy to share pilot duties but there was a price to pay, seemingly.

Willis: 'We did not reach our objective, being forced by the failure of our starboard engine to come down at about 23.00 hours at Mizerieux, near Villefranche (in Vichy France).' Stuart Parkes produced the perfect wheels-up landing in the snow. 'After destroying secret documents we burned the aircraft.' Having failed to set her alight with Very pistol cartridges in the fuel tanks, they got her going with matches and an impromptu wick. They remembered to set the homing pigeon away with a message but forgot to retrieve their survival rations before it was too late.

We went to the village of Mizerieux and tried to knock up the Curé but he slammed the door against us. We set off to walk to Villefranche with two or three feet of snow on the ground. After about six miles we met a soldier who took us to the gendarmerie at Trevoux and later that morning we were handed over to the commandant of the aerodrome at Amberieux, where we were very well treated both by the gendarmes and the aerodrome staff. We were told that we were to be taken to a quiet place in the mountains for a few weeks until the Germans stopped looking for us. Instead we were sent to St Hippolyte (St Hyppolyte-du-Fort, Hérault).

Back in Suffolk Mackay was on his first flight as captain, to Wilhelmshaven again.

We had a shock when we were boxed in. You had a line of searchlights either side then they closed the box with more searchlights fore and aft. You were trapped and they threw everything into the box. The dodge was to change the pitch of the propellers and put the engines out of synch. The difference in the sound gave the impression you were diving and the searchlights dipped to follow while you flew straight on and got away. That was the idea, anyway. When we got there we bombed and reported that ours had fallen half a mile north of the target although how we calculated that I've no idea.

There was no planning at all – you chose your own height. We generally flew at twelve thousand feet where you didn't need oxygen all the time. You could struggle up to eighteen thousand in a Wellington but it took a long time getting there when you could have been on your way to the target. You chose your own directions, too, according to the skills of your navigator and, if several squadrons were attacking, anything could happen. Occasionally you'd see something flash past your window and it was a load of bombs. Haphazard – that's what it was. A bit of a shambles, and we knew it.

The weather made Ops nigh on impossible in the second half of January and it was snowing in Vichy, France, where all six of Parkes's crew were still together at the prison camp in St Hippolyte.

Willis: On 26 January the six of us climbed a fifteen-foot gate at the back of the camp and went to the station. Unfortunately we ran into a party of gendarmes. The camp Commandant was not annoyed that we had tried to escape but rather that we had not gone out through a gate, and at midday when internees were normally allowed out. At noon that day we left again, this time through the gate, and met a British officer in a café. We split into twos and walked to Sauve, where we got the train to Nîmes and changed there for Marseilles.

From there the usual route was to Perpignan and thence on foot over the Pyrénées into Spain, first stop Figueres.

A scheme was afoot for getting to Gibraltar by aeroplane and Sgts

Parkes, Goldingay and Bratley hoped to use this way of getting out. The rest of us went – with the British officer, an army private and a Belgian named Alexander Halot – to Perpignan. We waited four days for the snow to clear and the wind to die down. Two Spaniards took us in a taxi to within four miles of the Spanish frontier. While the taxi went through a customs post we made a detour on foot. But we were seen by gendarmes, who challenged us as we were getting in the car again. We believe they were searching for one of the Spaniards, who was wanted for murder and smuggling. They arrested the taxi driver but the rest of us got away and began our walk to Spain. The gendarmes, still searching for us, found us, confiscated our money, took us, handcuffed, back to Perpignan and then back to St Hippolyte.

At Honington, Wingco Arnold took over as CO from Healy. Largely nothing much of operational importance occurred except on the night of 10 February when two hundred aircraft raided Hannover.

Mackay: There was a very heavy fall of snow so we all thought, 'Good-oh, a night out in Bury St Edmunds!' but the CO said no, you're flying tonight, and he had all the erks (ground crew; term derived from aircraftman) and WAAFs in lines, twelve abreast, walking up and down the airstrip all day, stamping the snow down with their feet. That night we sat and watched the first pilot take off, knowing that if he managed it, we'd have to. And he did.

Mackay bombed a Hannoverian flak emplacement. On the way back he ran into some more flak of a different sort. 'As was our routine we came down to a thousand feet as we crossed the coast, the argument being that we were less likely to be spotted by a nightfighter. And flying flat out, or as flat out as a Wellington could go, we offered less opportunity for the flak outposts to get us lined up.'

Mackay had a new observer, George McRiner: 'It was a beautiful night, full moon, and we were all very happy to have left the enemy coast behind.'

Mackay: We were going fine when Bill Ainsworth in the front turret chirped up, 'Suffolk coast ahead, five minutes'.
McRiner: I said that was impossible. I had our position as thirty miles away.
Mackay: Bill gave his considered opinion that the navigator was off his chump because he could see searchlights and gun flashes: the coast was being attacked. As this discussion was becoming animated, we reached this coast and saw that it was a convoy, one of ours, being attacked by

a couple of German aircraft. As soon as the ships saw us, they banged away at us also. So Milly (Millington, second pilot) fired off the colours of the day. The ships just carried on firing while the Germans saw our flare and turned on us, too.

Shells ripped through the fragile fabric of O-Orange from friend and foe alike and it could have been either who knocked out the starboard engine and damaged the port one.

We staggered along, but we were dropping lower and lower and as we crossed the coast at last it was obvious we weren't going to make it home. We also realised we'd been flying very low over the sea and we'd forgotten to inflate our Mae West jackets. Must remember next time, we said. It was blackout, of course, deep, deep darkness and we looked for somewhere to lob down. It was flat country and there were some decent patches of different coloured black that looked as if they might be good fields so I put the undercart down and had a go.

McRiner: We hit something – a tree, or a pole put in the field to stop people landing in it – and spun around. Milly hurt his knee, but that was the only injury.

Everyone clambered out and had a look. Against the sky they could make out a house.

It was after one o'clock in the morning but there was somebody out walking, who just said goodnight as if he met a bomber crew every evening around there. We marched up to the farmhouse and knocked on the door and an old boy leaned out of an upstairs window with a shotgun and told us to bugger off. He let us in eventually but we had to remove our flying boots in case we dirtied his carpet. We found out that we'd crashed between Martlesham and Woodbridge, twenty miles or so from Honington, but more important for us a mile or two inland.

Mackay and pals were soon back in business. 'The worst job was if you were tail-end Charlie, the crew with the camera. At the briefing they would say, 'Tonight, it's you,' and you were given the company camera, which meant being last man in and flying straight and level until George McRiner said he'd got a good shot.'

Cloud continued to make target-finding very difficult while offering protection from searchlights and guns but the lack of proper navigation aids was not only a reason for poor bombing results: it also killed a lot of airmen who couldn't get back. Ten went to Cologne, 1 March. F/O Hugh

Lawson had been on squadron since the New Year. ORB: 'A signal was received from the aircraft that the Operation had been completed at 00.58 hrs. Nothing more was heard from the aircraft until he asked for a homing bearing at 01.57 hrs. This was passed, but not acknowledged.'

Lawson had set off almost three hours after the first aircraft. The rest were back home when, around midnight and all alone, Lawson was bombing Cologne, and they were asleep in their beds when Lawson's ETA at base came and went while he, in low cloud and a strong wind, was circling over the Humber estuary looking for an airfield in Suffolk. The aircraft ran out of petrol, ditched and sank to the bottom, taking the crew with her.

On this day, 1 March, St Hippolyte-du-Fort was the scene of yet another daring escape bid by Sgts Willis, Vivian and Blaydon, beginning with an official recreational day trip to Nîmes under the supervision of a British officer.

Willis: He put us in touch with a Frenchman, who took us to a hotel in Port Vendres. Owing to some financial difficulty, guides could not be secured so we met the officer again in Nîmes and he gave us three thousand francs. We set off for Perpignan. On the way Sgt Blaydon was arrested in a waiting room at Narbonne and sent back to St Hippolyte. We (Willis and Vivian) spent four days in Perpignan. A guide allowed us to sleep in his room but we had to be out by 08.00 and we spent the rest of each day hanging about cafés. Two other guides agreed to take us across the Pyrenées and, after twelve hours' walking, we came to a farmhouse where we could rest and eat. The farmer's son, aged about 12, conducted us to a village station whence there was a train to Barcelona.

Without papers, they were arrested on the train and interned. Meanwhile, Sgt Blaydon had hopped over a prison wall, reached Perpignan and, with a guide, walked over the mountains to Figueres, where he jumped a passenger train. Without papers, he too was arrested and interned: 'A German in civilian clothes asked my name, birthplace and age, and expressed an interest in the organisation which had got us into Spain as too many had been getting over. I said there was no organisation and if there had been, I would not have been before him. He mentioned various names, but I denied knowing any of them.'

Shortly he would be freed and would travel home, Gibraltar to Greenock, with his mates Willis and Vivian. Blaydon and Vivian would return to 9 Squadron. Vivian was to last out the war while Willis, awarded the Military Medal for his evasion, was too sick after his time in Spanish jails to resume duties. Sgt Blaydon would become the w/op of a Lancaster and, as Flying Officer Reginald William Blaydon DFM, come down in France, 8 August 1944, near Le Havre. The pilot and bomb aimer would evade but second time around Blaydon would not be so lucky.

Alan Mackay was going on his longest trip. He and some sun-seekers took off in a new Wimpy for Benghazi via Malta, 9 March.

Mackay: They'd been appealing for volunteers to go to the North African theatre and we thought that sounded a lot warmer than Suffolk in winter. George McRiner didn't want to go, so Alan Butler came with us, who'd been observer with F/O McIntosh DFC. We set off with a load of mail for the soldiers in Africa, petrol and miscellaneous supplies, but we were hardly up when the airspeed indicator packed in.

Butler: We were no more than a hundred feet off the deck. Our wireless and R/T were fitted up for the Middle East so we had no means of communication with the ground and they'd doused the flarepath lights. We fired off all our Very cartridges, got nothing and lost sight of the aerodrome. This was my first trip with Alan Mackay. Landing without your ASI in daylight is bad enough when at least you can see roughly how fast you're going. At night, in pitch blackness, it promised to be very ticklish.

Mackay: Our new observer said where he thought the aerodrome should be. I did a quick turn and we saw the church, so I told the crew to prepare for a crash landing and be ready to get out fast as we had over a thousand gallons of petrol on board.

Butler: We were just over the perimeter hedge when the flarepath came on and Mackay lifted us neatly over a cement mixer which threatened our undercart. He made the perfect landing. White as a sheet, maybe, but quite calm.

Mackay: It was a very close thing, landing on estimated speed with a lot of petrol swishing about. We only just made it so we expressed our relief by going on a bender. We were all fully recovered by the time we set off again next night, except Milly who was feeling a bit rough.

Malta had come under renewed attack and was no longer considered suitable as a stopping-off place.

Butler: We were briefed for Benina, near Benghazi, 1,920 miles away and at the limit of our endurance. I think it was the first time anybody had tried it non-stop. In any case, we had no margin for error.

Mackay: They removed some of the supplies and told us we were to make the journey in one hop of twelve hours. A long time in a

Wellington and for me it was largely without the help of the second pilot who was laid out on the cot saying he would never go drinking with us again. Little did we know what a prophet he was.

Butler: We were fired at over Free France, otherwise there was no problem on the trip. We crossed the French coast bob-on ETA and likewise the Tunisian coast with ten tenths cloud below. We were pointed more or less due east when the sun rose and we were duly impressed with the speed it came up in southern parts.

Mackay: One of our wing tanks didn't empty so we were flying heavy on one side for a lot of the way and, no matter what I did with the trim, I still had to make constant and continuous corrections and physically hold the kite level. It was very tiring and Milly was u/s with a self-inflicted alcoholic wound.

Butler: Jim (House, w/op) wasn't having any joy with contacting Benina so we had to go down below the cloud to see exactly where we were. We broke out at a thousand feet, over the sea. Jim got a QDM from Malta but thought it was a bit fishy, possibly a German signal to mislead us.

Mackay: We hit the Bay of Sirte (Khalij Surt, Libya) at a spot which, when we'd left England, had been occupied by the Eighth Army. They'd been doing a rapid retreat while we'd been airborne but nobody had told us. We came in at a thousand feet and the Germans were very welcoming. They shot the aircraft full of holes from the ground and an Me110 added some more from the air with Steve Bevan, our rear gunner, trying to make some holes in return. Amazingly they missed all of us crew and there was just about enough Wellington left to land so we came in on the beach, got out, shot some Very cartridges into the remains to finish her off and waited.

Butler: That was twice in thirty-six hours Mackay had made the perfect landing instead of killing us all. Then what seemed like the entire Afrika Corps came at us. They were in a great semi-circle, infantry, tanks, motor bikes, armoured cars, the lot. They obviously expected six British airmen to cause a lot of trouble.

Mackay: The senior officer came up to me and actually said, like they do in the films, 'For you ze var is over.'

Mackay had decided the crew should not tell the enemy that they were new and part of a reinforcement. They were North Africa veterans, been there months. 'Sitting in the noonday sun coming straight from a British winter did nothing for our story and, if that wasn't enough evidence, on our drive to Tripoli, Jim House cried out, "Look! Camels!" The officer said, "You have not seen camels before?" and Jim said, "Oh yes, but only in the zoo."

Before the war Sgt Alan Mackay had been a sub-editor at D C Thompson, the Dundee publisher. In Stalag Luft III and later at Heydekrug, he would promote himself to editor and produce the *Daily Recco*, a remarkable camp newspaper, at first handwritten and pinned up on the notice board every day. It was paid work, too. Like all POWs his back pay would mount up. His basic was fourteen shillings and threepence a day, plus three shillings pilot-qualification pay and threepence good conduct pay equalled 17s 6d a day. Less two bob a week for next of kin fund and £1 17s 6d a week income tax equalled £4 3s 0d a week net or £215 8s 0d *per annum*, tax paid.

The war was far from over for those left behind at 9 Squadron and March saw the arrival of the new Wellingtons modified to carry the 4,000lb blast bomb, the 'cookie', and the earliest attempt at what later became known as the Pathfinder method. With only six aircraft on the raid Sq/Ldr Wasse and F/Lt Morgan went in with incendiaries to mark the target at Emden so that No. 149 Squadron could follow in and drop the first ever cookie. There was a spectacular explosion. One of 9 Squadron's most experienced pilots, Sgt Fairfax, took a cookie to Cologne a few days later. Wellingtons struggled with such a load, pilots found the aircraft harder to handle and cookie trips were considered dicey. In a couple of months the Mark III with Hercules engines would solve the power problem but not the navigation problem.

Joe Anderson: To Cologne, 19 March. Good bearings from German beacons. Got a running fix and observer said it was about a mile out. On our way back I rose up and accidentally pulled the leads from the terminal block. I was about half an hour putting it right and so was too late to get a fix, but did manage two QDMs. Landed with my trailing aerial still out to make the crowning success of the evening.

To Berlin, 23 March. Long trip so we had to conserve oxygen. Could not find any beacons that worked, only German ones that I didn't know the position of. Unable to get fix on way back and I tried Hull, Tangmere and Pulham. Dawson got lost and was sending P-priority, short of petrol. Morgan got lost and was sending SOS. Nothing was heard from Wasse for three hours. I eventually got a bearing from Hull and we landed at Feltwell. Everybody did reach home in the end, although Stark flew back from Hannover on one engine.
George McRiner: Morgan was another who was near the end of his tour, and it showed. Thoroughly decent chap, but Ops had got to him. We younger ones were always astonished to find out that these old men, these ancient warriors who'd flown a tour, were only those few months older than us.

Losses in March from the rest of the force were heavy – five, six, seven eight aircraft and crews almost every night – but 9 Squadron came home; then the gods picked the number nine out of the hat. Flying over Belgium on the way home from Cologne, *Oberleutnant* Walter Fenske espied WS/K. The skipper was F/Lt John T L Shore: 'At twelve thousand feet my starboard engine packed up. It started again then, five seconds later, both engines stopped. It was impossible to start them again and at eight thousand feet I began getting rid of my crew, leaving the aircraft myself at fifteen hundred feet.'

The listening station at Hull picked up a message at 22.48: 'I am forced to land GN' (goodnight), sent by Sgt Beeves just before he parachuted clear. Also among those jumping was P/O James 'Cookie' Long, second pilot, out of the war after less than four weeks, but not yet dead. Shore found himself in a football field with a sprained ankle, a few miles from Heusden en Maas in Holland. He tried to destroy his parachute by burning it 'but they appear to be treated with some fire-resisting substance. It is best to cut them into shreds with a knife. I kept about twelve yards of my parachute cord concealed at the back of my tunic.' After failing to wake a farmer by throwing stones at his bedroom window, failing to get into a locked church and unable because of his ankle to accept an invitation consisting of civilian clothes, papers, money and an open bathroom window, he ended up in the police station with the rest of his crew with the exception of Sgt Tomkins.

Tomkins had a 4.5 Smith & Wesson on him and, as he was a navigator, he would know where he was. He could speak good French and also had the rations as they had been laid out on the navigator's table in front of him. His parachute had been found by the Germans and I should like to draw attention to the fact that every parachute is stencilled with the owner's name, number and rank, so that the Germans knew that one of the crew was missing.

After some fairly easy-going questioning, they were taken to a barracks in Amsterdam, where they were put in separate cells. 'We communicated by hammering on the walls. After an hour some food was brought – ersatz coffee, bread and sausage – but I was not searched. The guards were very slack and if I had not been lame, I could have got away. Cigarettes were provided and a novel to read: *The City of Beautiful Nonsense*.'

Personal effects were confiscated but not kit and, after breakfast next morning:

On our journey to the station the Dutch waved and cheered. We went by train to Frankfurt-am-Main, arriving there at about 20.00 hours, travelling in second-class carriages and being issued with bread, sausage and margarine. The guards were very lax and put their rifles on the rack. We did not see any bomb damage at Cologne. At Frankfurt I noticed that one of the Germans was carrying the navigation bag of my aircraft. I cannot think how they could have got this but they said it had been found twenty yards from the crash. In the Red Cross buffet we were given water while some twenty (German) soldiers came in and out and were given soup. Though we asked for some of this, we were refused.

Their guards, young Luftwaffe boys, did not enforce the no-talking rule in the buffet or the bus that took them to Dulag Luft. 'While driving through Frankfurt, I noticed that the blackout was fairly good but not so good as ours.' At the camp they were issued with bed clothes and food and assigned to rooms. The commandant, Major Rumpel, came to see John Shore the next afternoon in his new quarters. 'I did not answer any of his questions and he said it did not matter what squadron I came from, 9, 10 or 11. He tried to put me at my ease and asked me about the bombing of our towns, the number of my squadron, my mission, place from where I started, etc. His attitude was deliberately friendly and casual.'

The Germans also tried to elicit information using fake Red Cross forms and friendly chats with the half-dozen interpreters around the place. Discipline was lax, there was no searching of rooms, parcels and letters were as per and officers who gave their parole could go outside for walks. 'We were issued with Rhine wine and Dunkirk whisky. We also had beer at the little inns on our walks. Everybody seemed very happy at Dulag Luft.' Even so, two tunnels were being built.

> 'I say, old boy, did you notice those
> Spitfires we overtook on the way down?'
> P/O Sharp

Shore: The train (to Stalag Luft I, 15 April) started and I went into the lavatory. There was a small window on two hinges and I loosened the screws, leaving the window like this until I needed it. There were ordinary railway maps in the carriage and we were allowed to look at these for a while. As I wanted to go to the Swiss frontier I had to get out of the train fairly soon, during the daytime. I jumped out of the window but unfortunately they heard me and pulled the alarm cord while I made for a wooded bank, crossing the line to get there. The guards came out of the train and started firing their revolvers. I was caught by a *Feldwebel,* who was very annoyed when he got hold of me and pushed me down a bank. We arrived late at Kassel and missed our connection. When the next train came in at about six o'clock we (the officers) were put in one carriage and locked in. (During the journey) we could go and speak to the sergeants if we wanted to and arrived at Barth on the morning of 17 April.

While John Shore was being processed at his new home, there was bad news at Honington. Heaysman was lost at Berlin and Sgt Stark was due over the same target at about 01.00.

ORB: At 23.57 hours the letters NAP* were sent. Nothing more was heard from the aircraft until 00.14 hours when they requested a fix, which put them in the neighbourhood of Texel. A further fix was requested at 00.30 hours, which showed that they were not quite half-way across the North Sea, and finally an SOS message was sent by the aircraft at 00.58 hours, a fix of which was then some thirty miles off the English coast. A search was organised, in the course of which a parachute was seen in the water a few miles off Lowestoft and a dinghy was seen within two or three miles of the estimated position where the aircraft went down. It is difficult to connect the parachute with this particular incident, however. The attention of some destroyers on convoy duty was directed towards the parachute but there was nobody attached to the parachute harness. A ladder was hanging over the side of the dinghy but there was no wreckage anywhere.
*NAP = *unable to bomb primary and so have bombed target of last resort.*

No one attached and no sign anywhere of six more souls lost in the sea because they couldn't find their way even though they'd been flying successfully together for three and a half months. Their names would be forever connected with this particular incident by an inscription on the Runnymede Memorial.

Sgt Damman arrived on squadron as a new pilot and went on a 'second Dicky' with Sq/Ldr Cruickshanks, to Brest against the *Scharnhorst* and the *Gneisenau,* and another with Sq/Ldr Wasse. A second Dicky was a pilot as second pilot or, later in the war, as passenger. Before going on Operations as captain of his own aircraft, the new man was sent out with an experienced and well-regarded skipper, not necessarily a senior officer like Wasse, to get the feel of flying over enemy territory. Your compulsory joy-rides were your second Dickies because you, the novice, were second to Dicky, the pilot, and you generally had two such trips or, in some cases, three. Very occasionally, the second Dicky trip found someone out. A pilot, who seemed fine in every way, when exposed to the German defences might lose his nerve. He would be quietly shipped off to a rather less glamorous job, out of sight.

Traditionally pilots had become aircraft captains after a spell as a second pilot of half a dozen trips or more. Damman's second Dickies represented a quicker, more urgent way and he went out as skipper for the first time to Emden in R1281. This was a brand new Wimpy, also operating for the first time, in a raid featuring four Wellingtons.

ORB: At 00.57 hrs the NGZ* signal was received and an hour later the aircraft obtained a third-class fix from Hull, which made its position to be a few miles west of Berlin. This was probably fairly inaccurate owing to the distance, but it did indicate that the aircraft had been going in an easterly direction after bombing.
*NGZ – *we have bombed the target.*

It certainly did indicate an easterly direction. The target, Emden, was on the Ems estuary, a couple of minutes from the Dutch border and the North Sea coast. To be a few miles west of Berlin, instead of heading for Honington, Sgt Damman had to have flown for an hour at top speed to make something like two hundred and thirty miles the wrong way.

The stars, millions upon millions of them, shining with a piercing clarity unknown on the ground, gave crews a deep feeling about their status and their relative significance in the order of things, as well as offering the navigator a check on position with a sextant. Some of the crew might take an interest, too. It was not unknown for a pilot to put red on black, that is, to look at his compass and fly a course 180° out, whereby you could fly to Berlin instead of Suffolk.

'At 02.14 hrs the aircraft came up on the station wavelength and obtained a QDM of 272, which was passed as a first-class bearing and the aircraft was believed to have been then forty miles off the station.' This was a remarkable belief. Either the Berlin fix had been wrong by two hundred miles or Damman had just flown a Wellington at 400 mph for 75 minutes.

However, we now know this was impossible and no doubt the aircraft was on the other side of the skip distance* which appears to indicate that by asking for a QDM he thought he was nearer to base than he actually was. At 02.23 hrs he again obtained a third-class fix from Hull, which put him just south of Emden and the word LOST was sent from the aircraft. By this time the aircraft only had about an hour and a quarter's petrol left and a message was sent to him to fly at low boost

for the nearest point of the English coast as there was a strong easterly wind behind him. This message was not acknowledged and nothing further was heard from this aircraft. It is noted, however, that the German High Command communiqué claims to have captured† the crew of a Wellington aircraft in occupied Holland.

Skip distance: invisible error caused by the Heaviside layer (ionosphere) undulating, usually at dawn or dusk.

Sgt Fairfax finished his tour and said goodbye. John Fairfax was one of the best and would duly have his DFM in August, his promotion to Pilot Officer, his posting to 21 OTU and his twenty-first birthday, only to crash his Wellington shortly after take-off on 4 October. He, two trainee pilots, a w/op, a gunner and two ground crew would all be killed.

In RAF Bomber Command it was an inflexible, unquestioned rule that the pilot was the captain of the aircraft. In May 1941 two rare exceptions occurred to prove it. Sgt Copson, observer, had been flying with F/O McIntosh, whose second pilot was Sgt Lewis. It was the ambition of most but not all seconds to become firsts and Lewis had had his wish granted with two Ops in April. Next time out, 3 May, Wellington R1224 went to Brest with Lewis as pilot and the observer Sgt Copson as captain. Four German Ops followed for the same team.

Copson and Lewis went for a spot of leave. Joining an attack at Boulogne was pilot Sgt Green with observer George McRiner as the captain.

McRiner: In the Polish airforce the navigators were the captains. I'd had a lot of experience with quite a few different pilots and then suddenly they gave me this chap Green who was, to be frank, green in more than name. I wasn't the first navigator to feel that, as I was running the show, I should be captain. The CO was in agreement and Green was quite relaxed about it, perfectly amenable. We navigators used to refer to the pilots as drivers, airframe. We saw ourselves as the brains behind it. We gave the directions and the drivers turned left or right accordingly. There was an old joke. In a group of aircrew, how can you tell which are the navigators? They're the ones who can read and write. Of course, the pilots might have argued that we didn't say much when evasive action was required.

Last to take off that night was Sgt Les Mitchell, after five Ops as a second pilot, doing the job of skipper for the first time. Mitchell bombed the docks

†*The aircraft force-landed, out of petrol, at Ommen, Overijssel; all crew taken POW.*

all right but when he brought WS/Y home and attempted his first operational landing, he found he couldn't get his undercart down properly. He went in near the bomb dump and the aircraft burst into flames. Mitchell was killed but the rest survived, two of them thanks to the station commander and the MO, Group Captain Gray and Sq/Ldr McCarty, who climbed aboard the burning aircraft and pulled them out. The two senior officers received the George Medal.

The Group Captain used to like the occasional Op, hitching a lift with one of the flight commanders to see what it was like over Bremen or Brest. Aiden McCarty, although highly respected and well liked, had a reputation for being somewhat irascible, believing that no illness or injury should interfere with the peaceful, orderly life of a medical officer such as he. A phrase with which he used to greet each of his morning queue of patients passed into squadron lore and became its second motto: 'There's always bloody something'.

While Frank Whittle watched the first air test of his jet aircraft down the road at Cranwell, captain McRiner and crew went together under piston power to Kiel. 'That was a dicey one. We had to drop our bombs from two hundred feet, which is well below where they can hit you with heavy flak* but they made up for it with everything else, and as bomb aimer the captain/navigator sees everything at close quarters.'

Heavy flak – unlike the continuous, visible streams of light flak, this was a shell primed by the gunners to explode at a given height and so was unseen until it went off in a black and red cloud. One direct hit would usually down a bomber.

There were no losses in May but life in the air could always turn nasty, brutish and short. 9 June: four went to attack enemy shipping off the Belgian and Dutch coasts, taking off around 3.30 p.m. Sq/Ldr Pickard reported 'all bombs brought back. Six Me109s encountered four miles NE of Calais. Evasive action taken by turning into cloud. Rear Gunner reported seeing aircraft, believed Wellington, being attacked by two 109s. Black smoke seen coming from Wellington.' It had to be 9 Squadron. Theirs were the only Wellingtons on that trip.

The smoke wasn't coming from P/O Robinson's aircraft. They had a running battle for half an hour and the three men at the guns, Sgts Blakemore, Clarke and Bell, kept the fighters at bay without suffering any damage to themselves at all. So the doomed Wimpy was either T2620, F/O Douglas Lamb DFC, or R1758, which was the squadron CO. Wing Commander Roy George Claringbould Arnold, age 30, was on one of his occasionals with a scratch crew including F/O Dominic Bruce, the squadron's navigation leader and F/O Bax, the gunnery leader. Arnold gave the order and held her steady at very little feet while they all jumped but he was unable to get out. He crashed and was killed.

For Bruce, navigation from German POW camps now became the preoccupation and he would make many attempts, including one from Colditz, where he was seen trying to cut through the wires. Rifle and machine gun bullets flew as he prostrated himself and yelled his surrender. To everyone's astonishment, the Germans stopped firing. Perhaps they were laughing, because instead of shouting 'Ich gebe auf' – I give up, he'd shouted, 'Ich über gebe' – I'm going to be sick.

Now a Wingco, Wasse came back to take over the squadron and oversee a summer of almost entirely German targets.

McRiner: Wasse was one of the old school, a military man as well as a flying one. There was a scruffy little sergeant pilot – I'd never seen anyone so scruffy – and he did something to upset Michael Wasse, who called him into his office. Whatever was said, it infuriated Wasse even more and he pulled out a revolver. He didn't shoot the scruffy sergeant. He only put a bullet through the ceiling.

Sgts Parkes, Goldingay and Bratley were back from Vichy France and flying again. Sgt Goldingay would retrain as a bomb aimer and, as Flight Lieutenant Leslie Dennis Goldingay DFC, fall in April 1944 serving with PFF (Path Finder Force). That nightfighter killed in one hit a DSO, a DFM, two DFCs and two DFCs with Bar.

8 July 1941: 'AC1 Macdonald J M was killed after being struck by an aircraft Wellington R1591, which was landing on return from operations.' That was Sgt Parkes, coming back from Cologne. Sgt Stuart Martin Parkeshouse Parkes would become Squadron Leader Parkes DSO. Also in Pathfinders, 97 Squadron, on the night of 25 August 1944 he would take off for Darmstadt in a new Lancaster full of the latest kit and be sought out by a nightfighter. There would be a crash landing as the veteran and highly regarded Parkes tried to come down with wounded crew but only the flight engineer would survive.

Back in rural Essex the family Saich may have started to save coal for the winter, thoughtfully rationed by the government that July. Their 20-year-old son, Sgt Jack Saich, was out to burn more than coal on his third as a captain, 14 July, Bremen, with Bob Telling his second pilot.

ORB: Whilst over the target area they were held in a cone of search-lights . . . violent evasive action . . . again caught in searchlights and sustained a number of hits in the fuselage and mainplanes. The aircraft was set on fire in the rear portion of the fuselage and on the fin. The

forced-landing flare in the port mainplane was set on fire. The pilot, thinking that the port engine was on fire, switched off the petrol to that engine and switched the engine off. But the fire eventually went out, so he turned on the petrol and restarted the engine. It was found that the bomb doors were open, the hydraulics having been shot away. The navigator (Sgt Smitten) succeeded in extinguishing the fire in the fuselage. They had only been able to drop one bomb, and the rest, consisting of six 500lb bombs, they were unable to drop by any means. Three members of the crew were hit by shrapnel but only slightly injured.

So far, so good: the fires were out, injuries were slight and the aircraft was in the air on two engines. It was home time.

The captain set course for base but, owing to the bomb load still being on and the bomb doors open, his airspeed was very low and he was using as little throttle opening as possible to conserve his petrol as he did not know if he had been hit in the tanks. There was a shell hole in the starboard mainplane, which was blanketing off the aileron and which made the aircraft difficult to fly.

Sgt Saich got a fix near Texel and, after the crew discovered how slowly time could pass in a crippled aircraft flying over the North Sea, another fix which put him just off the English coast.

The captain, being satisfied that he was going to reach land before running out of fuel, decided to test his undercarriage, which he lowered, thus detracting still further from the aircraft's speed. He was unable to bring it up again as the main hydraulic system had been shot away. On reaching the coast and his petrol gauges having shown nothing for some time, he thought that he was about to run out of fuel and decided to force-land immediately rather than attempt to make an aerodrome. He selected a large field where he could land into wind and after attempting to lock the undercarriage down with the emergency hydraulic system he executed a forced landing in the selected field.

Thank God for that, lads. We're down, in the selected field.

In the half-light of dawn, the pilot had not noticed that the field was obstructed by poles and ropes. He struck two of these poles prior to touching down, which were carried away successfully. On touching down the starboard leg collapsed and the aircraft, striking another post, swung round and broke in two. All the crew returned to Honington with the exception of the rear gunner (Sgt English), who was taken to Norwich Hospital after the captain had ensured that a guard had been placed on the aircraft.

Next day nothing of operational importance occurred. Saich and his crew could sleep through first, the rain and drizzle, later becoming fair and, if they wanted, through the occasional showers in the afternoon. After a few days' leave and with a new second pilot and a new rear gunner, Saich was off to Hamburg.

25 July 1941: a future 9 Squadron observer near the end of his training, Sgt Ken Chamberlain, aged 19, was flying his last cross-country before posting to active duty. His skipper, P/O Rowland Mytton Hill, also 19, direct descendant of the Penny Post originator, noted that the temperature and pressure readings on the port engine were very unusual.

Ken Chamberlain: Our rear gunner (Frank Crook), an old man of 24, was an engineer in civilian life so Roly called him on the intercom for advice. 'I would say your port engine's about to catch fire,' said Frank. 'Oh, do you really think so?' said Roly. 'Look,' said the gunner. 'There's a perfectly good airfield down there. Let's land and have it looked at.'

Young and a mere trainee, Roly Hill would have felt a fool landing at a strange airfield and asking about his engine so he said no, he'd throttle it back and it would be fine. Chamberlain gave him the course for the next leg of the cross-country but as forecast the engine caught fire. Chamberlain was in his navigator's seat overlooking the port wing.

The flames were leaping past my window. The altimeter started to unwind and the airspeed built up. We were obviously in deep trouble and Eric Shipley in the front turret said, 'Roly, do you think I might come out?' Roly said, 'Well, if you want to,' and he came and sat on half of my seat. Roly said, 'It's all right, Ken – I can see an airfield' and I said, 'Roly, there are no airfields around here.' 'I can see a flarepath.' 'Roly, there are no airfields.' The next I knew there was an almighty crash and I came to, lying in a field with the aircraft burning steadily beside me. It turned out that Roly had mistaken the railway yard at Spalding for an airfield and tried to land on that. To his eternal credit, once he realised, he did manage to get the aircraft over the last houses in Spalding before we went down in an orchard but he was still killed, as were all the rest. The Wellington had broken its back and thrown me out, but kept all the others inside.

F/O Smith: 'We stayed sober all evening.'
F/O Jones: 'There was a bar present?'
Smith: 'Yes.'
Jones: 'But no barmaid, obviously'
(after a visit to the Duke's Head, King's Lynn)

Back at Honington and bringing with them the old jinx on flight commanders, two new ones arrived, Acting Sq/Ldr Ball and Sq/Ldr Bufton. Kenneth Ball went down on his third. Bufton was a prewar regular with seven years' service and he went to Cologne in the last remaining of the four Wellington Mark II aircraft belonging to the Squadron.

ORB: The aircraft bombed the target at 01.22 and at 02.07 an SOS was received stating that the aircraft had engine trouble. Several QDMs were obtained, but at 03.12 a signal from the aircraft faded out and nothing further was heard.

Sq/Ldr H E Bufton: We had engine trouble just before reaching the objective but were able to unload our bombs. Shortly afterwards one engine caught fire and the other seized. We accordingly baled out over Catillon (Nord), fifteen miles south east of Le Cateau.

Sgts Stickles (second pilot), Murray (w/op) and Wright (gunner) gathered together and made for a farm, where the Germans found them and sent them to POW camp. Sgts Crampton (observer) and Read (gunner) headed south. Next morning the squadron went for a sea sweep, all of them in the belief that Bufton had come down in the southern North Sea. By that time, he had already had discussions with local dignitaries.

As it grew light I approached the Curé of La Groise in his house next to the church. He directed me to the mayor, who advised me to report to the police. I went on and at the first house in Catillon found shelter and was given food and an overcoat. Two miles further on, heading south, a farmer took me to his house, gave me a meal, a map and directions for the next twenty miles. It was then about 09.00 hours. A friend of the farmer's said that he had heard of another British airman and guided me to a barn. At first I hid as the Germans could be seen searching, but as soon as they disappeared I entered the barn and was joined by Sgt Crampton, who was still in uniform.

Crampton: After I climbed out of my parachute I destroyed a document bearing my name and the name of the squadron. On the road I took a bearing on my button compass on the direction in which I thought the others had come down, and walked till dawn. Failing to find a hiding place in the fields, I went to a house but the people there were too terrified to take me in and gave me only two raw eggs. I walked further along the road and learned from a man who brought me a flask of wine that three members of the crew were in hiding a little way off. I made towards the place he indicated, but another man met me and took me to a loft, where he brought me food, coffee and cigarettes. Later I was taken to a tank in the yard where Sq/Ldr Bufton was hiding.

Sgt Read landed alone, walked fifteen miles and more and met a Belgian, who hid him for a day at his house. In the evening the news came that three of the crew had been captured and so Read set off again, walking twenty-five miles over the fields to reach the village of Orsinval.

Read: There I spoke to a baker's boy who took me to the bakery. The baker befriended me and I lived with him from 28 August to 10 October. During this time there were six German soldiers billeted in the village. I was put in touch with The Organisation and after a short visit to Lille for clothes and identity card, was taken to Burbure, where I was kept until 30 October.

Reunited, Bufton, Crampton and Read would have a journey of many stops by bicycle, car, train and foot, crossing the Somme bridge on forged passes. Their party eventually enlarged to thirteen soldiers and airmen in Marseille. A goods train would take the RAF contingent plus five Poles to Barcelona, then Madrid and finally Gibraltar and home.

Ken Chamberlain, still in training for the flying life after his sole-survivor crash, had had a month's sick leave, gone back to his unit to join a new crew and was in the air for a minute.

We took off for our first night flight and the aircraft in front of us went straight in, bang, and we flew through the flames. I went to the MO next morning and said enough was enough. Certainly ninety-nine out of a hundred doctors would have classified me as LMF (Lacking Moral Fibre) and ninety-nine out of a hundred station commanders would have agreed and thrown me out. I just happened to have the one doctor who took an interest, and the one station commander who was willing to take the time and persevere.

They left the shocked and shaken Chamberlain in the navigation section and let him fly when he was ready. In a few months' time, the luckiest navigator in the air force would arrive at 9 Squadron.

F/Lt Wilberforce had now stepped up to be a flight commander, Sq/Ldr

Inness was posted in to the job and it quickly began to look as if the jinx would have him too.

ORB: Wellington R1279 . . . was flying over the Mannheim area at 23.20 at eleven thousand feet. After bombing they did some jinking in cloud to avoid flak and searchlights and got severely iced up. The captain (Inness) lost control of the aircraft, which turned on its back, but having managed to regain control of the aircraft, he told the crew to stand by ready to abandon aircraft. Unfortunately, the aircraft again got out of control but it was eventually back under control at two thousand feet.

While losing nine thousand feet in a free-falling Wellington, three of Inness's crew stayed at their posts, praying and waiting for orders from the fully occupied skipper. 'It was then found that owing to some misunderstanding, the navigator (Sgt Corser) and the wireless operator (Sgt Clarke) were missing and had, in fact, been seen to bale out by the front gunner (Sgt Blakemore).' Inness's own report of the Op is somewhat less detailed. 'Believed bombs to have dropped in the Mannheim area but no results seen.'

Oberleutnant Helmut Lent got Jack Saich at last, in the very early hours of 8 September, on the way back from Berlin. This time the fires could not be put out, he could not land in the selected field and the injuries were not slight, but fatal for all as they crashed to earth in Friesland. 'A message NAP was received from the aircraft at 00.50 hrs but from then onwards nothing further was heard.' Sgt Saich had seen, and done, more than enough to earn his DFM, awarded a few days before, and he was still only 20.

Kit Kitson DFM went to Genoa. He'd completed his first tour of Ops and come back to 9 Squadron to do it all again. A few minutes after 02.00, 29 September 1941, he was over the Alps. 'A message NAP received from the aircraft at 01.36 hrs and this was followed at 02.08 hrs by a message SOS engine trouble. Nothing further was heard from the aircraft.' New Wellington Mark IIIs were arriving with their much more powerful Hercules engines, but Kitson's troublesome engine was a Pegasus and he was flying the last Mark IC to be lost by 9 Squadron.

Sgt Wilmot briefly thought it might be his turn, on his third with a new observer, Canadian Graham Welsh, bombing the floating docks and searchlights at Kiel.

Welsh: We were over the sea on the way home. I was taking astro sightings to confirm our position and saw the second pilot* going back to the rest area. We were just flying along so I thought I'd go up to his

seat and get his view of things, and I'd not been there long when Tommy (Wilmot) signalled for me to take over. I did have some experience flying twin-engined aircraft, but I had no idea Tommy knew about it. Anyway, I climbed up and carried on flying. He went back to the rest area too, and after a while suggested to the fellow there that he might get on with his navigating. It gradually dawned on the two pilots that it was the new observer driving and their feet didn't touch the floor or the sides of the aircraft as they did the length of a Wellington in point one of a second.

The much-increased efficiency of the German defences was generally causing losses to rise at a frightening rate. They had installed a great wall of searchlights called the Kammhuber Line, after its designer and commander, which caught the bombers as they flew, one at a time, over France, Holland and Belgium. A chain of radar stations had been set up all along the coast from Denmark in the north to France in the south, which transmitted their sightings to a series of small ground-control stations covering the Danish, Dutch and German frontiers. Each of these stations made a two-element team with a nightfighter assigned to a box of airspace. Any bomber flying alone through a box could expect to be intercepted as the ground controller, with one *Würzburg* radar following the bomber and another tracking his fighter, could guide his man close enough to an individual British aircraft for the pilot to be able to see it. The *Würzburg* could gauge height as well as direction; the earlier *Freya* system could only plot direction. The Germans also guided their anti-aircraft guns with radar.

One in five bombers failed to return from raids on the most heavily defended sector, the Ruhr. Tom Kirby-Green, now a squadron leader with No. 40, was one such. Returning home, his Wellington was hammered by a fighter and everything went dead. With the aircraft spinning out of control, Kirby-Green gave the order to jump. His parachute opened only moments before he hit the ground, injuring his spine so badly he couldn't move. A few seconds later, thirty yards away, his aircraft crashed. The rear gunner, F/O Peter Campbell-Martin MC, aged 44, was dead in his turret. The rest of the crew got out slightly before their skipper, which put them above higher ground. Their parachutes opened but, with much less distance to fall, they were all killed instantly.

F/Lt Shore was determined to rejoin the war and his numerous mad schemes for escape earned him the nickname 'Death'. Taking time out from

*Sgt Leslie Silver, who would be killed aged 20 in April 1942, going back to Kiel.

scheming, he had firm ideas about improving the comfort of fellow prisoners.

> **Suggestions for Red Cross parcels. No carrots or Maconochie stew* should be sent. Too much tea is sent. Too much bramble jelly, which is insipid. Provisions which would be appreciated are self-raising flour, dried eggs, custard powder, coffee, cocoa, raisins and currants, salt and pepper mixed in _waterproof_ packets, thin transparent lavatory paper, curry powder.**
> _*Maconochie Brothers, contractors to the War Office, supplied army rations – tinned meat and vegetables – in the Boer War and onwards. The statement on the label, 'The meat in this tin is prepared in its natural juices', caused much discussion._

Death Shore teamed up with Jimmy James in a halfway sensible tunnelling scheme which failed, and then another.

> **I noticed there was a tunnel started from the rubbish bin so I approached the man who had started it. At 10.30 every day there was a football match and the boys watching used to stand on the sloping top of the incinerator. Under their cover we kicked open the trap door and dropped in. We left the door open a little for air and James and I worked from 10.30 to 17.00 when another twelve people stood there while we got out. On Sunday we could not dig as there were no football matches. We used a table knife and took the earth out on a board and put the earth in the incinerator. The Germans had been told to look out for people hiding in the refuse cart so they paid no attention to the incinerator being half full with earth. It took us four days to dig the twenty-five feet with just enough room to crawl along. I had to wash my clothes after each day's digging but luckily I had two pairs of trousers.**

During this time the Germans emptied the incinerator, throwing the earth and burned rubbish mixture into a cart and taking it away, a novel method of soil disposal in the history of wartime tunnel making.

Now the escapers had to wait for an air raid, when a complex system of guard-trebling, sentry go and curfews gave them greatly increased danger and a time limit of five minutes to get through the tunnel but also provided darkness. Part one of the plan was to crawl through trap doors they had made in hut walls, out into the compound and on towards the incinerator. At 22.30, 19 October, bombers were heard and the lights went out.

I started crawling through my trap door wearing my greatcoat, which prevented me going back so that a German guard came along and nearly stepped on me before walking towards the gate. I got up and walked after him, making my footsteps coincide with his. I went along to James's hut and called him, and he came out just behind me. I got into the incinerator, but James did not come.

James was unable to come. He'd seen Shore go in but had had to hide from the guards whose Alsatians soon found him. The tunnel had six inches of water in it but Shore rattled through, emerged into the football field, rolled into the ditch at the edge and dug his way under the wire buried in the bottom. In the first convenient wood he waited for James but was forced to run when he thought the Germans were coming with dogs. Squeezing lemon onto his boots and clothes to destroy his scent, he set off on a long march to the sea. After many mistakes and alarms and a poor attempt at stealing a bicycle – 'all bicycles in Germany creak for lack of lubricating oil' – he reached the docks at Sassnitz and tried to pass himself off as a Swedish sailor looking for a berth. This was not working at all well when 'an SS man came up and asked me for my papers. I said, "Ich bin Schweder. Nicht verstehen." He brought two Danes from a nearby ship so that they could show me what he meant by papers. Another Dane, drunk, appeared and put his arms around me and the SS man.'

Shore saw his chance and slipped away towards the railway lines that led to the spot where the ferry would dock in the morning.

I saw two Pullman coaches and got in one and had a drink and a wash in the lavatory. I was feeling rather despondent by then and got into a second-class carriage and went to sleep, not caring much if I was discovered. I woke at about 03.00, went out, scrambled into a tarpaulin-covered truck full of piping, looked and saw the funnels of the ferry. A line of trucks was being taken aboard so I jumped out and ran fifty yards to scramble onto a low truck with a German lorry on it. I spent the voyage sitting in the cab of the lorry.

In Sweden – Trelleborg – Shore was spotted, arrested and given money and a first-class ticket to Stockholm. Soon he was back in the UK. As Wing Commander Shore MC, he would be killed in a postwar crash.

> 'Came so close to the ground in a dive
> that we had to elevate the front guns'
> P/O Canton

On the day Shore arrived in Blighty, 29 October 1941, Wellington Z8368 of Middle East Command, 148 Squadron, was on a mission to German-occupied Crete. The skipper, Conk Canton, gave the order to bale out when terminal engine trouble developed. 'I was in the sea for about five hours and lost consciousness (before being) picked up by some Cretan fishermen, who gave me some food and left me in a hiding place amongst the rocks. A child gave me away to the Germans, who arrested me and took me to Crasalum, where I was interrogated.' Canton went to several prison camps via Athens, ending up in Stalag Luft III. His five crew were not so fortunate. Their bodies were never found but their names would be carved in stone, at Runnymede.

No. 9 Squadron's raid on the night of 7/8 November showed what could so easily happen if the weather wasn't favourable. Six flew blind to Berlin, taking off between 17.52 and 18.35.

Sq/Ldr Inness: Reached point north of Berlin but unable to locate target owing to 10/10 cloud. Returned via the Ruhr and bombs dropped on a large red fire. Bombs seen to burst.

P/O Wilgar-Robinson: Bombs jettisoned on Berners Heath (bombing range) owing to all instruments being u/s.

Sgt Roberts: Unable to reach primary owing to 10/10 cloud and severe icing. Bombs dropped on Jüterbog, but no results seen.

Sgt Carter: Primary not located owing to 10/10 cloud. Bombs dropped on concentration of light flak twenty miles west of Magdeburg. No results seen.

Sgt Wilmot: Searched for half an hour in target area and bombs dropped singly on ETA. Flash of 1,000lb bomb seen.

Sgt Dalgliesh: Bombed believed target area on ETA. Bursts not seen.

Graham Welsh was Wilmot's observer on this trip.

We'd had no weather warnings at briefing but after crossing the enemy coast we could see a large cumulus cloud ahead of us, with its promise of icing and strong winds, so I ordered a changed course to the south. I don't know if every crew did this, maybe not. Our diversion meant we would not have sufficient fuel to return if we spent too much time around the target. We made frequent checks on our dead reckoning along the way using enemy radio beacons; their frequencies changed by the day but we were given the codes. We reached Berlin, dropped our bombs singly in a line, and used the same methods to get home.

On starry nights I could use my clockwork sextant. You wound it up then, once you had your celestial object sighted and stabilised, you pressed the trigger and signalled the wireless operator, who recorded the exact time. The clockwork took a series of regular sightings until it ran out, when the time was recorded again, and you averaged the readings and got your position that way. It was one of the tools we had, and an invaluable one.

On this night the awful weather had been forecast at HQ, even if nobody told 9 Squadron, and Bomber Command's C-in-C, Sir Richard Pierse, had been severely lobbied to cancel the Berlin part of the schedule which was to feature two hundred of the record 392 aircraft on Ops. Other targets were then admitted but still 169 went to the Big City, more than half of which couldn't find it, and another record was broken. Altogether, 37 losses were suffered, twenty of them on the Berlin raid, with no noticeably compensating result. The Berliners counted some damaged industrial buildings, fourteen houses knocked down and eleven people killed, while the RAF was counting rather more. Into the Valley of Death rode the four hundred. Casualties on such a scale, almost ten per cent of the biggest ever raid, caused mutterings in high places about bomber commanders.

For a while Ops would be few. The dreadful damage suffered by Bomber Command over the previous several months had forced an order for restricted operations onto Pierse, while those above pondered questions about the usefulness of bombing. Since early July, No. 9 had lost ten Wellingtons, a squadron's worth. Bomber Command had lost over five hundred aircraft and crews. If there had been no replacements, there would have been none left.

The Butt Report in the August compared 600 bomber photographs with crew reports and Bomber Command raid assessments. D M Butt, a War Cabinet civil servant, had never flown on a bomber Op, of course, and his investigation was done at a desk, but he came up with some shattering statistics. Of the two-thirds of crews on a given Op who claimed to have bombed the target, between five per cent (no moon) and forty per cent (in moonlight) actually bombed within five miles of it. The rest were further away and figures were even worse for the Ruhr, where smoke and haze were ever present.

The Prime Minister, the War Cabinet, the Air Ministry and the RAF top brass took the report at face value. In sum, it said that RAF bombing was an inconvenience and occasionally a hurtful nuisance. The Germans from first-hand experience might have given the bombers rather more credit, while naturally assuming that the RAF would get much better at it and planning accordingly. Churchill said that the only plan was to persevere which, since Bomber Command was the only force fighting the Germans in Germany, was spot on.

Meanwhile, No. 9 was active in the pursuit of getting better. The Squadron had been selected for the field trials of a new piece of wonderkit, the navigation aid for which the bombers had been desperately waiting, known as 'Gee'. The system was based on radio signals. A Gee box in the aircraft received pulses from three far-apart ground stations on mainland UK. By analysing the phase differences between the signals, the box calculated where the aircraft must be. It was confidently expected that this would fulfil the bombers' dream of being able to navigate with certainty, in large numbers, to pinpoints in Germany and especially to the Ruhr, a massive industrial area where individual targets had very few identifying features when looked at through smog from twelve thousand feet in the blackout.

Of course the field trials centred round whether the thing would work or not, but there were also serious tactical considerations. It would take some time before every bomber had Gee, so there would have to be raids where the Gee-equipped led and the Gee-without followed. If 9 Squadron, for instance, were to lead a Gee raid, would it be better for them to start fires with incendiaries for the unequipped to bomb, or should they drop flares? Or should they lead the force in formation and instruct the others when to bomb?

These matters would be resolved with intensive practice. There was still a war to fight: 27 November, ten of 9 went to Düsseldorf. Though fighters were about Sgt Ramey, American pilot from Milwaukee, didn't need them. 'Bombed target area and bursts seen. Starboard engine caught fire after crossing Dutch coast and crew baled out over Herne Bay, two of crew being drowned and the rest safe.' Safe but injured, except for the front gunner. Warren Ramey and three of the crew lived to fight another day for 9 Squadron, knowing that for them death was more probable than life. They'd flown half a dozen Ops together; this was their fourth with Ramey as captain. Could they have kept going if they'd known, for instance, that they had inflicted no casualties in Düsseldorf?

Every available 9 Squadron aircraft and crew, including a new second pilot called Runnacles, went to Aachen on 7 December with the city-centre Nazi HQ as their aiming point. On the way, after crossing the enemy coastline at Knokke, F/O Hodges and his men had a weird and extremely unnerving experience with an unusual kind of fighter escort.

. . . broken cloud above ten thousand feet, three-quarter moon on starboard bow. Searchlights and light flak had just ceased and no star shells or flares were illuminating Wellington when three unidentified low-wing S/E E/A* all carrying amber downward recognition lights appeared from astern at six hundred yards range. They took up inverted vic formation around Wellington with one astern and one on each quarter, maintaining a distance of approximately five hundred yards and same height. This formation was held for forty minutes, although Wellington climbed in and through cloud and remained mostly in cloud during this period. E/A made no attack or attempt to close nearer than three hundred yards. On reaching Aachen area, the two E/A on beam broke away upwards and rearguard machine faded away later.

single-engined enemy aircraft.

Whatever that was all about, no one hit the target and there were no casualties in Aachen. A Cologne trip was a certain navigator/captain's last. F/Lt George McRiner DFC had completed 34 trips, 202 hours 26 minutes of operational flying, and was signed off by Wasse as above the average. He didn't have much of a rest. In January 1942 he was to go to 149 Squadron on Stirling. 'A disappointing aircraft, the Stirling. It was poor on height and there was always the likelihood of something going wrong with the undercarriage. You always felt very nervous when landing in one.'

Around the country, this was an especially merry Christmas, with extra rations allowed of four ounces of sugar and two of tea. On 28 December ten went to Germany, including Sgt Ramey with a new second pilot and rear gunner to replace his dead men, but the rest the same. This was one month after swimming in Herne Bay. It was to be Tom Purdy's last night, being shot down by a fighter over Holland. Warrant Officer Purdy DFM, biplane pilot from prewar days, survivor of 9's first raid to Brunsbüttel and 28 years old, had lasted a long time, longer than anyone except his wife, Ellen, could have expected.

3

THE END OF THE BEGINNING: 1942

During the old year, in very round numbers, two hundred Fairey Battles had been lost, seven hundred Blenheims, five hundred Hampdens, seven hundred Wellingtons and four hundred Whitleys. Exact figures were 2,331 aircraft and crews lost on Ops; 2,795 altogether.

The New Year began in frustration. Once again the priority was the German warships *Gneisenau*, *Scharnhorst* and *Prinz Eugen*, which were in Brest harbour for repairs after many successes in the Atlantic. Between them they had sent the carrier *Glorious* and well over one hundred thousand tons of merchant shipping to the bottom. No. 9 Squadron went to Brest three times and never saw a thing through ten tenths cloud. Sgt Wilmot finished his tour; up at 04.03, bombs dropped on estimate, down at 10.00, could they get the interrogation over before the bar shut in the sergeants' mess? There would have been no thought of the morrow. Even if there had, Wilmot would never have guessed that in two years' time he'd be back with 9 Squadron as Flying Officer Wilmot, Lancaster pilot.

Wing Commander K M M Wasse DFC moved on and his place was taken by the promoted flight commander, W/Cdr W I C Inness. Graham Welsh: 'Michael Wasse was popular with all and a real inspiration as our CO. His successor was very different. He could be described as dour and distant, especially towards non-officer aircrew. He was an old India hand, flying Hawker biplanes against marauding Afghan tribesmen.'

Day and night the squadron was doing top secret Gee box exercises, carrying special crews, which meant that any loss was a blow way beyond the usual. On the morning of 19 January part of X3370's starboard wing fell off and she came down at Folly Farm, Thetford. All seven aboard were killed. The pilot was Bob Telling. One of three observers in training with Gee was Harry Tarbitten, who had started the previous May and was on his second tour. Another was John Amphlett, who had ditched in Herne Bay with Ramcy.

Gee or no, the old days hadn't gone yet and the individualist method could still produce results. Sgt Doughty set off for Soesterburg aerodrome but attacked Schipol instead from four hundred feet at 260mph. 'Machine-gunned enemy aircraft about to land. Tracer seen to enter enemy a/c that burst into flames and burned out on the ground. Hangars and buildings bombed from four hundred feet. Three searchlights shot out and one light gun emplacement silenced.' Sgt Dalgliesh saw a dummy aerodrome, picked up Soesterburg and watched the flarepath being switched on and off for landings and take-offs. 'Bombed flarepath from five hundred feet, also machine-gunned 'drome. Repeatedly followed E/A circling 'drome and fired at no less then seven, including two on ground. Balance of HEs* and incendiaries dropped on concentration of lights or fires on the aerodrome.'

*HEs – high explosive bombs.

Dalgliesh was given a new and unusual rear gunner. Four Royal Artillery officers were seconded to 9 Squadron, with the job of assessing the effectiveness or otherwise of the German anti-aircraft gunnery. The senior man, Captain George Rupert Buck, never did find the answer. He, Dalgliesh and all the crew were killed when their Wellington went into the sea off Clacton on a training flight. The others, 2nd Lts Southgate, Pullen and Mullock flew many Ops and were all captains by the time they left. Mullock, as Major Mullock, would come back in July 1943 to do one more Op – a unique one.

For Bomber Command things came to a head in February 1942. It was those ships at Brest. All in all, 1,875 sorties had been flown against them and two thousand tons of bombs dropped. The net result was 43 British bombers shot down, much repair work to the warships but no permanent damage. Hitler decided he wanted his ships nearer home and on the morning of 12 February, they set sail, heavily escorted by naval and air forces, through the English Channel. Here they were in the Straits of Dover, the twenty miles of sea where the Spanish Armada was defeated, which the British always regarded as their personal property. The Germans had purposely picked a bad-weather day and, accidentally, one on which almost all of Bomber Command was on a stand-down. The order said that these ships were to be attacked by every available means and so, after a mad scramble, 242 aircraft were sent in pursuit. Sgt Casey of 9 Squadron was one of the 203 who missed sighting the boats at all. 'To attack enemy battle cruisers off Dutch coast. Unable to locate target owing to heavy rain, snow and icing.' True, Sgt Casey, but the position you had been given was wrong by some sixty miles.

F/Lt George McRiner was in a 149 Squadron Stirling. 'We were briefed to fly at six thousand feet, which was above the cloud and we couldn't see a thing. Our skipper said we'd go down below the cloud, which was a bit hairy, wave hopping, but we still couldn't find the ships.' Of the 39 of Bomber Command who did find the targets, sixteen were destroyed and the rest caused zero damage. It was no good pointing out that the weather was so foul no one could have done any better, especially as none of the bombers were equipped with low-level bombsights, or that *Scharnhorst* and *Gneisenau* had been badly hurt by mines laid by Bomber Command, or that many crews had shown the greatest heroism.

Unfavourable and grossly unfair comparisons were made with the success of the Japanese at Pearl Harbor, 6 December 1941 and, four days afterwards, their destruction of HMS *Repulse* and HMS *Prince of Wales*, the first* capital ships ever sunk on the open sea by air power alone. The British public saw only the failure in home waters and was appalled by the incompetence and the shame. The fall of Singapore, symbol of Empire, took second place in a week of disasters.

Other firsts were the Royal Navy destroyer HMS Gurkha, sunk off Norway by Luftwaffe bombers, 10 April 1940; the damaged cruiser Königsberg sunk in Bergen harbour, 11 April 1940, by Skua dive bombers of Fleet Air Arm Squadrons 800 and 803.

Something had to be done. Churchill could order the resumption of all-out bomber attack on Germany, which he did, but what would be achieved if a grand total of 2,117 sorties couldn't put a disabling dent in a warship? Clearly, Sir Richard Pierse, lately the bombers' C-in-C, had been a good officer but was now seemingly out of his depth. He had also taken the blame for that Berlin night last November. Churchill had no confidence that such a man could reinvent Bomber Command and so Pierse was transferred to India. The top desk was vacant.

New technology was needed and new techniques plus better organisation and teamwork, better target finding and, once found, much better marking of targets with reliable flares. Bombers needed to know more precisely where they were and they needed a better bombsight. If they were to succeed in a long-range war of attrition with the German air defences, they needed better aircraft. They needed better PR, too. Those in power had to believe that Bomber Command funds and priorities could not be more usefully allocated elsewhere. Above all, if they were to get all of these things and be able to deploy them to succeed at their job, they needed new leadership.

Ten vital days began with 13 February, the night after the battle-cruiser debacle. The *London Gazette* announced 'the award of the Distinguished Flying Cross to P/O H L Tarbitten, since deceased' and the final trial of Gee was held. For 9 Squadron exercises had been going on pretty much every day of the month, requiring crews to arrive at a distant dummy target at an exact time. All their pilots and observers had been on an intensive Gee course at Marham. They were ready and, in an experiment code-named Crackers, twelve aircraft of 9 Squadron, guided by Gee, arrived over a target on the Isle of Man and each dropped a flare. They circled and came in to drop another, hopefully more accurately with the help of the illumination of the first, and repeated this to keep the target lit for twenty minutes. As an afterthought, they also dropped some flares in bundles of eighteen. The single-flare method proved adequate as a beacon but nowhere near bright enough for visual ID of the target. The bundles were much better.

> 'Ah! Heavy flak!'
> P/O Wilgar-Robinson
> (on finding a pea in his soup)

Crackers II was mounted on the night of 19/20 February, aiming for a railway station in North Wales. Unlike during Crackers I, there were no ground station faults nor was there half a gale blowing. Crackers II was a success. Although noting these historically significant flights in the 9 Squadron ORB only as 'At night aircraft carried out navigation exercise', 3 Group, whose 9 and 115 Squadrons had done the pioneering, could now offer a plan to turn the bombing war. For a quarter of an hour waves of Gee aircraft would light the target with flare bundles dropped at ten-second intervals. An incendiary force would bomb by the light of the flares and the main force would bomb the incendiaries.

Three days after Crackers II, a former deputy chief of air staff, Air Vice Marshal Arthur Travers Harris, arrived from his liaison post in Washington DC, 23 February 1942, to take up his new job as Commander-in-Chief, Bomber Command. A week later a new aircraft, the Avro Lancaster, flew its first Operation and a new bombsight, the Mark 14, began trials.

Like his two predecessors, Pierse and Portal, Harris was formerly with the Royal Flying Corps and keeper of order in the Colonies. Now Chief of Air Staff, Portal expected a close partnership with Harris, a partnership founded in the early days when they'd both commanded bomber squadrons on the same station. Portal was one of those men who could get things done without raising his voice. Harris was quite different, single-minded, crusty, brusque, determined, unstoppable, and charming when absolutely necessary. The strategy – destruction of factories, transport and cities – was no different to what had gone before. It had been long laid down in a directive from the Air Ministry.

Bomber Command was instructed to 'focus attacks on the morale of the enemy civil population and, in particular, of the industrial workers'. There was a list of cities to be destroyed: Essen, Cologne, Gelsenkirchen, Duisburg et cetera. An additional brief was to 'take on particular targets of immediate strategic importance, such as naval units, submarine building yards and bases . . . specified factories in France'. Harris did not bring the strategy with him. He had been appointed because the previous man had failed.

Up to the end of February 1942, Bomber Command had dropped 13,614 tons of bombs on German industrial towns with results officially described as negligible. The percentage of built-up area destroyed was so small it was not worth calculating. On average, bombers were attacking a target at a rate of forty an hour and dropping a ton of bombs each. Such a performance was not very different from that achieved in the earliest days of the war so the only major change up to Harris coming in had been a vast improvement in the extent and efficiency of the German defences, which would continue for a long time yet. No diplomat and no compromiser, Harris set about the job in a way that might turn the grand idea into a reality.

Britain and the British needed some good news. The Japanese were doing what they liked in the Far East, as had the Germans in Europe. U-boats ruled the Atlantic but, at last, the German machine had been halted, in Russia, by the fanatically devoted Red Army. The western war would now become a case of prosecution, to liberate Europe, rather than of defence, to save the British Isles from invasion. Harris: 'The bomber force of which I assumed command on 23 February 1942, although at that time very small, was a potentially decisive weapon. It was, indeed, the only means at the disposal of the Allies for striking at Germany itself and as such, stood out as the central point in Allied offensive strategy.'

The process of increasing numbers and re-equipping with heavy bombers had been started long before Harris took charge. Even so, the force was less than four hundred aircraft, of which only seventy were the four-engined Stirling and Halifax types, which had made slow progress through their early difficulties. The twin-engined Manchester had made no progress at all and would shortly be withdrawn. On any given night perhaps three hundred bombers were available for duty and between them in a month they managed to drop a mere two thousand tons of bombs on Germany. With such a force, it was little wonder that Pierse and Portal had failed to destroy any German cities and how was Harris supposed to do any better? Harris again: 'It is not too much to say that, owing to the small size of the force and the primitive methods then at our disposal, we could no more assail the enemy effectively by air than by land or sea. His defences were sufficient to prevent us from operating in daylight and by night we could not find our aiming points.'

The new technology, the Gee system, looked good and the Ministry was very happy. The instructions said that Gee was 'to be regarded as a blind-bombing device and not merely as a navigational aid'. With the help of Gee, Harris was expected, for example, to destroy Essen, including the vast sprawl of the Krupp works employing two hundred and forty thousand people to make iron and steel, railway locomotives, guns, shells, aero-engine parts, all sorts of engineering production vital to the war.

To destroy Krupp would have been a remarkable improvement but an Op against the Renault truck factory at Billancourt, western Paris, by well over two hundred bombers in less than two hours, caused severe damage and raised hopes that a new dawn was breaking in Bomber Command. Getting on for half the factory was destroyed, production was stopped for weeks but still there had to be a downside. Air raids there had not been expected. They hadn't even bothered to install any flak. The sirens went off almost nightly as bombers flew to Germany and the workers were used to false alarms. They stayed in bed, but tonight it wasn't false. Despite the greatest care many bombs fell among nearby workers' quarters and around four hundred were killed or died later of injuries, twice as many people as had ever been killed in a raid on Germany when no such care was taken.

George McRiner: I was back in a Wellington, with Group Captain Evans-Evans as skipper, and a cookie for the first time. We didn't seem able to get up any speed at all. Crawling along, we were. Anyway, the Group Captain got us sorted eventually and we did two runs. I got six photographs and everybody seemed delighted.

For McRiner Ops were almost over. After various training posts he would fly in Dakotas and Liberators with Transport Command, ferrying aircraft – Canada via Greenland – and bussing soldiers to and from even more distant places. 'Two little army boys asked me if they would have parachutes. I said no. "Oh," said one, "my mother said I should never fly without a parachute." Hard luck I said, get aboard.' The group captain would last almost to the end of the war, going down at Gravenhorst aged 43 in February 1945.

With Gee they should be able to do even better than the Renault job and, on the night of 8 March, the first Gee attack was mounted: on Essen. This was the 3 Group plan, as proved on the railway station in North Wales. Fourteen of 9 Squadron went, Gee-equipped and led by Sq/Ldr Turner, the same Turner who had flown Heyford biplanes in 1938 and was Grant's second pilot at Brunsbüttel, the first raid of the war. He was back with his old squadron as a flight commander responsible for marking the target for the rest of the force with a line of flares. Another line, laid by 115 Squadron, would make the form of a cross and then they'd go round again in a wave of incendiary-dropping aircraft, bombing the cross and starting some good fires for the main force to hit.

At Essen, P/O Hale reported, 'Flares were illuminating Krupps works.'

Sgt Davidson saw 'Flares clearly illuminating town' and F/Sgt Casey 'Town clearly seen and very big fires started.' The crew of X3411 and skipper Sgt Lovell, who had been on squadron since November, never saw the lights. On the way there they went down, into the sea. Fatally demonstrating the lack of magic in the new black box was X3641, captain Sgt Doughty, who had such fun strafing Schipol. Taking off at 00.31 for Essen and not getting very far with his navigation aid 'The aircraft requested a fix at 01.12 hrs and a further fix at 01.27. After that time nothing further was heard. As soon as daylight permitted, a sweep was carried out without success by aircraft from other stations over the North Sea.'

Sgt Jim Cartwright and crew were very nearly the third loss of 9 Squadron's Essen night. 'Flares dropped east to west across town. Bombs dropped on same course.' On the way back things became more exciting.

SECRET 9 Squadron Combat Report
8/9 March 1942. Essen. Wellington X3643. Captain: Sgt Cartwright. Visibility good, moon astern, no cloud but some haze beneath. No flak or searchlight activity and IFF* off. A Ju88 without lights approached suddenly from below and ahead and opened fire at 200 yards. IFF was switched on and E/A climbed above and attacked again from astern. Rear gunner (Sgt Nicholas) fired one short burst at 600 yards and two longer bursts when E/A approached to 400 yards. E/A dived below on port quarter and front gunner (Sgt Sadler) fired three short bursts. E/A disappeared into haze and was not seen again. During the attacks our aircraft took evasive action by turning in towards E/A's attack and then descended steeply into haze. Both gunners saw four streaks of tracer coming from nose of E/A and consider them to be cannon not machine gun fire. Rear gunner claims hits on E/A in centre of nose. No damage to Wellington.
*IFF – Identification Friend or Foe.

Not so lucky over Essen that night was a Stirling of 15 Squadron, skippered by 9 Squadron ditcher and crash survivor from 1940 George Nicholson, now a flight lieutenant on his second tour. The flak got him and he and all his crew died.

> 'I don't need a duty signaller. I do everything myself'
> P/O Nicholson

The survivors from 9 Squadron returned from Essen around 7 a.m. Like everyone else they'd missed the factories and at 7 p.m. they took off again to attack the same place. Jim Cartwright and crew, one day older, had engine trouble over the sea, turned back and were twenty miles from home when, with most of their petrol still aboard, they crashed near Harleston, Norfolk. Every one of them died in the flames.

At Essen the flare-laying was fine but many of the incendiary wave of raiders were late. Not only was their timing out; so too were the flares by this time. They scattered their fires in the wrong places, wide and short of the target, some in Essen and some in twenty other towns not mentioned at the briefing, and the main force bombed the same.

ORB: Information was received that P/O R P Hoult (observer) reported missing in aircraft X3411 (Sgt Lovell) on 9 March 1942 has been picked up by a trawler after thirty-three hours in the sea and admitted to Lowestoft General Hospital suffering from exposure. No news received of the other members of the crew.

At Kiel they tried the same bombing method, attacking the Deutsche Werke U-boat building yards. Eight took off, four came home with engine trouble, one found he was short of petrol and bombed anywhere. The U-boat yards were hit, but Canadian pilot Sgt Gerry Webb had yet to round off a fairly dismal night for 9 Squadron:

The flak was heavy over the target but we managed a straight bombing run. Our observer, P/O Victor Saul, called bombs gone when sparks and flames leapt from the engine and back across the wing. I switched it off, of course, and hit the extinguisher button, and flew on one with full port rudder and the port wing down. The engine fire went out but we were losing height too fast to get home. We'd be in the sea long before, so I unfeathered the starboard prop and tried starting the engine, only to be presented with another shower of sparks and tongues of flame. The same thing happened when I tried it later. At the third attempt, with a prayer to the Good Lord as we were almost in the drink, it started.

The engine would only run on low power but it was enough for the moment. With careful nursing it might take them home.

I was utterly exhausted so I handed over to my second pilot, Sgt Vickers, and went to sleep in the bomb aiming compartment. Vickers woke me as we crossed the coast at a thousand feet so I could take her in, but I made the most terrible landing of my life and the Wimpy was a write-off. But at least we were all right.

So they were, but three of the crew would go with Saul as an observer/captain and prayers would be no help to them.

Crashing, totally wrecking a new Wellington only four Ops old, was not viewed as anything which might psychologically affect a pilot and his crew and Gerry Webb was on 9 Squadron's next Op, back to Essen, when he had to come home early and land again with a dicky engine. This time he got down safely.

Over the next few weeks the squadron flew 77 sorties to Essen in eight raids including another double, home and away again in a few hours. Runnacles: '10/10 cloud all the way. *TR faded so bombed on ETA. Exact position unknown but definitely in Germany.'

*TR1335 was the early term for Gee.

In five weeks six crews, half of the squadron's normal airborne strength, went down for Essen, plus one for Cologne. Over the whole of 1942 ten per cent of the RAF's bombing effort would be expended on Essen; 3,724 sorties, 201 aircraft lost with, as Harris put it, 'no important damage inflicted on the Krupp works and little on the town'. Gee was very useful, especially in the hands of the best navigators, but it was not accurate enough to allow all navigators and pilots to be sure that a fire below was not one of the many very good decoys the Germans lit, or one of the RAF's own making in the wrong place. There was also the smog produced by industry, which meant that flares and incendiaries adequate for less polluted regions did not shine clearly enough for the main force to see them properly, in the right spot or otherwise.

Gee was a godsend for finding the way home. Aircraft took increasingly accurate fixes the nearer they flew to base. Exhausted crews with Gee, who previously might have got lost and ended up in the sea or crashed because they couldn't find the aerodrome, now came back safely.

To start with, ten squadrons had Gee. Fully functioning, it could take them to the right area, within a mile or even better, but to mark a target precisely still required visual identification. Lübeck, a moderately important Baltic harbour and trading town, was easily recognisable from the air. It was not covered in coal-fired haze and, as Harris pointed out, 'its defences could not be compared with those of the Ruhr. The attack was planned primarily to learn with what success the first wave of aircraft could guide the following wave by starting a conflagration at the aiming point.'

The first wave would go in and mark the target with incendiaries; the second and third would smash the place to pieces. The raid would feature 234 aircraft and they all had to bomb in two hours. Such restrictions and discipline had never been known. In the Gee-equipped incendiary wave on that Palm Sunday, 9 Squadron found the town already alight. Sgt Webb, his engines purring, 'dropped incendiaries about centre of town but could not see aiming point owing to smoke and fires'. Sgt Ramey dropped his 'in centre of island but no bursts seen, owing to fires which appeared to be solid'. Runnacles: 'Own incendiaries dropped in centre of fires in town. Fires were spreading rapidly on leaving and were visible 90 miles away.'

Lübeck, with an old town centre of narrow streets, was ideal for burning. When thousand upon thousand of incendiary bombs fell in back alleys and city lanes fires started straight away, spreading widely and wildly, beyond any control. Germany had never seen anything like it and, small-scale though it was, those sent to inspect afterwards were shocked to their souls. Something like 3,500 buildings were destroyed or badly damaged. The Germans had been right. The Tommies were bound to get better at bombing.

Harris: The raid was an unqualified success and proved that under good weather conditions a fairly important, but not vital, German town could be at least half destroyed by a relatively small force dropping a high proportion of incendiaries. The loss of thirteen aircraft* on an operation of this type, involving as it did deep penetration in bright moonlight, was moderate in relation to the achievement.
*The thirteen were mostly shot down by fighters on the way back and it could so easily have been more.

SECRET 9 Squadron Combat Report
28 March 1942. Lübeck. Wellington X3649 WS/D. Captain: Sgt Davidson.
(Near Westerhaven) Me110 appeared 400 yards level on port bow, dived below and came up below and astern of Wellington, opened fire at 200 yards to which rear gunner replied. Rear turret badly damaged and rear gunner wounded (Sgt Rushton). Me110 came in again from starboard beam below and gave Wellington long second burst of about seven seconds both cannon shell and machine guns, wounding second pilot (P/O Dowdell) in right arm and navigator (Sgt Pullen) seriously in both legs. Wellington took violent evasive action by sharp diving turns thereby losing Me110. Wellington eventually reached base and made good fuselage landing as hydraulics damaged. Intercom, longerons, rudder and geodetics also damaged.

The Captain of the aircraft commends the great courage and devotion to duty of the Navigator Sgt Pullen who, although seriously wounded in both legs, refused to leave his table and navigated the aircraft back. Only when English coast was reached did he allow himself to be placed on the rest bed.

Five days later immediate DFMs for Davidson and Pullen were announced, then it was 31 March and Essen again, in daylight but using cloud cover predicted by the Met.

Graham Welsh: We had these not-so-good engines and were trying to reach the clouds over the North Sea when the red light came on. To continue at that height without the cloud cover would have been pure suicide so we came back, jettisoning our bomb load at Berners Heath. We landed and expected to be directed to taxi to dispersal, but no, we were told to stay put. The CO, Inness, came out and he was in a towering rage. 'I will take over,' he announced and we took off again and circled the base at two thousand feet. Without the bombs, some of the fuel and only going up to two thousand, needless to say the red light didn't come on. He landed and tore an almighty strip off the skipper, Ian Pearson, for returning 'without just cause'. That was, I'm afraid, typical of the CO.

ORB: '1 April 1942. Nothing of operational importance occurred. Weather fair and fine with frequent showers between midday and midnight.' As the month opened, the squadron's strength was eighteen crews with two more expected. There were veterans such as Taylor, Eliott and Hale and new boys like Brooke, Mactaggart and Barnes. Ramey was there, Pearson, Runnacles and Davidson would be back. CO Inness and flight commander Turner could be reasonably pleased with their blend of enthusiastic youth and hardening experience; Sq/Ldr Holmes would arrive shortly to share the burden. They'd tasted real success at Lübeck and could look forward to making a similar impact on the most-wanted target: the Ruhr.

At 9 Squadron the practice had been developed of giving new crews a relatively safe-ish Op or two to ease them into the job. Such Ops were generally against French targets while the rest of the Squadron went to Germany. P/O Brooke, for instance, went to St Nazaire to attack shipping and then dropped leaflets over Paris. P/O Mactaggart and Sgt Barnes went to Le Havre twice. Sq/Ldr Holmes went there too, to get his hand back in. As April went on, the supposed point of the practice seemed to go rather astray.

When Paul Brooke went to Cologne on his first German Op after two French cake slices, he found the experience of little use and was shot down between the target and Bonn. Essen was Alistair Mactaggart's first German Op and his last. He crashed to earth at Himmelgeist on the banks of the Rhine, far from his home harbour of Port Ellen, Islay, where the people were instructed to keep back their Laphroaig and Lagavulin whiskies while allowing their sons to sail to war.

12 April, Essen yet again, when Sgt James, rear gunner, was the only survivor from the crew of the man who, a fortnight before, had saved them from fighter attack and achieved a belly landing in a virtually unserviceable aircraft, university graduate Sgt Fred Davidson.

For a while that was the last of Essen. In the recent campaign, over one thousand five hundred sorties resulted in more than a thousand crews claiming to have bombed the target area. To compensate for the sixty-plus aircraft and crews lost, one fire had been started in the Krupp works.

April 1942 was halfway through. The squadron had lost three of its twenty crews. In that same fortnight Bomber Command had lost over ninety aircraft on Ops, mostly Hampdens and Wellingtons, plus several more in accidents. It was hard to see how the war would ever be won this way.

If the Commander-in-Chief was to fulfill his brief, 1942 would have to be a year of rapid development. Bombing raids over Germany needed to be kept up plus a visible improvement made in tonnage dropped and hits scored, but the really big battle would have to wait. He needed to convert his current crews from medium to heavy bombers, step up the training of new crews and greatly increase the rate at which heavy bombers went into service.

There was also a tactical change, approved before Harris's day but implemented by him. This was to make every Op a Lübeck, to do away with many of the freedoms previously given to bomber crews and have them concentrate, fly together to the target and bomb together. The idea was sound enough. The Germans had their nightfighter patrols strung out in a line. With hundreds going through a small hole in the line they would not be able to cope and when bombing was done in an hour, the fire fighters and other resources below would be similarly overstretched.

On the other hand a packed bomber stream increased the risk of collision and being hit by others' bombs, and there would be traffic jams at homecoming. In any case general navigation hadn't been good enough for crews to keep together in the dark, to know they were keeping together and to arrive over the target at a given time. With the introduction of Gee the bomber stream had become practicable and, with more work, bombing could be done without the moon.

During 1942 the Whitley and Hampden medium bombers were withdrawn from service, although the Hampden carried on as a torpedo bomber with Coastal Command. In came the two great aircraft of the post-Battle of Britain period: the De Havilland Mosquito and the Avro Lancaster.

Despite its lack of creature comforts, aircrew and especially pilots grew to love the Lancaster. For an aircraft of its size it was highly manoeuvrable; more than one pilot flipped over onto his back by storm or tempest found that the Lancaster allowed him to turn her back again. Once over her teething troubles, she was as trustworthy and reliable as any machine of the time could be. This would be the aircraft to do Harris's job. This was the bomber, not just of the RAF. This was the bomber of the war.

German U-boats were winning the Battle of the Atlantic, destroying the lifeline of Britain, the convoys of merchant ships bringing everything from America which could not be produced on the besieged islands sufficiently or at all, including huge quantities of food and general supplies, weaponry, vehicles, petrol, name it. Admiral Dönitz's *Unterseeboote* were increasing in numbers and effectiveness, his wolf-pack tactic bringing him great success. A pack of twelve U-boats once sank 32 ships in four nights. It was common for a U-boat to sail into home base with three, four or even six victory pennants flying from her rigging. In 1942 U-boats would sink 1,094 ships. Such losses could not continue without bringing about the defeat of Britain. Starving within the year seemed likely.

If U-boats could not be caught at sea in sufficient numbers or hurt in bomb-proof shelters on the French coast, how might they be stopped? The Royal Navy was exerting heavy pressure on Bomber Command to put a brake on U-boat production.

Back in February, 9 Squadron had been ordered to start practising something quite extraordinary: formation flying. Bomber Command operated at night and certainly not in any kind of formation but, without explanation, the crews of 9 Squadron had been up almost every day, flying together as a team and doing extra gunnery practice too, air to air and air to sea over the Wash. On 5 March low flying was added to the agenda. On 7 March they gave the citizens of Newmarket a fright as they skimmed over the rooftops. Ops interrupted on 9 March, then more formation flying, then it all stopped, again with no explanation. For the pilots, whose concentration had to be intense and flawless for hours on end, it had been exhausting work; also for the navigators, who only had a small patch of rapidly moving ground to look at.

Someone, somewhere, had decided the Wellington III was not the right aircraft after all for whatever trip they were planning. The target was too far. If flown in daylight, it would have to be at zero feet, confusing the enemy radar and restricting fighters' angles of attack. Low flying used a lot of fuel. The Wimpy Mark III could carry more petrol and fly faster than the IC but wherever it was they had been scheduled to go, they wouldn't have got home.

Could the new bomber do the job, the Lancaster? It turned into the first Lancasters-only raid, on Augsburg, 17 April 1942, featuring the biggest contingent yet, 12 aircraft of 44 and 97 Squadrons. This Bavarian town of about 185,000 people was home to the MAN works, where the famous diesel engine manufacturer now turned out power units for U-boats.

It was the deepest penetration yet by the RAF with six hundred miles of enemy territory to cross and it was a glorious disaster. Seven of the twelve Lancs were lost and the leader of the Op, Sq/Ldr John Nettleton of 44 Squadron, was awarded the VC. Graham Welsh: 'There were mixed feelings at 9 Squadron when we heard about the Lancs and Nettleton. Our training had been for nothing, and we and our faithful Wimpys had obviously been passed over in favour of this new kite. On the other hand, there but for the grace of God . . . '

At the time the raid was a fantastic fillip to British morale and a dire warning to the Germans. The damage done to the capabilities of *Maschinenfabrik Augsburg Nürnburg* was insignificant but British bombers had actually got there and hit their aiming point rather than missing by miles. The losses, though, had shown long-distance daylight raids to be impracticable without fighter cover. Since there was no long-range fighter cover, such raids were impracticable, full stop.

Sq/Ldr Turner: 'No wonder you never find the target, Saul.'
P/O Saul: 'But sir, I always do.'

A new pilot, Sgt Harvey Holmes was assigned a crew of old hands – Sgts Swiderski, Rutherford and Evans, and P/O Saul, observer. Victor Saul was the officer, so he was made captain, and he would direct Holmes on his night-time Le Havre learner's trip. It did not go well. The wireless went u/s and they only got as far as thirty miles north-west of Worthing.

Most of the rest went to Cologne, which was Owen Barnes's third German Op and Hale's umpteenth. Hale went down near the target with only one killed. The skipper would turn up at Stalag Luft III with all those other 9 Squadron former pupils. Sgt Owen Cicero Charles Barnes fell in Holland trying to get home with flak damage; he died with his second pilot and his navigator was fatally injured.

Worst of all was Ramey. American Sergeant Warren Thompson Ramey, outstanding pilot, been there since early November, struggling back and crashing at Sapiston, half a mile short, with only the rear gunner surviving. The next day they found Sgt Russel, still in his turret, in the back of a hedge.

Like Lübeck, Rostock offered a smaller and less heavily defended, identifiable and German target on which to test Harris's methods. There were important dockyards and a Heinkel aircraft works to hit, in the April moon on four successive nights. No. 9 Squadron went twice. Coming home proved to be the most dangerous part of the mission; South African P/O Taylor was out of enemy territory, over the sea and homewards.

SECRET 9 Squadron Combat Report
23 April 1942. Rostock. Wellington X3449. Captain: P/O Taylor.
No cloud, bright moonlight, visibility excellent. Wellington was suddenly attacked from astern and below by an unseen enemy A/C, firing a five-second burst of cannon and machine-gun bullets. Rear gunner Sgt Watson was killed before being able to return fire. Second attack was from astern and below, firing five-second burst. Wellington's rear turret was on fire and owing to other damage lost height rapidly. E/A made no further attacks, presumably seeing tail of plane on fire considered it destroyed. The pilot, P/O Taylor, although wounded in left thigh in first attack made no mention of it. He succeeded in bringing the plane back to base despite serious damage and made a belly landing without further injury to the crew. Meanwhile the observer, P/O Simpson and the second pilot, P/O Musselwhite, attempted to rescue the rear gunner and to extinguish the fire that had spread along the rear of the fuselage. The fire extinguisher proved insufficient for the purpose and although the rear gunner could not be extricated, he was seen to be dead. To prevent the flames spreading, the astro hatch was removed and the slipstream blew the flames straight out of the back. The fire was beaten down as much as possible but was still glowing when A/C landed. Main damage to A/C: rear turret, tail, port elevator and aileron badly shot up, entire rear of fuselage damaged by fire. All instruments u/s except altimeter *W/T and compass. No lights or hydraulics.
*W/T – *wireless telegraph.*

At long last the loss of young men was possibly becoming balanced by a significant effect on the enemy. The Germans called the four-day blitz against Rostock *terrorangriff* (terror raid), a term they had never used before, and photo-reconnaissance suggested that more than half of the town had been laid waste. There had been something over five hundred sorties with fifteen bombers lost. It was a real success, but it was only Rostock. C-in-C Harris: 'Three great problems remained to be solved: (i) could the defences of a vital industrial area be saturated by a similar operation on a much larger scale? (ii) were the high concentrations, now seen to be desirable, a practical proposition? and (iii) how could the weather limitations on finding and marking the target be overcome?' Problems one and two would be resolved at the end of the following month but efficient bad-weather target finding and marking was some time away yet.

Pearson, Welsh and the boys had flown nine Ops in the month, including three in four nights. Rear gunner Harry Stuffin had missed a few but otherwise they were the same crew throughout.

Graham Welsh: It was basically a twelve-hour shift, from briefing to post-Op interrogation, with an early breakfast after and straight to bed. It was difficult to sleep in the daytime particularly if you knew the squadron was operating again that night.

We were slated for another Op to make it ten in April and I was apprehensive. When we reached the aircraft I realised Ian (Pearson) was drowsy, Webborn, now well into his second tour, was almost in tears and Howarth was in a poor way. I had a strong premonition that, if we flew we would not return, and so I did the unthinkable. I ran back to the CO and told him the pilot, the rear gunner and wireless operator were unfit to fly. I half-expected Inness to promise me a court martial, bearing in mind the previous incident of 'returning without just cause', but he sent the three to the MO, who confirmed my opinion and we all were given a week's leave.

Saul and Co went mining in the Heligoland Bight, 3 May, and on the way back bombed a lighthouse. Five went to Hamburg, three did not attack. Sweeney: 'Hamburg not attacked owing to rear gunner being badly frozen.' P/O Cooper attacked all right, both the town and the *Luftwaffe*, and observed a Junkers aircraft looking surprised.

SECRET 9 Squadron Combat Report
3 May 1942. Hamburg. Wellington X3463 WS/X. Captain: P/O Cooper.
(We) attacked a Ju88 in conditions of clear visibility with no cloud and a bright moon on the port quarter. There were no S/Ls, flak or flares and the Ju88 was first seen approaching at four hundred yards on the port quarter, two hundred feet above the Wellington. The Ju88 did not appear to see our A/C and the rear gunner (Sgt Walker) got in first with a four-second burst, firing as the E/A came in to one hundred and fifty yards, when it broke away to starboard, peeling off downwards. It appeared too surprised to return the fire and our A/C's bullets were seen to hit the belly of the E/A.

4 May: Saul to Nantes. Too foggy to see it, so bombed the waterfront at St Nazaire.
5 May: six to Stuttgart. Two came home with technical troubles. Sweeney: 'Bombs dropped on target identified by bend in river.' Casey: 'Bombs dropped on very large fire in believed Stuttgart.' Eliott: 'Bombs dropped over town, possibly Stuttgart.' More likely it was the very effective decoy some miles to the north.
8 May: eight to Warnemünde, near Rostock. Seven were home between 04.40 and 05.40. Sweeney saw the assembly buildings and workshops,

where Heinkel was making aircraft. Casey believed he hit Warnemünde. Everyone there saw and believed this was a very well-defended place, especially so for a Baltic target, and that the plan they'd been told to follow was impossibly complicated. In their confusion the searchlights found them out and the flak shot down eight Wellingtons, two Halifaxes, one Stirling, four Lancasters, two Manchesters and three Hampdens. One hundred aircrew were killed on this Op, including the five 9 Squadron men in the long serving F/Lt Eliott's Wellington.

> 'While flying at low level over Warnemünde,
> the rear gunner observed a German soldier's
> hat blown off in the slipstream of our aircraft'
>
> Anon

15 May: six went mining at the south end of the Great Belt (*Store Bælt*, the channel dividing Copenhagen's island from mainland Denmark). A man who was to make a deep and lasting mark with 9 Squadron was Kiwi P/O James Cowan, here a fresher second pilot to Sgt Langton. Graham Welsh was the observer.

The normal drill for mining was to assign two aircraft to each drop zone but we seemed to be alone when we got there. I knew from experience that the Germans were ahead of us in guessing where we'd be mining next, and put flak ships in what they rightly saw as their vulnerable areas. So I told Langton, who was only on his third as a captain, that we should reconnoitre the area carefully before making our run and sure enough, we saw a flak ship right beside our drop zone. Standard procedure was to find a prominent land feature and calculate a timed run from there to the drop zone, flying at four hundred feet. I said to Langton, the second we've dropped, climb hard to starboard, and our rear gunner, Harry Stuffin, would be able to rake the ship with fire. As we began our run in, there was a flurry of flak ahead of us so we assumed our partner aircraft was there, doing the business too.

So it was. Sgt Richards, on his second Op and without the benefit of Welsh's experience, was shot down with all his explosives aboard.

17 May: two new crews skippered by Sgts Trustrum and Wanostrocht to Boulogne. Trustrum couldn't find it. Nothing was ever heard from Sgt Wanostrocht, who had been a second pilot on the Squadron for a long time. Five more names for the Runnymede sculptor to carve.

19 May: Trustrum had another go, to St Nazaire. 'Aircraft returned early, owing to pilot's escape hatch being open. Furthest point reached 69

miles from base. Bombs jettisoned on Berners Heath from two hundred feet.'

29 May: huge influx of new crews. P/O Cowan, P/O Mullins, Sgt White, Sgt Goalen and P/O Haward, plus Trustrum and the recently arrived new flight commander Sq/Ldr Ledger, went to Dieppe. None of them could find it. Sq/Ldr Ledger jettisoned three of his sixteen bombs to make landing easier. New boy Sgt White jettisoned all of his. Meanwhile Turner and Saul went to the Gnome & Rhône factory at Gennevilliers, taking off half an hour apart and bombing thereabouts in low cloud. The factory remained in its entirety.

This was a typical month and not what the C-in-C had in mind at all. Ever since he had first sat in his commander's chair, or maybe before that, he had been devising a mighty blow, one which would have huge public-relations value as well as inflicting dreadful damage on the enemy. Harris proposed the first 'Thousand Plan' raid for the last day of May, a Sunday, in the moon. The Plan went all the way to the Prime Minister and, only two days after it was proposed, was approved by him and those who sat on his right hand.

Harris's own right hand, Air Vice Marshal Saundby, had the job of collecting a thousand bombers and crews when there were only a few more than four hundred on regular Ops. Initially, including the tour-completed men now teaching at the training schools and two hundred and fifty from Coastal Command, the thousand looked feasible. At the last minute, the Admiralty intervened on the grounds that flying two hundred and fifty serviceable aircraft to a very large, well-defended German city was unlikely to do much for the future growth and prosperity of the anti-U-boat campaign.

Things might have been different if Harris's preferred target, Hamburg, had been selected. They built one hundred U-boats a year there, but continued bad weather forced the decision to Cologne, the third largest city. By including many crews who had not completed their training, some with second-tour or instructor pilots, others with pilots who were some way off being posted to squadrons, the magic number was reached. Soon after noon on 30 May the order went out.

A few hours later more than a thousand aircraft set off; twice as many as the *Luftwaffe* had ever mustered for a raid on Britain. About half the force was made up of training and conversion units' aircraft, featuring just about everything in the country that flew and could carry a bomb, or used to be able to. Wellington 602, Halifax 131, Stirling 88, Hampden 79, Manchester 46, Whitley 28 and 73 of the new Lancaster type made 1,047.

It could have been 1,048 had not the brand new Wellington Z-Zola been pranged – by a 9 Squadron flight commander, no less – after an air test.

This officer was the dashing type, colourful, prewar regular, old school. He enjoyed dogfights with faster aircraft like Me110s and was indeed an impulsive character, once firing a revolver at a target on a hanger wall, forgetting that such walls were rather thin and narrowly missing an aircraftman next door. The lowly erk came belting in and tore a strip off the exalted squadron leader and, quite rightly, got away with it. On this day, he decided he'd show anybody watching how to land a Wellington from a very steep approach, and so Sq/Ldr Bob Turner, 9 Squadron fixture, tipped his kite on her nose. Never mind, they all climbed out and got into R-Robert.

On the way to Cologne the weather varied from bad to dreadful but cleared towards the target as forecast. This was the first use on anything like this scale of the bomber stream tactic, where everyone flew the same route at the same speed, at different heights and times. Pheasants were flying over the guns in a many-layered kind of single file that was, perhaps, hard on the lowest, but very good for the highest.

Slightly under nine hundred found the spot and bombed, dropping almost 1,500 tons of bombs in an hour and a half. It was a great success, with the three aiming points – Hansaplatz, Eifelplatz and Neumarkt – clearly and correctly marked with incendiaries by 9 Squadron and those others equipped with the latest kit.

The 'Thousand Plan' destroyed hundreds of acres of Cologne for the loss of forty aircraft and, contrary to fears expressed in gold braided meetings, there had not been a traffic jam and a mass of collisions. In this one raid the damage done was not very much less than the aggregate total of all such damage inflicted by Bomber Command so far in the war.

Harris: It proved that in a successful operation the damage increased out of proportion to the numbers involved. It also showed that the destruction of German industrial centres by bombing was a realisable aim if sufficient resources were devoted to achieving it. From this time onwards one target, against which practically all available forces could be used, was selected for each night's operation. Co-ordinated plans for each attack and common routes were laid down at Command HQ, in consultation with Groups and the planned concentration of bombing was set at ten aircraft per minute.

Analysis also showed that German fighter activity on that night over Cologne had been much greater than usual and that – as usual – they had been able to pick out and stalk single targets, but they had been so overwhelmed by the numbers that they had shot down a smaller proportion than they would have expected on a normal-sized raid.

No. 9 Squadron lost two out of fourteen Wellingtons. F/O Hodges and crew had gone on their first back in October. With their tours very nearly complete, they were attacked by a nightfighter on their way back and fell by the River Maas in Holland. After eight months of Ops over Germany and France, twice coming home on one engine, once crashing and killing a gunner, Michael Ryland Hodges was still only 19 when he died.

Graham Welsh had flown almost all of his tour as observer with Sgt Pearson, who had been commissioned and posted. In January 1944, F/Lt Ian Maclaren Pearson DFC would die at Berlin, skipper of a 7 Squadron Lancaster and one or two Ops short of completing his second tour. Now Welsh had three to finish his first tour with, it turned out, Sgt Langton.

Welsh: We were on our way home (from Cologne) when there was a big explosion on the port wing. On one engine we lost a lot of height and Langton, for some reason, insisted on flying as slowly as he could, fractionally above stalling speed, which meant we were ever mushing towards the ground. I was really the senior man, observer in a five-man crew with no second pilot, and I kept warning him. When we dropped below a thousand I ordered everything loose to be thrown out, but it didn't help much and soon we were level with the squirrels. I think Langton had frozen. We were going straight for a farmhouse and he didn't see it. I was standing beside him. I saw it all right and shouted, and he pulled up on the stick and the wing dropped, and bang, we were down in the farmyard.

They had crash-landed in Belgium, not far from Antwerp, with bad injuries to Langton, who was thrown out of the aircraft as she slewed along the ground. The rear gunner, Sgt Pexman, was killed. Welsh: 'Front gunner Johnson was uninjured. I'd taken a blow on the ankle and Howarth the w/op had a badly lacerated hand. We three spent almost a week evading capture but they took us when we were looking for a doctor for Howarth.'

The last Wellington Mark 1A to fall in this war was shot down by a nightfighter coming back from the Cologne 'Thousand Plan' raid, near Apeldoorn. Five of a scratch crew from Central Gunnery School were killed, including Tiny Cooling's old tail-end Charlie, John McKenzie McLean.

An Essen raid, featuring thirteen of 9 Squadron, was the second of the three-phase 'Thousand Plan' and 956 went to find low cloud smothering the target. Bombing was scattered, again doing a lot of damage but not where it mattered most.

Hoping to do better was an American pilot, one of the gallant few who had volunteered for the Royal Canadian Air Force before Pearl Harbor.

He'd got his old headmaster from Deerfield Academy, Massachusetts (founded 1767) to write him a reference, 3 October 1940, to help him go to a war in which his own country was not yet a participant. The headmaster obliged: 'Anderson Storey is from one of our oldest and best New England families, a young man of high character, fine personality and good scholastic ability. He is very sincere in his desire to be of service at this critical time.'

Sergeant Anderson Storey was certainly a high character, around six foot four with fair hair. Away from school, however, he was rather shambolic, the kind of man who would automatically cause ulcers in the vital organs of sergeant majors, adjutants and other types of bull-and-blanco expert. He was also a bit of a comedian, liable to fool around, with something of the dilettante attitude associated with the sons of old, wealthy American families and these aspects of his character would prove faults rather than assets, initially at any rate. Before the war Anderson Storey had spent holidays in Britain, loved it, and had joined up for purely altruistic reasons. He felt that he couldn't sit back and do nothing so he trained, came to 9 Squadron and went as second Dicky with P/O Cooper to Bremen, 3 June.

Traces of the old hurrah-chaps, gifted amateur, tally-ho style were still apparent in some officers of Bomber Command. It was an established ethos, a way of dealing that needed to be changed. Bombing had to make that switch, from being a potentially lethal game into a potentially lethal job of work. Take the next four days on 9 Squadron.

4 June: Weather fine apart from slight ground mist around dawn. The Squadron was not called upon to produce a main effort today so training was carried out by day and by night. The only operational effort was Sgt Macdonald in aircraft 'M', who attacked DIEPPE. Nothing outstanding occurred during his trip and he returned without incident.

5 June: Weather fine. Once more the Squadron was not called upon to operate so an intensive flying and ground training programme was embarked upon. A ground defence exercise was arranged for the Station and a number of aircraft contributed to the party with SCI sprays using training mixture. The spraying was 100% successful.

6 June: Weather fine with only small amounts of medium cloud in the late evening. Operations were resumed today when fourteen crews were briefed for an attack on Emden in the north-west on the River Ems. The Squadron particularly wished to make a good show this evening as it was the occasion of a visit by two officers of the US Army Air Corps, Major Chilvers and Major Douglas. As it happened luck was right out on this day. Sq/Ldr Ledger and Sgt Hannaford collided with each other

while taxiing from dispersal. Sgt Runnacles burst a tyre while taxiing and one of P/O Haward's engines refused to take any interest in the programme for the evening.

When 'M' and 'D' had been parted from their loving embrace, the path from dispersal was cleared and the remaining aircraft became airborne and proceeded to the target with the exception of P/O Cowan, who was last to take off. This crew had a remarkable escape. Immediately after taking off and before a height of one hundred feet had been reached, the revolutions began to fall on his engines. Height was lost and the aircraft crashed about a mile south of the aerodrome. The bomb load of incendiaries immediately ignited and the flames spread so rapidly that, although the fire tender was on the scene within two minutes of the crash, it was a hopeless task to subdue the fire. As no enemy aircraft were in the vicinity to be attracted by the blaze, it was allowed to burn out, which it did in about an hour.

All members of the crew escaped from the aircraft. The Observer, P/O Brown, injured his back and had to be carried by other members of the crew and P/O Cowan received a gash in the forehead necessitating a few stitches, otherwise no one was hurt.

Before the excitement from this episode had ceased, Sgt Macdonald returned early under the impression that he was obtaining a phenomenally high petrol consumption. Subsequent investigation showed faulty petrol guages. To wind up a perfect night, Sgt White endeavoured to land at Horsham St Faith and crashed on landing (in R-Robert, which he'd brought home on one engine three days before).

Altogether not a very successful evening but some consolation was found in the fact that the attack on EMDEN appeared to be quite successful. All aircraft returned without incident (including Sgt Trustrum, who seemed to be fully functional at last).

7 June: Weather fair-to-cloudy all day. No flying took place today with the exception of Sq/Ldr Turner, who proceeded to Horsham St Faith to collect the crew that had crashed there the previous night. A little excitement was caused on his return owing to the aircraft being rather heavily laden. Sq/Ldr Turner decided that a landing with the load aboard would be a little tough on the undercarriage so unloaded a few gallons of petrol over the aerodrome. This caused consternation, disgust and other mixed feelings amongst the car and motor cycle owners on the Station.

Perhaps the writer would not have been so flippant had he known that Bomber Command had lost over one hundred and fifty aircraft and crews in the week that had started at Cologne, or that almost all of the 9

Squadron men he mentioned in his record of four June days were fated soon to be killed in the air war. Nor did he know that the war was exactly halfway through, nor that three quarters of Bomber Command casualties were yet to come.

Emden had Storey as second Dicky again so he was ready to take his own crew, which included that luckiest of navigators, the one who had escaped Roly Hill's crash at Spalding, Sgt Ken Chamberlain. Their first Op was to Dieppe, 8 June. They made a stuttering start to their tour, coming home early with the rear turret u/s and missing out on the gardening, as mine laying was known, of 11 June.

All aircraft laid their mines as ordered except Sgt Hall, who accidentally brought his back. In addition Sgt Paddison discovered a convoy off the Fresians, which he proceeded to shake up a little with two 500lb GP bombs and a few rounds from his guns. And Sgt Macdonald received a little attention from a flak ship, which he returned with interest in the shape of two 500lb GP bombs. P/O Saul did not return from this trip. Stations at Heston and Hull heard signals from his aircraft but they were being jammed by another and could not be clearly distinguished.

Aircraft were stood by to search for P/O Saul and crew but, other aircraft having reported finding an empty dinghy in the search area, our aircraft did not take off. It is reported that the enemy have picked up a crew in the same area, which it is hoped will prove to be P/O Saul's. Officers' movements: F/Lt Stubbs posted from No 20 OTU (after a tour with No. 75 Squadron and a DFM as Sgt Stubbs).

It wasn't Victor Saul and his boys who were rescued that day. The only sign of them would be their names carved at Runnymede. One was Sgt James Rutherford, Ramey's front gunner when they ditched in Herne Bay, survivor of Gerry Webb's crash after Kiel and at last disappearing, still only 20.

Storey flew to the Rouen area to drop leaflets and was briefed for gardening and ship attacks around Borkum Island. 'Sgt Storey in aircraft T did not take off.' He did take off on 19 June, one of four to go to Emden again. 'Sgt Storey had a minor encounter with two FW190s, but did not claim a victory.' It was minor in the sense that the Wellington, carrying five hundred and forty 4lb incendiaries and three 500lb bombs, beat off the first attack. 'Horizontal visibility was good owing to Northern Lights. Rear gunner (P/O Moorhead) fired three short bursts as our A/C prepared to make a diving turn into the attack. The E/A broke away without firing and was not seen again.' After bombing came the second half of the minor encounter as another FW190 flew in at high speed from one hundred yards, misjudged the approach under fire from P/O Moorhead, could not get in a shot and was not seen again.

> 'It's not fighters or flak I'm scared of
> when I'm flying with that crew'
> P/O Moorhead

SECRET 9 Squadron Combat Report
20/21 June 1942. N of Bergen, Holland. Wellington Z1663. Captain: P/O J Cowan.
Fair visibility, no moon, bright Northern Lights, no cloud. Me110 observed level six hundred yards dead astern and made a sudden attack. After one burst our rear guns jammed and Me110 made about ten more attacks mostly from port quarter. On instructions from rear gunner (Sgt Brown) bomber made sharp diving turns into the attack losing height (9,000 feet) rapidly, pulling out into climbing turns in the opposite direction in an endeavour to break off the engagement.

There was damage to the port engine, the starboard wing, fifteen holes in a petrol tank and a few more miscellaneous knocks, which you were bound to suffer during a dozen attempts on your life while you endeavoured to break off the engagement with half your guns jammed.

Just another night at the office, it would seem, with mixed opinions as to success. There had been lots of flak but that was not worth mentioning. So have we forgotten something? 'The Squadron was most unfortunate in losing its Commanding Officer, W/C James, on this trip. Nothing was heard of him all night. This was W/C James's 27th raid and the first of his second tour of operations. All other aircraft returned safely.'

Wing Commander Leslie Vidal James DFC, called Jimmy of course, looked the archetypal part with his handlebar moustache. He'd done his first tour with No. 149 and many of the Ops had been in his Wellington 'The Ozard of Whiz', with said character depicted on the side as a prominently uddered dancing cow. He had arrived as the new 9 Squadron CO a month previously, bringing with him his second-tour observer, John Baxter DFM. The crew all died in the crash in Holland, unable to break off the engagement with a nightfighter flown by *Oberleutnant* Egmont Prinz zur Lippe Weissenfeld, who scored three that night.

22 June and life took an odd turn, which was eventually to have the ultimate consequence. Ken Chamberlain and the rest of the crew went for an air test with Andy Storey at 11.15 in Wellington T, and another in the same aircraft at 16.50 with F/Lt Stubbs. In between the two air tests the crew had changed skippers. Storey's early flying career had not gone well.

His crew had lost confidence in him and, likeable good company that he was, they could not see themselves regaining it. Instead they went to see the new CO, Wingco Southwell on his first day and said that for the sake of their own preservation they would like a new skipper. Stubbs – very experienced, extremely competent, highly professional – was everything Storey was not. Storey went back to school for some revision and his crew boarded their Wimpy that night for Emden with Stubbs. 'A very good crop of photographs resulted from this raid, P/O Mullins bringing back a particularly good one of the target.'

That Stubbs's men might be a lucky crew must have occurred to them when it was announced that the squadron, being an aircraft short, had borrowed a Wellington from the OTU up the road. Ken Chamberlain: 'Instructor pilots, showing off to their sprog pupils, had been throwing this thing all over the sky and it was not in tip-top, over-Germany condition. Worse, it was the early Pegasus-engined version (2 x 1000hp), not the much better Hercules-engined version we were used to (2 x 1675hp). The proposal at 9 Squadron was to draw lots for it, but Dick Stubbs said there was no need. He'd have it.'

Ground and air crews worked hard to get her into shape, ready for the third and last 'Thousand Plan' raid, to Bremen, 25 June. 'Over the target we were hit by flak and the port engine stopped, often a disaster in the Pegasus Wimpy, being so underpowered. Stubbs told us not to worry; he would get us home, and he did.' Bremen featured more than eleven hundred aircraft, mostly depending on 9 Squadron and their Gee-equipped colleagues to mark the aiming points because, contrary to forecasts, there was cloud when they got there. They did pretty well and there was considerable damage to shipyards and Focke-Wulf factories but losses were heavy at fifty. Of the 'Thousand Plan' raids, Cologne had been the only big success but the raids assured the future of Bomber Command. They proved that it could be done. Setbacks were certain in times to come but after Cologne the only way was onwards and upwards.

29 June: Fine with ground fog around dawn, becoming cloudy. A certain amount of training was carried out and crews were briefed for Operations, the target once more being Bremen. P/O Sweeney crashed on the flarepath in taking off, but luckily his incendiary load took no action and apart from a slight facial injury to the rear gunner no one was hurt. On return Sgt Goalen made a bad landing, which proved too much for his undercarriage, which folded up under the strain. Apart from laying out the rear gunner, no injury was sustained by any member of the crew.

Sweeney's rear gunner was Lovis, John Alfred Cronin Lovis, the only man to escape unhurt from a crash in September 1941. That was it for him; tour expired. His replacement was Harry Stuffin, who had flown with Saich. Both would become second tour men and would share the fate they all expected, over Berlin, two years hence within a few days of each other.

It was Bremen yet again on 2 July. Stubbs and Chamberlain were in the flak. 'We were coned by searchlights and hit by flak again and Sgt Newby, our bomb aimer, was wounded very badly.' Anxious to avoid over-statement the ORB noted that 'several aircraft reported slight peppering'. 23 July 1942, thirteen aircraft to Duisburg: Haward, Sweeney, Hannaford, Macdonald, McKeen, Pink, Goalen, Mullins, Brown, Hall, Cowan, Stubbs and second-tour Sq/Ldr Clyde-Smith. Haward was first up at 01.00. 'Conditions at the target were not too satisfactory, there being few breaks in the cloud although several crews saw the docks and the Rhine. One of our aircraft did not return. Three photographs had detail on them.'

Conditions indeed were not too satisfactory. Within a few months, all but two of these thirteen captains would be dead and the great majority of their crews with them, starting this night with Henry Brown after four weeks of it.

The first of a pair of Hamburg Ops, 26 July, went reasonably well. 'Target visible in moonlight with docks and lake showing up well.' On 28 July fourteen went again in weather so foul some of the squadrons on the raid were recalled. Among those who didn't get the message was No. 9, of which three failed to return. James Mullins, 21-year-old Canadian and his men were shot down by flak south of the target and all were killed. The two that collided from that bad June show in front of the American majors also finished their business on this raid. Those whose aircraft had been parted from a loving embrace, Sgt Henry Hannaford and Sq/Ldr Harry Ledger, were joined fatally and finally with only Ledger's rear gunner, F/Sgt Hunter, taken prisoner. Hannaford's rear gunner Bill Warren, a Wexford man, was the only body found from their sea burial. Losses for 3 Group that night were fifteen per cent. Hazell on his second, Runnacles, Macdonald, Hall and Stubbs bombed in intense flak and returned for a couple of days' rest before 9 Squadron's final Wellington raid.

The end of July was the end of an era. The Squadron was to move to a new home, from Honington grass in Suffolk to Waddington tarmac in Lincolnshire; to a new Bomber Command Group, from No. 3 to No. 5; and convert to a new aircraft. The last of the old-style Ops was to Düsseldorf, where the 630 bombers included 113 Lancasters of which two were lost, and thirteen Wellingtons of 9 Squadron, of which two were lost. Those returning were diverted to Hunsdon, minus P/O Pink, the accidental mine man Sgt Hall and their crews, for whom Düsseldorf was not so much the end of an era as the end of a short aircrew life. The only man to escape that fate was Hall's observer Sgt Levy, who managed to contact a member of the Belgian Resistance who, it turned out, was hiding a Jewish woman. When the dreaded GFP (*Geheime Feldpolizei* – secret police) found all three, the sergeant must have thought he'd had it with a name like Levy. As was proper, they sent him to POW camp.

Sgt Kenneth Hobbs flew the squadron's last Wellington. He brought his Mark III X3341 in to land at 05.38 on the morning of 1 August after overheating in both engines, and that was the closing act of almost two thousand five hundred sorties in the much loved Wimpy by No. 9. Hobbs was a new pilot, with two second Dickies and two Ops, like so many of them a replacement for a replacement for a replacement. Casualties had been heavy. In the previous four months, No. 9 had lost the equivalent in aircraft and crews of nearly two entire squadrons' operational strength. The thought of the new bomber was a welcome inspiration. Away went the Wellingtons; in came the Lancasters.

Pilots began training by flying the Manchester. Bomb aiming had started to become a specialised trade and it was completely so by now with the new and excellent, semi-automatic Mark 14 bombsight. There was a dedicated flight engineer rather than a second pilot to look after the complexities of the Lancaster's four Rolls-Royce Merlins. Gunnery and wireless operating became separate trades. Observers became navigators.

There were two full-time gunners, one in the rear and one in the dorsal or mid-upper turret. Harry Irons came straight from gunnery school, without going through an OTU, and joined up on eight shillings a day with Dick Stubbs.

Irons: They (the converting crews) were teaching themselves really. There didn't seem to be any organised instruction. Stubbs was one of the most experienced blokes on the squadron, halfway through his second tour. Our flight commander was Cowan and he'd never flown a Lancaster either. I was just the office boy so they put me in the mid-upper turret.

At first there had to be some swapping and improvisation as the Wellington men stepped up to the best bomber in the world. Things became more settled as the newly trained crews came through, but if the Old Wellingtonians thought life would be any less dangerous in the Lanc, they were much mistaken. They would also find that Gee had become little more than useless for target finding. The Germans were jamming it. Its main purpose now was finding the way home, if home was an option. So, the old squadron became one of the two dozen operational heavy-bomber outfits and one of only nine at that time which had the Lancaster. Whatever the ship, Stubbs expected to continue in lucky vein with his extended crew, including Harry Irons, except he wasn't Irons. 'There was a chap, name of Galloway. That was me. I went in on the wrong name. I was under-age at 16 when I joined, and I used my mother's previous married name to help me fool them. Later on, when I changed back to Irons, Ken Chamberlain used to call me Knife and Fork, or Knife, Fork and Spoon if he was feeling talkative.'

'D'ye no think ah had better bung up the air hole
to stop the petrol evaporating from ma car?'
F/O Bridgewood

Lancaster Ops began for No. 9 on 10 September 1942, led by the well-liked CO W/Cdr Southwell, to Düsseldorf. It was a first for everyone, a first in a heavy bomber for the Wellington boys like Harry Stuffin, now gunning for Southwell, and a first Op of any kind for the rest.

The moment came near. Time to collect parachutes and flying kit. Rear gunners had electrically heated flying suits, which they certainly needed in what was the coldest part of the aircraft. Bomb aimers, in the cold, cold nose, and mid-upper gunners could have heated waistcoat and slippers, and both gunners had heated gloves.

Crews and individuals had their mascots – teddy bears, homemade cuddlies, lucky rings and badges, an old girlfriend's silk stocking – which were at least as important to them as parachutes. There was time for a goodish draw at the Gold Block, or for a Woodbine. Most aircrew smoked; virtually all of them did. Just about the entire product range of the British Empire tobacco industry was represented on that tiny piece of Lincolnshire, where they waited for a WAAF in a truck with seats that did for a bus, to take them to their dispersals.

Player's, Woodbine, Park Drive, Senior Service, State Express, Kensitas, Three Castles, Craven A, Silver Fern rolling tobacco for the Kiwis, you name it, were in battered tins or maybe cigarette cases, brass, leather-covered, shining silver, and pipes were filled with every tobacco from Warhorse Block to Bottomley's Light Shag. For some of the men there that night it might be their last cigarette or their last pull on the old briar.

The smiling, cheerful WAAF arrived with the truck. She knew what was required of her and it certainly wasn't a sincere and serious 'Jolly good luck, chaps'. These WAAFs were the nearest thing to a stress counsellor and they did it with their manner, their kindly and considerate bearing, their warm softness in keenly sharp contrast to the cold hardness of an Op.

The crews were dropped off on the circuit of dispersal points around the aerodrome perimeter. The WAAF drove away, no doubt thinking her usual thoughts, wondering which ones she would never see again and which would return transformed from the chirpy young fellows she'd just been with to the threadbare old men she'd pick up a few hours hence. One of them might even be her boyfriend. Perhaps she would catch herself hoping that if somebody did get the chop, it wouldn't be him.

Some crews had rituals to perform before boarding. The standard one was for each member in turn to pee on the rear wheel, even though it had been officially forbidden by head office memo complaining about the corrosion it caused. Aircrew tended not to pay too much attention to head office memos. The author in this case clearly didn't see the irony of his instruction as the urinators idly wondered if theirs was an aircraft which would last long enough ever to need a replacement rear wheel.

They also had their 'wakey-wakey' pills, routinely administered to all Bomber Command aircrew before every Op by the medical officer or the padre, which kept them awake and, more importantly, made them feel H.A.P.P.Y. about going. Officially, wakey-wakey pills were just that. In fact, they were benzedrine, another name for amphetamine. No one had heard of 'speed' in those days.

With anti-sicks and wakey-wakeys safely ingested and beginning to take effect, crews climbed up the little ladder to the door on the starboard side of the fuselage towards the rear. Six young men turned right and headed up the aircraft. One, the rear gunner, turned to his left and went downhill to his turret.

All around the dispersals the two-wheeled trolley accumulators were plugged in, buttons pressed, propellers turned and there came the huge, darkness-shattering giants' shouts of Rolls-Royce Merlin engines. The shy lights of the runway were lit. The usual little crowd of WAAFs, other non-operational people, the station CO and the squadron CO if he wasn't flying, gathered to see the boys off. The aircraft began to taxi around the perimeter track, steering with blasting engines and squealing brakes, undercarriage legs groaning, a cacophony if ever there was one. This shuddering, supremely clamorous caravan of din and destruction headed for the north-eastern end of the main runway. Stubbs's aircraft W4122 WS/U, brand new of course, would shortly be transferred to a training unit and would see out the war there. Oh, that aircrew could look forward to a similar future.

Irons: Stubbs was a strange character. Didn't drink, didn't smoke, didn't chase women, didn't swear, but when he was in the air he changed completely. From the time we took off until the time we landed his language was unbelievable. So off we went to Düsseldorf and I'd

never been so frightened in my life. I didn't know what was going on. Never been to OTU. Stubbs said, 'You'll learn as you go along' so that was the extent of my operational education. I couldn't credit the flak and the searchlights and all the aircraft blowing up. I had the best view from my turret.

We were hit by flak and on top of that we had a lot of engine trouble with the Lanc. There were immersion pumps in the fuel supply and they were not reliable. I was in a daze when we got back but Stubbs was right. You did get used to it.

You had to get used to it, and the enemy had to get used to much more effective air raids. In this one, in round figures, fifty industrial firms were put out of action, two thousand five hundred houses destroyed or badly damaged and two hundred and fifty people killed.

The night of 14 September was black and soundless at the wire fence of Stalag Luft III as Conk Canton and his pal Johnson slowly snipped their way through with wire cutters made in the camp.

I had on a French soldier's jacket and F/Lt Johnson* was wearing blue battledress. We were to make for Czechoslovakia. Once outside, we walked south for about sixteen kilometres and then followed the railway line Sagan-Breslau for four days.

F/Lt Johnson managed to board a train going to Breslau and I got on one that then reversed. I was discovered and arrested but evaded my guards on the pretext of getting a drink of water. I used this opportunity to jump onto another train that took me to Gorlitz, where I got off in a siding and started walking south for the next two days. I reached the outskirts of Reichenberg, where I ran into a party of peasants who stopped me. An SS car appeared and took me back to Gorlitz. After four days in the cells there I was sent back to Stalag Luft III, where I served fourteen days in the cells.

*F/Lt S P L Johnson, probably Coastal Command, didn't get away either.

Twelve Lancasters of 9 Squadron set off for Essen, 16 September. Two turned back, including Stubbs.

Ken Chamberlain: One of the flight engineer's jobs was to watch the four red lights that indicated flow of fuel to the engines. If a light came on, something was wrong with the system, that engine was being starved and Tom (Parrington, engineer) had to switch it to a reserve tank. As we took off across married quarters, with a 4,000-pounder on board, all four red lights came on. It was a toss-up who was coughing and spluttering the most, Tom or the engines. Anyway he got them all switched to the little 100-gallon wingtip tanks and we flew out to the Wash to jettison the bombs but the engines kept cutting out two at a time and the lights kept coming on. We flew home with all four engines running off one wingtip tank and landed on the last smell of petrol. Next morning I was due to be interviewed by W/Cdr Southwell for my promotion. 'What do you think of the Lancaster?' he said. 'Well,' I said, 'I don't think much of the fuel system.' 'Ah,' says he, 'you'll be in Dick Stubbs's crew.'

Clearly, bombing was as hairy as ever but was it becoming any more effective on night raids over Germany? Was it yet the precisely applied science it needed to be? 'Altogether this was the squadron's most successful Operation thus far in Lancasters. P/O Runnacles actually brought back a photograph showing the corner of Krupp's works and P/O McKeen was only 1,000 yards further away. Another photograph was less than four miles away. But these successes were not without cost and two crews are missing.'

Both aircraft had been at Waddington less than a week. One of the crews was new, too, P/O Musselwhite's. His was an especially bitter fate. He'd been second pilot with P/O Taylor on that moonlit night in April when they went to Rostock, were shot up by a fighter, rear gunner killed and 'seen to be dead' and Musselwhite burned in the attempted rescue. He'd come back in June, trained as a Lancaster pilot and was killed on his first Op as skipper. The other crew were just as dead in a suburb of Düsseldorf but even more notable historically. Some of them had flown the last 9 Squadron Wellington to land, on the morning of 1 August, Sgt Hobbs and four of his men. Now they all had the cachet, post-mortem, of having flown the first two 9 Squadron Lancasters that failed to return.

The squadron was having a bad year, as were many others, and had they been able to read the tea leaves they would have seen no improvement. In the future, until the war was over, lay 135 operating weeks and a 9 Squadron Lancaster bomber lost for very nearly every one of those weeks.

Harry Irons: People thought there must be something that could be done to reduce the losses. A couple of fellows came to us from Cambridge and installed a magic box,* a radar detector in the rear turret. Brian (Moorhead, rear gunner) would have a red light come on when a fighter was near us. Very good, we thought. Very clever, these university chaps.
*Probably a prototype of the Boozer device.

Anderson Storey, back on squadron and promoted to flight sergeant, shared a room in the mess with Tom Parrington and Harry Irons. 'Andy Storey was a real gentleman. We often used to go for a few beers together, our crew and his.' He took that new crew on their first Lancaster Op, 19 September. ORB: 'The target was Munich, the Nazi shrine. The aiming point, appropriately enough, was the beer cellar. Navigation seemed to be of a high order for everyone returning had located the target and dropped their bombs.' Stubbs's port inner engine failed shortly after bombing but they flew along with no incident until almost home.

SECRET 9 Squadron Combat Report
20 September 1943. 40 miles SE of Rheims. W4157 WS/V. Captain: F/Lt Stubbs.
Ju88 attacked from port quarter up. First seen at 150 yards. Rear gunner fired two short bursts. Ju88 broke away to port beam. Evasive action slight turn to port. Ju88 fired machine guns and cannon that passed over port wing. Mid-upper gunner fired burst as Ju88 crossed under to starboard beam. Ju88 attacked from starboard to port underneath, using free gun. Evasive action turn starboard. Ju88 re-crossed underneath from port to starboard and finally disappeared.

Harry Irons had a more informal, less restrained view of it.

We were in ten tenths cloud, all the way there and most of the way back, then we broke into clear weather. And there was a fighter, a Ju88, thirty yards away, maybe nearer. Me and Brian opened fire at the same moment. The Junkers had his nose slightly up and was too close really, so his cannon shells went over us. We both belted away at him and he dropped away to port and he stayed there for a few minutes, then he dived and went right across us underneath and I had about twenty bullets just miss my arse. Stubbs corkscrewed all over the sky and we got rid but that fighter could not have followed us all that way through thick cloud unless he knew blind where we were. Either he had a better red light machine than we did, or he could home in on our signal. So we landed full of holes, but we had holes in the aircraft anyway, from the flak. You always came back with holes in.

The corkscrew was a piece of violent evasive aerobatics taught as a standard tactic. One of the gunners would spot an incoming fighter and order the pilot to corkscrew port or starboard, whichever was into the direction of the attack. The pilot stood the aircraft on her left (or right) wingtip, dived and turned to the left (or right) at the same time, then rolled her back, climbed and did it the other way. Properly executed at the limits of the Lancaster's performance this combination of slamming dives, sudden steep climbing turns and wingtip to wingtip half rolls was something a mobbed sparrow hawk would have been hard put to emulate.

If they saw the fighter in time a Lancaster crew might corkscrew out of trouble, especially if the fighter pilot tried to follow them through the winding match. If he was older and wiser he sat there while the bomber pilot tried to deform his aircraft into a twist of barley sugar and, at the moment she was frozen in space – between a climb and a dive, like a car at the top of the big dipper ride – let her have it. Ken Chamberlain: 'The gunners and the pilot were professionally occupied at times like that; the rest of us just panicked and offered up a silent prayer while all my pencils fell on the floor.'

Prayers proved powerless that night for Lewis Haward, one of whose engines had refused to take any interest in the programme for the evening back in June. He and all but one of his crew were henceforth unable to take any interest in any programmes at all.

Ten went on 23 September, an eight-hour trip to the aerodrome and Dornier aircraft factory at Wismar, flying across Denmark at rooftop level in bright moonlight, thunder and lightning. When they hit low cloud there were violent discharges of static – Stubbs's crew counted fifteen electrical storms – like heavy flak going off. They bombed from only 1,400 feet. 'Bombs seen to burst and pieces of building thrown into the air.'

Harry Irons: The flak was very bad and we got some more holes, but we definitely got a direct hit on the factory on our first run, which was good because Stubbs wouldn't go home until he was sure he'd got a hit. He'd shut the bomb doors on the way in, not satisfied for some reason of his own, then go round again and again if he didn't think the aim was spot on, and by that time Jerry really had us in his sights. We saw one of our squadron shot down on the way in. We were in ten tenths cloud going back, absolutely nothing to see, and the Gee box was no use this far out. Ken got us home. Brilliant navigator. And then we got a piece of paper from the group commander because we'd hit the aiming point. That's what they gave you, a sheet of paper with a drawing on it.

The aircraft Harry Irons saw was R5907 WS/M, piloted by the Kiwi P/O McKeen of the thousand-yard photograph, hit by flak three miles short of Wismar and all killed. F/Sgt White, crashing star of that June week, would likewise be endeavouring no more. They fell into the Baltic Sea.

Destined for posting to 9 Squadron as beginners was a crew led by F/Sgt Jim McCubbin, with bomb aimer Ken Dagnall known as Joe, but they were diverted at the last moment to Coastal Command, which was desperately short of crews to combat the U-boats.

Dagnall: I was just over 18. Jim would be 22, a little older than most. We'd done OTU and instead of sending us to Lancaster finishing school they sent us to fly in Whitleys looking for submarines. That was a shocking aircraft, shocking. And to think people used to fly over Germany in them. We were going to fly over the Atlantic, not so dangerous but we were liable to be attacked by Junkers 88s. There were squadrons based on the Atlantic coast at their equivalent of an OTU and the learner pilots used to come out and try to find people like us. If they had done it would have been Charlie Stewart's and my job to deal with it. So while the Junkers cannonfire was knocking hell out of us and Charlie was doing his best, alone in the rear turret of a slow-moving object with four machine guns, I was to wind myself down into the belly turret, grab hold of the Sten gun there and help him shoot the enemy down with that. Our plan, needless to say, was to escape into the clouds rather than fight.

McCubbin, Dagnall and Co would go on their first sweep and never see a thing. Next time out would prove exactly how shocking a Whitley could be.

The new month at 9 Squadron started with a further go at Wismar and an attack on Krefeld. Yet again Stubbs and his men, with an extra this time, second Dicky Sgt Doolan, went through the briefing, the pre-Op tension, the waiting, the take-off, only to have engine trouble. The starboard outer caught fire, there was an oil leak on the port inner so Stubbs had to coax the Lancaster home early, which meant the Op didn't count on a crewman's tally of thirty, now the definition of a tour of Operations replacing the two hundred hours. Well, they hadn't reached the target so it was DNCO (Duty Not Carried Out). Spending half a day thinking about it, and an hour and a half flying in a fire-disabled aircraft meant nothing at all.

A rookie pilot, Sgt McDonald had a different idea. '(He was) compelled to cut the starboard outer over the English coast on the outward journey and proceeded to target on three engines. He brought back a photograph and this was considered a very good effort for this pilot's first trip as captain.' Very good effort, or foolish beginner's luck? What might have happened to him if he'd met up with three Me109s all at the same time, the first one no more than fifty yards away? Another debutant that night was Flight Sergeant Gibson and for his very good effort he needed all four engines.

SECRET 9 Squadron Combat Report

5/6 October 1942. 50 miles west of Aachen. W4158 WS/O. Captain: F/Sgt Gibson.

One Me109 attacked from port quarter slightly up. First seen at 50 yards by mid-upper gunner (Sgt Broadley), who fired a short burst and the enemy returned with a short burst of red tracer. E/A passed over MU and broke away to starboard beam, where it was joined by another Me109. Both E/A then turned and came in on the starboard quarter, MU firing a short burst at each. Another one attacked from the port quarter, MU firing a short burst. During these encounters violent evasive action was taken until cloud cover found and E/A lost.

Stubbs's status as a reliable pilot was recognised again on the next Op when he took the New Zealander P/O William Bruce Cowan as second Dicky. Identical-looking, he was two years younger than his brother, F/O James Cowan, who was nearing the end of his tour but still had enough left to allow a special distinction to 9 Squadron: two brothers skippering on the same Op. This was a trip to Cologne, when 'all crews with the exception of F/Sgt Storey definitely identified the target'.

Harry Irons: Stubbs and his men from the Wellington days were getting near the end of their tours now and we had a passenger going to come with us, Cowan the Kiwi, the other brother, at the start of his. I still had a lot of trips to do, but we all could look around and see the same thing. You saw the whole operational squadron when you were waiting to be taken out to dispersal. You'd sit there, having a smoke, knowing that a crew or two wouldn't be coming back. You'd wonder who all these new faces were and if you'd ever get to know who they were. Flying experience in itself didn't necessarily count for much because you'd get pilots coming in from Transport Command, thousands of hours on the clock, and they'd do two Ops and bang.

We took a *Daily Express* reporter with us once, who went down into the bomb aimer's compartment with Bill Colson to see what a raid was like. He fainted when we got into the flak and he missed the whole thing. Another time we took an artillery officer, who was interested in the German guns. When he saw the flak he had the fright of his life. 'How can you get through it?' he said, which was what I'd thought at Düsseldorf on my first trip. It was one solid wall of explosion. I could not believe it was possible to come out the other side but it became part and parcel.

There was a great deal of special training now, in low formation flying with several other squadrons. No. 9 was to form the first wing on an unspecified attack with Nos. 49 and 61, and few if any of the pilots had had experience of close formations. Against widely held private expectations and a certain amount of talk from mid-upper gunners about sitting in a boiled egg while your top was sliced off, there were no accidents to the Lancasters.

> **Harry Irons:** There were ninety of us, flying in a gaggle at about twenty feet, around Lincoln, over The Wash, and these Spitfires came at us. They came in from behind in a mock attack and we were too low to take evasive action. As the Spits tried to break away, they hit the slipstream of ninety Lancs. If we'd been at a hundred feet they'd have been all right. As it was, some of them just flipped over and went straight into the deck.

Stubbs, Storey and seven others trained until they had proved they could fly at zero feet, almost touching each other, at full speed for hours on end. Then they were told the target: the Schneider works at Le Creusot, the biggest iron and steel manufactory in France, Krupp of the South, making guns, engines and armour. The factories were to be hit by 88 of the 94 Lancs while six bombed the power station. The crews had all heard about Nettleton VC and the Augsburg raid, to which the current venture bore many similarities. Irons: 'Rumours had been going round about a daylight then there was all this special practising. We shared the aerodrome with 44 Squadron, we shared the mess and everything, so they told us all about Augsburg and Nettleton VC and losing five out of six Lancasters.'

ORB: 'Flying at 0 feet over the Channel, ran into sea fog, which cleared forty minutes later with all aircraft still in sight and squadron formation regained by French coast.' Stubbs and company were approaching said coast, near La Rochelle, the wave tops seemingly near enough to paddle in, when another Lanc swerved across them.

> **Chamberlain:** The slipstream forced our aircraft into an instant half roll. She went through ninety degrees in less than the wink of an eye and everyone swore that the downward wingtip was in the water. Stubbs got her back, brilliant flyer that he was, and resumed formation as if nothing had happened. We'd just settled ourselves and our nerves from that when there was a terrific bang. The front Perspex had a great hole in it and Tom Parrington, our flight engineer, was covered in blood. It wasn't flak, though. It was our first and only experience of heavy seagull.

Irons: Tom was knocked out, and he was out for quite a while. Brownie (Sgt Brown, w/op) went up with the skipper while Tom recovered. We were in a loose gaggle about a mile wide, easy meat for any fighters, but we never saw any and it was crystal-clear weather. We could see for miles and miles. We never saw our escorts either; we were supposed to have a couple of hundred Spitfires but they didn't turn up.

The Lancs were still flying at nought feet and French people waved cheerily. In two minutes 9 Squadron were in and out of the target, bombing at 18.15: 'We were given 4,500 feet as our height. The highest was 5,000 and the lowest 2,500, but one Lanc* went in really low. I don't know if it was his own bombs or somebody else's, but he blew up and went into the houses.'

This was 61 Squadron's Sq/Ldr Corr DFC attacking the transformer station.

ORB: 'Buildings were disintegrating in all parts of the factory and almost all bombs fell across the works, creating tremendous damage.' Rolling mills, turbine-building works and machine shops 'had been well hit and were in flames', true enough, but 'almost all bombs'?

Irons: Quite a few of the bombs fell short, onto the housing estate which was at one end of the factory. There were plenty of civilian properties destroyed, as well as the target.

The Saturday after Le Creusot we went to Milan, travelling more or less the same route, eighty-eight of us this time, all Lancs, carrying the same load, six one thousand pounders. They were so surprised in Milan they didn't even sound the air raid sirens. We did see some fighters, Italian air force, but they stood off and didn't interfere. We were there in the middle of the afternoon and people were in the streets. Some of the Lancs went down with machine guns after they'd bombed. We didn't but some of them did, and there was no opposition. The Press were all around us when we got back and they published a picture of our crew and Squadron Leader Tubby Fry and his crew in the *Express* and various national papers on the Monday. Later in the week the Italian papers had the same picture, but they'd changed the headline to 'English Gangsters' and they put that in the *Daily Sketch* as well. I think that raid really shook the Italians. Ninety Lancs hitting a fairly compact town, coming all the way from England and wrecking the industry in broad daylight. Well, I think they lost a lot of their appetite for the war.

Jim McCubbin, Ken Dagnall and the others of his Whitley crew, unknowingly, were taking an extremely dangerous route to Bomber Command and 9 Squadron. Their navigator was Dr B J Sherry.

29 October 1942. Took off from St Eval at dawn for an anti-submarine sweep down The Bay (of Biscay). We set course from Bishop's Rock lighthouse on a twelve-hour patrol, heavily laden with fuel and depth charges. We flew at between five and seven hundred feet through showers and squalls until around 11.00 when Jimmy McCubbin, the skipper, discovered the port engine was leaking oil. At this point we were nearly five hundred miles from land. Jim decided to turn back to try and reach base before darkness. The wind, head-on during the trip out, now veered and was against us also on the return course. At 15.00 the wind strength increased, visibility shut down and the sea was running with a heavy swell and breaking wave tops. With groundspeed reduced considerably, more serious trouble developed when the oil pressure in the leaking port engine dropped rapidly and the engine packed up. The feathering mechanism (in an ex-Training Command Whitley) was clapped out, so coarse pitch had to be selected and the propeller left to windmill, which reduced speed further.

Dagnall: We were going backwards. There was a terrific easterly gale, which was very rare. Our cruising speed was about seventy knots, but the wind was gusting up to a hundred and our navigator Bart Sherry, an Oxford PhD, said we weren't going to make land.

Sherry: We were still a good hundred miles from the Scillies with a head-wind rising to gale force. After jettisoning depth charges, guns and ammunition, the Whitley was only just staying in the air, wallowing along at thirty knots. Air Sea Rescue was advised of our position in case of ditching. We clawed our way back to forty miles off the Scillies when the starboard engine, which had been running alone and on full throttle, overheated and the engine temperature gauge shot into danger. Andy (Smith, w/op) transmitted our position with a final SOS and locked the morse key on transmit.

Dagnall: Jim gave the order for ditching stations, which for me meant sitting against the main spar and acting as a relay for the skipper calling out our height because without our intercoms plugged in the rest couldn't hear him. 'Hundred feet!' he shouted and I shouted, 'Hundred feet!' and hoped they could hear me. 'Fifty feet!' and before I could get it out, a wave came up and hit us. I think that was the gentlest landing Jim ever made. So we got in the dinghy and watched the aircraft break in two and sink.

Sherry: The starboard engine caught fire and seized. In a matter of seconds we hit the sea and, after the initial inrush of icy cold water, the dinghy was launched with all crew members aboard. The retaining cord was severed to allow us to drift downwind and clear as the aircraft sank. We were now exposed to the full force of the gale and started to ship water fast. Flying helmets were used to bale out the water and we were soon bitterly cold and exhausted.

Dagnall: We sat with our feet carefully arranged between each other and settled down to wait for our rescue. We were well equipped. We had a Very pistol, a little compass, and we had a pigeon in case nobody had heard the wireless. Sherry wrote down the latitude and longitude and set the pigeon off with this vital information. Well, we'd ditched at about half past four on a late autumn afternoon. It was nearly dark and the waves were fifty and sixty feet high in a gale force wind blowing the opposite way to home. If we'd had a pigeon fancier among us, he might have told us the bird had no chance of bringing about our salvation.

Even if the pigeon had flown straight back through the night in record time, it might still have been too late. They didn't think to tie themselves in until a wave broke on them.

Sherry: We were caught by an extra large wave that overturned the dinghy and threw us into the sea. It floated upside down some twenty feet away and, after a concerted effort we righted it and climbed back in, but it was a most exhausting process and we lost a lot of gear although salvaging the emergency rations. Our priority now was to survive the night. I don't think we would have had the strength to deal with another dinghy capsize. So, cold and miserable, soaked to the skin, every muscle aching, we managed to keep ourselves going, alternately baling and pounding each other to keep warm. Around midnight we were heartened to see flares dropped by an aircraft and, rising on the crest of a wave, could distinguish a searchlight winking about a mile off. These welcome signs of rescue activity died away.

As dawn broke the crew felt that the wind had slackened a little and they might therefore have a chance of getting through their ordeal.

Sherry: We checked the rations and the skipper started to get things organised. There were six pint tins of water, a clear graduated beaker, two tins of emergency rations – Horlicks tablets, barley sugar, chewing gum – a telescopic mast and flag, a first aid kit, two marine signals which proved useful as paddles but were little good otherwise, and two escape outfits. We decided to do without water that day and to start tomorrow at the rate of one pint tin divided between the six of us per day. Three Horlicks tablets per man per day was the basic ration.

They would run out of everything after a week in the dinghy. Such a forecast was superfluous. If they weren't found sooner than that, they'd be dead anyway.

We divided into watches of two, each pair on duty for two hours at a stretch, sitting diametrically opposite each other. There was one wristwatch: my Service waterproof. As for the crew, Joe and Andy were apparently quite complacent; Charlie was wearing his usual poker face while Jimmy had the McCubbin cheesed-off expression. Mac MacKenzie, the spare pilot, was the big problem. We had only met him when he joined us shortly before take-off. He was very pessimistic about being rescued and became more depressed as time went on. After a while he refused to exercise to keep warm and even refused to converse.

It was soon dusk and the wind had continued to freshen when, at about midnight, MacKenzie became restless, mumbling to himself. He sat up, struggling with the ration tin, trying to throw it overboard, shouting about setting the control column before the plane hit the sea. He was quite delirious and struggled furiously. It was all we could do to keep him and the ration container safely down in the dinghy. Finally, he quietened down and dozed off.

31 October. Dawn came at last and everyone began to sit up and stretch except Mac, who lay back, very white and drawn, with his mouth open. When he didn't respond to shaking we started to rub and slap him to get his circulation going, but we had no effect. He was now quite cold with no heart nor pulse beat: dead. We slipped him overboard after removing his Mae West, identity tags and some personal items.

Sgt George Cameron MacKenzie of Edinburgh was 19 years old. The RAF issue dinghy was a circular inflatable with adequate room for three or possibly four, but it was very cramped with six. Now they were five, and the fact that they didn't quickly become four, three or fewer was a marvel in itself.

Dagnall: Our second pilot died on the second night and we had to let him go. We only tipped over once more in four days, which was how long it took them to find us. If we'd been in some sort of a boat rather than the inflatable we'd have been smashed to pieces long before. As it was, we rose up and down with the waves like a cork, sixty feet at a time, which was absolutely horrendous, like the very worst kind of fairground ride but it saved us.

A Liberator went over at one point but didn't see us or our two Very lights. If a German had seen us in that sea they wouldn't have been able to rescue us, so they would have shot us. That was good practice. It stopped us getting back as trained aircrew ready to fly again. Yes, so they'd have knocked us off all right.

Sherry: At 16.00 a plane appeared heading roughly in our direction, which we identified as a Whitley. When almost abeam he turned towards us and circled. After three circuits he appeared to lose sight of us and drifted down wind. He did a square search and again missed us, due to the broken nature of the sea. We took heart that the sighting would be reported and the search would continue. I was able to judge our course fairly well with the aid of the small escape compass and announced that we were heading in the general direction of South America at a rate of two knots and into the area of anti-U-boat patrols so our chances of being seen were improving.

Next day, at about 09.00, Joe spotted another Whitley. We ran up the distress flag on the telescopic mast and waved it about. Just as we thought we had been missed again the aircraft altered course and headed towards us, marking our position with a smoke float and climbing up to transmit our position. At midday three Hudsons of Air Sea Rescue arrived, laid down a smoke float, then dropped three yellow containers linked by a flotation line downwind across our drift path. The middle container burst open and a dinghy began to inflate, so we paddled to the flotation line and hauled ourselves along to the dinghy, which was the much larger Lindholme sort. The Hudsons departed, leaving the Whitley standing by. We stored the other containers' supplies in the smaller dinghy and got into the Lindholme, which gave us more leg-room. Apart from water, new rations consisted of more Horlicks tablets, another first aid kit, a pack of cards, a torch and, more importantly, a goose-down waterproof sleeping bag and two chemical hot water bottles. We bundled Charlie, now the weakest of us, into the sleeping bag and activated the hot bottles by filling them with sea water.

About midnight it started to rain so we collected the rain water into the dinghy canopy, drank it with great relish and settled down again to doze. Andy, who was on watch, wakened us and announced that he could hear a plane approaching. We had heard that some aircraft were fitted with radar capable of picking up a dinghy or a conning tower on the screen, and of course we knew that U-boat hunters had a Leigh light. They gave us a demonstration of their radar-guided accuracy as the plane approached and pinned us with a brilliant light first time. We were marked by a flame float and continued to be so marked every fifteen minutes. It was still dark when we became aware of an unusual shape that resolved itself into the outline of a ship. Her searchlight homed in on us, followed by the rattle and smack of a boat hitting the water.

Dagnall: We'd put all our belongings together in the pigeon tin, which was like a big biscuit tin, with over a hundred pounds in notes so it wouldn't get quite as saturated as ourselves. As we came alongside the rescue boat I stood up, which I thought I could do, holding the tin. But I collapsed and the tin went into the sea. 'Bugger it,' I said, which was the only comment made on the matter. None of the others said a dicky bird. In our state material things meant absolutely nothing. Anyway, I got on board the ship and they laid me down on the steel deck and it was the most comfortable place in the world, and they gave me a big glass of something to drink. I was teetotal at that time and I didn't know what navy rum was.

Sherry: I was woken at noon and in no time was tucking into a bowl of beef tea. The Navy looked after us extremely well. We were aboard HMS *Cutty Sark* – a frigate – bound for Devonport. The captain, Commander Mack, looked in to see how I was getting on and I had a long chat with the ship's navigator, Lieutenant Maurice Green, whose bunk I was occupying. I gave him my flying boots as a memento and spent the time dozing and drinking until we docked at Devonport at 14.30. We had ditched thirty miles short of the Scillies and in three and a half days had drifted another hundred and ten miles to the south west.

Dagnall: I woke up in Dartmouth hospital. They had to get our legs back to normal. They'd been under freezing cold salt water for four days and we'd got a kind of trench foot.

Through the rest of that autumn 9 Squadron went to an assortment of targets. Some were hard; some, like the series of raids on Italian ports and production centres to reinforce the army's fight at El Alamein, were lightly defended and relatively easy, if long. Storey went to Genoa five times in three weeks. 'On 6 November crews reported an uneventful trip with quite a large amount of light flak, which was ineffective. Slight amounts of heavy flak were fired seemingly at random.'

What the Italian gunners could not achieve, the thoughtlessness of the RAF's head office planners could achieve for them. The crews of 9 Squadron were back from their nine-hour flights at around 07.00, briefed for another Op at 15.00, and away again to Genoa at 17.30. Coming home from their second Italian long haul without a proper break between, F/O Mackenzie DFC and the newly promoted P/O Macdonald, both Wellington veterans and very experienced pilots, collided in midair and crashed on the southern edge of the aerodrome. There were no survivors. If the officer who wrote the account of the 6 June poor show was still there he might have noted that, with the death of Macdonald, of the seven pilots he mentioned only Runnacles and Cowan were still alive.

Out of hospital and back at camp McCubbin, Dagnall, Sherry and Co. found that they'd been presumed lost and so their kit had been the subject of the usual redistribution of wealth. There was nothing left but their uniforms.

Dagnall: My father was a watchmaker and he'd made me one that was worth £35, seven times his weekly wage. Of course that was gone, and my post office savings certificates worth £96. I tried to complain, but the sergeant told me to sod off, we had a war to fight. And we had, because we were posted to Lancaster training. They gave us two days to get there, and the train tickets. Because we'd been in the drink they were all right about issuing official kit but there was no chance of anything else apart from a week's wages in advance.

Ken arrived at Paddington and had to find his way to Euston. He had no idea if that was five minutes or five miles and was standing there, wondering what to do when a taxi drew up. Inside were two smooth and shiny gentlemen.

One said, 'What are you looking for, airman?' So I told him Euston, and I had an hour to get there. 'Driver,' said the chap. 'Detour to Euston, please.' So I got in, and on the way they told me all about the East End and how grateful, truly grateful, everyone was for the work we airmen did fighting the Germans. 'This is Euston,' he said. 'Jump out and I'll pass you your kit.' So I did, and the taxi drove off.

For the second time, Ken Dagnall was stranded with very little to his name.

I'd put my railway ticket in the left breast pocket of my tunic and half my wages, one pound twelve and six, in the right. And that was all I had. I didn't even have my gas mask. They'd cut the bag away with a razor and left me with just the strap. The RAF had had to believe me the first time I'd lost the lot. The second time I had to buy it.

Life went on at 9 Squadron and Storey had 'a very pleasant journey' to Milan, and three trips to Turin. Stubbs and the boys went too.

Harry Irons: We were cruising around looking for the target, which was the Fiat works, and our bomb aimer, Bill Colson, I think was suffering a bit. Tired and emotional, you might say. We used to call him Guinness. He kept saying he couldn't see anything, and the flak was starting to come up in earnest, and then I saw a big row of factory sheds, loads of them, dozens. I said to the skipper, 'Look, starboard side, factories as far as you can see.' The flak was pretty strong, the skipper was getting edgy, Ken Chamberlain was getting edgy, and Bill said, 'Oh, right, that's what we want, down there.' Ken came up to me afterwards and shook my hand. 'If you hadn't seen that lot, we'd have been bleeding shot down.' We had a couple of hours' kip and then we were on again to go back there. We had Flight Lieutenant J A G Skinner DFC with us on that one, the signals leader. He was something of a character, Joe Skinner. He'd been on the Milan daylight as a gunner with the CO.

Nancy Bower was a WAAF serving as barmaid in the officers' mess. 'Joe Skinner was one of the cheeky ones. He had a big RAF moustache, a big smile and a famous glint in his eye.' Harry Irons: 'What he was most famous for was putting footprints on the ceiling of the officers' mess.'

In between was the Royal Visit; the notice went out that King George VI was to inspect RAF Waddington on 12 November. There would be a rehearsal parade after which a tale swept the station about Anderson Storey. Everyone else was buffed and polished, clipped and snipped and pressed to perfection. Andy Storey turned up in carpet slippers, claiming that the RAF could not provide uniform shoes big enough for him, and with a small dog on a long lead. At the real thing the American met the King without incident but an R/T WAAF in Flying Control, Leading Aircraftwoman Beck wasn't present. She was mounting her own little protest about extremely valuable and scarce aircraft petrol being used to scrub out the hangar His Majesty was to inspect. Following her night shift, she stayed in bed, so there.

On 22 November Stubbs had yet another dangerous failure early on the way to Stuttgart, home of the Bosch spark plug factories, VKF ball bearings and Daimler-Benz aero-engine and armaments plant. Both starboard engines cut out. Getting them home on the two port motors was the good news; the bad was DNCO and one more trip added on to the end of their tour.

F/Sgt Ken Chamberlain now became a pilot officer. 'On my first day in the officers' mess, some bastard pinched my gloves. I said to Dick Stubbs, look, all this time in the sergeants' mess and never any bother, and now see what happens. He gave a knowing smile and said I should never trust an officer.'

Cowan the elder seemed to be well out of it. He'd crashed in his

Wellington full of incendiaries and been blown clear; he'd also flown through the blast of an exploding mine and experienced all the usual alarms and near misses. Cowan finished his tour and went off to 1661 Conversion Unit, leaving his kid brother to carry on the family tradition. His brother would survive the war and go back to New Zealand a squadron leader DFC. A third brother, Neville, five years younger again, would also become squadron leader DFC after a Wellington tour with No. 148. Flight Lieutenant James Cowan had his DFC but never the time to become a squaddie. The 30-year-old from Hastings, Hawke's Bay, would survive only a matter of months until 12 March, when his Lanc would crash at Cromwell killing all the eight men in it and two ground crew.

The prevailing poor weather went into reverse on 17 December and the promised cloud failed to appear for a moling trip. These Ops were an idea left over from somewhere, a nitwit stratagem whereby Germans not normally in the firing line should occasionally be reminded there was a war on. There were eight targets, including Cloppenburg, Nienburg, Soltau and Diepholz, north east of the Ruhr, for 27 Lancasters. Stubbs went to Haselünne and came back all right.

Irons: It was low level, moonlight, no cloud, and we had twelve one thousand pounders. The flak on the Dutch coast was murderous, light flak from hundreds of guns. From a distance it looked like twenty firework nights all at once, purples, blues, yellows, all different colours. We were each given a village, and we went in at two hundred feet and there was a train puffing in the station and we machine-gunned that and caught it afire, and we dropped our bombs right along the high street. They told us that the German factory workers were being transported to these dormitory villages so they could get a good night's kip.

Sgt Hazell had 'a very successful and amusing trip when we attacked a train, a town and a railway station'. It was not so amusing for the crews of Sgt Wilson and Sgt Allen and for seven Lancs from other 5 Group squadrons. One third of the attack failed to return. Bomber Command sent a team to investigate.

They interviewed Stubbs and asked him what he thought went wrong. 'Quite simple,' he said. 'If you had a good navigator you got there and came back. If you didn't, you didn't.' Chamberlain the navigator thought Stubbs should have some credit. 'The briefing had said to fly the route at 10,000 feet, assuming cloud. The cloud wasn't there so the experienced skippers either went much higher or much lower. The others stayed at the given height, clearly visible and easy targets for the flak gunners.' Sgt Allen had three Ops and two second Dickies behind him. Sgt Wilson had had the same amount of practice. So, how did you ever get to be an experienced skipper?

Perhaps the Fates had not approved of Sgt Hazell's use of the word 'amusing'. On his next time out, to Duisburg as a pilot officer, as he circled to gain height he collided with a 44 Squadron Lancaster. Everyone was killed, including Hazell's three Wellington originals who were, like him, over 30 and married. Harry Irons: 'We were right above it. Tremendous explosion, full petrol loads, full bomb loads, and they went into each other head on. We were more than close. I don't know how we got away with it, and the funny thing was, with an incident like that, you still carried on with the Op.' No question that Stubbs would carry on. It was his penultimate.

Stubbs had the two necessary ingredients for a successful Lancaster pilot. He had reactions like lightning, so when we saw a fighter he was into his evasive action before we'd got half the order out. And, he had ice instead of blood. We were running into Germany one night with a full bomb load and all four engines cut out at once. Stubbs said, 'That's a nuisance, four engines gone,' or words to that effect. We dropped like a stone and I think Tom must have blanked out because he didn't do anything. So Stubbs said, very calmly and quietly, 'How about changing the fuel tanks over?' which Tom did. The engines all started up again and we carried on as if nothing had happened. Stubbs was only three or four years older than me but he seemed more, a lot more, like he'd had ten years' experience of this terrible job.

> 'Ask that fellow what he's talking about.
> He's fast asleep'
> P/O Lovell

Eight went to Munich, 21 December. 'G (F/Sgt Fenwicke-Clennell) failed to return.' Edward F-C made it five squadron losses in a fortnight and it was the end of Stubbs's second tour. 'Town definitely attacked, but with what degree of accuracy impossible to say.' Out of his Wellington crew he still had with him Chamberlain and Brown, and rear gunner Moorhead had completed on the trip before. These were three who had transferred from Anderson Storey and proved so lucky ever since. With all their engine failures Stubbs had had 35 starts, Chamberlain 34, to get to 30. Brian Moorhead's luck would change for the worse, and bomb aimer Bill Colson's, and Stubbs's.

Harry Irons: 'The skipper came to me and we shook hands. He said, "Harry, I'm off, but I wish you luck and hope you survive the rest of your tour." Which was nice of him.'

Some months later, used to their peaceful jobs, Chamberlain would see Runnacles and suggest they volunteered as a two-man Lysander crew, flying Special Operations Executive people and supplies. 'I quite fancied the idea of navigating a light aircraft to a bloke with a torch in a field. John Runnacles said no, he wasn't volunteering for anything. He'd lived through a tour; he didn't believe in tempting Fate by going back early.' Sadly for Runnacles, Fate would make her own decisions as she had in the cases of 44 bombers and crews of 9 Squadron during 1942, and things could only get worse.

LACW Pip Beck knew F/Sgt Storey's name and voice from her job of bringing the boys in to land and she recognised him as the gangling, slightly uncoordinated one, who stood out in any military company. In the sergeants' mess at the NAAFI do on New Year's Eve, she met him.

Everyone who wasn't commissioned went. They were good, the dances in the sergeants' mess. There was a band, playing Glenn Miller and all the popular tunes, and the bar, and lots of tiddly blokes wandering around. This very tall, non-tiddly man asked me to dance and we did, and we were sitting later with a drink and he was telling me about his life in America without a trace of an American accent. One of his gunners came up and grabbed his leg and gave it a twist, and ran off. It must have happened regularly. Andy just said that he was big but not very well put together, and that there would be no more dancing. He hobbled across to the bar for more drinks and that was the way the evening went.

Pip Beck had no sense of premonition. Sometimes aircrew seemed to go about their business with the Black Spot almost visible on them and Pip had had a close encounter with this. 'I once had the eerie experience of dancing with a quiet, pleasant Scottish sergeant pilot and suddenly knowing he was for the chop. I knew it with a certainty. I wondered if he had any suspicion of it himself. Sure enough, on his next Op, he didn't come back.'

Storey told Pip about his family, his school days at Deerfield and college days at Harvard. There might have been romance in the air but Pip already had a boyfriend and Storey perhaps felt that a bomber pilot was not the best of propositions. After the ball was over he walked Pip back to her billet. 'He dropped a chaste kiss on my forehead, stroked my hair and turned quickly back to the road.'

1943

When my fighter squadron was based in Lincolnshire we often rubbed

shoulders with these bomber boys, in crowded pubs or on the rugger field. There was something different about these men. They tried to hide their feelings under a forced gaiety, but sometimes snatches of conversation revealed the strain. 'Our third flight commander in three weeks . . . our squadron's grounded until we train the new chaps . . . ' When we attended their long briefings about the weather, enemy dispositions, navigation, communications and armament we could feel the pressure steadily mounting. We had the greatest admiration for these bomber boys, whose job was infinitely more dangerous than ours.

Air Vice Marshal Johnnie Johnson DSO and two Bars, DFC and Bar.

At the start of the year, the experienced crews on 9 Squadron were led by Lonsdale, Storey, Gibson, Southwell, Meyer, Doolan, Marshall, Cowan, McDonald, Hobbs, Jarrett and Fry. New crews, arrived and arriving during January, were led by Carswell, Chilvers, Foote, Walsh, Thomas, Lyons, Nelson, Jacombs, Boczar, Hunter, Van Note, Cox, Davis and Lind. That was 26 pilots and crews altogether. Only fifteen would be there to start February.

3 January: Lonsdale and Storey were part of a very small force at Essen, bombing on the experimental Wanganui skymarking flares for use in ten tenths cloud, which were dropped by Mosquitos using the equally experimental Oboe navaid. The 9 Squadron Wanganui pair was almost across the enemy coast when *Underoffizier* Költringer spotted Lonsdale's kite. Költringer blasted her and set her on fire and, unlike the Turin time when Lonsdale was hit by two incendiaries from above, this fire could not be extinguished. Everyone died in the crash. Douglas Lonsdale DFC was 31, married, with the end of his second tour in sight. Storey, thinking about the end of his first tour, came back to Waddington alone.

Harry Irons: They used to give you a mining trip for a bit of a breather, a piece of cake, but they were very dodgy. You'd go out into the Baltic or somewhere and there'd be these flak ships waiting for you. And you had to fly low to drop the mines, so you didn't damage them, which gave the flak ships the piece of cake: us.

Storey went mining in the Baltic when his trip counter showed 28 up, two to go. He came back unscathed, but 'Sgt Doolan in R was unfortunate in having a direct hit on the tail causing the death of the rear gunner.' Perhaps, rather than Sgt Doolan, it was the rear gunner, Sgt Robinson, who was unfortunate.

Harry Irons: Reggie Robinson, called Robbie, was a bit older than me. He'd be 20, from Brixton. They brought him back but there was nothing left of him apart from some of his upper body. We gunners knew each other. We went to his funeral. The parents had declined the offer to see his body. They wanted to remember him as he was. His skipper was Sgt Doolan, who we'd taken as a second Dicky. He was famous as a pilot who couldn't land. Aircrew considered landing an important skill and weren't keen on flying with him. So he came in the mess and said they'd put a nice new turret on his Lanc and would I like to get in it. Some of my pals said, you're not going with him, are you? I said there wasn't anybody else.

Pip Beck: I met Andy Storey around the camp sometimes, stopping to exchange news, but nothing more. His tour was almost complete. I asked him one day if he'd take me up in his Lanc. He promised he'd take me for a flip when his tour was finished. I had a 48* due. When I got back, Andy would almost certainly have done his last Op.

*48 hour leave pass.

16 January: a force including 190 Lancasters, twelve of them from 9 Squadron, went to Berlin. So far this was the largest number of Lancasters in one raid and the first on Berlin for over a year. It was a long way, the Big City, the target with the most flak guns anywhere. ORB: 'The target, Berlin, was received with delight by the squadron. Met forecast good conditions over the area and crews very satisfied with the prospect after so many Wanganui trips.' Cowan: 'Entire route well defended and heavy flak appeared at most frequent intervals from Mendo* Island to Swinemünde and on return from Berlin to Langeland (Denmark).'

*Mandö, Denmark.

Going second Dicky with Hobbs was F/Sgt Frank Goheen Nelson, 24, of Wilkinsburg, Pennsylvania. He must have wondered if they were all like this. 'Believed Berlin, 20.10 hrs, 16,500 ft. Red flares seen (Neuwerp). DR* run to target. Fires below cloud. Impossible to tell whether target or dummy. No results seen although fires appeared where incendiaries dropped. 60 x 4lb incs hung up and were brought back. Starboard inner engine oil pressure failed at Danish coast. Feathered.'

*Dead reckoning.

Whether these smaller disasters were portents of major ones, the crews couldn't tell. They knew most of them were doomed, but who? The next night they set off again with nine more among a doubtless equally delighted force of 170 Lancasters that achieved another record, one which would not be broken for seven months: the largest number of Lancasters lost on a single Op. Following the same route as the night before, Carswell was first up at 16.54, followed by Chilvers 16.56, Sq/Ldr Fry 16.57 with novitiate Sgt Boczar beside him, the Aussie Trevor Gibson at 16.58, six more, and Anderson Storey last at 17.20. Two of 9 Squadron's contingent had technical troubles and returned early. That left nine for the Flying Control staff to wait for.

W/Cdr Southwell was on his second successive occasional, with a distinguished crew including Nav Leader F/Lt W I N G Doig, Bombing Leader F/Lt Higginson DFM, Gunnery Leader P/O J P Crebbin and second Dicky Sgt E C Davis. They missed Berlin altogether, bombed Bützow, a small town with a steelworks not far from the coast, and gave freshman Ernie Davis a master class in night fighting.

SECRET 9 Squadron Combat Report

. . . returning from Berlin, visibility good, thin cloud at 12,000 feet, moon on port beam. (Me210) attacked from green bow down firing with fixed guns in nose and free beam gun. Our aircraft dived steeply. Rear gunner fired burst of 200 rounds across trace of enemy aircraft's nose guns, then further burst of 200 rounds from 150 yards as enemy was breaking away. Large number of sparks were observed coming from enemy aircraft's port engine. From size of holes in our tail plane, enemy beam gun would appear to be 7.9mm. Rear gunner P/O Crebbin. Captain W/Cdr Southwell.

Sgt Carswell crashed about 25 miles from Magdeburg; he and four of his crew were taken prisoner. Nothing was heard and no trace found of John Chilvers's aircraft, likewise that of the experienced P/O Gibson, who once flew through the Alps on three engines rather than over, who flew his way out of an attack by three Me109s at Aachen in October, and who went down with yet another second Dicky, a New Zealander called Jacombs.

Pip Beck, away from Waddington on her 48 and so not at her post on that dreadful night of endless anxiety, was not to have her flip with Anderson Storey. Though he had just this one Op to do, he and all his men were not posted to safe jobs. Instead, a nightfighter found them near Neumünster in Schleswig-Holstein, on their way to Berlin, and posted them all to Hamburg Cemetery.

4

THAT'S MORE LIKE IT

Harry Irons: My first raid with Stubbs had been Düsseldorf, and my first raid with Doolan was Düsseldorf. It wasn't the same Lanc with a new rear turret after all; it was ED477 WS/O. John Pratt was our flight engineer, John Buckley was our bomb aimer – (he was a schoolteacher), Chap Chappell was our w/op. We had a sprog in the mid-upper, Moseley, replacing Sgt Baines, who had refused to fly with Doolan any more after Robinson was killed and had gone off with another pilot. We were a compact unit, all sergeants, playing cards in the mess. When we got a Lanc of our own we decided we'd call it 'Robbie's Reply'.

30 January, Hamburg: a nightmare. Five out of eleven, including Doolan, came home early with bad icing and mechanical trouble.

Harry Irons: We were almost there. Well, we were there but not over the target. We could feel the aircraft getting more and more sluggish, then we reached that point where the weight of ice became too much and we dropped like an express lift. We could see Hamburg coming up fast underneath us. We dumped our bombs, the ice fell off and we came home. It was DNCO, duty not carried out. I thought if I have to do as many trips that don't count with Doolan as I did with Stubbs, I'll never get to the end of it.

Nothing was heard from the Aussie Jack Thomas, who had lasted to his fifth Op and went down near Vechta with all his crew. Messages did come from the American Frank Nelson, diverted to RAF Leeming, but they flew into the Hambleton Hills and were all killed on their second Op together.

In this month of January, only nine Operations were flown by 9 Squadron with nine cancellations. A total of 63 sorties resulted in the loss of nine Lancasters and crews plus one rear gunner, one pilot, and a Lancaster with a new crew who hadn't operated yet. Of those 72 men, ten lost crews plus two, only five individuals survived as POWs and 28 of the bodies were never found. At this stage of the war, ten Lancs and crews amounted almost to an operational squadron, the force that a squadron could contribute on any one night of men and aircraft all present, correct and serviceable. New crews and new aircraft arrived as fast as they could be trained and made, but of the ten lost in January, seven were new anyway.

2 February, Cologne: P/O Robert Van Note, American volunteer, clocked up number one, as did Boczar, a Canadian known neither for his beauty nor his height. Canadian aircrew were paid more than their RAF native colleagues although not as much as Americans in the USAAF. Americans like Van Note counted as Canadians. The extra money was of limited use in a country where the beer was liable to run out before the session got properly started. Commodities like cigarettes, nylon stockings and chocolate, taken for granted in Canada and the USA, had acquired high luxury status for the civilian population of wartime Britain. What scant quantities of these goods the ingenious transatlantic servicemen could glean and garner were reserved for that most deprived section of the populace, the young and pretty women.

After two scrubs, they at last got off for Wilhelmshaven, 11 February. There had to be a certain *frisson* about Wilhelmshaven but they didn't lose anybody this time. 'Two crews reported large flashes below the cloud after bombing and a glow as they left the target area.' For the first time H2S worked well so the marking was spot on. H2S was an early form of air-to-ground radar, which displayed on a screen the profile of the landscape flown over. The flashes and the glow came from a German navy ammunition dump, which went up with a terrific explosion and caused devastation all around. 'T (F/O Wilmot) was unfortunate, the trimming tabs being u/s necessitating 25° of flap to keep the aircraft level, the electrical and R/T circuits of the rear turret being also u/s.' This was the same Tommy Wilmot, who had already done an eventful tour with 9 Squadron in Wellingtons as a sergeant, and that was a slow and cold flight home for Sgt Taylor, rear gunner, appreciating how much an electrically heated suit could do for you if it was working.

F/Lt Richard Noel Stubbs DFM, DFC-in-waiting, now of a fighter affiliation unit, took off in his Spitfire on a training flight, 27 February. Stubbs came over to 103 Squadron, recently converted from Halifaxes to Lancasters and, not surprisingly, was not entirely satisfied with the performance of the learner Lancaster pilot in reaction to his spoof attacks. He landed the Spit. Stubbs would demonstrate the procedure and took up with him the full crew. He climbed from the 'drome at Elsham Wolds (north Lincs, near Brigg) and began to throw the Lanc into skid turns. It might have been the stress of high speed manoeuvring, or less than thorough maintenance after the aircraft's previous night's Op to Cologne, or a combination of the two. Whatever it was, a rudder fell off.

Stubbs ordered everyone to bale out. They did, and would one day be lost at La Spézia, but Stubbs decided he would land the thing. This was the bomber pilot who wouldn't leave the target unless he flew the perfect run, who would go round as many times as he needed to get the aiming point in the sights. He would have been thinking, 'If I jump, a rudderless Lanc could crash anywhere.'

Stubbs overshot on his first pass and was executing a measured, controlled turn into his second circuit when the other rudder fell off. The aircraft flipped over onto her back and went straight in, missing the local manor house Elsham Hall and smashing into some woods. Dick Stubbs, two tours of Operations completed, was still only 22.

There was a story about a mix-up with parachutes, that they'd believed they were one short, that there wasn't one for Stubbs. Another story was that he was taking the Lanc far beyond her normal limits, trying to turn much too fast. A chute was found in the wreckage but to Harry Irons none of the stories sounded like Stubbs. 'Stubbs was a stickler. He would stand no slackness of any kind, about parachutes or anything else. He was a single-minded flyer but single-mindedness is one thing. Being a daredevil and a show-off is quite another.'

By March, of the New Year starters at 9 Squadron only Boczar, Van Note and Walsh were still around and Cox had been posted. The month began with Berlin and it was quite a night. Three had engines on fire over the target. Boczar's crew were exercised too. 'Red and green TI (Target Indicator) markers clearly seen but unfortunately not in bomb sights when bombs were dropped owing to violent evasive action becoming necessary.' Perhaps that was the reason why Boczar was still on the list. He'd be flying along on his bombing run, through the most numerous and most efficient anti-aircraft defences in the world, and he'd say to himself, 'By Jove, I do believe violent evasive action is becoming necessary.'

Bill Meyer, an alderman of the mess at 32, whose faithful Lanc U-Uncle had a pawnbroker's sign painted on her side, was interested to espy the buildings of Berlin illuminated by the flashes of the guns firing at him. They hit him as well, in the bomb bay. Jim Verran, on his second tour of Ops after 35 Whitley trips with 102 Squadron, was three or four miles from home when he crashed at Heighington. The Lanc was in pieces all over a ploughed field, three of his crew were killed and he went through the canopy, suffering broken bones and various other serious wounds. Verran became a Guinea Pig, a patient of the legendary surgeon Sir Archibald McIndoe, and was off the 9 Squadron rota for good, if not done with bombing and crashing for good.

He would join 83 Squadron Pathfinders as Sq/Ldr Verran and set off for Königsberg, 26 August 1944. On the way back an Me110 would find him.

The rear gunner would shoot down the fighter but be killed in the process. With the aircraft burning fiercely, the bomb aimer would bale out of the front hatch and Verran would try to do the same, only to be sucked by the slipstream into the open bomb bay. Somehow freeing himself to jump, he would be the only survivor, but very badly burned, his skin grafts and major surgery this time being supplied by a German doctor.

Much to the C-in-C's liking and setting the example of how it should be done was the bombing raid on Essen, 5 March 1943. A mixed force of over 400 aircraft – Lancs, Halifaxes, Stirlings and Wellingtons – were shown the way by a target-marking group equipped with the Oboe system, through which ground stations in England could guide an aircraft to within 300 yards of the target by calculations based on a radar signal sent by the aircrew's operator. The system's drawbacks were that nightfighters could home on the radar signal and the ground stations could only handle a few aircraft, making it unsuitable for general bombing but a brilliant improvement on target marking and therefore on results.

The route to Essen was given as from Egmond on the Dutch coast to a point fifteen miles north of the city. The bombers flew in a thin stream about one hundred and fifty miles long, intending to bomb at a rate of one aircraft every six or so seconds. Pathfinder Lancs dropped yellow markers on the point where the bombers had to turn to come in on their run. As they came up to the target, they saw red indicators dropped blind by the Oboe Mosquitos, or if they couldn't see those, they aimed for greens dropped by the Pathfinder Lancs. This was a decisive raid. 'Target area covered with mass of fire. Violent explosions lit up the sky. Huge fires were raging and explosions were countless. Glow visible from 120 miles.' It was the first time the RAF had been able to find and mark Essen properly and they wrecked a hundred acres of Krupp's works and environs.

Harris: Nothing like this had ever happened to Essen in any previous attack and as a result of the bombing concentration achieved, only fourteen aircraft were missing from this operation. Years of endeavour, of experiment and of training in new methods, had at last provided the weapon and the force capable of destroying the heart of the enemy's armaments industry. It was an achievement comparable only with the 'Thousand Raid' on Cologne and marked an important turning point in the bomber campaign.

While Harris at last felt he had something like the force he wanted, there were still limitations on what could be done. The main flak concentrations and nightfighter deployments, and the approach of summer's shorter nights, meant that the risks and distance of a target had always to be weighed most carefully against its desirability. There was the possibility of overconcentration. Repeated attacks would bring beefed-up defences, moved from less bombed areas, so surprise and secondary targets had to come into the plan to keep the defences spread as widely and thinly as possible. Even so, the Essen crossroads was the last one on the way to the Battle of the Ruhr. Over the next few months, Bomber Command would knock a large part of the industrial stuffing right out of the German war effort. Harry Irons: 'That was a swine, that was, Essen. With haze over the target you had to take your time and things were getting rough by this part of the war, really getting rough. Flak, fighters, and you watched them shooting down our aircraft, especially on the run in. The poor old Stirlings took a hell of a banging. And every time it was raining shrapnel. It clattered into you and it was amazing it didn't set the bombs off.'

For James Douglas Melrose, known as Dougie, joining the RAF apprentice boys scheme in 1938 turned out to be a long way round to becoming a Lancaster pilot. This Edinburgh lad had lived and breathed the idea of flying ever since he'd found out it was possible and had gone into the RAF at the youngest age he could, 16. Perversely, as the war moved on and while civilians his age were joining aircrew training, the scheme kept him away. It wasn't until four years later that he flew an aircraft.

From his earliest days Melrose saw himself as the career flyer, the serious, dedicated pilot who lived for his work and the RAF. A different sort of a boy, Raymond John Harris, left his Eastbourne school at 14 and messed about at this and that until he was 16 and a quarter. To Ray, reaching this age seemed a perfectly logical reason for going along to the RAF recruiting office in Brighton and telling them that he was 17 and a quarter, which they believed. Ray was the carefree type and at the time being a pilot sounded like a great idea. The RAF said he was fine except for his maths so he went back to his old teacher and sat in his room for a few weeks. Ray's teacher told the RAF when he thought he was up to the mark, and that was that.

Everyone who wanted to be a pilot had to start by taking twelve hours with an instructor in a De Havilland Tiger Moth, the marvellous old light biplane so forgiving in the hands of learner drivers. At the end of the twelve hours, there was a sort-out. Those who had managed to go solo with success went on to the next pilot's stage; those who hadn't transferred to other courses and usually became navigators or bomb aimers. Melrose distinguished himself at this early point and there was never any doubt that he would be going on. Harris didn't quite manage the solo flight but some-how was selected anyway. Melrose went to South Africa, Harris to Canada.

Back in June 1942, at the South African No. 5 Air School (Witbank, near Kimberley), early practical training had consisted of flying a Tiger Moth, sometimes with an instructor, for about forty-five minutes each day, gradually working through the canon of manoeuvres. Over a couple of months this built up to three or four sessions a day. On 7 July 1942 Melrose passed his first air milepost when Flying Officer Stretton certified without further comment that he had witnessed Corporal Melrose execute his first solo spin and recover successfully.

By the end of the month Melrose had over forty-eight flying hours, half of them solo. He was ready to move on to the next level of difficulty: side slipping, forced landings, aerobatics, low flying, instrument flying, night flying and, with his fellow students, formation flying. Instrument flying was simple. They just covered up the cockpit so the student pilot couldn't see anything; thankfully, the instructor could. By the end of that September, Corporal 573259 Melrose had flown 38 hours solo and another 41 dual. He was passed as an above average pilot with no points in flying or airmanship that should be watched.

One engine became two when he transferred to the Airspeed Oxford, a low-wing monoplane and the aerial equivalent of a Bedford minibus. It cruised at 150mph and reached 180mph in a dive. On 1 October 1942 Melrose flew his first solo in the Oxford and went through the whole sequence of manoeuvres again with an extra emphasis on night flying and night landings, the most hairy experiences so far.

His introduction to bombing came by way of the camera obscura. Taking turns to fly the Oxford, he and a fellow pupil pilot, usually his pal Woolford, did dummy runs on sunny days over a small building with a wide-angle lens fitted in the roof. The lens projected a picture of the sky onto a horizontal screen inside the hut. When the lads dropped their imaginary bomb, a light flashed and the hut's instructor marked the time and place, and calculated the target error. It was a long way from dropping bombs at night over Germany while under attack from fighters and flak guns but they had to start somewhere.

Coming up to Christmas 1942 at No. 21 Air School, Kimberley, Melrose was passed again as an above average Oxford pilot with 154 hours' experience but this time with formation flying as a point to be watched. Training now largely consisted of steep turns, forced landings, night flying, instrument flying, air gunnery and bombing. Things were becoming more real. Melrose was a proper pilot now, not so much learning to fly as learning how to apply his flying to the job he was to do. With a grand total of 240 hours 45 minutes of solo and dual flying, plus 43 hours 25 minutes on the Link trainer (flight simulator), Melrose qualified as an above average Group II pilot. He was commissioned and received his wings, his RAF flying badge, on 13 March 1943, which was the day Hobbs and Lewis went gardening.

Spring was on its way and the allotments had not to be forgotten. Howard Lewis, the boy from Ann Arbor, Michigan, and Sgt Arthur Hobbs set forth with their mines for the Baltic and the fancifully named Spinach plantation off Gdynia. Hobbs couldn't find the right spot in the sea fog and came back. Lewis and all his original crew were on their sixth Op together. No one will ever know if they found Spinach in the fog.

For the next week it was training, practising, cancellations, and a new boss arrived. W/Cdr Kenneth Brooke Farley Smith DSO was a 30-year-old regular from before the war, an Oxford graduate and a man who took his responsibilities very seriously indeed. Arriving with him was Jim McCubbin's crew, the lads who flew Whitleys backwards and spent four days in a dinghy. They sat in the mess and listened to Sgt Turp, veteran of one Op, telling everybody how an incendiary bar dropped from above went through his starboard wing and how the rear and mid-upper gunners from another Lancaster fired a four-second burst at him.

Berlin, 27 March: W/Cdr Smith took passage with Sgt Swire and his fortnight's experience. Someone accidentally hit a secret *Luftwaffe* supply dump in the middle of some woods that the PFF had marked as central Berlin. The Germans were dumbstruck by the quality of Bomber Command's information and their ability to hit a small spot in a forest.

As had been forecast by those opposed, including the C-in-C, some of the best mainforce crews were siphoned off for Pathfinders. In March two went from 9: Wilmot, second tour pilot with a first tour crew, and F/Sgt McDonald with Tom Parrington, navigator Victor Nunn and gunnery leader John Crebbin. For some it would prove a good move but for the men they left behind, April would turn out to be another January.

2 April: Paramore, Fox and McCubbin to the U-boat base at Lorient, first Op for all of them and the last time Lorient town would have to suffer. Most of the people had fled as they had from St Nazaire. Harris hated these raids which he saw as mere diversions because he didn't yet have a bomb which could penetrate the concrete roofs, eighteen feet thick and more. He summed it up beautifully. 'These attacks were generally very well concentrated and left little undestroyed in either town except for the U-boat bases.'

Ken Dagnall: Lorient was a clear moonlit night and the first time I'd ever flown so high. The old Whitley could only struggle up to 12,000 feet, and here we were in the top of the sky, millions of stars, and I thought, if this is war, it's a picture. And the next night we were on for Essen which, the grapevine said, was just about the most heavily defended place we could go to. Only Berlin was worse.

3 April, Essen: Bill Swire was picked up on the way back over Holland by nightfighter pilot *Oberleutnant* Eckart-Wilhelm von Bonin and that was that for the 20-year-old and all his crew. Sq/Ldr Geoffrey Jarrett was 34; he'd been in the RAF in the biplane years. Having almost completed his second tour in a Lancaster he too fell to earth with every one killed.

SECRET 9 Squadron Combat Report
4/5 April 1943. Hëide. Lancaster 'W'. Captain: Sgt McCubbin.
Interception by a S/E E/A took place very shortly after bombing the target, Kiel. The pilot was carrying out continuous weaving at 21,000 feet. The E/A, believed to be Me109, was seen 200 feet below and directly astern at 100 yards by the rear gunner (Sgt Stewart). He warned the captain, who executed a diving turn to starboard while the rear gunner fired two three-second bursts at the E/A, the second of which was seen to hit. The fighter immediately dived away and disappeared while still at 100 yards range without opening fire.

No moon, visibility fairly good. Layer of 10/10 cloud at 6,000 feet illuminated a little astern of our aircraft by searchlights.

Rear turret 450 rounds, no stoppages.

Ken Dagnall: That was the first time we went in W-William, which we christened *Cutty Sark* after the frigate that picked us out of the sea. We found out that cutty sark was Scottish for short skirt, so we had a picture of a young lady wearing one painted on W's nose. And that was three Ops on the trot so they gave us a week's leave.

In Doolan's Lanc was Harry Irons. He was due something more than a week's leave. Kiel had been his last. The combined Messrs Galloway and Irons had officially had his thirty.

Including the DNCOs it was more like 36. I said goodbye to my skipper and told him he never would learn to land an aircraft and I went as a gunnery instructor. Then I was on pulling drogues for the artillery to shoot at, which was my most dangerous posting of all. We pulled this long streamer about two hundred yards behind us, at three or four thousand feet, and the artillery aimed at the streamer. We lost quite a few shot down – aircraft that was, not streamers.

Harry survived again and would do his second tour on Halifaxes. Lancaster ED654 WS/W-William AKA Cutty Sark would also have a long career, 62 Ops, twenty of them with McCubbin, but would eventually end as almost all of them did, in February 1944.

'Everything will be OK while I'm on leave.
The other air gunners are taking over my job'
P/O Tozer, Gunnery Leader

A move down the road was imminent, to a new airfield at Bardney. The advance party was sent there on 7 April and the next day a party of five Lancasters was sent to Duisburg, then six more to Duisburg on 9 April.

Meyer, Brown and another Hale, Johnny Hale, came home, each with a second Dicky. They didn't know that it was no use waiting for the others. Arthur White, the Kiwi, had met a nightfighter over Utrecht; all killed after one month. A newer Arthur, Paramore, had also met a fighter over Holland, a few miles north of Eindhoven, and he and all his crew were killed. The third Arthur of the night was quite a different case. Sergeant Hobbs, not to be confused with Sergeant Kenneth Hobbs, the Wellington pilot who was already dead, nor F/Lt Murray Hobbs DFC who had earned his gong while flying a tour of thirty Ops with 75 Squadron and was still alive.

Sgt Arthur Roy Hobbs had very nearly finished his tour. He'd been on squadron since October when he'd second Dickied with Lonsdale and again with Hazell, two long servers who nevertheless had ended up the usual way. Hobbs had gone on his first Op planting vegetables with the same crew as came with him on his last, apart from one. Tonight they were in a new Lanc, ED566 WS/J-Jig, only nine Ops, and she and they were lost without trace. The letter 'J' was thus free, ready to be taken by a Lancaster hoping for a kinder fate. Among the airmen lost this night was one Curly Jones, w/op to Tiny Cooling, now of 460 Squadron, later of the Runnymede Memorial.

Only a small contingent was available to follow Group orders on another five hundred raid to Frankfurt: Robertson, McCubbin, Fox, F/Lt Hobbs, the American Van Note approaching the twenty Ops mark, Hale and Wing Commander Smith.

Ken Dagnall: The squadron lost six aircraft in action in the first ten days of April. We suddenly became one of the senior crews and we'd only been on four Operations. The Wingco had us all assembled in a room for briefing. Normally, a squadron might be a hundred or more needing the village hall to meet in. We fitted in somewhere like your dining room at home. He said, 'I'm going with you tonight, to find out what's wrong', which was a bit daft. He wasn't going to find out what was wrong that way. What was wrong was that Jerry was shooting us down, that's what was wrong.

W/Cdr K B F Smith DSO, mentioned twice in despatches, OC

9 Squadron, did indeed find out what was wrong. He went in near Mainz.

Ken Dagnall: The Wingco might have been like quite a few of them, I think, senior officers brought up on biplanes and Empire business, you know, fighting the old fuzzy wuzzies in the Middle East somewhere. They were fearless and determined but perhaps not all of them had grasped the essentials of flying at 20,000 feet at night over Germany.

On 12 April the new man, W/Cdr Burnett DFC came from 5 Group HQ, his reputation as a strict disciplinarian going before him. Pat Burnett, a regular officer from before the war who had indeed flown biplanes on Empire business over Egypt but also a full tour over Germany with 44 Squadron, was respected rather than loved.

No. 9 moved from Waddington to their new aerodrome at Bardney, taking with them some of 44 Squadron's aircrew and station men, including adjutant F/O Rushton and experienced pilot F/Lt Wakeford. Aileen Walker was a WAAF waitress in the officers' mess at Waddington, then Bardney. 'He was rather posh, Rushton. He said to me, "Are you coming with us to 9 Squadron?" I said I didn't know. He checked the list and he said, "Aileen, your name's not on it but it will be in ten minutes. You're coming with us." So I did.' WAAF Nancy Bower, officers' mess barmaid, also moved to Bardney.

Flying Officer Rushton drank pink gin. Well, I didn't know what it was and he obviously expected me to know so the first time he just ordered it and said nothing. I got the gin and wondered how to make it pink and Rushton pointed to the bottle of Angostura bitters. I thought, it must be like the Worcester sauce in a Bloody Mary so I poured it in. When he settled down after watching that, Rushton told me, four drops only. Ever after that he used to say, 'Four drops, Nancy, four drops.'
Aileen Walker: So I was in the officers' mess in the dining room, waiting at table, and Flight Lieutenant Wakeford was there with his back to me. He was a big man, great mop of red hair – they called him 'Red' – and an educated man. Without looking round he said, 'Aileen, are you there?' I said, 'Yes, sir.' He said, 'I'm bringing a dog back from leave, and when I go on Ops I'm taking that bomb aimer with me, the one you're going out with. So you can look after my dog.' That bomb aimer was a Sergeant, Harry Hawkridge, a 20-year-old from Leeds. The only officer in the crew was an American, *F/O Reeves, whose first name was Jonah, which didn't sound too lucky.
*From Durhamville, New York.

Red Wakeford had been the first officer I served in the mess at Waddington. My first lunch and I walked through the door of the dining room with two plates of soup expecting maybe a dozen or twenty men and there seemed to be hundreds, and they all gave wolf whistles, which they always did with a new WAAF. I put this soup down in front of Wakeford and nearly spilled it all over him. He asked me if I was all right and I put the other soup down, and walked out and kept walking until I was in the rest room. The sergeant in charge of me asked me what on earth and I said, 'I'm not going back in there.' She said, 'Oh yes, you are. You're going to get some more soup and you're going in, and you're going to give them back what they give you.'

Burnett supervised the move while managing to send six aircraft on Ops from Waddington to La Spézia that came back home to Bardney. Ken Dagnall: 'We were a bit shocked at Spézia. There was a terrific anti-aircraft barrage, really heavy. And then, as soon as our first bomb hit, everything stopped.'

Swire, Jarrett, Walsh, Ingram, White, Paramore, Hobbs and Smith – eight skippers, eight crews, no survivors, all in less than a fortnight, and still the eager apprentices turned up. Five skippers went to Stuttgart and took four second Dickies. Being on his first Op, George Saxton didn't. Geoff Stout, little George Nunez, John Evans and Herbert Wood could hardly have had better, more experienced pilots to show them the way, but they were all Joe'd for the terminal prang, the only difference being that one would have a long and distinguished career first.

The Škoda works at Pilsen (Plzeň, modern Czech Republic) had become much more important to the German war effort since Krupp had taken such a beating. Ken Dagnall took with him a little score to settle with his skipper.

Going to Kiel a fortnight before we'd run into a jetstream, which is like a tidal current in the air, and we'd been thrown off track and we were late. Skipper wanted to get on and get out when we found the place and my bombing photograph didn't look too good. Jim denied all responsibility, of course, and I'd had a bollocking from the CO. So I was absolutely determined that we'd hit that factory at Pilsen smack on and I made him go round four or five times until I got the perfect shot. It was perfect, too. I was given a certificate, signed by Air Vice Marshal Cochrane (OC 5 Group), to say that we'd hit the aiming point. I told the intelligence officer at the interrogation that there'd been a lot of smoke so we'd had to go around again.

John Evans, 20, went on his second trip as captain to Stettin, 20 April. 'Flack over target. Bombs jettisoned at 200–500 feet without captain's knowledge owing to breakdown of intercom. Port outer engine caught fire. Fire started in cockpit and under pilot's seat. Port wingtip hit. Port side of fuselage hit. Fires extinguished. Explosion of jettisoned bombs caused severe damage to aircraft, but captain succeeded in bringing it back.'

At Stettin former 9 Squadron skipper McDonald, now a pilot officer with his new Pathfinder squadron No. 83, was attacked by a nightfighter. Petrol leaking fast, they decided to try for Sweden, so made a landing attempt at Malmö and ended up ditching. McDonald, with his 9 Squadron vets Parrington, Nunn, Paley, Coles and Crebbin, was pulled from the sea, interned briefly and sent home to carry on to more adventures.

A new Lancaster arrived at Bardney, W4964. She was assigned the letter 'J' and given to W/O Herbert Wood for Stettin, her first Op. J-Jig came home, Wood came home, 'outline of factory seen', and two careers began; one would prove very much shorter than the other. At Stettin lots of factories were seen, first by the light of the excellently placed marker flares, and then by the light of the flames. Out of Oboe range this was professional bombing.

Results were coming, though bought at the same dear price. The odds against an airman completing a full tour, averaged over the whole war, were four to one against. The average life expectancy was thirteen Ops.

The new aircraft W4964 had odds of 250-1 against what she was going to do; fly over one hundred Ops. At the start of a tour of thirty Operations, a crew member and/or a new Lancaster seemingly had no chance of finishing it. Churchill, the War Cabinet, the Air Marshals and all the other top brass deemed it acceptable that heavy bomber losses should run at an average of five per cent per operation, one in twenty. That was to say, acceptable to those who did not fly in bombers, or love those who flew in them, who did not repair and maintain them, or work on bomber aerodromes.

Take any twenty bombers and crews and after twenty Ops there shouldn't be any left. New boys, sprog crews, were more likely to be lost than old hands, that was observably true, but the powers-that-be counteracted that by giving the worst jobs to the old hands. Even so, some had to have the luck to survive the thirty, a reassuring thought for those who felt themselves to be very lucky. Perhaps it was like batting in cricket. If you scored nineteen not out, you were more likely to reach thirty and less likely to be out than you had been when you came in on nought. Also, the lost Lancasters were replaced so you could say, each time you went you were one of twenty again, 19-1 against being the one who had a prang, bought a packet, bought the farm, went for a Burton, got the chop. Was killed.

Nightfighters were perhaps the deadliest foe. Some crews completed a tour and never saw one but, for many more, the one they didn't see was deadly. Full of sparks, the exhausts from a Lancaster's engines could be noticed from a mile and a half away. A fighter might close in that first half-mile and see the bomber silhouetted against the stars to confirm the signal he was getting on his radar. Once the fighter fastened on, after maybe stalking his victim for half an hour, the odds were hugely in his favour. Comparatively slow and clumsy, the Lancaster was armed only with rifle bullets, .303 inch calibre (about 8mm). The fighter had those too, plus cannon shells of 20 or 30mm.

Darkness was the bomber's friend as well as the fighter's. Darkness allowed the fighter to get close but might fool him into getting into range where the four machine guns at the back and the two in the mid-upper turret could pour quite a volume of rifle bullets.

Flak was ever present at every target. A crew who strayed off-track might happen over a well-defended urban area on their own, a deadly fate and losses were often suffered this way. The straight and level bombing run was a gift to the flak gunners and, especially in the minds of the bomber crews, the gift was wrapped and beribboned by the extra time they had to fly after bombs gone, waiting for their photoflash bomb to explode, their camera to click. This was not only to help RAF Intelligence assess the damage; it also proved that a crew had been where they said they had and that they were indeed straight and level as per procedure.

There was also mortal danger from self-inflicted wounds; the crashes on take-off and landing, mechanical failures in the air that could easily finish you for good, and the almost certainly terminal possibility of being flown into by another aircraft in the dark. There was also the chance of being bombed out, hit by bombs dropped from above by a colleague. You could fly into a stuffed cloud, one with a cliff or a hilltop inside it. You could be fired at by your friends, who might be in a Royal Navy ship, or manning an English or Scottish coastal ack-ack gun, or flying an RAF fighter. All three types of friend occasionally executed bomber victims.

If any member of a bomber crew spent much time thinking about this he would have to conclude that whatever the mathematical odds, he would be very, very lucky indeed to get through it, which was one good reason why most of them hardly thought about it at all.

McCubbin and the experienced P/O Brown, with four from other squadrons, went mining to St-Jean-de-Luz near Bayonne.

Ken Dagnall: The moon was shining brightly. We circled twice around a lighthouse on the Spanish border then we started in on our run, which was one minute 48 seconds. We could see the anti-aircraft fire ahead.

They were throwing everything at us, light flak, heavy flak, machine guns, everything. The aircraft in front of us was blown out of the sky and we flew right through the explosion. We were shitting bricks, absolutely shitting bricks, and they never hit us with a single round, not a bullet.

Squadron ORB states, from McCubbin: 'Found French coast north of Biarritz. Circled twice. Timed run of 1.8 mins. Planted vegetables near Cape.' It doesn't state anything from Ralph Brown because his was the aircraft blown up. In the squadron, and possibly in the whole of Bomber Command, his crew was unique. Although mostly in their early twenties, six of the seven were married, including the squadron's Bombing Leader, Ron Higginson DFM, filling in for the regular man.

The tiny West Indian Sgt Nunez got his first taste of skippering when he went to plant some veg, and his second and last at Essen. Ten Lancasters lost in April 1943 and not a crewman surviving. At the beginning of the month they had managed to get a dozen on the runway for Ops and at the end they were still thereabouts. The effort and determination, while faced with losses in staggering ratio to resources, can only be marvelled at. And still they came, the new ones, Duncan, Derbyshire, Gill, Hall, Head, Livingstone, Lyon, Woodhouse, Wakefield and all their merry men, high in hopes, low in expectations.

May began well. They put fourteen in the air to Dortmund, a raid thought to be a good show and was, with well over three thousand buildings hit and the steelworks and docks badly damaged. The next five Ops were cancelled. 12 May: a dozen went to Duisburg, another good show, so good they didn't need to go there again for a year. Things were starting to look up. The second Cowan brother certainly thought so; he'd finished his tour. At last the business of bombing seemed to be fully functional. Crews reported target indicators well placed, good concentration of fires, Gee fixes working. P/O Hale reported that he made three runs over Duisburg, 'but bomb doors failed to open each time. All bombs brought back'.

SECRET 9 Squadron Combat Report
12/13 May 1943. 52° 21'N, 05°47'E. Lancaster 'G'. Captain: P/O Hale. Lancaster intercepted by T/E E/A identified by both gunners as Ju88 on the outward journey to Duisburg. Pilot executed standard corkscrew to starboard on rear gunner's executive order and RG was able to lay a good, steady aim halfway through the dive and fired a short burst at 300/250 yards. The Ju88 opened fire with one short burst of cannon and machine guns at 200/150 yards.

This burst from the E/A was fairly successful although the hits from cannon and small-calibre guns were confined to that portion of the mainplane behind the port outer engine. The main spar boom was shot through in two places and the hydraulics, ancillary controls and the port outer engine rendered unserviceable. It appears that the defensive manoeuvre employed was sufficently effective to confine the hits to this comparatively non-vulnerable part of the aircraft.

After firing this burst the E/A broke away, pulling its nose up and making a steep turn to port, level with the rear turret at 75 yards. This gave both rear and MU gunners a very good shot at the belly of the Ju88 and they both fired short bursts between 75 and 150 yards range. The Ju88 continued its turn to port and eventually got into position to make a second approach. At 600 yards pilot recommenced corkscrew with a diving turn to port and RG opened fire with well-sighted burst at 25/150 yards range. This was seen to hit the fuselage of the E/A and tongues of flame were seen in the cockpit of the machine.

Although the Ju88 was in a position to open fire, no burst was seen and suddenly it was seen to climb steeply, stall with the port wing up and then spin perpendicularly downwards. The E/A was not seen again and is claimed as probably destroyed.

The E/A appeared to ignore the position of the half moon that was about 25° above horizontal on the starboard quarter of our aircraft.

MU gunner: Sgt Clark, 25 rounds no stoppages.

Rear gunner: Sgt Jones, 300 rounds no stoppages.

> 'It is generally recognised that the gunnery
> leader should have squadron leader rank'
> P/O Tozer, Gunnery Leader

More new crews came to Bardney, for more raids, more losses. Then something new happened when seven hundred bombers, including sixteen from 9 Squadron, went to Wuppertal, heavily industrialised but not raided before. Derbyshire saw a 'large circle of concentrated fires'. Stout thought the fires 'very concentrated'. Duncan saw 'many good fires'. Whole districts turned into rubble and the local services were completely overwhelmed. Three quarters of the Barmen side of Wuppertal, something like one thousand acres, was burned to the ground. There had been half a dozen major industrial employers; now there was one. There were two hundred fewer industrial buildings and four thousand fewer houses than before. Over three thousand dead was by far the biggest total of the war. Witnessing what amounted to the first firestorm, the more observant and prudent Germans might have foreseen the zenith of horror which would inevitably be reached when Bomber Command absorbed the lessons of Wuppertal and put them into practice over a bigger city, such as Hamburg.

Tommy Overend was Derbyshire's bomb aimer, back from the concentrated fires.

Drink, women and leave were the three subjects uppermost in our minds, usually in that order, and drinking at the local was a big part of our lives. In fact the RAF could have saved themselves a great deal of trouble, had they sent our pay direct to the landlord of The Jolly Sailor. I was strolling one night down the garden to the outside toilet when I espied three pairs of ladies' nether undergarments, red, white and blue, hanging on the line. 'How patriotic,' I thought. My intention, of course, when I unpegged the blue pair was simply to show them to my crewmates Eddie (Oakes, w/op) and Fred (Cole, mid-upper), hoping to improve my dull image, and then to repeg them unbeknown. Alas my short-term memory was affected by the camaraderie of the evening and it was not until after the fish and chips that I put my hand in my pocket and felt something silky.

'Aha!' I cried. 'Look what I got this evening.'

'Bloody hell!' said Fred sheepishly withdrawing the white pair.

We looked expectantly at Eddie who very slowly produced the red ones. Next morning when we went out to the aircraft Fred had been before. The white pair fluttered from the whip aerial. From then on, whenever we were on Ops one of the pairs similarly fluttered and Fred used to fly the red pair as a flag out of his turret as we took off.

Aileen Walker: Now Squadron Leader Derbyshire was a perfect charmer, a real gentleman. We could always spot the gentlemen. If they got a knife that had a mark on it, they'd discreetly give it a rub. The other sort would say, 'Here, polish this.' Derbyshire was tall and thin, little black moustache. Some of the officers would talk to us, tell us about their girls back home, but he was very quiet, a very reserved person.

Not at all thin – in fact quite the opposite – was a visiting Group Captain.

He was fat enough for two chairs. As a visitor, of course, he had to be served first, so I was walking up with a tureen of cauliflower in white sauce when I caught Muriel's foot and stumbled forwards. The cauliflower shot out of the pot like a missile and landed right in his lap, white sauce and all. I had no idea what to do. I took a spoon and started ladling the cauli back into the tureen from beneath the overhang of his great stomach. Well, I was only 18. I didn't know what Group Captains kept in their trousers. Anyway I hadn't got very far with it when he shouted, 'That's enough, WAAF, that's enough!'

For some months, Harris, the managing director, had had the resources to do better with the objective given him as the progressive destruction and dislocation of the German military, industrial and economic system and the undermining of the morale of the German people to a point where their capacity for armed resistance was fatally weakened. At last Essen and hundreds of Krupp buildings were wrecked and Krupp would never recover. Dortmund, Duisburg, Gelsenkirchen and others were all heavily damaged and battered. Regardless of losses, destruction and dislocation was progressively achieved, as directed.

Ken Dagnall, bomb aimer: The natural tendency was to bomb short. An eighth of an inch in your bombsight was half a mile or more on the ground and, being somewhat nervous while being shot at, your instincts told you to get rid of your bombs sooner rather than later. Of course, after my rough ride with the CO over that photograph, I was even more nervous of coming home to another, so I perhaps went a little the other way, much to my skipper's annoyance.

Generally, though, with bombing short, the result was that the bombing carpet tended to creep back. So they dropped the markers further up.

F/Lt Dicky Bunker DFC arrived for his second tour, his first having been in Hampdens with 83 Squadron. Bob Van Note was nearly at the end of his first, Bochum, 12 June being his penultimate. For Herbert Wood, first operational pilot of W4964 J-Jig, on the squadron since April, Bochum was the ultimate. On the way home a nightfighter picked him up and had him over Gelderland. Pilot and rear gunner were killed, the rest became prisoners.

The American Van Note had had a quite remarkable career. During a time when there were losses on virtually every German raid by Bomber Command – 45 Lancs went down on his last three raids alone – Van Note suffered hardly a scratch worth reporting. If the odds on finishing a tour at all were long, what were they on finishing a tour without ever having an engine on fire, without being shot up by a fighter, without having a crew member wounded or killed, without any of the things which happened all the time to everybody else? Then there was Oberhausen, a new town of the industrial revolution, population 190,000, iron and steel, coal, chemicals and the centre of a spider's web of railways. After bombing such an unlovely place through cloud, Van Note and crew might have had the sudden thought that the great bookmaker in the sky had made a final recalculation.

SECRET 9 Squadron Combat Report
14/15 June 1943. Oberhausen. Lancaster 'A'. Captain: F/O Van Note.
Our aircraft was intercepted by a T/E E/A on the return journey from
the target at 01.54 hours in bright moonlight at Soesterburg, 23,000
feet, rectified airspeed 165mph. The Boozer* had shown Yellow and
the pilot had been doing a moderate weave for about ten minutes when
the rear gunner (Sgt Dale) reported E/A 500 yards astern flying the same
course. On instruction from the rear gunner the pilot made a diving
turn to port and the E/A followed the bomber down. At 400 yards both
the rear and mid-upper gunners fired bursts that appeared to enter the
fuselage of the E/A. The pilot then started a barrel corkscrew and the
E/A broke away starboard quarter, from which direction it made
another attack firing short bursts with cannon and machine guns, the
tracer of which was observed to pass well above the bomber. Rear and
mid-upper gunners fired long bursts and the tracer was seen to enter the
E/A which broke away in a dive and was not seen again. No damage
was sustained by the bomber. The E/A is claimed as damaged. No
ground co-operation of any kind was observed and no unusual
phenomena.
Mid-upper turret 250 rounds, no stoppages.
Rear turret 1200 rounds, no stoppages. *Airborne fighter detector.

With calamity all around, Van Note and his crew completed their tours,
twenty out of the thirty in their faithful ED493 WS/A, with as much fuss as
if they were manning a Green Line bus. In August the skipper would get his
DFC, along with his navigator P/O Graver. F/Sgt Tubbs, the bomb aimer,
would receive a DFM. Harry Hounsome, flight engineer, would be killed
flying between Mildenhall and Solingen, Bonfire Night 1944, on his second
tour with 15 Squadron.

While Van Note and his men could celebrate Duty Over, nothing was
ever admitted to be over by Conk Canton, who was on the break again.

**F/Lt Johnson and I joined a de-lousing party, who were marched out of
the gates. This was part of the first mass break from this camp. We were
well equipped, being disguised as Hungarian workers, and had papers
and money with us.**

We managed to get away and reached Sagan station, just missing a
train going north towards the Baltic ports, for which we were making.
We had to wait at the station for half an hour. When we boarded a train
I was recognised by a German doctor who had seen me only the day
before. He stopped the train and we were arrested and taken back to
the camp, where I served fourteen days in the cells.

The success at Le Creusot by 5 Group led to another special show for five crews led by McCubbin, Hobbs, Hale, Wakeford and Boczar. Their target was the Zeppelin sheds at Friedrichshafen, where the enemy was making radar sets. It would be the first of a new kind of raid called shuttle: go, bomb, fly on, land far away, hit somewhere else on the way back, and there were two more new ideas to try. If accurate dropping of markers was followed by accurate bombing, the markers could be blown out or become obscured by smoke, so 5 Group invented offset marking, marking a spot some distance from the target and doing a timed run from that. Another innovation was a raid manager, someone who would watch and direct not just his own squadron but all of the aircraft there, so at Friedrichshafen was the first instance of the master bomber technique (Guy Gibson had managed the much smaller Dambusters raid in similar fashion).

Sixty Lancasters went. The original master bomber, Gp/Cpt Slee had to return early and hand over to his deputy W/Cdr Gomm, who decided, because the defences were so strong in the moonlight, to attack from higher up than planned and practised for. The first wave of aircraft bombed on TIs dropped by a PFF Lancaster. At the greater height the new wind made a difficult job harder and results were poor. The second wave included 9 Squadron. F/Lt Wakeford: 'Bombs aimed by indirect method, time and distance run from predetermined point. We thought we got a hangar. Good fires seen.' They got a hangar all right and altogether destroyed about half of the factory's equipment plus some of the Maybach tank-engine works.

The five had taken off around 21.45, bombed at about 02.45 and landed at Blida in Algeria around 07.45. They had a couple of days off, came home and hit La Spézia, Italy's chief naval base and a centre for manufacturing torpedoes and other naval armaments, on the way.

Ken Dagnall: I was taken out of this world as we came back across the Alps. We were at something like 18,000 feet and it was a beautiful moonlight night, with a white ocean of cotton wool below, and sticking out of the cotton wool was the top of Mont Blanc. I couldn't help but watch it, on the port bow, until it vanished.
Aileen Walker: We were all waiting for them to come back from Africa and when Red Wakeford's crew came in, they were all carrying bunches of bananas except my young man, Harold Hawkridge from Harehills. Nobody had seen a banana for years. They were like treasure. The wireless op, Alec Backler, he'd brought some for my friend Muriel. They were very close, Alec and Muriel, not like me and Harold. Anyway, I said to him, 'Well, if you can't be bothered to bring me some bananas back, I can't be bothered to see you any more.' He said, 'I've

sent you something a lot better than bananas, but you'll have to wait for it, just a couple of weeks'.

While this was happening, one of 9 Squadron's shorter careers was blossoming. 19 June: Sgt H Denness, aged 20, and crew arrived from 1660 CU. 21 June: Sgt H Denness, actually not H at all but Kenneth, on second Dicky with F/Lt Bunker in ED699 WS/L to Krefeld to help destroy half the town in one go. 22 June: target Mülheim, Sgt Denness and crew all killed when shot down in same Lancaster, ED699, near Krefeld after completing three hours of operational duty.

Young Ken Denness had had no chance to gather that essential to survival: experience. Tom Gill, on the other hand, had been lucky enough to get through his initiation and was now showing what an old scholar of a month's study could do.

SECRET 9 Squadron Combat Report
22/23 June 1943. Noordwjk area. Lancaster 'E'. Captain: Sgt Gill.
T/E E/A sighted starboard beam slightly down, range 500 yards, firing with cannon and machine guns as it approached. The Lancaster was weaving systematically at the time and the enemy fire appeared to pass above. The MU gunner told the pilot to commence a diving turn to starboard and at the same time gave the enemy three accurate bursts. Tracers appeared to enter the E/A which broke off the attack at 400 yards and took up a position on the starboard beam flying parallel to the Lancaster. Our crew now observed that the E/A was on fire as a red glow was seen in its nose. Both rear and MU gunners now opened fire on the E/A, which went into a dive obviously in flames. The captain, bomb aimer and flight engineer then saw the E/A explode in the air. This aircraft is claimed as destroyed.
MU gunner Sgt Davis 250 rounds
Rear gunner Sgt McKee 100 rounds

Sgt Duncan didn't like Mülheim much either. 'Caught in searchlights, aerial shot away, lost 4,000 feet evading lights and flak, very bumpy as flak became more accurate.' At least it got no worse than very bumpy and down below things were very bumpy indeed with two-thirds of this iron and steel town, population 138,000, reduced to dust.

Wingco Matheson's aircraft was fresh out of the factory. Aiming for the Elberfeld side of Wuppertal, 24 June, she refused to reach the proper height. They jettisoned the cookie half an hour short of the target and went on to bomb with what was left.

Aircraft hit by heavy flak over the target. Port inner and starboard outer failed. Navigator (Sgt A G Boyd) wounded in the face. Holes in roof, cockpit and fuselage. One hole at least in every engine cowling. While navigator was unconscious (oxygen mask knocked off and bleeding) steered south to get well clear of defences after being coned. Lost height to 5,600 feet from 12,000 feet weaving and diving in searchlights. After navigator came round set course for nearest point in France. Finally got organised and set course for home. Jettisoned everything possible including camera.

On two engines, he made a perfect landing. Over thirty bombers had made the other sort of landing but there was hardly anything of Elberfeld left.

F/O John Sams, an Oxford graduate, arrived 25 June. He'd only been there a couple of hours when he learned he was to fly that night as an extra man with Sq/Ldr Murray Hobbs DFC, veteran's veteran, Kiwi character, on his 14th with 9 Squadron and his 46th altogether. Who better for a drive to Gelsenkirchen? They got there all right but a fighter had them on the way back, at the Dutch coast and all were killed.

Bob Wells was a new skipper with a new crew in an elderly Lanc that had done six months of Ops, and they were off to Cologne on 28 June. Coming back, flying at 22,000 feet, a Ju88 flashed across their view from right to left. It wasn't attacking them but Wells took a diving turn to starboard anyway while his gunners, Bill Gough and Steve Moss, poured 800 rounds into it and watched it burst into flames then explode. If only they were all like that.

The one which attacked them sixteen minutes later came in from dead astern, but gave Moss enough time to order a corkscrew and they never saw each other again. Five minutes went by and an Me109 dived on them from the port quarter. They saw it, Wells dived and turned hard towards the attack and Gough and Moss fired 350 rounds, but missed. Three fighters in one night and one of them destroyed. Any crew collecting that quantity of mess-room stories on their very first Op surely deserved to survive.

Deserving, of course, had nothing to do with it, as the leader of the Zeppelin sheds raid, Red Wakeford, found out at Cologne, where a new German tactic was introduced. Rather than relying on radar and control from the ground to infiltrate the bomber stream, the fighters would lurk above the area being bombed. They would watch for their prey picked out in the glare of searchlights, flares and the glow of fires below. There would be a hopeful arrangement with the flak gunners not to fire above a certain height.

Major Hajo Herrmann was the proponent of this scheme and, above

Cologne, he found himself in the thick of the flak. 'It was like sitting in a cage of fire and glowing steel.' That should have been no surprise, having been a bomber pilot himself. 'I was so close to a Lancaster I could see the rear gunner in his turret, watching the burning city.' Perhaps it was Wakeford's Lanc that he saw; maybe it was George Dohany watching the burning city. In any case no gunner would have expected a fighter attack in among all this flak and, unopposed, Herrmann gave the Lanc a burst of cannon fire and down it went. There were other victories, too for Herrmann and his small band, enough to encourage the formation of a new *Geschwader*, JG300, which came to be known as *Wilde Sau*, the wild boars.

A second Dicky, Sgt Tom Porter, aged 21, died beside F/Lt John Alfred Wakeford DFC, just one year older but a year was a very long time in Bomber Command. They smashed into the Rhine, where the Germans found two bodies, WAAF Muriel's boyfriend w/op Alec Backler and rear gunner Sgt Dohaney. The rest, including the bomb aimer courting Aileen Walker, Harold Hawkridge aged 20, became a matter of record only.

Regardless of RAF losses the raid was an outstanding success. Almost 6,500 buildings were destroyed and 15,000 more damaged, the worst Cologne had had to suffer and the most forceful pointer yet to the result of this war.

Aileen Walker: Wakeford's little dog was called Snifter. I wanted to keep him and my mother in Nottingham wanted him as well, but he had to go to Wakeford's mother in Devon, and I was given the job of sending him. I had to put him in a box and take him to the railway station, and I had to walk all the way because I couldn't get the box balanced on my bike. When I got there I handed him over and I had to apologise for how wet the box was with my crying tears. And that wasn't the end of it. I was setting up the tables in the dining room when a letter came for me. It had stamps and postmarks all over it, and it was in Harold's writing and it was from Algiers. I shouted, 'Muriel! They're alive!' but when I opened it, it said that by the time I got it, Harold would be on leave at home. Harold wrote that he'd kept his distance long enough and he was coming back for me and we were going to get married. I was reading this and he was dead. And still I wasn't finished with the tears because a few days later there was a little box in the post and it was from his mother. The letter said thank you for making her son's last hours happy ones and hoped that I'd accept this necklace as a small token.

Some parts of Cologne were still standing, so it was there again, 8 July.

Ken Dagnall: 'It was ten tenths cloud, couldn't see a thing, and it happened that we were in the first wave. The PFF hadn't turned up yet so there were no flares or TIs. We dropped on a Gee fix, which was very inaccurate. Our navigator, Sherry, told me on the intercom when we were there and that was it. What else were we supposed to do? Hang around all night at 21,000 feet circling over Cologne?'

While Wells and Co were attacked for the fifth time in three Ops by fighters, Sgt John Duncan of Saskatchewan and crew in ED480 U-Uncle were hit by flak over Gelsenkirchen, 9/10 July, after yet another unsuccessful attempt to blast the oil refinery. As they had struggled through a dozen Ops together so they struggled as far as the Pas-de-Calais but the loss of fuel made home impossible. They jumped. The engineer Sgt Blunden was wounded and mid-upper Sgt Warner taken prisoner. The others would all evade and come home, including Canadian rear gunner David McMillan, who landed badly in a meadow, sprained both his ankles and struck a blow against the Wehrmacht. 'My legs for a while were quite inert from the shock sustained on landing but when I could move them freely, I started off in the direction of a clock chime some distance off. I thought that if the chime came from a church I would try for help there.'

McMillan's plan with the church didn't work. A young German soldier found him and took him to a guardroom where he was searched and documented. There was no transport to take him onwards and so he set off on foot with the soldier. 'My ankles were paining me considerably and after going a little way I sat down on a low stone wall, took off my flying boots, showed my swollen ankles to the German and rubbed them.' There was no sympathy. McMillan accidentally knocked one of his boots off the wall. 'Feeling for it in the darkness I also felt a large stone. I put the boot on and reached back for the stone.' Pretending severe pain and disability he held out his left hand for help.

The German offered me his left hand. I pulled him towards me and crashed the stone, which I had kept all the time in my right hand, against the left side of his head. He dropped with a clatter. I tried to get the bayonet off his rifle, but failed. I searched him hurriedly and recovered my cigarettes and watch, but found nothing else of use. He was quite senseless, bleeding a little from the nose, and I put him over the wall. I was feeling shaken and left the town at once. I nearly went back for the German's boots but decided against it.

I reached Busigny and went to the station. There was an elderly Frenchman in the ticket office. I said, 'Un, Paris' and put down four of the 50 franc notes from my purse. He gave me the ticket without comment, handing me back two of the notes and some small change. I asked him, 'Train, quelle heure?' and he wrote 4.30 on the back of the ticket.

While waiting for his train McMillan was picked up by some young Frenchmen, who arranged a journey to Spain for him.

No. 9 was briefed for Italy again, 15 July, to bomb an electrical installation at Reggio nell' Emilia, a small, joint Op of two dozen Lancs to several north Italian targets with 50 and 61 Squadrons and 617 flying for the first time since the Dambusters raid. They wouldn't have anything like the duration to get back so they would fly on to North Africa.

Aileen Walker: I got a telephone call saying there were two officers coming back off leave who were on Ops that night and could I get them some lunch. I hung around and gave them their lunch. They'd been there since the middle of May but I hadn't got to know them. One was a Kiwi, Flying Officer Head, and one was from Nottingham like me, well, he was Beeston actually, Flying Officer Shaw. He said when he got back we'd have a lot to talk about.

Although bombers were sent to targets in numbers with general orders and a general purpose, each was on its own once anything happened not covered by the orders and each crew felt themselves to be an independent team. The Op to Reggio nell' Emilia illustrated the point perfectly. Only three went from 9 Squadron. Burnett was up first, 22.15 in ED700 O-Orange, then Head at 22.20 in P, then F/Lt Bunker, 22.21 in L. Bunker was about halfway when he had trouble. His starboard inner went u/s and he had the Alps to cross. He wove his way through in the dark, between the mountains on three engines or, as he put it, '(the Alps) were negotiated below safety height. After crossing the Alps the aircraft was of necessity far off track. Amended course was steered in an attempt to get on track again but no pinpoints were seen, owing to poor visibility. Course was then set for the coast and pinpoint was made 20 miles south of Genoa. Centre of Genoa bombed from 6,000 feet at 04.03.'

F/O Head sent a message from near the target saying he'd collided with another aircraft. This was DV167 VN/M of 50 Squadron, which went in straight away, killing all the crew including a mid-upper gunner, Reggie Goff, who was 18 years old. Head's message said they were going to try and make Algeria. 'After attempting to continue flying for a further 20 minutes, I was compelled to give orders to bale out, at about 05.00 hours. I came down in a field about 3 miles from Miràndola (about 25 miles from the target). I ran as far from the burning aircraft as possible but was rounded up after being at large for about half an hour.' Flight engineer Ted Edwards was killed when his parachute failed to open but the rest landed safely. The w/op, Johnny Merchant, had been a close friend of flying control WAAF Pip Beck.

I landed by a canal and hid my parachute and Mae West in a culvert. I saw the rear gunner (F/Sgt W J McCoombs RCAF) and we decided to hide in the bushes, but the Italians were out searching for us and we were picked up immediately and taken into Miràndola, where we met the rest of the crew.
Head: I was interrogated first by some Italian officers and then by Italians in the presence of a German. When I refused to speak I was threatened by the German, but no force was used and the interrogation was not pressed.

Burnett couldn't find the target either and 'bombed a small marshalling yard in an unknown town'. He and Bunker landed in Algeria after their ten-hour trip with no further bother but, in Italy, Merchant, Head and the rest were still in difficulties.

Merchant: We were taken to Bologna for one night and then Poggio quarantine camp. The treatment at this camp was good but the food was very scarce. From there we were sent to Rome and on to POW camp at Chieti.
Head: (At Poggio) we were first placed in solitary confinement and then in pairs. We were also interrogated. In Rome we were in a large house, some sort of private residence. There was mostly RAF here, but we suspected some so-called Army officers to be stool-pigeons.

Operation Gomorrah, the offensive against Hamburg, was to be destruction and dislocation on an entirely new scale. The raid was meticulously planned in four phases demanding meticulous flying, now made more likely by H2S offering some really distinctive ground to look at. H2S was a complex and temperamental box of tricks. If it was still serviceable when the target was reached, it required a skilled, experienced and intuitive operator to match the picture on his screen with the actuality below. As the H2S box was on board the aircraft and didn't need any ground stations, it had no limit to its range. Oboe was much the better blind bomber but it only worked up to about three hundred miles from home.

There would never be enough H2S kits made for every bomber and installation was confined to Pathfinder Force and a small proportion of mainforce aircraft. As with Oboe, the H2S radar signal was used by the Germans for homing and tracking. The danger was acknowledged but the benefits greatly outscored any additional peril for H2S crews.

In the darkness of the night of 24 July 1943, 740 Lancasters and Halifaxes flew across the North Sea and turned in towards the enemy coast at a point fifteen miles north-east of Heligoland. In the PFF Lancs with H2S the bomb aimers watched the radar screens as the bright clock hand swept around and around, leaving a green trace behind for the coastline and adding more blotches of light as the cities of Germany came into its view. There at last, in the middle of the screen, was Hamburg.

No. 9 Squadron sent sixteen Lancasters, including W4964 WS/J-Jig, skippered by Sgt Charles Newton, a barrister in civilian life, who always insisted his beloved J could come home, no matter how much damage she suffered. The first use by Bomber Command of a new RCM (radio counter measure) called Window was in the hope that a great many aircraft of every letter would come home. Window was a simple device: strips of aluminium foil about eight inches long and an inch wide, black paper on one side and shiny foil on the other, dropped in bundles from the sky. It was believed enemy radar would be so confused by the reflections as to become almost useless.

Window's introduction had been delayed, partly because British forces' various priorities on precious aluminium were much struggled over, but mainly because it was thought that the Germans would soon cotton on and use a similar thing on the British, which argument would have prevented the introduction of every weapon since the boomerang. Oddly enough, the Germans had developed a similar system called *Düppel* and had similarly feared its discovery by the British. Under orders from Göring himself, they had had the papers locked in a safe. Window had been ready for use for well over a year. How many bombers had gone down and how many men been killed in that time by radar-assisted fighters and flak guns?

The Germans had watched Bomber Command getting better and better at its job and were fully aware that the Fatherland's defences absolutely had to turn Tommy's bombing into a loss-making activity. Now the *Luftwaffe* and the *fliegerabwehrkanonen* had their chance. Since late afternoon they had been standing by for a very big raid. Which city would it be tonight? Their radar would soon tell them. As the RAF threw out bundles of Window, fighters took off to intercept the bomber stream which, the radar said, was coming in towards the north of the Netherlands. The Tommies were over Amsterdam. No, they were west of Brussels. No, they were still out to sea. No one knew where the bombers were and the ground controllers were frantic. Every *Würzburg* set was completely jammed and *Freya* was almost useless too, but the nightfighters had contacts on their Lichtenstein apparatus (airborne radar) screens. Wilhelm Johnen was one such pilot, with wireless/radar operator Facius.

At 15,000 feet my sparks (Facius) announced the first enemy machine in his Lichtenstein. He then reported three or four more pictures. I hoped I should have enough ammunition to deal with them. Then he suddenly shouted, 'Tommy flying towards us at great speed. Distance decreasing . . . 2,000 metres . . . 1,500 . . . 1,000 . . . 500 . . . '

I was speechless. Now Facius had a new target. Perhaps the other had been one of ours. Facius shouted again, 'Bomber coming for us at a hell of a speed. 2,000 . . . 1,000 . . . 500 . . . he's gone.' 'You're crackers, Facius,' I said, jestingly, but I soon lost my sense of humour for this crazy performance was repeated a score of times.

At last the Germans saw the real thing but the radar-guided flak was all over the place. They called in the fighters to a thousand-bomber raid but by the time the fighters got there, the bombers had gone and the city was ablaze. In the morning millions of little strips of foil were found all over Holland, Belgium and northern Germany. People said they were meant to poison the cattle.

Over Hamburg Window proved a great success and losses generally were well below what would have been expected without it, but the USAAF, combining with Bomber Command for the first time to attack the same target but flying by day, lost bombers at the usual rate. Coming home high above The Wash, crews could see the fires of Hamburg, three hundred miles away.

A trip to Essen in between the Hamburg battles was meant to maximise the surprise value of the new Window; Geoff Ward was there. 'Fires in target not fully visible owing to enormous pall of smoke which reached to higher level than aircraft. At 01.42 hours Lancaster had almost reached Dutch coast on return when an enormous explosion was seen back in target area that lit up the sky.' Krupp had taken its worst punishment yet. Dr Krupp himself had a stroke and, like his works, never recovered.

Among the 18 Lancs sent by No. 9 to Hamburg on the second raid, 27 July, was one with a most remarkable crew. The pilot was the squadron CO, Wingco Burnett and besides the nav and gunnery leaders he had the Royal Artillery officer from the Spring of 1942, Major Mullock, on a one-off trip in the mid-upper turret. Another crewman was a rather distinguished Kiwi, the station CO, Group Captain Samuel Charles Elworthy DSO DFC, who would one day be Marshal of the RAF The Lord Elworthy of Timaru, Chief of the Defence Staff, Lord Lieutenant of London. Today he was the flight engineer.

The official German report by the 21st Army Group makes graphic reading.

... the fact (of another raid on Hamburg) in the night from July 27 to 28 was not surprising. Its magnitude and consequences, however, were far beyond all expectations. At least 800* planes attacked the city in several waves from all sides. The main weight of the attack was this time at the left shore of the Alster. Within half an hour the whole left side (of the city) was in a terrible situation by a bombardment of unimaginable density and almost complete annihilation of those town districts was achieved by the enemy in a very short time ... the alternative dropping of blockbusters, HEs and incendiaries made fire-fighting impossible. Small fires united into conflagrations in the shortest possible time and these in turn led to fire-storms which went beyond all human imagination. The overheated air stormed through the streets with immense force, developing into a fire typhoon such as was never before witnessed, against which every human resistance was quite useless.

*Actually 787. This included 353 Lancasters, the largest number so far on one raid, of which eleven were lost.

For the squadron there had been no losses over Hamburg despite the frantic deployment of the part-trained JG300, the wild boars. Perhaps the idea that it was a piece of cake tempted an aircrew member called Rossie to hitch a ride with F/Lt Charles Fox on the third raid, 29 July. F/O Anthony Rossie was a navigator but only a passenger on this trip. The rest had been with Fox since joining from Lancaster finishing school in March, all that time ago. They had been through it and come out of it every time, until now.

Ken Dagnall: We were flying along and there was a Lanc right next to us. I said to Jim (McCubbin), 'Isn't that Fox?' and Jim said, 'By God, I think it is.' It was really unusual to spot anyone from your own squadron on a night raid, much less actually know who it was. Anyway, we looked down at our instruments again and bang. Flak. Direct hit. And we knew who was in there.

The final Hamburg raid was on the night of 2/3 August. From 9 Squadron's point of view it was a mess. Most took off on time but three were recalled after taking off late. Those who got away, including Newton completing WS/J's full set of four Gomorrahs, flew through severe icing conditions and electrical storms then found heavy cloud over the target up to 25,000 feet. Hamburg was hardly touched but it didn't matter.

'If the five months of The Battle of the Ruhr were months of severe trial for the enemy, the virtual annihilation of the second city of the Reich within six days at the end of July was incomparably more terrible.' Those were the words of Arthur Harris. Hitler himself might have thought back to his words of 1940, in a different context. 'Thousands of fires. They will unite in one huge blaze over the whole area. What will their firemen be able to do once it's really burning!'

The fighter pilot, Wilhelm Johnen, saw the truth of it.

'40,000 people* were killed, a further 40,000 wounded and 900,000 were homeless or missing. This devastating raid on Hamburg had the effect of a red light on all the big German cities and on the whole German people. Everyone felt it was now high time to capitulate before any further damage was done, but the High Command insisted that the Total War should proceed.'

Actually around 42,000 but almost all of them on the second night. Over a million fled the city afterwards.

Harris was being proved right and the policy likewise. Hamburg was hardly there any more and the other industrial centres were wrecks. The would-be conqueror was defeated. Industry, morale, everything, was indeed fatally weakened, for example Krupp at Essen.

Harris: By the end of July 1943 (Bomber Command) had reduced this great industrial complex to a veritable shadow of its former self (including) the largest single unit in the whole works, the huge Hindenberg Hall, where locomotive production ceased and never restarted in spite of the fact that locomotive production then had equal priority with aircraft, tanks and submarines.

Krupp could also make no more large shells, no more shell and bomb fuses, and gun output was cut by half. There was no way out. Albert Speer: 'The first heavy attack on Hamburg made an extraordinary impression. It was I who first verbally reported to the Führer at that time that a continuation of these attacks might bring about a rapid end to the war.'

Every senior officer of the *Luftwaffe* wanted all aircraft production and all efforts of every sort directed to defence against the bombers, night and day. The first problem was that they had a lunatic in charge of Germany and he instead ordered that top priority be given to revenge. 'The British will only be halted when their cities are destroyed. I can only win the war by dealing out more destruction to the enemy than he does to us,' said Hitler. The second problem was that they had no means for carrying out his priority. The *Angriffsführer England* was almost powerless to do anything. After a series of meetings with his most senior aides Göring issued the order: defence was to be everything, whatever Hitler might say. They had to stop the bombers.

'I can shoot them down without using the sights'
P/O Tozer, Gunnery Leader

August 1943: pilot Stanley James, looking very young to be a Flying Officer, arrived from 1661 CU, as did F/Lt C J A G Brain DFC, to start his second tour after an eventful time in Wellingtons with 99 Squadron, including a parachuting abandonment in dense Suffolk fog. If Brain gave it a thought, he might not have reckoned much on James's chances. The boy probably thought Brain was some sort of god, over there in the mess asking Sq/Ldr Bunker DFC if he could be given a lift on the next show to get his hand back in.

SECRET 9 Squadron Combat Report
10/11 August 1943. Nürnburg. Lancaster 'W'. Captain: Sgt McCubbin. As Lancaster was running up to bomb a Ju88 attacked from the port quarter up. The rear gunner opened fire and told the pilot to commence diving to port. The Ju88 continued firing and shells hit the rear turret, rendering it u/s and injuring the rear gunner (Sgt Stewart). The mid-upper gunner (Sgt Lynam) had been killed, probably in the initial burst of fire from the fighter. The enemy aircraft then dived to port and took up position beneath the Lancaster approx. 600 feet below. It then continued to move from port to starboard and from starboard to port, and the front gunner* (Sgt Dagnall) was able to get in several good bursts, the last of which brought sparks from the enemy aircraft, which dived and disappeared below. *The bomb aimer's second job was the front guns.*

Ken Dagnall: I was down, ready for bombing. There was no noise, no warning, you just saw it, a line of tracer going right through the aircraft, and it hit Dicky Lynam. On the intercom I heard him make his last sound, like a sort of breathy retching, and then this German fighter flashed past us. I should say he was a new boy or not very experienced anyway. He'd overshot and he was looking round, wondering where we'd got to. I grabbed my guns and blasted at him. Well, you've never seen such a hopeless mess. He was over there and my tracer was nowhere near. Jim had gone into the corkscrew, the fighter was swinging from side to side and all those instructions we'd had about getting your target in the sights were a load of rubbish. I tried to imagine the fighter's flight path. I aimed for the sky where I hoped he would turn up, and he flew right through my bullets.

As soon as he'd seen the tracer from the Junkers, Dagnall pressed the bomb release, universally known as the tit, and scrambled for his gun turret, not noticing the release hadn't worked and the bombs had not gone. The attacks lasted eleven minutes with a full bomb bay. Dagnall hit the Ju88 on the starboard engine and watched thick black smoke pour from it as it vanished below.

We were in a hell of a state. Everything was u/s for navigation and we found our way home by watching the defence boxes, the groups of searchlights and guns, and working out which city they belonged to. It was lucky for us that somebody flew over Paris because when they opened up, it wasn't anything like Germany and we could definitely tell where we were, and then Andy (Smith, w/op) said he'd got Tangmere. We threw everything out we could into the sea, including the bombs which were stuck and had to be released by hand and we scraped in at Tangmere. I walked back through after we'd landed and saw Dicky. He was splattered all around the inside of the aircraft.

Rear gunner, Charles Stewart ('Arse-end Charlie', as his crew-mates called him) was badly wounded in his legs and there was high activity getting him out. Back on *terra firma* Ken Dagnall wasn't entirely himself.

What we'd been through must have hit because I was standing there in a daze. A ground crew flight sergeant came up to me and gave me my first taste of counselling. He belted me across the face and said, 'Sergeant, get on with your job! You're all right.' I felt so ashamed.

I was something of a loner, partly because I didn't smoke and I didn't drink, and partly because mathematics was my hobby. I used to take an algebra book with me on our Ops. I saw very little of it, but I used to take it. I'd signed the Sunshine Pledge and I kept to it until Dicky was killed. When we got back from that I was off to do my usual routine for stress, which was to set myself a few mathematical problems from one of my books and bury myself in them, but Jim and the boys wouldn't let me. I had to go down The Railway with them, so in I went and ordered an orange squash. They said, 'You're bloody well not having orange squash,' so they laid me on a table and poured a double Scotch down my throat, after which I found life easier if I had what they gave me. So, for my first drinking session, apart from the navy rum on HMS *Cutty Sark* that I didn't taste, I had a minimum of eight large ones, and was I ill! I was sick during the night, what a mess, and I stuck to beer after that.

Two replacement gunners had to be found. F/Sgt Houbert was the new mid-upper. Dagnall: 'You had to get on with it. Here was somebody coming in for a dead friend, but you just did your job. So you're here for Dicky, you'd say. Well, I hope you bring us some luck.' Dagnall, McCubbin, Owen, Sherry and Smith, with new team members Houbert and Elliott, would be going to Nürnburg again in a week or two.

For some time the War Cabinet and their advisers had been deeply concerned about what might be going on at the experimental establishment at Peenemünde, an isolated two-mile peninsula on the Baltic coast, east of Greifswald and almost into Poland. In fact, it was where Wernher von Braun was trying to make a successful rocket, the one Londoners would eventually know as the V2. Information was coming to British Intelligence from some of the slave labourers there, who were building launching platforms and so on, and who were seeing things which were inexplicable in ordinary aeronautical terms.

It appeared that the enemy was preparing a pilot-less, automatically guided weapon that could hit London from two hundred miles away. There was even information suggesting a rocket that could reach New York. Some senior figures, including Lord Cherwell, Paymaster General in the British government and personal scientific adviser to Churchill, argued that such a project could not be because according to known science it was impossible. Others said that perhaps the Germans knew some different science. In any case it was pretty obvious something big was going on, whatever it was, and it needed a big effort to crush it.

The first full-blown, large-scale raid with a master bomber was Peenemünde in the full moon, 17/18 August and 9 Squadron sent twelve Lancasters. The target offered much the same route as the one to Berlin and so a small dummy raid was made on the capital to disguise the real target for the night. Eight Mosquitos of 139 Squadron flew high over Denmark dropping vast amounts of Window. That, coupled with the foreknowledge from spies that a big raid was on for northern Germany, plus the radar signals showing a large force of bombers massing over the North Sea, convinced the Germans that Berlin was in for a Hamburg experience. When the Mosquitos reached Berlin and began dropping their pathfinder flares on the city, millions ran for the shelters and every available *Luftwaffe* fighter was sent to the capital.

While all this was going on Group Captain John Searby of No. 83 Squadron (PFF) flew low over Peenemünde and thought what a dump it seemed. He hadn't been told what was really happening down there. He and the four thousand or so aircrew of six hundred bombers had been briefed that it was a research station producing some special nightfighter kit. Searby didn't like the weather. Instead of the clear night forecast there was cloud about.

There were three aiming points, all buildings of various sorts: 'F' was houses (where the scientific staff lived), 'B' two big workshops, and 'E' was more workshops (the development laboratories). All three made a line with a small island to the north of Peenemünde called Ruden. If the bombers timed their runs from the markers dropped on Ruden they would have an extra check on accuracy, especially those coming in later to find fire, markers, smoke and explosions to baffle them. These would include 9 Squadron, whose most experienced dozen crews had practised intensively at Wainfleet, doing timed runs from a landmark.

Searby called his marksmen in and was dismayed to see some of the Ruden flares go wrong by a couple of miles. He judged which markers on the houses were correct and called in the first wave of bombers, ordering them to bomb the accurate greens rather than the inaccurate reds. Red spot fires were the smaller, brighter flares that burst on the ground as opposed to the TIs, which burst at about a thousand feet and cascaded down like giant Roman candles. The next lot of markers were again a mixed bunch; some overshot. Searby broadcast his orders to the second wave: 'Bomb the greens to the north, not the greens to the south.'

Meanwhile over Berlin there was madness and mayhem. Berlin's anti-aircraft batteries were blasting away at the hundreds of aircraft in the sky overhead, all of which were *Luftwaffe*. Knowing that such an intense battery would not be deployed without good reason, the fighter pilots redoubled their efforts. Great claims were made for Mosquitos shot down but however many twin-engined aircraft were destroyed that night over Berlin, only one of them was a Mosquito. The Mosquitos had gone home.

German flyers saw the pathfinder flares going down one hundred miles away on the Baltic coast and realised they had been duped. Of course the RAF wouldn't attack Berlin in the full moon. Berlin was the most heavily defended city in the world. What were the authorities thinking of? Some sent wireless messages about the raid going on between Rostock and Swinemünde but in the control rooms all was confusion. A few set off for the raid anyway and eventually all capable twin-engined aircraft were ordered to set off, heading for the flares and fires without knowing what the enemy was so interested in on that bleak stretch of coast.

Searby, the magnificent Searby who had orbited the target dozens of times, trying to make sense of what his pathfinders were doing while co-ordinating six hundred bombers in three ten-minute waves, watched as his third set of markers went down and believed them to be correctly placed. The first wave over Peenemünde had started at 00.17 and finished at 00.27, going for aiming point 'F', the houses, while the pathfinders marked aiming point 'B', the factory. No. 9 Squadron, including W4964 WS/J-Jig with Newton, now an officer and still a believer in his aircraft, was in the third wave. They went in between 00.44 and 00.57, at between 6,000 and 7,500 feet, looking for aiming point 'E', the research and development shops. Sq/Ldr Bunker was leading 9 Squadron. 'Commentary heard from the Master of Ceremonies was that attack was going well and to bomb the greens.' F/Sgt Hall: 'Three concentrations of fire seen at APs 'F', 'B' and 'E', fire at 'B' being most impressive.'

The greens were out of line and they missed the workshops. Wernher von Braun was in there, sheltering. The man who almost single-handedly invented that intellectual benchmark, rocket science, escaped with his life and his design drawings.

As the last bombers turned for home the fighters arrived from Berlin. It was havoc. Lancs and Halifaxes were picked off with ease, flying low, doubly visible by flame and moonlight. The combat report of Lt Musset, pilot of an Me110 with w/op Cpl Haffner, says it all.

From the Berlin area I observed enemy activity to the north. I promptly flew in that direction and positioned myself at a height of 14,000 feet over the enemy's target. Against the glow of the burning target I saw from above numerous enemy aircraft flying over it in close formations of seven or eight. I went down and placed myself at 11,000 feet behind one enemy formation.

At 01.42* I attacked one of the enemy with two bursts of fire from direct astern, registering good strikes on the port inner engine which at once caught fire. E/A tipped over to port and went down. Enemy counter-fire from rear gunner was ineffective. Owing to an immediate second engagement I could only follow E/A's descent on fire as far as a layer of mist. *Local time.

I make four claims as follows:

1. Attack at 01.45 on a 4-engined E/A at 8,500 feet from astern, range 30–40 yards. E/A at once burned brightly in both wings and fuselage. I observed it till it crashed in flames at 01.47.

2. At 01.50 I was already in position to attack another E/A from slightly above, starboard astern and range 60–70 yards. Strikes were seen in the starboard wing and E/A blew up. I observed burning fragments hit the ground at 01.52.

3. At 01.57 I attacked another 4-engined E/A at 6,000 feet from 100 yards astern. Heavy counter-fire from rear gunner scored hits in both wings of own aircraft. Burning brightly in both wings and fuselage E/A went into a vertical dive. After its crash I saw the wreckage burning at 01.58.

4. At 01.59 I was ready to attack again. E/A took strong evasive action by weaving. Enemy counter-fire was ineffective. While E/A was in a

turn to port, I got in a burst from port astern and range 40–50 yards that set the port wing on fire. E/A plunged to the ground burning brightly and I observed the crash at 02.01.

A few minutes later I attacked another E/A that took violent evasive action by weaving. On the first attack my cannon went out of action owing to burst barrels. I then made three further attacks with machine guns and observed good strikes on starboard wing without setting it on fire. Owing to heavy counter-fire from rear gunner, I suffered hits in port engine. At the same time I came under attack from enemy aircraft on the starboard beam, which wounded my wireless operator in the left shoulder and set my port engine on fire. I broke off the action, cut my port engine and flew westwards away from target area. No radio contact with the ground could be established. As I was constantly losing height, at 6,000 feet I gave the order to bale out. As I did so, I struck the tail unit with both legs, thereby breaking my right thigh and left shin-bone. After normal landings by parachute my wireless operator and I were taken to the reserve military hospital at Güstrow. At 02.50 my aircraft crashed on the northern perimeter of Güstrow.

At least fifteen bombers went down a few miles from the target, in a short and sharp turkey shoot. As the rest flew back over Denmark, the fighters scored again. A German force of about thirty aircraft shot down more than their own number of Lancs and Halifaxes. The total score was 38 heavy bombers lost directly to enemy action during or after the raid, including 29 aircraft of the third wave. On the way there, three more came down and another two crashed at home. Five Me110s from a *Staffel* of *Jagdgeschwader 1* shot down twelve bombers between them. Had the whole two hundred fighters that had been waiting over Berlin instead waited over Peenemünde, and had they shot down a similar share of bombers, the RAF would have lost an unbearable number, perhaps half the force. Those eight Mosquitos and their Window had saved Bomber Command from utter disaster, or allowed an attack, a moonlight attack, which could not otherwise have been contemplated.

The bombers crushed a hundred buildings, including laboratories and workshops, at the research station and forced the troubled project to pack up and relocate, setting it back by crucial months. The bombs for aiming point 'F' largely missed the houses where the scientists lived and instead hit the slave-labourers' quarters. Certainly those spies were never heard from again.

In the end the raid was classed as successful but with hindsight, it was a terrible waste. Without a nuclear warhead, the V2 was a hugely expensive way of delivering a small payload.

Harris returned to his proper job. Most of the easier-to-reach targets in the Rhineland and the Ruhr had been given a thorough pasting but H2S allowed large forces to be sent against Leipzig, Frankfurt, Hannover and Mannheim and of course, Berlin. Harris saw Berlin in the same way Hitler and Göring had London: destroy the capital and you destroy the country. For Bomber Command, powerful though it was beyond any air force ever known, Berlin was a fatal attraction. It was too big and sprawling, too well defended. After Peenemünde and up to the night of 3/4 September three attacks totalling 1,600 bomber sorties produced a lot of damage, yes, but an utterly dreadful score of 125 losses including one in six of the Stirlings on the middle raid. So many of the lower and slower Stirlings and Halifaxes were shot down that only Lancasters were allowed on the last of the three, 24 failing to return out of 316. The Stirling was sent again over Germany but as heavy bomber its uses would soon be redefined and strictly limited.

Many of these losses were to the wild boars. In two months Major Herrmann's tactics had gone from experiment to saviour of the Reich. Until they worked out a more permanent counter counter-measure or a radar set to see through the Window, the fighters tried to find the bomber stream, sometimes guided by the Window droppings, and flew beside it, not going in but giving a running commentary for the ground stations to relay. Others flew above the bombers, dropping cascades of flares. Over the target area there was a more co-ordinated searchlight policy. The sky in general was lit, rather than concentrating on coning individual bombers, allowing the fighters to spot their prey. This tactic worked especially well in a cloudy sky when silhouetted bombers on their bombing runs appeared to the fighter pilots as so many back-lit black crosses moving in straight lines at a snail's pace.

After the bombers had bombed, radar wasn't needed to work out where they were going next. The homeward journey especially was often illuminated by those clusters of parachute flares dropped by the fighters, very bright but only of short duration. When a bomber crew saw some, they knew there was a bandit close by. 'If we fail, we shall be overrun,' said Generalfeldmarschall Erhard Milch, deputy to Göring and the *Luftwaffe* chief of supply.

On his second tour of Ops Harry Irons saw the power of Window over the radar guided flak guns.

There'd be two hundred of us in a line, dropping Window, going round in a giant U-shape ready to make our bombing runs. This one Halifax, must have been a sprog skipper, decided he was late or in the wrong position or something, and he tried to cut across from one leg of the U to the other. I'd never seen flak like it. The guns suddenly had

something clear to aim at. Pop, pop, bang, he was gone. So you could say that without Window we'd all have been shot down.

SECRET 9 Squadron Combat Report
27/28 August 1943. 01.03 hrs. Nürnburg. 23,000 ft. Lancaster 'S'. Captain: F/O Brill.
Bomb aimer sighted Ju88 port bow down, range 600 yards. Order given for Lancaster to turn to port. Ju88 passed Lancaster and disappeared starboard quarter down, next seen starboard beam up. Lancaster immediately turned to starboard and rear gunner opened up at 400 yards. His shots struck the port engine that caught fire. He continued firing and the starboard engine also caught fire. Ju88 went into a steep dive and was lost to view in the smoke over the target. This aircraft is claimed as destroyed. The mid-upper turret was u/s owing to a burst oil pipe.
RG F/Sgt Battle 400 rounds.

Such a crew might feel elated especially as they were on their first Op. They might relax. Home, F/O Brill, and quick about it. The river Oise was below and the coast a mere seventy miles away.

SECRET 9 Squadron Combat Report
27/28 August 1943. 03.06 hrs. St Quentin. 23,000 ft. Lancaster 'S'. Captain: F/O Brill.
Unidentified T/E A/C sighted dead astern, 400 yards; instructions given to commence corkscrew port. E/A followed Lancaster down and rear gunner opened fire. Shots were seen to strike nose of E/A, which broke away port quarter down and was not seen again.
RG F/Sgt Battle 200 rounds.

At around mid-tour, Brill and five of this crew, including F/Sgt Battle and Doolan's old w/op Chap Chappell, would transfer to Pathfinders and, like many, find tours just as hard to finish there.
In the crew of Lancaster EE136, the long-lasting WS/R Spirit of Russia, McCubbin was on the last Op of his tour, as were Sherry, Smith and Owen. Ken Dagnall had a couple more to do that he'd missed with the mumps, so moods were mixed as they set off for Mannheim. Everything went to programme. Dagnall called bombs gone at 23.30 from nineteen thousand feet, and one minute later he called camera gone. For the last time, almost a year after the four-day ordeal in the dinghy, five months after the first bombing trip with 9 Squadron, Jim McCubbin put his Lanc into a climb and turned for home.

SECRET 9 Squadron Combat Report
5/6 September 1943. Mannheim. 23.32. 20,000 ft. Lancaster 'R'.
Captain: P/O McCubbin.
S/E E/A sighted by RG (Sgt Elliott) following Lancaster. Pilot informed
and Lancaster commenced to corkscrew. E/A closed on Lancaster from
port quarter and RG opened up with a long burst at a range of 400
yards. E/A continued on a course to attack and broke away to port
quarter after firing a long burst. MU (F/Sgt Houbert) fired a few rounds
only before being hit and took no further part in the combat. More
attacks ensued making five in all, firing long bursts in each attack and
the Lancaster's RG also firing long bursts. During the final attack the
E/A burst into flames as shots from the rear turret hit him. He dived
beneath the starboard wing, obviously on fire. This was confirmed by
the flight engineer and bomb aimer. This E/A is claimed as destroyed.
No searchlights or flares were seen to be connected with this attack.
The Lancaster suffered considerable damage, the bullet holes being too
numerous to count.
MU gunner 20 rounds
Rear gunner 3,000 rounds

With bullet holes too numerous, Jim McCubbin could look forward to a
quiet-ish time at a training unit. They had bagged themselves a wild boar.

Sgt Knight and his crew, P/O Gill and his fell to earth near
Ludwigshafen, next door to the target in Mannheim. Knight had had four
Ops in a week, including one in the indestructible W4964 WS/J, then a
week off, then three in a week, then the chop. Back in May P/O Gill had
been Sgt Gill when he skippered his first Op. That trip had been in W4964
and they'd stayed with J for quite some time, taking her to Essen and
Düsseldorf, Bochum, nice places like that. Perhaps they should have stuck
with her.

That made six crews down who had flown in J, while the aircraft had not
yet reached twenty trips, and one officer who wouldn't be served by Aileen
Walker that night.

**They'd ring and say such an aircraft was home, two officers, so we'd
get the bacon and egg ready. We'd hear them come in, then the toilet
door would go, then they'd drag themselves into the dining room, flying
boots undone, hardly able to walk upright and they'd flop into chairs.
Tea and cigarettes, they mostly wanted. Some wanted their food right
away, and one might say I want so-and-so's egg. He got the chop. You
had to wonder how they could adjust their minds and be ready to do it
all again tomorrow.**

On 5 September a most unusual fellow arrived, First Lieutenant Eric Roberts. At least, he was unusual in being USAAF. In two months Roberts would be as usual as the rest of them. He went second Dicky next night with Newton, but the main event featured skipper Bill Siddle and his rear gunner Clayton Moore. After dropping their bombs on Munich they had a heavy flak shell explode very near. Lancaster Y immediately went into an involuntary sideslip to starboard. Siddle got her back again but she was full of holes. One engine soon had to be feathered and at least one fuel tank had been emptied, but the damaged instruments didn't show it. Almost out of petrol they reached Bardney. A second engine packed up but started again.

As they were coming in, about a mile from the aerodrome and at two hundred feet, all three good engines stopped. A crash landing was inevitable. The starboard wing hit a tree and the shock broke off the tail section of the fuselage, sending gunner Moore and his turret spinning through the air before landing, guns down, in a field. The main part of the Lanc ploughed on through various obstacles and finished up as a scrap heap in the field next door. Every crew member was injured, some seriously, and they thought Moore, spreadeagled and unconscious in his wrecked turret, was dead. The fitter ones and a curious cow gazed at the fallen gunner, who called out, 'When you've got a minute!'

Eventually Siddle's aircrew would reassemble from hospitals and sick leave with a new bomb aimer and flight engineer to replace those invalided out, and a temporary mid-upper, the American Sgt Gerry Parker. Sgt Moore had the cost of flying goggles and a boot, lost in the crash, deducted from his pay.

Still in Italy was Johnny Merchant.

During my stay (in Chieti) the Italian Armistice was signed but the prisoners were forbidden to leave the camp. A small party of Germans arrived and took the camp over. There were three escape tunnels built and when the Germans were moving us out, 60 POWs hid in these tunnels and were left behind. We went to Sulmona.

Malcolm Head: Whilst at Sulmona a Lt Ward, eleven Sikhs and myself attempted to escape by climbing through the window of the latrine. We would only have had to penetrate the outside wire to get away but as we saw that the Germans had observed us and had sub-machine guns trained on us, we gave up the attempt. We were placed in cells for three days.

Merchant: We were put on a train in box cars to be sent to a prison camp in Germany. During our trip north the men in our box car broke a hole in the side. In company with Sgt G E Pearson (RASC), I escaped by jumping off the train close to San Benedetto val di Sambo, where we contacted a civilian and stayed with him for a week.

F/O Head, the eleven Sikhs, Lt Ward and three Army captains took the cover off a ventilator on the train and got out when it stopped before Goriano Sicoli. By the time Ward got out the train was passing through the station and doing about twenty miles an hour. The Sikhs made a run for it while the others went to find Ward. Head: 'We found him surrounded by Italians, who were very helpful and took us to a deserted house, the idea being that we would remain hidden there until our own troops arrived. We were joined by two Sicilian officers, who wanted to get down to our lines and fight with the British.' For a fortnight they would remain in the hut, fed by the station master and his staff.

At Bardney, squadron life and death resumed. Flying their first to Hannover, 22 September, Sgt Crabtree and crew had an ancient Lanc with four hundred hours up. At Bad Münder-am-Deister, about fifteen miles from the target, they crashed and died without knowing what it was like for seven friends to complete an Op and come home. The Recorder of Operations did as required, filling in crews, times, heights, observations on the trip. Nothing further had been heard from Edward Crabtree but the R of O didn't know his initials nor those of most of his crew. Here yesterday, gone today, first Op, and nobody had had time to write down their names.

Ken Dagnall was looking for a trip as spare bod. The CO said he'd take him to Hannover. They bombed at the exceptional height of twenty-two thousand feet and came home.

SECRET 9 Squadron Combat Report
27/28 Sept 1943. 00.17 hours. 1,500ft. Bardney-Horncastle area. Lancaster 'O'. Captain: W/Cdr Burnett DFC.
As Lancaster approached Bardney outer circuit lights, with navigation lights on, an unseen aircraft attacked from port bow slightly below and opened fire with cannon and machine guns. Attacking aircraft was not seen by any member of the crew. The visibility was very bad at the time and it was raining heavily. Three engines were damaged and both mid-upper and rear turrets put out of action owing to severed pipelines, and there were numerous holes in the machine.

Even with numerous holes W/Cdr Burnett's aircraft, ED700 O-Orange, was a particularly reliable machine. Also with numerous holes (three to be precise) but unaware of them was Ken Dagnall.

We were coming into the circuit when tracer flew across and the runway lights went off. Burnett got on the radio. 'Put the bloody lights on,' he said, 'I'm coming in to land.' Our starboard outer went, which was not too bad because we were circling clockwise. Then the port

inner went and just as he turned in on the landing approach, the port outer packed in. There was no panic. He said, 'Ambulance, fire engine ready,' and touched down as the last engine stopped. He told them we needed dragging off the runway and said something about a pretty close thing, which I certainly agreed with, then I stood up and something started running down my leg. 'Skip,' I said, 'I've been wounded,' and he said, 'All right', and that was that. Never saw him again. They gave him the DSO. He certainly could fly a Lancaster.

The Doc slammed me on the table and started poking around, no anaesthetic or anything, hole here, hole there, but he couldn't find any bullets or bits of shrapnel. He had this metal probe with a little ball on the end, which he pushed into my wounds. There was a nurse there so I couldn't say anything. They put a sticking plaster over each hole and I had a message to say I'd finished my tour.

For a year Ken would be an instructor then he would join 227 Squadron reformed, with skipper W/Cdr Balme DSO, DFC and Bar.

Balme was a brilliant flyer who, unlike some COs, always put himself in the way of the worst jobs. He was an expert at the Immelmann Turn, a German World War One fighter manoeuvre. You were in your ten-foot-long Fokker Triplane and you found you had a Sopwith Camel on your tail. You did an instant half loop and a half roll, and you were on his tail instead. Balme used to execute it in a Lancaster to get us out of a searchlight cone. They did say that when you were coned, you had ten seconds to get out of it or you were dead.

Stuttgart, 7 October was the last of Bunker's second tour. Ahead of him lay 620 Squadron and leadership of a flight of twelve Stirlings at Arnhem, and 190 Squadron at Great Dunmow, where he would be CO. With the end of the war just around the corner Wing Commander Richard Henry Bunker DSO, DFC and Bar would be killed on 20 April 1945 when his Stirling took off, loaded with supplies for Brussels, with a flat tyre on a tail wheel. The wheel caught fire, the fire spread, the rear turret fell off and the Stirling headed for the village of Windlesham in Surrey. Bunker managed to pull her away from the centre but could not prevent her from crashing by Woodlands Lane or keep himself and his men from death.

Bill Siddle and some of his crew were back from their crash. One of the older Lancs needed to be air tested before going on Ops. Let Siddle's men take her up, test her properly and get their air-confidence back at the same time. The tests were fine and everything went to plan until they came in to land. Memories of the crash proved too vivid for pilot Siddle, who pulled her up at the last minute after coming in too high and overshooting. After several more attempts the entire base was on alert, everyone watching, and Wing Commander Burnett, the disciplinarian, was trying to talk Siddle down. On the ninth pass they made it and the Wingco was on the R/T wanting the skipper in his office – now.

The skipper ordered his crew to leave except for the new replacement flight engineer Jock Wilson, experienced but on his first flip with Siddle. He was to check the landing gear and climb back in, which he did. After three more take-offs, circuits and landings, Siddle was satisfied his demons had been exorcised although he knew the satisfaction was likely to be purely personal and of no further interest to the RAF. He was in for a court martial, that was sure, and in easier circumstances such would have been inevitable. In a war, especially in difficult times, the Wingco could not afford to lose a good pilot. After a thorough, fully embellished Burnett-style rollicking, Siddle was given one more chance, provided he could find a crew willing to go up with him, which was unanimously no problem at all.

Hannover that night would be a very shaky do with nineteen lost in an all-Lancaster raid of 360, at that time the record number to go. One of those nineteen was the 5,000th bomber loss of the war. It could have been Brain's old girl, ED499 WS/X, herself a record holder, the longest lasting Lanc on the squadron with 57 Ops, flight tested and given a record number of circuits and near-bumps by Siddle. For a time too she had been Robbie Robertson's, when she was named Panic II and by virtue of Robertson's Portuguese childhood, given a painted proverb in that language: 'God looks after drunks and little children.'

Now she was entrusted to Howard Gould for his first trip, but the paperwork couldn't keep up with this crew either. The Recorder of Operations only knew the initials of one of the dead seven, the officer. The w/op Norman Beer was listed as Sgt Reed. Still, plenty more where they came from.

Arriving with F/Sgt Glover's crew and expecting his first Op shortly, Sgt Frank Belben had it sooner than expected. The veteran Ervine was selected to take Lou Glover as second Dicky to Leipzig, 20 October, then his regular engineer went sick so Belben had to fill in at the last minute, making his most unusual debut as a fully functional member of an experienced crew while his own skipper stood behind the seat and watched.

Frank Belben: It was reassuring for me having an old hand like Ervine as my driver on my first, but I don't know what he thought about it. He didn't say anything but I guess he might have had the odd worry. He let me get on with my job, though, not checking up on me. The weather was utterly dreadful. We weren't shot up as such although there were

some near misses, but you had to expect it over that type of target. I was glad to get it over, my first one. Losses were very high and it was rare for a crew to get through a tour, but we'd known that all along.

Belben had joined the RAF as a ground crew fitter/engineer and been posted to a Coastal Command squadron in Cornwall flying Lockheed Hudsons which were long-range reconnaissance bombers.

The Hudson was developed from a prewar airliner. They still had their windows along the side. Then there was an idea in Bomber Command to form a daylight unit* and so they collected together some Flying Fortresses, which were much better armed with guns than our own bombers, although they couldn't carry anything like the bomb-load. I was posted there, but it didn't last long. There was no long-range fighter support and we couldn't get spares so they were only going up four at a time. The losses were relatively heavy and it fizzled out. When our own four-engined heavies started coming in, they asked for volunteer flight engineers from among us ground lads because we knew part of the job already.

*This was 90 Squadron, reformed in the spring of 1941. The idea was high-altitude daylight raids using seven-man crews rather than the American ten, a not very successful experiment lasting only a few months. The squadron's first loss was on a high-flying test when a Fortress shook itself to pieces (22 June, the day Germany invaded Russia) and a passenger, the squadron MO, survived after jumping from a free-falling section of the fuselage. There were two more training losses before death in action began on 8 July, with a fighter interception over Brest at 32,000 feet, then a record, when three aircrew were killed during the fight. Six B17s were lost for 52 sorties, 11.5 per cent.

> 'I saw the target and bombed it
> through a hole in the cloud'
> P/O Deaves

SECRET 9 Squadron Combat Report
Unidentified T/E A/C passed across stern of Lancaster from starboard to port same height 300 yards range. RG opened fire when A/C was dead astern and fired two long bursts, tracer appeared to enter A/C. Fighter was not observed again as two scarecrow flares exploded close to the stern of the Lancaster and momentarily blinded the RG. RG Sgt Robinson fired 600 rounds.

According to Intelligence scarecrow flares were a German comedy weapon, a huge but harmless oil-filled flare, which made a great flash but was nothing to worry about. It was only a daft German idea to try and frighten crews of incoming bombers, as if British bomber crews could be frightened by such a thing.

Scarecrow was an official myth. The reality was called *Schrägemusik* (music played slantingly or transversely). It was a method of attack, from below at the unprotected belly of a Tommy bomber, using a pair of upward-firing 20mm cannon adjustable up to 72°, mounted behind the cockpit of a twin-engined aircraft. The pilot fired them using a reflector sight in the cockpit roof and thus had much more flexibility in his attack than with the conventional method. Even without *Schrägemusik* he would often approach from below but would have to line up his aircraft with his target to fire his fixed guns, bringing himself into the bomber's field of fire. Thanks to an inventive sergeant armourer called Paul Mahle, with *Schrägemusik* the fighters could attack in secret and without danger to themselves.

When Mahle persuaded the sceptical airmen on his unit to try it out, one crew claimed two bombers shot down; another claimed four. The news soon got around and Mahle became very busy until his invention was officially adopted and he was given five hundred Deutschmarks and a diploma.

The art was to get directly beneath the bomber in the blind spot and out of any slipstream turbulence. With the bomber crew oblivious to any danger, the pilot could take his time aiming. A volley of cannon shells into the fuel tanks or loaded bomb bay meant instantaneous and total destruction. The bomber blew up in the sky in a massive flash, leaving no evidence that an aircraft had ever been there and momentarily blinding Sgt Robinson.

After a few fighters had got themselves too close to their bombers and gone up with them in the big bang, fighter crews started to ensure their own safety by firing from a little further away and aiming specifically at, say, the port or starboard inner engines, which ran a lot of the hydraulics. They still achieved results but not always so spectacularly. Rumours that scarecrow flares were a Ministry cover-up were confirmed as bomber crews observed the curling coloured hoop of upward tracer and their colleagues going down by the more usual method: on fire and exploding on impact.

Harry Irons: On one of my early trips, to the Ruhr I said to the intelligence officer at interrogation that I'd seen fifteen of our bombers go down. 'That's not right,' he said, 'don't you go spreading rumours about bombers being shot down.' I said, I was just telling him what I saw. He said I'd seen decoys, scarecrows. He gave me a right rucking.

Well, I was only a sergeant and he was a flight loo – I had to agree with him.

John Merchant reached England via a year in Switzerland and was repatriated to Canada, but Malcolm Head's ride would be a little more bumpy.

The Italians told us they did not think it safe to remain at Goriano any longer. We were walking along the railway line when we were called to halt by a German patrol with an officer in charge. We were taken back to Goriano and locked up in a barn. We were interrogated, chiefly with a view to discovering the names of those who had helped us. We gave no names away and the interrogation was not pressed. (They were sent to an improvised POW camp at Castel di Sangro). Here Ward escaped, but was recaptured. We also commenced to dig a tunnel, but it was discovered.

Dougie Melrose was now Pilot Officer 51126 Melrose. He had been posted back to Blighty from South Africa to move up to yet another level of difficulty, still in Oxfords, but the last before the great leap: from Oxford airbus to Wellington warplane.

A boy called Robert Woolf had joined the Royal Australian Air Force on his eighteenth birthday, done his initial training in Sydney, then been posted to No. 2 Wireless School in Calgary, Canada, in August 1941. After qualifying as a w/op he went to Bombing and Gunnery School in Saskatchewan, where he passed his Air Gunner course and was commissioned. Posted to Vancouver and the Coastal Command OTU, he joined a four-man crew flying the Handley Page Hampden in its torpedo bomber version.

After three months on Hampdens he came to England for more training. 'I was expecting my Coastal Command role to carry on, only we found that our whole group of wop/AGs had been taken over by 5 Group of Bomber Command. They'd lost a lot and we were the replacements.'

It was early November 1943. Bob Woolf would now be training at Silverstone in a Wellington. The question was, with whom? Heavy-bomber crews were neither allotted nor selected by any scientific method because there was none. Instead, inside a large room, part-trained aircrew stood and sat about in their groups. The bomb aimers were together, navigators together, wireless operators together, and the pilots started drifting between them. It was like a quiet party with no drinks, one of those occasions where the idea is to circulate, not to have a good time.

At the party, this skipper decided he wanted this wireless operator, but the w/op didn't quite feel right about the skipper. No go, just don't fancy it. Sorry. Another wireless operator thought differently and agreed. Good. Gradually the groups diffused and mingled. A few settlements were made, crews began to assemble themselves.

Bob Woolf: I met our future navigator first, a fellow Australian called Jimmy Moore. Jimmy was a good deal older than most, perhaps ten years older and I liked that. The maturity was comforting, as well as feeling better among all these strangers with another Aussie. Jimmy was a gentleman. He seemed stable, sincere not excitable. That suited me very well.

Anyway, this short, stocky, fit-looking chap appeared in the doorway, very short he was, but a young man of military bearing with a great big RAF moustache, which helped him look older. His eyes scanned the room. What was he looking for? And what were me and Jimmy looking for?

They would have to make a decision, using no information and no experience, which could well seal their fate. Luck had something to do with whether you came back from an Op or not, but the pilot could have even more to do with it. The chap with the 'tache saw Bob and Jim and advanced towards them with a beam on his face. Clearly he thought he'd seen exactly what he was after. He introduced himself as Dougie Melrose. There was a light Edinburgh touch to his classy English accent, not that two Aussies would have noticed. 'He looked like a pilot, like a pilot should look, like a skipper, and acted like one of the more determined sort. He asked if Jim and me would like to join his crew. We said yes without hesitation.'

Among the bomb aimers was a young and athletic specimen that appeared to the Aussies to be a rather typical Pom, like Dougie. Unlike some of his kind he had not only been to the right schools but was also highly intelligent. Sammy Morris was the bomb aimer. The four moved on to Turweston Satellite Drome, where the gunners arrived.

'Dougie liked Bert Hoyle, possibly because he seemed to know everything there was to know about armaments. He'd been in training initially as an armourer. And he had a great sense of humour. The other theory we had was that with Bert in the crew, Dougie would no longer be the shortest. He would be equal shortest.'

Ernie Stalley was tall and shy, very likeable, and he had another quality Melrose admired in a gunner: excellent eyesight. The decision as to who would be mid-upper and who would be tail-end Charlie had to be a corporate one. Bert and Ernie had their preferences; the skipper and the rest of the crew had no strong opinions. Bert became mid-upper; Ernie would bring up the rear.

While the pilot's training took the longest, gunners had the briefest. In an aircraft hangar were arranged ten gun-turrets in rows of five facing the long walls. They had intercom between themselves and between them and the instructor, who was in a little cubicle by the door. On each long wall was painted a continuous white snaking, looping line in an attempt to reproduce the effects on gun-aiming made by a corkscrewing bomber trying to get away from a fighter trying to avoid being shot at. Trainee gunners concentrated here on turret manipulation following the twisty lines, fast. Turret movement was the one advantage a bomber had over a fighter, whose pilot had to line up his aircraft for a shot.

Mastery of turret driving was the trainee gunner's goal and evidence of achievement was unofficially shown with a pencil attached to the end of the gun. Using only his turret controls, the tyro would make a drawing of a familiar reproductive organ or, in the case of the inhibited, sign his name.

Breakdowns were expected so trainees had to assemble two different types of machine gun, parts mixed together, blindfold. These examinations passed, the students went up in the air. Four trainee gunners would be in an Oxford or an Avro Anson and they took it in turns to operate the gun turret, firing cine film at pursuing RAF fighters pretending to be Germans, or live rounds at a drogue being towed along abeam of them by a Fairey Battle or some such. After fifteen or so hours of this, spread over a month, it was off to practise in a Wellington.

So, here was a Melrose-led crew of six. They'd had theoretical training and rigorous tests in their respective trades to make sure they knew the job backwards, hoping that vital matters would become instincts, but all the training in the world could never be enough. There had to be a judgement, too.

The Melrose men had a few months to go yet, as did F/O Malcolm Head.

We were put on a train moving north, confined in a sort of sub-compartment of a guard's van, a *Feldwebel* and six men being in the main compartment. When the train was passing through a tunnel we lowered the window and felt for the latch on the outside of the door, which we released. After being in the train for about two-and-a-half hours it was dark enough and the train moving slowly enough for seven of us to get out. The Germans fired several shots at us and, in the confusion, I lost the others but soon picked up Lt Ward and one of the Sicilian officers and we three moved together. Later we found Capt Cheer. We stayed about eight days in the mountains near where we had jumped then moved south with a guide, who took us across the Sangro

river. Near Forli del Sannio we were shot at by Germans. I was hit in the left arm, which was broken, and Capt Cheer was hit in the arm and the leg and captured as he could not run.

The remains of the party would contact British troops and Head, via hospital in Bari and Cairo, would reach the UK in February 1944.

Berlin, November 1943: battle was joined in earnest. Between now and the end of the war a huge number of aircraft would be lost over Berlin but the total represented only 6.2 per cent of aircraft sent there. It could be put another way: over eight thousand bombing sorties were flown against Berlin in eighteen months, and only five hundred aircraft were lost, or one in sixteen. In the official view, considering the magnitude of the task, this justified the use of the word 'only'.

There was further justification too when it was considered how vast were the numbers of men and weapons deployed to defend German cities when, without the British bombers, they could have been deployed in the enlargement of empire and the defeat of the Allies. Estimates are difficult to make and equally hard to rely on, but there must have been between one and two million potential frontline men tied up in Germany repairing bomb damage and another huge number in flak regiments. Something like forty per cent of German navy effort was expended on sweeping the mines dropped by Bomber Command and up to a third of the output of German gun factories was anti-aircraft production. Add in all the fighter squadrons and a picture emerges of an enemy seriously distracted from positive action. So, perhaps it was a case of 'only'. In 1943, No. 9 Squadron was losing only one Lancaster a week.

That November Arthur Harris, universally known as 'Butch' in the RAF, began his final assault on Berlin with four raids. With another four in December, six in January 1944, one in February and a final one in March, the Battle of Berlin would be resolved. There would be bombing in bad weather, too bad by normal standards for the wild boars but such standards could not be allowed. As autumn grew into winter the reputation of those famous tactics which had made Herrmann into a Lt Colonel would fall as quickly as it had risen. Single-engined fighters, flying blind in cloud and rain, could find it very hard to get home. Many would crash on landing; pilots would bale out rather than try to land. Profits and losses would be out of balance and the redeveloped Lichtenstein apparatus, able to see through the Window, would arrive to restore faith in the old faithfuls, the Ju88s and the Me110s.

Arriving at 9 Squadron ready for the battle were fresh crews led by Phil Plowright, Denis Froud, John McComb, Harry Blow and Bob Lasham: 'I refused to carry a good-luck charm and I broke off my engagement to Joyce until times were more settled.' Quite right, you never knew. McComb, for example, was killed on the second of his two learner/passenger flights.

Nancy Bower: 'Phil Plowright always wore his striped scarf, which was in his college colours: green and orange. That was his good luck charm, and it worked for him.'

There could be no war, no German resistance, if there were no Berlin. That was the belief. So, on that significant afternoon of 18 November, seventeen crews of 9 Squadron were briefed to take off around half past five for the long haul to the Big City, including the new squadron CO, Wing Commander Porter, who had been in the job for all of four days. Pat Burnett DSO, DFC, 45 Ops completed, had set off upstairs, where he would become head of Air Ministry intelligence when the war was cold and the enemy Soviet Russia.

Bob Lasham had done his early training in Florida, was in Miami the day the Japanese attacked Pearl Harbor, came back to England, flew Ansons full of trainee w/ops, went to nightfighter school and eventually completed as a Lancaster pilot with several hundred flying hours more than most including a lot of night experience. Whether such extra qualification could influence his fate, only time would tell. Lasham was with Mitchell in ED700 WS/O, which Wingco Burnett had landed on one engine with numerous holes: 'I stood behind the pilot's seat all the way on my second Dicky. He didn't say much and I couldn't see much. It was a quiet night, ten tenths cloud. It's not a good observation point, behind the seat.'

The Berlin force was 440 Lancasters, sixty more than had gone to one target before, but both sides got off lightly. Ten down out of 440 was light unless you were one of the ten, like 9 Squadron's P/O Lees on only his second trip, colliding with one of his own and parachuting. Or P/O Gordon Graham, Canadian pilot with a good many Ops behind him, dying with all his crew.

Harry Blow, on the other hand, could bomb on this raid with both turrets u/s and not see a fighter. Blow would fly a round dozen to Berlin and come home twice with a fin bent at right angles after midair collisions. He would have a wing badly damaged by a bomb falling from above and would have unexploded shells from a 30mm Mauser cannon lodged inside his fuel tank. Jimmy Ling would do ten Berlins without serious incident. Ling's luck would run out eventually, but not over Berlin.

The next Berlin was 22 November and it was a big one. They sent 764 aircraft including 469 Lancs, another record, including from No. 9 Wells with Sgt Plowright second Dicky, Comans, Warwick, Newton, Ward, the American W W W Turnbull (known as 'Tex'), Blow, Chambers, Anstee, Reid, Ling, Bayldon and James. It was a good attack. Once again there was cloud, huge banks of it, but they bombed accurately and set large parts of the place alight. Tiergarten, Charlottenburg and Spandau suffered the most and there was gratifying destruction at a *Waffen SS* college, the barracks of the Imperial Guard, the Ministry of Weapons and several Siemens factories. A gasworks blew up and killed a hundred people. A direct hit on a shelter killed another five hundred and probably about two thousand died that night.

Inside one of the eleven Lancs shot down, Z of 156 Squadron, was a very experienced crew with three DFCs including the warrant officer in the rear turret, John Lovis DFC. His experience ran from a 9 Squadron crash with Gingles in a Wellington on a grass strip in Suffolk in 1941 to the Runnymede Memorial, and he was still only 22. Likewise there was lots of experience lost in Lancaster C of 83 Squadron with a wing commander DSO, DFC and Bar as pilot, a squadron leader DFC bomb aiming and a flight lieutenant DFC in the rear turret who was John Percival Crebbin, ex 9 Squadron gunnery leader, first tour in Wellingtons, second in Lancs.

The next night it was Berlin and on her fiftieth operation, ED656 WS/V almost made it home. With ten miles to go she crashed to the ground at Scamblesby. Only the two gunners escaped alive. Pilot Norman Robinson from County Kildare, passenger pilot Charles Hinton and the rest did not. Later, the second-Dicky practice would be stopped. In the meantime the Germans could shoot pilots down in pairs and invariably get one with long experience and one whose three years of training were instantly and completely wasted, leaving behind a headless crew who, in this case, had been on the squadron for four days. No experienced skipper would want to take on a raw crew fresh out of OTU.

> 'After slight folly on take-off, my undercarriage
> collapsed on making a perfect landing'
> Sq/Ldr Wasse

The Short Stirling was withdrawn from German service, leaving Harris eleven squadrons shorter. The Americans wouldn't help by going to Berlin during the day so the Battle of Berlin was looking ever, ever harder. The night of 26 November was the worst so far for Lancasters. Having gone the long way round to try and convince the Germans that Frankfurt was the target, they found that it worked, but backfired. There were few fighters over Berlin but the many ready to defend Frankfurt had time to readjust and pick off those who strayed off track on the way home. As a direct result of enemy action or, in the case of at least one a midair collision, 31 Lancasters were lost away from home. A further sixteen were written off through crashes when trying to land at base after the raid, some with total casualties; others none. For 9 Squadron all returned safely to Bardney. A

Lanc of 106 Squadron was one that did not make it and in the back was the steady, reliable Harry Stuffin. Victor Nunn, navigator, Swedish internee, Norfolk parachutist, was in T of 83 Squadron and, three days after his pal John Crebbin, met the same fate.

Going to the same target over and over again was not good for the spirit of a man. Berlin, Berlin and Berlin: three and a half hours there and four and a half back into the prevailing headwind damaged the self-defences that allowed aircrew to fly on a succession of nights, keeping the thought firmly in the backs of their minds that it would be the other crew who would get the chop. Good for them or no, it was Berlin yet again on 2 December, with Lasham on his first in ED654 WS/W, the one in which Dicky Lynam had been killed, Plowright on his first with his flight engineer, Sgt W C 'Sticky' Lewis who was destined for a very long and very unlucky career.

The Frankfurt detour hadn't had the right effect so it was back to route one. Plowright's rear gunner was Norman Wells.

When we went into the briefing room and saw we'd got Berlin for our first, we thought Christ Almighty and yet, at the same time, it was something good. We were going to Berlin. That was the heart of the war. But when we got there, God, it was horrendous. We all thought, we can't get through this. It was a mass of searchlights, and with the flak and the photoflashes* going off and the bombs exploding, it was as bright as day. Nothing hit us but we could see plenty of other aircraft going down, plenty. I wasn't expecting fighters over the target, not with so much flak, so I could rotate my turret and I could look kind of forward, past the wingtip. Of course I didn't do that for long and soon we were on our way out of all the light and mayhem. And we crossed some sort of invisible line and there we were, instantly, in black darkness, where we knew the fighters were waiting for us, and I realised that in all the light over the target I'd lost my night vision. Pretty scary, that first one. When we got back and walked down those steps and stood on the ground, we felt elated. We felt, thank God for that. Then we said, 'Wouldn't have missed that one for the world.' Well, we could say that, couldn't we? We were home.

*A lot of aircrew didn't like the photoflash and not only because it meant extra straight and level flying time. It was a reconnaissance flare, removed from its parachute and modified as a small bomb, full of aluminium flash powder approximately worth 20 pounds of HE. The story was that it had an inappropriate American fuse and one had blown up where it was fitted, in a chute in the aircraft floor. In fact it was safe, or as safe as anything could be in a loaded bomber, but the story still stuck.

Bob Lasham had a routine trip, assuming what Norman Wells saw for the first time to be routine, until he got home.

Our fuel gauges were registering almost empty when we reached Bardney and there was a queue waiting to land so we were peeled off to Fiskerton. In fact there was plenty of petrol; it was just the gauges that were wrong. Fiskerton was only a few miles from Bardney so they put us in a car and whisked us back home for the interrogation, and we went to bed. We hadn't been asleep long when the SPs (Service Police) came charging in, making a lot of noise and packing up the kit of the chaps we shared with, who were sergeants out of F/Lt Wells's crew. They'd been lost that night. And we were told later that one of the survivors of Warwick's crash at Gamston was in hospital and refused to give anything but his name, rank and number because he was convinced he was in Germany and the doctors and nurses were Gestapo dressed up.

I hadn't heard much on the trip from my rear gunner, Eddie Clark, who was older than the rest of us. We were late teens and early twenties but he was in his thirties. Anyway, after we landed we found out why he'd been quiet. His oxygen supply had partially failed and one of his heated shoes had packed up completely and his foot was frozen. He had to have some toes amputated and we never saw him again. If this had happened later in my experience I might have investigated more and come down lower, but my orders were to stay at that height and being new, that's what I did.

Leipzig, 3 December. Plowright swapped from L-Love to W4964 J-Johnny, J-Jig as was, now with a name change. She was one of those Lancasters that lasted long enough to acquire a special identity with nose painting to match by the station artist, A flight ground crewman Corporal Pattison. She was J-Johnny Walker, still going strong, with a large picture of the top-hatted and monocled whisky gent striding along beside those rows of mission symbols accounting for thirty-four trips so far.

Now it was the December moon so there was a bit of a lay-off. Normal operational service was resumed on 16 December except it was worse than normal, the most going and the most falling, a night to be remembered as Black Thursday. The battle order was posted with thirteen crews named. Berlin, again. God, who would it be this time? Old hand Comans? Newton the barrister? Hadland? New boy Plowright? Turnbull? Would Tex turn out to be an American like Van Note or an American like Storey and Roberts?

Bob Lasham: 'I always used to go into the intelligence office to see if there was any new gen on flak emplacements or whatever. I used to see

Pilot Officer Blow in there, and Bill Reid, but I never saw any of the others, not even when it was Berlin.'

Of the record 482 Lancasters going on 16 December 1943, a record 54 crashed or were shot down. EE188 WS/B, a veteran of 45 Ops was the Lancaster in which Sgt Robinson had fired six hundred rounds and been temporarily blinded by scarecrows. On this trip Ian Black was her skipper, with rear gunner Douglas Gordon, who had shot down three nightfighters on their journeys together. They reached Berlin but not Bardney, going in at Rheine, not far from the Dutch border.

Richard Bayldon, aged 20, and his crew were killed when they fell 25 miles from Berlin. The mid-upper gunner Raymond Baroni had no need to be there at all. He'd left his home in Glendale, California, volunteered through the RCAF, chased off German fighters on several occasions (twice in one night at Kassel) so he could have said he'd done his bit, helped them get this far. Now, like the rest of them, he was of no further use to the cause, like pilot David Brill, rear gunner Ernest Battle, mid-upper Gordon Little, w/op Chap Chappell, ex 9 Squadron, now PFF, killed at Berlin.

The explanation for Black Thursday lay not entirely with the human enemy and his machines but partly with the powers of nature that could assist or oppose. Had those who fell in the usual way managed to struggle to the home coastline they would have found the entire region covered in thick fog and confusion. There was nowhere to land. Some couldn't wait and, short of fuel, baled out or took a chance on finding a friendly spot beneath the blanket of mist.

A Pathfinder crashing at base had 9 Squadron men. Among the dead was P/O John Towler Pratt DFM, flight engineer with Doolan and Harry Irons all those months before, and dying with him in F-Freddie was bomb aimer F/O William Alfred Colson DFM. Bill Colson, married, aged 28, a bricklayer by trade, had already done a full tour in Whitleys and another in Wellingtons and Lancasters with Dick Stubbs.

At Bardney, flight control might have wondered if the new lad Lasham had suffered the same fate. He wasn't back but he was on his way, with the Gee box u/s and the navigator completely lost. Lasham put out a 'Darky' call. Darky was an emergency distress code word, requiring urgently a place to land because of technical failure or being lost, or because damage done by the enemy had at last become unsustainable. Darky calls were made on a special radio telephone channel under the control of the pilot.

After a quarter hour of this there was an answer – Churchyard – and a searchlight to show them the way to what turned out to be a tiny grass airfield almost on the beach at Donna Nook, a Coastal Command Beaufighter station between Mablethorpe and Cleethorpes. Lasham's first duty when he got down on this inappropriate landing ground was to telephone Bardney.

One of the Donna Nook people asked me if I'd missed my own base before. 'Oh yes,' I said, 'on purpose and by mistake. Four times altogether.' 'So how many Ops have you done?' he asked. I looked at my crew all standing round me with stupid grins on their faces, trying not very hard not to laugh. 'Four,' I said.

SECRET 9 Squadron Combat Report
20 December 1943. 19.45. 20,000 ft. Frankfurt. Lancaster G. Captain: P/O Glover.
Shortly before approaching the target the bomber was swept by cannon and machine gun fire, which set fire to the rear turret and the port inner engine and damaged the intercommunication system. The rear gunner was injured by splinters in the face and slightly burnt and the mid-upper was hit by a machine-gun bullet in the leg. The attack came from astern well down and as soon as the pilot saw the tracer he commenced a corkscrew port, losing height rapidly to gain extra speed, having a full load on. Both gunners saw a Ju88 come in from astern down but rear gunner could not fire as guns had been damaged and MU could not get guns to bear. E/A broke away down and again attacked from same position opening fire at 600 yards and closing in to 100 yards. E/A's trace all passed above the bomber and he broke away astern down and was not seen again. The pilot resumed course on three engines and bombed the target from a very low altitude before returning to base.

Visibility clear but dark. No moon, flares or searchlights. No indication on any special apparatus. Damage to own aircraft: rear turret badly smashed. Port inner engine u/s. MU turret and fuselage holed in many places. Intercom shot away. No rounds fired by either gunner.

Captain's ORB report: 'Bombs were dropped on written instructions from navigator (F/O J S Middleton) when over centre of target area.' He also noted the results of the raid. 'Fire and incendiaries seemed fairly well concentrated.'

Lou Glover was awarded the DFC for carrying on to bomb from a very low altitude while reading a note from his navigator after being swept from stem to stern by cannon and machine guns and corkscrewing out of trouble on three engines in a fully loaded aircraft, defenceless against what was obviously a skilled and experienced foe before returning to base. He would be back on duty nine days later.

Edward Argent, skipper of ED700 WS/O on the aircraft's fiftieth, bombed Frankfurt and was on his way home.

SECRET 9 Squadron Combat Report
20 December 1943. 21,000 ft. Frankfurt. Lancaster O. Captain: P/O Argent.
While crossing a belt of flares north of the target the MU gunner saw Me210 diving in from port quarter up and immediately gave pilot order to corkscrew port. Both gunners and the E/A opened fire at the same instant at 200 yards. E/A's tracer was seen to pass above the bomber. The gunners' fire was seen to enter the E/A, confirmed by the Wireless Operator who was standing in the astrodome. E/A went into a very steep dive and disappeared port quarter down. As it broke away a burst of cannon and machine gun fire from port quarter up struck our A/C and the MU saw a Ju88 diving in from the same direction as the previous attack. The MU engaged the Ju88 with return fire until both his guns ceased to fire, cause unknown, after which he assisted the pilot by giving a commentary during the whole engagement, which lasted throughout approximately twelve very rapid attacks by the Ju88. The rear gunner was killed and the bomber received serious damage in the initial attack by the Ju88, but in all the remaining attacks only sustained slight damage in the starboard wing. The Ju88 finally broke away on the starboard beam and was not seen again. The pilot maintained a corkscrew throughout all attacks.
Visibility was very good in glare of flares. No moon. No searchlights. No indications on any special apparatus. W/operator reports Ju88 opened fire with beam guns on one occasion, but this is not confirmed by any other member of the crew. Damage to own aircraft: rear turret badly smashed and RG killed. Starboard fin and starboard wing badly torn. Fuselage holed in many places. Both starboard petrol tanks holed.
MU Sgt Trevena 500 rounds
RG Sgt Knox 400 rounds

During most of the incident Aussie gunner Alf Trevena could assist only by commentary rather than with guns, the other gunner could not assist at all and the w/op, George Fradley, hung on watch in the astrodome while his 20-year-old skipper did extreme aerobatics in a flying colander. Of course they had the advantage of good visibility, courtesy of the flares the German fighters dropped.

The relief of level flight and being left alone lasted almost to the English coast, but by then they had nothing in the bank and had to ditch off

Happisburgh. Vincent Knox, a 19-year-old Canadian, was the rear gunner who went down with his ship. The rest of the crew made it into the dinghy and managed to keep going through four dark hours of a December night before an Air Sea Rescue launch picked them up. They were given ten days' leave.

Nightfighters often operated in pairs. One would attack while the other held off, waiting for the Lancaster's gun flashes to give away her exact position and altitude. Another trick was for an Me110, say, to hang about out of range with its lights on. While the bomber crew were looking at it and wondering what it was up to, another fighter would attack from the other side. Norman Wells: 'One time the second fighter was a FW190 and it came screaming past us ablaze from nose to tail. Somebody behind us had learned from experience.'

A prewar sergeant armourer, who had been in France with Fairey Battles when the Germans invaded, now Acting Pilot Officer J H Maguire known as Mick, was plucked from a series of squadron postings and Air Ministry R&D jobs. He was told he was armaments officer for 9 Squadron and was to report immediately to Waddington.

I didn't know quite if it was Christmas or the third Tuesday after muck spreading. I'd been out of Bomber Command for a while and when I'd been in it, we'd had light bombers. Up there in Lincolnshire I knew it was one big brawl. Heavy losses, constant losses, unremitting battle. I thought I could imagine the pressure but I didn't have a clue. First, I had to report to a senior armaments man, who shall remain nameless. It was a maximum effort Op that night and that clearly caused him maximum panic, which I had to sit there and watch. Eventually he dropped it all and took me in a little van across the dark Lincolnshire countryside in the blackout to Bardney airfield and into a tiny shoebox of an office with the standard dim blue light. He scuttled round and round this office to no purpose. From the noise of engines, an Op was imminent. He shouted, 'I've got to go. There's trouble at Skellingthorpe!' and left me alone. I'd been there two minutes. The whole place was palpitating with noise. I'd been on stations with a hundred Spitfires, but a dozen or so Lancs at night seemed a lot noisier.

Stranded in a strange land, Maguire sat on the edge of the desk and wondered where they kept the tea. The phone rang.

Every instinct said don't answer it but I answered it. 'Maguire, armaments officer.' A voice said, 'What?' 'Acting Pilot Officer Maguire, new armaments officer, just arrived.' The voice shouted,

'Well, get over here right away!' and then the phone went dead. I didn't know where over here was, or how to get there in the dark.

He soon worked it out. At a time like this, such voices would be coming from the control tower and if he got down on his knees, he could discern faintly against what little starlight there was, an outline.

It turned out to be flying control with stairs up the back, and inside I found the voice, the Station CO, a little group captain, striding up and down, demented. 'Who are you?' he said. 'Where are you from?' Well, I guessed he wasn't expecting me to say 'Belfast, sir', so I told him I was from Fighter Command. He couldn't have given me a more apoplectic look if I'd said I'd been in the King's Own Martian Dragoons with Popeye the Sailorman. 'Fighter Command?' he said. 'Fighter Command? There's an aircraft out there with a u/s rear turret and you've got forty-five minutes!' I didn't like to mention that I'd never been close to a Lancaster before so I asked if this one could be held back to be the last to take off. He gave me that look again, only with extra steam. The other people in the tower were studying the night sky with enormous concentration. The group captain, whom I soon found out was called Pleasance, took two steps towards me and almost screamed 'It's already done!' and I half fell backwards down the stairs.

The Lancs were warming up their engines. Take-off for Berlin looked rather less than forty-five minutes away as P/O (Acting) Maguire stumbled back towards the only place he knew, that office with the blue light and the telephone. There he bumped into a large sergeant with a dog end dangling from his bottom lip and an air of exhaustion and frustration about him.

'Who are you?' I said. He looked at me, clearly at the end of his tether, and spoke in a strong Liverpool accent. 'I'm Sergeant Gallant, but more to the point, who the ****ing hell are you?' So I told him and said we had to fix this turret and I'd never seen one before. 'Follow me,' says he, and off he went with me straining to keep up. We passed a little crane with a man inside and the engine running. 'Don't ****ing move,' said Sergeant Gallant and next thing we were diving into the MT section and a truck. In two ticks we were beside some hangars and another crane came out with a rear turret hanging from its jib, and a small low-loader appeared. 'Where's the aircraft?' I asked. 'Over there. O's dispersal'* said somebody, as the low-loader spun around and the turret was put on it. The other crane turned up, hoisted the turret to the aircraft's rear end and two corporals got stuck into it. They had the new turret on and were connecting up the hydraulics and servos when the aircraft started sliding out of the dispersal. There was nothing I could do except watch as the corporals finished their work on the move, and Gallant suddenly appeared in the turret doorway with a can of hydraulic oil and jumped to the ground. I was just thinking that the whole exercise was pointless because the hydraulics would be full of air, when Gallant said, 'He'll bleed the bastard in the air. It's all right. He knows what he's doing.' When I asked Corporals Meadows and Delaney about Form 700, which certified the aircraft serviceable and without which it could not take off, they said they'd signed it in advance.

*ED700 WS/O had ditched three days before with Argent and had not yet been replaced.

We went back to the office. There was a bunch of armourers in there, smoking, loafing about, and I was the object of mild curiosity while they carried on talking about the problems they'd been having, and they did have problems. That turret business was just an example. I hadn't slept for twenty-four hours so I was half dozing when the CO walked in, Shorty Pleasance, and everybody kind of shuffled to attention, and he said to me, 'Sorry about all that. You managed.' I said I hadn't managed, they had, pointing to my new colleagues.

This was Bob Lasham's sixth Op. 'We reckoned if you got through six, you'd probably got the hang of things and the crew would be operating and co-operating well, and you might even think you'd get to the end of it. My navigator Joey Bosley had arranged to get married on Christmas Day so they had to give us all leave. Excellent piece of navigation, we thought.'

A familiar face looked around the door of the sergeants' mess. John Douglas Duncan had an extra crown on his uniform to denote the rank of flight sergeant but otherwise he was the same chap, returned from his *vacances en France*. As a Canadian it would have been standard practice for him to repatriate but he preferred the half a tour he still had to do. He was supplied with a crew including two officers from 50 Squadron and he could look forward to part two. All of them could, apart from one of those officers.

'I can take thirty beers easily before a session'
F/O Barnard

Next morning it was time for Mick Maguire to do some learning among his armourers and it quickly became apparent that here was a group of bitter men. What was the matter?

Life in Bomber Command was very tough, and tough enough without any extras. They told me that everything was always the armourers' fault. If an aircraft didn't take off on time, it was the armourers. The station armaments officer, who was theoretically responsible for the bomb dump, the shooting range and other non-aircraft matters, had been having to do my job as well, squadron armaments, and he hadn't been making a great success of it, they said, and we get blamed for it all. 'Who blames you?' I said. The Chiefy, F/Sgt Harrison, formerly with the Royal Navy Air Service, World War One and had been with the squadron since the Honington days, said, 'Old ghee guts up in the office' by which he meant the said station officer. The general opinion was that this man was afraid of explosives and hated aeroplanes, which was an odd combination for an armaments officer. 'Well,' I told them, 'from now on, if anyone gets any blame it will be me.'

Frank Belben went to Berlin, the first of his five such, on 29 December.

Berlin was very frightening. You knew it would be a sticky one, inevitably, by its very nature. You'd often be locked onto by fighters or you'd be coned and it was always doubtful if you'd get out of it if you didn't escape straight away. They were skilled professionals, the men with the searchlights. It was always touch and go who would win. Your pilot had to react instantly. It was the one time when the team didn't come into it. It was all up to him, and it was a regular thing over Berlin.

F/Lt Ervine had another example of a regular thing over Berlin.

Having received a red indication on special apparatus, commenced to corkscrew port. In the initial dive, the starboard tailplane was hit by flak. Almost at the same instant the bomber was struck by a burst of cannon and machine gun fire from an unseen A/C. A second burst of fire was seen to pass above the bomber. Both gunners failed to see the E/A having been dazzled by the flak burst.

Paddy Ervine, with damage to flying surfaces, hydraulics, instruments and R/T, and a wounded gunner, got back to England. He was near the end of his tour. A new pilot, hit by flak as he went into a corkscrew and then raked with shells and bullets, might not have been able to recover but Ervine had been on squadron for four months and more. It was a regular thing for him.

Composed in the 9 Squadron sergeants' mess, Bardney, Christmas
1943. (Sung to the tune of 'Bless 'em all')

They say there's a Lancaster out on the field
Waiting to go on a flight
With hydraulics leaking and engine revs down
But hoping to get there all right.
There's one or two cylinders running a temp,
One rudder adrift from its fin,
But with good navigation and much concentration
We're hoping to get to Berlin.

We know that the Hun has some very fine kites,
Of this we're no longer in doubt.
When ever a Focke-Wulf gets up on our tail,
This is the way we get out.
We go into a corkscrew, we dive and we weave,
We don't give the kraut time to think.
We show no repentance, just pass the death sentence
And shoot him right down in the drink.

When over the target our bombs hurtle down
As soon as we press on the tit.
There's searchlights upon us, there's fighters around,
Two engines have gone for a shit.
The crew's in a panic, they want to bale out,
All into the searchlights and flak.
There's no jubilation, complete consternation,
We know that we'll never get back.

The end of our story sees us at The Gates,
Where Peter imparts all the gen.
It seems they've no room for a whole bomber crew,
No billets for our type of men.
So that's it, we've had it, we won't get our harps,
We won't get our issue of wings.
Too late for repentance, there's no bloody entrance,
So join in the chorus and sing.

Bless 'em all, bless 'em all,
The long and the short and the tall.
Bless the air gunners, the wireless op too,

Bless the bomb aimer, the pilot and crew
'Cos we're saying goodbye to them all,
As into their aircraft they crawl.
They're off on an Op
And they may get the chop,
So cheer up, my lads, bless 'em all.

5

CREWED UP AND GOING UP: 1944

Happy New Year, everyone. In 1943, No. 9 Squadron had lost 55 Lancasters on Ops and 4 more in accidents. Bomber Command had lost 1,117 Lancs, 883 Halifaxes, 418 Stirlings, 327 Wellingtons, 67 Mosquitos, 20 Whitleys and 54 of other types on Ops, 2,886 aircraft altogether plus another 231 in accidents, plus another 764, mostly Wellingtons and Halifaxes, in training. Would 1944 be any better? Possibly. Possibly not.

New Year's Day 1944. 'Eleven aircraft were detailed to operate against Berlin at night. When the aircraft reached the target they found 10/10 cloud. 'V' (P/O Turnbull) and 'B' (F/O Manning) did not complete their mission but returned early, the former with technical trouble and the latter owing to the MU gunner (Sgt Zammit) being unwell (and one of the escape hatches blowing away).'

P/O William Wrigley Watts Turnbull was born in Pueblo in 1916, making him 9 Squadron's only Mexican pilot, moving to San Antonio, Texas whence he volunteered for the RCAF in 1941. DFC-to-be, he was remarkably skeletal and the motherly WAAFs worried about him.

Aileen Walker: That man, Tex Turnbull, I did look after him. He was so, so thin and spoke so, so slowly. I'd go to him and ask him if he'd like some second helpings and he'd say no, he'd had quite sufficient, so we could never feed him up. One night I came off duty and there he was, leaning on my bike. I said, 'What are you doing?' He said, 'I'm holding your bike for you. I'm going to walk you home.' Well, he walked me home, he was blind drunk, and when he stumbled and fell I took my tie-pin off and held it ready in my hand. He had a certain reputation, did Tex Turnbull.

Squadron Leader Brain finished his second tour and took with him a Bar to his DFC. Brain was what they called the press-on type. He'd pressed on through one tour, taught rookies how to fly Wellingtons at Cottesmore including Bob Lasham, and pressed on again right through a second at one of the more hazardous periods of the war. He and his ginger moustache would now become a noticeable feature of No. 30 OTU.

Mick Maguire was getting his department organised and was somehow catching up on equipment maintenance, which had been neglected under the pressure of constant operations.

I studied the Chiefy's unofficial Ops record book and came to realise how rough it had been in '43 and how rough it was still going to be in '44, as far as I could see. It takes years and years to mature wines and spirits, but for men a few weeks on a bomber squadron is all that's necessary. My lads were hardened by blood, sweat and tears and here was I, feeling, looking and actually being younger than virtually all of my great gang of armourers, whose morale had been lowered by not being led properly. Respect didn't come automatically along with the rings and baubles of an officer's uniform. Respect had to be earned, and I set out to do it in big ways and small ways. I decided that somehow I would squeeze myself onto an Operation or two, but little things also can mean a lot. One night, after take-off, just about the whole of the rest of the squadron had been to The Jolly Sailor in Bardney. We were walking back, ready for something to eat, and I discovered that the officers' mess was closed. There was a corporal who was about the same size as me. He lent me his jacket and I went into the airmen's mess and had supper with them.

SECRET No 9 Squadron Combat Report
14 January 1944. 19.30 hrs. 23,000 ft. Brunswick. Lancaster O. Captain: P/O Lasham.
The Lancaster was doing a banking search to starboard when it was struck by a burst of cannon and machine gun fire from the port bow down, which damaged the rear of the fuselage and the rear turret. The pilot immediately commenced to corkscrew and while climbing starboard was hit again on the port wing.

Bob Lasham: Sgt Swindlehurst was our rear gunner for the first time, which made him a regular, and we had two more first-time strangers in the crew who must have thought they'd joined the circus. A fighter had a go at us and did manage to wreck the rear turret and generally shoot us up but otherwise we seemed to be all right. I did my check around the crew. Everybody answered except Singleburst, as we called him. Doug (Nicholls, w/op) took the portable oxygen to see what was up but no reply came back. I sent Bill (Yates, engineer) who set off with the fire axe. Same result, nothing. I didn't know if they were falling out of a hole in the back end or what but I thought I had better get lower, below oxygen height, before I sent anybody else to see what was happening. I only had one of my own crew left, Harry Wilson the bomb aimer, so I sent him. He found two men unconscious through lack of oxygen, including Singleburst with a slight wound from a cannon shell, and Bill just coming round from his no-oxygen blackout. Bill decided we had landed in Germany and Harry was the enemy, so he attacked him with the fire axe. No harm done in the end.

The Fates were not to be gainsaid over Edward James Argent, aged 20, and they were doubly determined about some of his crew. After three weeks, P/O Argent along with originals Sgt Lyons, Sgt Fradley and F/Sgt Travena were all sufficiently recovered from their dinghy ride to go on Ops again, the team this time completed by three of Sq/Ldr Brain's old crew. They flew for Brunswick but they didn't make it back.

Bob Lasham: The Ruhr was finished so we were always doing long trips, seven or eight hours. Berlin wasn't especially different in that respect, and I could never sleep after a night flight. Most people seemed to put their heads down and be out like a light. Some of them could sleep on the aircraft. Coming back from Berlin once, on the northern route where you could see all the lights on in Sweden, we saw the most fantastic display of the Aurora Borealis. It was stunning, although it meant we were flying virtually in daylight, and it was all very fascinating except Joey fell asleep in his little office and so didn't give me a change of course. We were back half an hour after everybody else. I always took my own map with me after that.

We were coming home one time and a coolant tank burst and, as it would, set the starboard outer on fire. The coolant was glycol-based and burned with a brilliant light, which made you feel very exposed like you were walking down Piccadilly without your trousers. Following procedure, I said, 'Fire drill, starboard outer. Prepare to abandon aircraft,' expecting the flight engineer to feather the propeller and work the extinguisher. Bill (Yates, engineer) moved rapidly to feather the wrong engine, the starboard inner, and dived for the escape hatch with his parachute. His second mistake of the night was to pull the rip cord there and then, so silk streamed out behind him as he headed for the door. I'd have liked to have seen the expression on his face but I was too busy feathering the burning engine and restarting the good one. We got back a bit late but I still couldn't sleep. Next day we were on again and, on the way to the briefing, Sgt Powell, our mid-upper, told Bill Yates that the CO had issued special instructions that we were to take off thirty minutes before everybody else. Why, says Bill. To practise feathering, says Powell.

All things being equal in a doomed Lancaster, the bomb aimer should have had the best chance of survival, being positioned right over an escape hatch. A pilot could choose to have his parachute on his seat so it didn't need unshipping from the fuselage side like the others, but many pilots didn't like sitting on a parachute and the privilege was cancelled out by their obligation of honour to keep control of the aircraft while the others jumped. The flight engineer could step down and follow the bomb aimer. The rear gunner could swivel his turret and jump straight out. Worst off, in theory, were those in the middle of the aircraft, the w/op, the navigator and the mid-upper who usually tried to leave by the side door. Of course, if the thing blew up or crashed without notice, it didn't matter where you sat.

A fresh-faced lad who had walked into the officers' mess back in August had become a veteran, a flight lieutenant, a score of Ops, on his seventh Berlin, 27 January. The crew had come back from leave, had the good news at the briefing, up at 17.15, last heard of two and a quarter hours into the flight. Three were taken prisoner. James and the three others were killed. He must have lied about his age to get onto training because he was still only 19.

Few things excite as much as dodging death and, possibly, some men might get hooked.

Mick Maguire: I was in the billet, a Nissen hut I shared with Harry Blow, when he came in. 'Hello Harry,' I said, 'what are you doing here? You're on leave.' He ignored what I said. 'What's happening tonight?' he wanted to know. 'What's the target?' I hadn't been told. 'What's the bomb load? What's the fuel load?' You could guess the target with that information, or at least the kind of target. 'Any aircraft going spare?' He was quite a fierce little fellow, a Lincolnshire farmer. He came right up to me and said 'How do you think I feel, on leave, when the bomber force is going over my head at night? I can't stay home. I'll rake up a spare crew.' I told him his own crew would love him for that. And he wasn't the only one who did that sort of thing. Ron Mathers was another. He came in to see me in the office and said, 'Any chance of getting my aircraft out of the hangar?' I didn't know. I knew it had scaffolding all over it and was having all four engines changed. In any case, it would have to be air tested before it went on an Op. He was back a few minutes later. 'Will you put the bombs on in the hangar?' It was an HE bomb load that night. I wouldn't have been happy putting incendiaries on in a hangar. So he took the aircraft on Ops without an air test. No time. They had faith, those pilots. Must have had. Or something.

Out of almost 1,400 Lancaster sorties on the last three Berlin nights, 85 failed to return. Not too bad at six per cent unless you considered that 85 Lancs and crews was the equivalent of five entire squadrons going down. Add 27 Halifaxes out of 323 sorties, over eight per cent, and the Battle of Berlin looked like it was going the way of the defenders. Of course they were suffering. Thousands were dead, hundreds of thousands were homeless, public transport was a mess, all sorts of industrial and public buildings were wrecked. Among the mountains of rubble now lay the ruins of the new Chancellery and the Ministry of Propaganda, but it was not the stuff of victory. After 30 January, when 33 were lost at Berlin, all squadrons were stood down for a fortnight with a few minor exceptions.

Mick Maguire: Every time a new Lancaster arrived, which was often, we had to fit some special deep incendiary holders, part of the modifications which had gone on to double the Lanc's bomb load from the original spec. I was watching Corporal Willing, who was as good an armourer as we had even if I couldn't get him promoted, and he was dabbing a blob of red paint onto the corners of these things, and then they closed the bomb doors and opened them again. Wherever there was a spot of red on the inside metal skin of the doors, Willing attacked it with an axe. To me this was treasonable damage of His Majesty's aircraft. 'What are you doing?' I said. He looked and said, 'Bomb doors have got to shut. It's the quickest way.' This was the essence of everything. We never had any time. It led to magnificent achievement being routine, because the job had to be done whether we had the time or not. For instance, the armourers found that standard tools weren't adequate, so they designed and made their own. They could change a rotation motor in a turret faster than I could give the order.

The stand-down worked. Instead of sending a dozen or so aircraft as the best that could be managed under such pressure, the squadron fielded 21 Lancasters and crews, easily the best show so far. The target was Berlin.

Mick Maguire and his men were bombing up the last aircraft and had fallen a little behindhand when their favourite officer turned up, the one who was frightened of explosives and didn't care for aircraft.

He was a nice guy in many ways, but he'd been in a Vickers Armstrong drawing office and that had been enough for him to get over-promoted and put into one of the hottest spots in the war. He couldn't cope. Not his fault. Well, it was raining, it was cold, incendiaries were always a pain in the arse to load, and up rushed your man, flapping his arms about and saying we'll do this and we'll do that. He went up to

Corporal Willing and bawled at him to do this and do this. I saw Willing turn round and I heard what he said. His exact words were 'F*** off.' The officer said to me 'Did you hear what he said?' I said no, what did he say? And Willing turned around again and spoke again. 'I said f*** off.' So I ushered the officer away before a bomb fell on him.

This was the biggest effort yet on Berlin and the biggest of all except for the 'Thousand Plan' raids. As well as 9 Squadron's 21 there were 540 more Lancs, 314 Halifaxes and sixteen Mosquitos, making 891 aircraft and they had, as usual, mixed success. Bombs fell everywhere, in the centre, in industrial districts, on outlying villages, smack on the Siemensstadt, smack on some fields miles away. There would only be one more big raid on the Big City, one more thrust and parry in the Battle of Berlin. It was time to call it a draw.

Norman Wells: We were hit on our way in by flak on the starboard inner and it was u/s. Sticky (Lewis, engineer) went to feather it but it wouldn't feather, so the prop was being pushed round and round by air pressure, which caused a lot of drag on us, but we bombed and came home. It was bloody hard work, that sort of trip. Phil (Plowright) would be rocking the aircraft most of the time, side to side, so we could see underneath, and you did nothing for hours except stare and stare into the darkness, knowing that all the others in the crew, doing their various jobs, relied on the gunners to spot the enemy. You couldn't relax. Even when you saw the sea on the way home and you felt you'd made it again, the fighters could still be following you. Our own navy shot at us once when we were coming up to the English coast. Colours of the day went out and it stopped, but we could easily have been down. We had some leave then. When we came back, our Lancaster had gone.

Ops were cancelled, scrubbed, on three consecutive days.

Bob Lasham: We were sometimes scrubbed when we were in the aircraft, ready to start the engines. It was never explained why, or how we were supposed to wind down. Our answer was simple. Officially we weren't allowed off the station until told so, but we knew where to go and what to do. It was down to The Jolly Sailor to see Mr and Mrs Turner. Harry (Wilson, bomb aimer) was very friendly with them and we used to stop behind after time to help them wash up and so on. This was entirely out of the goodness of our hearts and nothing at all to do with the great rashers of gammon with eggs and chips that came out afterwards for our supper. Whisky was almost impossible to get in the ordinary way, as was gammon and eggs. It only needed the correct juxtaposition of professions, in this case innkeeper and farmer, and trade would result to the benefit of our good selves.

We thought of Mrs Turner as quite an old lady. She was probably mid-forties, which seemed old to us, and she used to put up aircrew wives sometimes in her letting room, but she stopped it. She had too many grieving widows to deal with when husbands failed to return. She couldn't stand it any more. I was in the flight offices one day when a gunner came in asking if he could have the morning off later in the week to get married. He was given a 72-hour pass, came back, and was killed on his next Op, so he had a three-day honeymoon and a three-day married life. Such things were everyday, commonplace. It happened all the time.

Leipzig, 19 February 1944; Lasham was there.

My navigator that night was Sgt Richardson who was a Jamaican and the only black man in aircrew I ever saw. There was a strong westerly wind and he got completely lost. We were almost at Berlin before he pulled us round. In the rear turret was Sgt Casson the famous dormouse, who became our regular rear gunner for a while but who couldn't get out of bed in the morning. I found out that the others were seeing to his guns for him, maintenance and so on, and I wasn't having that, and he became the only man, black, white or green, who I ever put on a charge.

Leipzig was another bad, bad experience for the bombers. Given that some of the force turned back early, losses were well over 10 per cent of those who flew on. Some arrived too soon and had to wait for the PFF. There were fighters with them all the way. The flak was especially effective, and the wheel had come full circle for Denis Froud. Leipzig was where Froud had been first time out. Now he and his crew, who had joined the same week as Plowright, were in Plowright's and Norman Wells's Lanc, W5010 L-Love and way off track, blown by the same wind that had taken Lasham away. A group of fighters had been to Kiel, following a small diversionary raid but they came scurrying back when it became clear where the main action was. The town of Stendal is on a line from Kiel to Leipzig and that's where Froud and his men were killed, one of the stunning, awful total of 78 four-engined bombers lost on the Leipzig raid.

F/Lt Paddy Ervine, DFC-to-be, finished his tour with the next trip, Stuttgart, site of one of the most wanted factories, Bosch. Ervine had been all the way through some of the worst of the war since he'd been second Dicky to Cologne with Sq/Ldr Derbyshire in July 43. Now, in February 44, he and that other everlaster, barrister Newton, were looking forward to their postings to a Lancaster finishing school. Ervine had been absolutely determined that he wasn't going down on his last, which made an interesting ride for the second Dicky he had with him, P/O George Denson, arrived on squadron only that day. Ervine came into interrogation and said 'I've corkscrewed all the way back from Stuttgart.'

Mick Maguire: I was becoming very concerned about the standard of gun maintenance. It was traditional on the squadron for the gunners, the aircrew, to look after their own guns while we looked after the bombs. I'd come from Fighter Command where guns were everything, and this tradition had to go. Look in a rear turret and you might find that each gun had a different girl's name painted on it. Watch a gunner cleaning his guns and you could see him using engine oil which, if you wanted your gun to freeze at high altitude, was the very best thing to use.

All the spare guns were collected up, which was a considerable number including all those that had been taken out of the useless ventral turret fitted as standard to the first batches of Lancs. We overhauled them, test fired them on the range, and began replacing the guns on the aircraft. I told the gunnery leader that it was my intention to have all guns serviced by armourers, and if any gunners wanted to service guns they could come down to the armoury to watch and learn. Every time a gun was fired, it would be taken out and serviced, properly, in the armoury. A Browning was a Browning. They were all interchangeable. I wasn't having this nonsense with personalised machine guns.

Schweinfurt, 24 February, population 50,000, was a market town too small to have had a Bomber Command raid so far but was a main centre of ball-bearing manufacture. PFF back-up markers undershot. Damage to the town was not significant. The ball bearings kept on rolling, unlike George Denson. He'd only been on squadron for four days, had the experience of corkscrewing from Stuttgart with Paddy Ervine and hoped he could confound the special risks attached to a new skipper taking his crew to Germany for the first time, but all he could do was confirm what everyone knew.

Only sixteen out of 460 were lost at Augsburg, 25 February, a rather better percentage than last time they were there. Lasham saw 'good fires in target area, no cloud, smoke rising to 15,000 feet'. Watching the success for the first time was Ginger Craig, second Dicky with Ling who was watching it for almost the last time. The marking had been near perfect, the bombing likewise, large parts of the target were no longer there and the MAN factories were severely damaged. Its very success caused arguments. The lovely old centre of town, the fine town hall and so on, were gone. The Germans protested again about *terrorangriff*. In the rest of the war, Bomber Command should perhaps restrict attacks to ugly and/or new bits of Germany and avoid being cruel to animals with big brown eyes.

Through November and December '43, Melrose and crew had flown almost every day and sometimes several times a day. The early flights had been largely for the pilot's benefit; the gunners' practice was done with an experienced instructor-pilot. Towards the end of the Wellington time they were introduced to a new game with the snappy title of Fighter Affiliation. Affiliate, literally to adopt as the son of, generally to connect oneself with, was the complete opposite of what they actually did. In daylight, a Spitfire or a Hurricane with a cine camera and a pilot intent on a bit of sport, would attack the bomber and the bomber pilot would desperately try to disconnect himself from the fighter while the gunners called the corkscrews and dives and tried to hit the fighter with their own cine film. The results indicated more than the skills of the players. A gunner who was not such a good shot or turret-driver, or a bomber pilot who lacked confidence in violent dives and turns, would give the fighter pilot an advantage, but timing and teamwork were just as important. The rear gunner in particular was the chief of defence for the aircraft; teamwork with the pilot had to be instinctive and trust had to be total. Norman Wells was Plowright's rear gunner.

In Fighter Affiliation you'd be just flying along and then a fighter would sneak up on you from below, or all of a sudden dive out of the clouds and come at you. We were told they were trainee pilots but I don't know if they were. Our job as gunners was to get him on the camera, and to tell the skipper which way to go. Whoever saw the fighter first, rear or mid-upper, shouted the order. You dived into the attacker, towards where he was coming from. Then the skipper would chuck the aircraft about, so we got chucked about as well, and there was quite a lot of G. It was difficult, really.

Frank Belben, engineer with Glover: 'We weren't supposed to go on Fighter Affiliation if we had a cold, because the extra forces and pressures generated could damage your eardrums. I only had a bit of a cold, thought I'd be all right, and bang. Very painful. Out of it for six weeks.'

Melrose and Co were off to Wigsley and 1654 Conversion Unit, where pilots were adapted from the two-engined Wellington to the four-engined

Stirling, a cumbersome beast largely relegated to training after being found wanting on Operations. Crews would move on later to Lancasters and Halifaxes, and they would most of them recall the Stirling with distaste. At Wigsley, Melrose needed to pick up his final team member, a flight engineer.

The engineer was a pilot in reserve as well as airborne mechanic and systems controller. Flight engineers were expected to have a full understanding of the aircraft's abilities, requirements and responses, and to be able to fly straight and level having had a few hours' practice on the Link trainer. Pilots were human. They could get migraines, or feel sick, or be killed come to that, and the engineer might have to do the job.

Bob Woolf: 'There was a whole gaggle of engineers in the hall as Dougie went in and walked around. He had a plan. He would have a brief chat and ask for the first three digits of their service numbers. This was Doug's subtle ploy to find out how experienced they were, because these digits corresponded to your entry year. He heard some numbers he liked from a young Scot and it wasn't until a few days later he realised that Jock had misheard him and given the last numbers.'

The communications problem persisted in the Stirling. A pilot in his early days of flying such a large aircraft needs things to go right in the cockpit, especially at take-off and landing which are the most dangerous aspects of flying anyway but particularly so in a Stirling. Melrose soon knew he had picked the wrong flight engineer.

Bob Woolf: We were just taking off and it was all standard procedure. 'Undercart up,' says our skipper. 'Aye, flaps in,' says Jock, and brought in the flaps and, of course, the Stirling began to struggle. The flaps provided lift at those vital moments as you were getting going. Well, she was mushing towards the ground and we all thought we were going to crash. 'Flaps back out, for crying out loud!' – Dougie was almost screaming at Jock, and he pushed all the engines up to maximum revs. We stayed airborne. Our little moment of crisis was over but Jock, we all knew, would have to go.

On the night Jock was transferring to his new crew, he came to the Melrose men's Nissen hut to say goodbye. Woolf: 'There was only me there and, as we shook hands, Jock broke down in tears. 'I wanted tae fly wi' ye. And I wanted tae die wi' ye.' A couple of months later we heard that Jock had been killed, on his second Op.'

A very tall, lean and fit fellow called Ted Selfe appeared at Wigsley, a flight engineer who had converted from ground crew on a Spitfire squadron. His mechanical experience appealed, as did his happy, optimistic attitude. His fine singing voice became an asset to crew morale as he combined with Bob Woolf over the intercom in perfect two-part harmony to provide Melrose and his men with their very own version of the BBC's *Music While You Work*.

Woolf: We were returning from a cross-country one dark early morning when a Stirling, right behind ours but slightly higher, met another one head on. The sky filled with the red and yellow light of the massive explosion. It was a fireball, a huge fireball. There were pieces of blazing aircraft thrown in every direction. As if that wasn't enough of a shock, we had some gargled comments on the intercom when Dougie and Ted, and Ernie in the rear turret, by the light of the fire saw another Stirling pass directly underneath us, no more than thirty yards away. Our skipper was able to make a decent landing shortly afterwards, which was a tribute to him and his skill and discipline, but he was one silent and shaken captain, and so were we all as we handed in our parachutes and waited to find out which of our friends had perished in those flames.

Stuttgart, 1 March. There was a lot of cloud all the way and amazingly, out of 544 Lancs and Halifaxes, only four were lost and the raid did serious damage to Bosch works, Daimler-Benz and what was left of the railway station. At least one fighter pilot could see through the clouds; he saw Glover, there with his usual crew including Frank Belben.

We'd finished our bombing run, slow, straight and level, and were turning for home when Harry (Wood, rear gunner) shouted 'Corkscrew port, go'. Lou put her into the dive and as he did, our cockpit canopy disappeared. The whole aircraft was riddled. How the rest of the crew weren't killed I don't know. Nobody was hit. I'd been standing up when the shells hit the canopy and the dive flung me back and threw me against the main spar. I was a bit dazed, frankly, and I crawled down to my position and saw that the starboard inner tank was losing petrol very fast. The self-sealing we had was helpful but no good if you got cannon shells through. The rear gunner could smell petrol, which they always could if you had a leak, so I cross-fed all the engines onto the leaking tank. Of course, you have to watch that or you'll empty the thing and all the engines'll stop, and you have to use up the other inner tank to balance the aircraft.

We'd lost ten thousand feet and hundreds of gallons of petrol, and I had to make an assessment of how long we could keep airborne. We'd normally have been going back in the stream on a set course but we didn't have the fuel, so we had to go directly from A to B on our own and hope we weren't attacked again. So John (Middleton, navigator) had to work out the best route allowing for the winds, and I had to work out if we could make it at certain revs at a low height. We all discussed if we should bale out or have a go. We got to a fighter station, West Malling, in Kent.

A big day for the squadron was 9 March, a specialised raid, a new kind of raid in a small, select force, and a long distance one to the aircraft factory at Marignane, near Marseille, nine and a half hours. Squadron CO Wingco Porter led a force of 44 Lancs, including 11 from No. 9. They'd had some practice on time and distance runs bombing from what was, to Berlin habitués, low level at around 8,000 feet but they had no real notion that they were about to meet the concept of raid management.

Lasham: It was a moonlight night and we usually stood down for the moon, and Porter was master bombing it, which was something entirely new to us because it hadn't really been tried since Peenemünde, before our time. Porter dropped a red spot fire from 6,000 feet and got it thirty yards from the aiming point.
ORB: The target was well marked by the leading crew, as a result of which a most successful concentrated attack was made. Bombs were seen to fall among factory buildings and many fires were left burning. Quite a number of good photographs were obtained. Little or no opposition was encountered.
Lasham: On the way back, after we'd got over the high ground we flew over France at two hundred feet all the way and thoroughly enjoyed it. Somebody was flashing VE signals on his downward identification lamp. We climbed when we got to the coast, of course, but we saw no fighters, no searchlights, no ack-ack, nothing. Piece of cake.

Stuttgart, 15 March, had them fly a roundabout route via the Swiss border to avoid the fighters, and it worked until they got to the target where Squadron Leader Backwell-Smith was spotted by Heinz Roekker, a *Luftwaffe* ace with many kills, in a Ju88. This kill was different from the usual pattern of stalk, shoot, and watch her go down in flames.

Roekker: My attack was at 23.55, to the west of Stuttgart. We came in from behind and below using our front guns. We saw hits but the aircraft did not catch fire. The pilot pushed her into a nose-dive then climbed, then turned sharply to port losing height, as the English pilots were trained to do in the aptly named corkscrew which was a successful defensive tactic. In pursuit of him, I attacked the fuselage with our rotating gun and hit the aircraft again but could not see any flames. The rear gunner did not shoot back, so either he had been killed in the first attack or he or his hydraulics had been disabled and he could no longer turn the heavy weapon machinery. The (mid-upper) turret gunner gave defensive fire but it went wide.

Finally, I lost sight of the enemy. It was the only time I failed to see my attack through to the end and confirm its success visually, therefore the kill was only provisionally awarded.

It might have been provisional for Heinz Roekker but it was definite for most of the crew. The w/op and the gunners were dead in the aircraft. The navigator and bomb aimer did not survive their parachute jumps. Skipper and engineer did.

> 'My interest in women is purely psychological'
> P/O Walsh

Stuttgart was Lasham's last with No. 9. He and his crew, not all of them terribly keen, transferred to Pathfinders and 97 Squadron. 'At this time of the war we were virtual certainties for a second tour if we got through our first. Some of the boys were reluctant, thinking that they might not get caught for a second, but I was sure of it. A second tour with Pathfinders was only fifteen Ops, we could stay together as a crew, we could get it over with, and we all got promotion by one rank. Seemed like a good idea at the time.'

At the time, in Pathfinders, was F/Lt William Alexander Meyer DFC, of 9 Squadron 1942/43, of U-Uncle with the pawnbroker's sign, who had been interested to see the buildings of Berlin illuminated by the flashes of the guns that were firing at him. He'd completed a tour and was flying on his second with a fully decorated crew. Every one of them had a DFC or a DFM, which made not a jot of difference when a nightfighter intercepted them forty miles from the target and sent them to their deaths.

Bob Lasham would be luckier. He'd end up with over fifty Ops, insisting that he kept going until all his crew had their forty-five, and all his pathfinding would be done on special attachment to 5 Group, or Cochrane's Private Air Force as it was known after its commander, Air Vice Marshal Cochrane.

Glover and his men were back for Frankfurt, 22 March, and a shaky do it was with 27 down. Jubb was lost, and Manning with the station commander, Group Captain Pleasance on board as a passenger. Although liable to get in a lather when under pressure, Shorty Pleasance was generally well regarded, a nice old boy, approachable. He'd done his years of Empire duties on the North West Frontier and was recently come from running a large part of the pilot training programme in Canada. With no need to go on Ops at all, this was his third trip to keep in touch with what his boys were facing routinely.

For someone following a normal kind of career, four months would be considered hardly getting your feet under the table. For Angus Jubb, after arriving on squadron in November, it was four months of constant raids over Germany. That constituted more formative experience than most men would want to see in several lifetimes. Although he'd had several different flight engineers, the rest of the crew were originals who all died with him.

Manning, the eleventh of WS/J's ex-captains to be lost, had been there a month longer than Jubb. He might have been justified in believing he was through it, especially considering what happened on his second trip, all that time before, when they were attacked by four fighters at once.

SECRET No 9 Squadron Combat Report
22/23 October 1943. Kassel. Lancaster B. Captain: F/O Manning.
MU and RG both sighted a Dornier 217, 300 yards starboard quarter up. RG ordered corkscrew starboard. Both gunners and E/A opened fire. As the E/A's fire passed above our A/C, the navigator, standing in the astrodome, sighted a second E/A port quarter up at 400 yards. As he warned the gunners the E/A opened fire and hit the Lanc all along the port side, killing the MU (Sgt Provis), disabling the RG and slightly injuring the navigator (F/O Hearn). As those two E/As broke away, the navigator saw two Ju88s closing in, one on either beam down. They fired but missed. Pilot continued to corkscrew throughout these attacks which happened almost simultaneously. Hydraulic pipes below pilot's seat severed.

They got away to fly Op after Op. Gunner John Zammit, without a skipper and crew since Mair went down in the October, replaced Gilbert Provis and had his sentence suspended until he flew with Manning to Frankfurt. This was the middle one of three raids, which, with the USAAF attacking during the day, more or less finished the place. A German report stated 'their combined effect was to deal the worst and most fateful destruction to Frankfurt, a blow that simply ended the existence (of the city)' which, for Manning, Jubb, Hearn, Zammit and the others, was the cause to die for.

Likewise not coming home was a Halifax of 578 Squadron. A Ju88 caught it and the crew jumped at 17,000 feet to be taken prisoner, plus their passenger, their station commander, ex-9 Squadron, ex-Loch Ness, ex-top corridor, Group Captain N W D Marwood-Elton, now a POW with all the rest.

On 24 March, 800 went to Berlin. Horne had his near incredible night in Lonesome Lola and for the rest it was not good at all. Of the 800, 72 were lost including 46 Lancs, a rate of 9 per cent. Strong winds blew them about, the stream divided into streamlets which strayed all over, even into the Ruhr, and the flak men had a great night of it. This was the last major offensive in the battle for the Big City. The Big City was a mess but not a write-off. Many, many aircraft had been lost, over 600, with three thousand men killed and 750 taken prisoner or, looked at another way, 25 entire squadrons in sixteen attacks.

Berlin and battles were the last things on the mind of F/Lt Les Bull DFC, the same Les Bull who'd flown his first tour with 9 Squadron in 1940, by now known as Johnny after the portly, waistcoated chap who supposedly represented the British spirit. Bull was at the exit hatchway of a tunnel called Harry, which he, Conk Canton and hundreds of other inmates had built over many painstaking months at Stalag Luft III. His job was to open the hatch, climb out, lie in the snow and control the escapes of the first lot of men. British bulldog spirit was in great demand just then because the hatch wouldn't open, swollen in the wet, and when they did manage it Bull popped his head out to find that the tunnel, instead of emerging in the woods, was three yards or more short. Everybody would have to crawl across open ground, in full view of the guards in the tower if they happened to be looking.

Bull solved the problem with a system of rope tugs, one end of the rope tied to the tunnel ladder, the other in his hand as he lay in the undergrowth at the edge of the woods. Everything went well at first if much too slowly, until the air-raid sirens signalled the Berlin raid sixty miles away and all the camp lights were switched off. Their tunnel lights went off too but at least it was black dark outside. More men pushed themselves along the tunnel floor on the little trolley cart running on wooden rails and it came to the turn of Sq/Ldr Tom Kirby-Green, Bull's contemporary in those early 9 Squadron days and now more anxious than he had ever been to meet his old pal again at the end of the tunnel. Judging by the passionate letter he'd written that morning to his wife Maria, his thoughts of her would have been making him utterly determined to succeed.

He was a big man, Tom Kirby-Green, six feet four and still big after months of Stalag diet, and when he unbalanced and derailed his trolley in mid-journey he dislodged some of the planks lining the tunnel. The roof caved in. Kirby-Green was entirely buried except for his head and it was a good hour before he was free and the tunnel repaired. The Lancs and Halifaxes had turned away from Berlin by this time and were into their next round of battles with the nightfighters, the lights were back on and around fifty men, including 9 Squadron's Jimmy James at Number 39, had gone through the tunnel: 'I stood at the bottom of the exit shaft and looked up and saw stars framed in the rough outline of the hole twenty feet above me. There had been much toil but worth every moment, I thought as I climbed the ladder.'

'There were so many aircraft
over the target the other night
that I couldn't keep out of the slipstream'
F/Lt Kirby-Green

James and a group of colleagues had a three-and-a-half hour walk in the perishing cold, through woods and open country, to a tiny rural railway station, while back at the tunnel there was another disaster, a second roof fall. Under it this time, and it seemingly had to be, was another 9 Squadron man, Cookie Long. Luckily the collapse wasn't anything like as bad as the first and more men struggled through until the first signs of dawn around 05.00 when they decided to stop. The eightieth man was about to emerge but discovery came before the halt was called. The previous three and the eightieth were marched back into camp by a truly astounded sentry and the escapers' expected four-hour start, between dawn and roll-call, was gone.

Graham Welsh: That left 120 of us who didn't get out, including me. My job until then had been intelligence, working in a team led by Roman Marcinkus, the only Lithuanian RAF officer in the camp. I knew German and so I was assigned to read the daily newspapers from Berlin, Frankfurt, Hamburg and Vienna for any little snippets about transport and communications which might help us make our escape good. Now we prayed that our work had been good enough. Roman was out, anyway.
Jimmy James: We were supposed to be a party of twelve on leave from a woodmill. The booking clerk at the little station couldn't believe we wanted twelve tickets but we got them eventually and travelled without incident to Boberöhrsdorf.

By 06.00 a *Grossfahndung* (hue and cry throughout Germany) had been ordered and every available member of the armed forces, the police forces and the local militias were out looking for British and Commonwealth airmen and more from occupied Europe including Poles, Norwegians and Dutch, 76 altogether. Kirby-Green was buying a ticket at Sagan station when they caught quite a few of the others while he managed to make it a little further. Jimmy James was away too, climbing through waist-deep freezing snow up the mountains that lay between him and the Czech border. Survival in thin clothes seemed unlikely. A tactical switch was made, to a railway station at Hirschberg.

As we (James and Greek airman Nick Skanziklas) approached the ticket office I saw two figures move towards us. We converged at the barrier. A policeman in teapot helmet and a civilian stood in front of us. We produced our passes confidently on demand but the policeman merely glanced at them, put them in his pocket, inspected the contents of our packs, and said 'Komm mit'. I protested that we were foreign workers on legitimate business and that our old mothers were waiting to see us, but we were marched away.

The end was almost inevitable. In twos and threes and fours they were rounded up. On 27 March, the score of escapers held at Sagan's town jail were taken to another jail at Görlitz where they were interrogated singly and, in the cells, found more of their fellows. It seemed they were not going back to camp yet. They were being collected.

Hitler, in a mad rage, had ordered that all the escapers were to be shot. Göring, with practical objections, succeeded in modifying this to more than half and the executions began, 29 March, with shootings of twos and threes. Les Bull was among the first day's cull, and Tom Kirby-Green who had been picked up at Zlin in Moravia (modern Czech Republic). He was to be taken by car to Ostrava but they stopped on the way and shot him in the back. Later eight of Jimmy James's woodmill party were shot, including Nick Skanziklas.

The war was still on and if that last Berlin night was bad, 30 March was terrible. It was another very big raid with 795 bombers attacking Nürnburg, a city not as famous for its industrial might as its special place in Nazi hearts. The defences were expected to be light and the weather was forecast as suitable for a moonlight raid; cloud to hide in on the way there but clear over the target. Warnings from a Met Flight aircraft changed the forecast but the raid was not scrubbed. Through a combination of erratic winds and human errors the force became scattered and the fighters were waiting. Over eighty were lost on the way in. Me110s with new improved Lichtensteins and *Schrägemusik* had a wonderful time.

Bombers that got there did virtually no damage to the target. Something like one hundred ended up bombing Schweinfurt by mistake. Duncan, now a Flying Officer: 'It is thought that position C was undershot due to considerable fighter activity along the route south of the Ruhr and to consequent defensive manoeuvres. It was considered that target had been reached early and no TIs or flares were seen and the area was orbited and bombs seen to be dropped by 40–50 aircraft. After orbiting another attack was seen in progress in the distance and it was thought that the correct target had not been identified. Time did not permit the latter to be attacked during the period during which PFF were operating and so bombs were dropped on the area orbited subsequently considered to be Schweinfurt.'

Duncan was attacked by a FW190 and then again by an Me110 (considerable fighter activity) but corkscrewed his way out of it (consequent defensive manoeuvres). He flew around and around above a well-defended city. A combination of unfavourable circumstances, confusion and devotion to duty took him into a fine old mess, in common with virtually all of his colleagues.

Frank Belben: 'That was a very stressful flight in, and even worse over what we thought was the target. From what we saw, we knew it was a night of heavy losses. We had a couple of fighter attacks but our gunners drove them off and we never got hit.' Crews reported seeing so many going down in flames that they could only suppose it would be them next. P/O Ginger Craig was in G-George.

SECRET No 9 Squadron Combat Report
Place: 50.33°N-08.00°E. Time: 00.37hrs. Height: 20,500ft. Speed: 155 RAS. Course: 082°T. Target: Nürnburg.
Rear gunner (Sgt Smith) sighted a Ju88 flying astern and below at 200 yards range. He ordered the pilot to corkscrew to port and opened fire. Only the right-hand guns fired and after 10 rounds there was a stoppage . . . while the Lancaster was still corkscrewing the E/A . . . opened fire at about 600 yards and broke away to starboard quarter level, the mid-upper gunner (Sgt May) opening fire at the breakaway at about 150 yards. Almost immediately the E/A attacked from the starboard quarter, MU gunner ordered corkscrew to starboard . . . five minutes later our aircraft was again attacked by an unidentified and unseen aircraft apparently from starboard quarter down.

Damage to own aircraft: Rear turret shot up, fire in rear of fuselage doused by M/U gunner who collapsed through lack of oxygen. RG fired 10 rounds. MU fired 200 rounds.

F/O Smith in T escaped the attentions of an Me410 by a combination of evasive action and the rear gunner, Sgt Roberts who fired 600 rounds. In V, P/O Forrest and his crew also had cause to remember Nürnburg, being attacked at exactly the same time as Craig and not very far away. Had they had the leisure for such things, they must have seen each other's tracer in the night sky.

SECRET No 9 Squadron Combat Report
Place: 50.30°N-08.40°E. Time: 00.37hrs. Height: 20,000ft. Speed: 155 RAS. Course: 082°T. Target: Nürnburg.
The Rear Gunner sighted a Ju88 at 250 yards starboard quarter down and gave the order Corkscrew Starboard. The E/A developed the attack from the position where it was first seen but did not open fire. The Rear Gunner fired about 500 rounds. The E/A was not seen to break away. Soon after our A/C had resumed course it was attacked and damaged by an A/C which only the pilot saw as it broke away to port low down. He identified it as a Ju88 and clearly saw the green camouflage and black cross on its wing. During this attack the M/U Gunner was hit and died of his wounds during the trip. Neither of the Gunners fired during this attack as they did not see the E/A. Continued on track over target and returned in concentration.
   Weather: 3/10 cloud. Half moon approx. Good vis. Searchlights: not exposed on the A/C.
   Damage to own A/C: Two holes about 2ft square, one just forward of the Elsan, the other just aft of the MU turret. Pipe lines in the rear turret severed and a fire occurred. This was put out when the A/C went into a dive after the second attack. The leading edge of the starboard tailplane was hit and the starboard side of the fuselage aft of the MU turret was holed several times.
Damage to E/A: none claimed.
MU Gunner: F/Sgt Utting did not fire.
R Gunner: Sgt Pinchin 500 rounds.

   Scanning the night for radar traces on his Lichtenstein SN2, the long-range model unaffected by Window, was radio operator Handke in an Me110 piloted by Major Martin Drewes of III/NJG 1. They had already downed one Lancaster not ten minutes before. Now Handke had another signal; there was a Tommy at 23,000 feet, quite a climb away. The Tommy, Lancaster X of 9 Squadron skippered by F/O Ling almost at the end of his tour, droned on. Well over one hundred miles to go yet. They'd seen the flaming torches of falling bombers. They knew there were fighters about. Where was the cloud they'd been promised?
   The bomber crew searched the sky but they didn't see Major Drewes. He was underneath with his *Schrägemusik*. He aimed with his usual care, fired, and his guns jammed. Ling instantly put the Lanc into a sharp bank then a steep dive. Minutes passed as he corkscrewed away from his invisible opponent. They'd thrown the fighter off. They must have thrown him off. No more shots, no sightings. Indeed, Drewes and Handke had had extreme difficulty in keeping up with Ling's aerobatics and several times they

thought they'd lost him but there he was again, settled into normal flight and clearly visible. Drewes dropped back a little, and down a little. He had no music to play so he lined up his Tommy, pulled up into a steep climb and raked the Lanc with his two nose-mounted cannon. Hundreds of 20mm shells hammered into the great bird's body. Immediately the Lanc was on fire and diving. One parachute came out. Seconds later there was an explosion. Bits of the burning aircraft fell into the woods of the Vogelsberg; most of it and six dead bodies hit the ground near Butzbach. The navigator was the only survivor.

Attempting a blow to Nazi morale rather than serious demolition of war production, the final score was one hundred bombers lost, including a few which struggled home but were too badly damaged ever to fly again.

Norman Wells: I don't know what made a brilliant pilot. We thought Phil Plowright was brilliant. Possibly they all were, or most of them, but most of them weren't lucky. When we were in L, our own aircraft, we were hit and came home on three, then we went on leave and she went down with another crew.* We went to Marseille in B, got a shell in the tail, came home, gave her back to her former owner, very experienced pilot** and down he went with the group captain on board, and we were there on the same Op, just like them, in among it.

We were nominated PFF Supporter for Stuttgart, which was muggins who flew in front of the pathfinders to draw the fire so they could drop their TIs undisturbed. After doing that, you had to go around and come in again to bomb. We were in J-Johnny, never got a mark on that Op, yet Backwell-Smith, a squadron leader, top man, FTR. Nürnburg, that dreadful, dreadful night, we never got shot at but we damned nearly got rammed by another Lanc heading for the same cloud as we were. He was so close we could hear his engines as well as our own. I went to Berlin seven times, Frankfurt three times. Goodness knows how many went down on those trips.***

*Froud and crew
**F/O Manning.
***Frankfurt: 53 Lancasters lost on those three Ops. Berlin: 243 on those seven.

Another time, we were flying almost wingtip to wingtip with this Lanc, straight and level on our bombing runs, and he had a flak shell burst behind him at the perfect height, then another in front, and the third hit him right amidships and he just went up in a cloud of bits. You were not supposed to deviate from your run in any circumstance. If you did, it would show on your photograph, it would be at a funny angle, and the skipper would be up before the CO. So that chap didn't deviate and they got the chop. He was close enough so even in the dark I could have taken his squadron letters, if I'd known that was going to happen. Everyone was supposed to report any losses he saw, give what information he could to the navigator. Usually it was no more than aircraft going down so many yards to starboard. I could have been really precise on that one.

In among all of this, aircrew still had their unfounded concern over the safety of the photoflash bomb and Mick Maguire decided to sort it out. He and his men took one to pieces, checked and rechecked the safety measures and pronounced them good. To reassure the flyers, he instituted a system by which he personally delivered the photoflashes after bombing up was finished and fitted them in their chutes himself.

A WAAF called June Taylor, one of the drivers, thought she would give me a hand loading these things in the truck. Before I could stop her she'd walked up to one in the fusing shed and then a very curious thing happened. WAAFs wore lace-up shoes, and the metal ferrule on the end of one of June's laces caught in the arming wire and the bomb went 'Wheeeeeee!' She was petrified. I bent down and put it to maximum delay and unscrewed the fuse. It was perfectly safe but June wasn't to know that and I was going to teach her not to mess about with bombs. I ran outside and put it somewhere I could get it later to re-fuse it, and came back in to find June still white as a sheet. She didn't need any more teaching. I finished loading the truck and she drove us around the dispersals. Next day I was the bravest man on the station.

Another time there was a thousand-pounder on the runway. A Lanc from another squadron had landed, opened his bomb doors and out it fell. We had a drill for this and we knew what we were doing and, if we did it properly, there was no danger. We had to be bomb disposal experts as well as armourers. Anyway, June drove us out and we started. I said to her, get yourself out of the way. Go to Flying Control. And if you hear a bang, don't bother to come back.

The first aerial attack in preparation for the Allied invasion of Europe had been on a railway centre, 6 March, and now the whole emphasis changed, especially for 5 Group and 9 Squadron. The job became mainly transport and armaments targets in France, tactical as opposed to area bombing, minimising civilian casualties, with a consequent increase in the responsibilities of the markers and the Master Bomber.

'He was a bloody fine pilot.
I gave him his Dual Night and Day'
Sq/Ldr Adams

There were three key elements of strategy necessary for the perfect invasion of the French coast. The enemy had to be prevented from being able to reinforce his armies; the landing place had to be rendered defenceless before the landing; and the enemy must not be strong enough to prevent the invaders from breaking out and advancing into open country. Perfection could not be achieved but Bomber Command was expected to create circumstances as near to it as possible. The first task was the complete paralysis of the railway system from the Rhine to the French coast and a list was drawn up of 79 targets in France, Belgium and Germany. The US 8th Air Force took on a large slice, the Allied Expeditionary Air Force took some, the US 15th Air Force took a few, and Bomber Command took the most. Marking was usually by high-flying Oboe Mosquitos although sometimes it was done visually at low level.

The rest of Germany was not entirely left alone and crews could find themselves flying on moonless nights to German targets and on moonlit nights to French ones: railways, armaments factories, garrisons, the logistics and resources which would be important to German counter-measures against the invaders. In 1943, the bombers had done six times the business their predecessors had. Now the rate was upped again, and 1944 would see twice as many heavy bombers as in 1943, doing three times the work.

Nevertheless, it was thought at HQ that raids over France would be much less dangerous for aircrew than flying over Germany. This would never do. Why, after originally defining a tour as two hundred operational flying hours then as thirty Operations, almost all of them over Germany, it seemed to some of the brass hats that occupied France was offering a new kind of tour, of thirty picnics. The prospect of waste, of seeing a crew transfer to safety, tour expired, after thirty Sunday School outings was too awful and so a French Op would henceforth count only as one third of a German one.

Such a raid was to an aircraft repair factory at Toulouse, 5/6 April. No. 9 Squadron sent ten Lancasters in a 5 Group-only attack of 150 aircraft. Wing Commander Leonard Cheshire, one of the great flyers of the war, marked the factory at low level. He flew in a Mosquito, judging the marking and acting as master bomber. The force destroyed the factory without much damage to the French town, using an 8,000lb blast bomb, a light case, high capacity weapon, or double cookie, which was the most powerful at that time.

Wingco Cheshire was a miracle. He'd started bombing in 1940 and had himself busted down from group captain so he could take operational command of 617 Squadron, his fourth tour. He would go ahead of the Lancasters and about ten miles from the target he would drop a white marker. The Lancasters would circle this marker while Cheshire went in to mark the target visually, and he went in very, very low. When he was happy he would call up the bomber pilots on radio-telephone, perhaps with a special instruction, bomb X feet to starboard or Y feet to port. The defences usually included heavy machine gun and light flak positions, to which Cheshire's ultra-low flying made him especially vulnerable so another development was needed. A pair of Lancasters would go in first, before Cheshire, and drop containers of 24-ounce anti-personnel mines to silence the machine guns. Partly because of their excellent and very experienced navigators, Russ Gradwell and Phil Plowright of 9 Squadron were the pilots selected out of 5 Group for this little extra job, after which they would have to go round again to bomb with the rest.

No one told them how they should accomplish their new duty so the crews sat down in The Jolly Sailor at Bardney and talked it through among themselves. Russ and Phil were on very good terms with the owners of the pub and had been ever since Gradwell's first night on squadron, 'when I went to the pub and asked for a slice off the ham hanging behind the bar instead of my change. We decided that whoever was in front when we reached the target would act as marker and put his navigation lights on, so the other could see him and concentrate on dropping the mines accurately. As the Germans could see him also, it would be expected that the second Lanc wouldn't take too long about it before he took his turn as lit-up decoy for his pal.'

After one particularly successful application of this technique, 9 Squadron was debriefing when Cheshire came over on the scrambler telephone to thank the boys for completely silencing the guns and making his job of dropping the markers so much easier.

Gradwell: Phil Plowright replied that it should be the bombers thanking the wing commander, who was so accurate with his marking that it made their Ops worthwhile. I said that I didn't believe the Wingco dropped his markers at all, but simply leaned over the side and placed them on the ground. Cheshire was highly amused but pointed out, in that rather posh sort of haw-haw voice of his, that if Flying Officer Gradwell had ever flown a Mosquito he would know that the wings got in the way of such a procedure.

Great strides had been made in bombing accuracy. By concentrating bombers together and improving strategy and technology, large-scale destruction of the target area had become the norm. Now, in the Spring of 1944, the ultimate seemed possible: to move from wholesale unloading of bombs onto one aiming point, to giving each aircraft its own specific target, knowing that it could be hit and knowing that the master bomber would manage affairs. In Bomber Command, 5 Group were at the head of this, often being given specific targets-within-targets while mainforce wielded the sledgehammer.

Traditionally, everyone aimed for the same markers and the results were as one might expect: very heavy damage in the middle of a circular or elliptical area, with bomb fall getting more sparse the further one measured from the centre. This was inefficient. The centre as marked might not be in the right place. Targets were not necessarily circular; they could be long and thin, like a railway marshalling yard. Regardless of how accurate the marking, there would be over-kill in the middle and under-kill elsewhere.

The introduction of the master bomber made each raid a work of dreadful efficiency. Master bombers were not selected by seniority, although they did tend to be senior because they needed a great deal of experience. Coolness under many different pressures counted highly, as did a record of good luck as they had to stay over the target longer than anybody else.

Within hours of the Toulouse attack Sir Arthur Harris sent a message to Air Vice Marshal The Honourable Sir Ralph Cochrane, Air Officer Commanding 5 Group, informing him that their method of marking and directing operations was confirmed as officially approved, and that 5 Group could now operate as an independent force. This suited Cochrane. He was, as Harris put it, 'a most brilliant, enthusiastic and hard-working leader of men' or, as others put it, cold, distant and hard to know. He loved to achieve. An aristocrat, son of a Scots baron, he had been a navy pilot in the first war, an Empire defender ever since, a flight commander under Harris in Mesopotamia, and AOC 5 Group from February 1943 when Harris fired the previous incumbent. That 5 Group attained a certain pre-eminence in Bomber Command might have been ascribed by cynics to close connections between high commanders but really it was due to Cochrane's leadership, an especially difficult job because, in common with all the Group AOCs, the men he was leading kept disappearing.

Of the 76 Great Escapers only three had succeeded in disappearing from Germany: one Dutchman and two Norwegians. There were fifteen who were sent back to Sagan, four to concentration camps and Jimmy James was one of another four who disappeared in a different way.

Order for the transfer of Prominent Prisoners. The following officers, Wing Commander Day, Major Dodge, Flight Lieutenant Dowse and

Flight Lieutenant James are to be transferred to Camp 'A' Sachsenhausen. To the outside world they are to be considered as escaped and not recaptured. The Commandant and his representatives are responsible with their heads for their secure housing and treatment.

Jimmy James 'had no idea why Dowse and I were considered to be Prominent Prisoners'. Come September, these four plus the famous Commando officer Jack Churchill MC, DSO and Bar, would tunnel out yet again, and yet again be the subject of a *Grossfahndung*, and yet again be recaptured but spared execution despite Himmler's direct order.

By mid-April, the other fifty men had been shot. Some faced firing squads, half a dozen or ten at a time, but many took a bullet in the back, in secret, out of the way, or sometimes openly by the side of the *autobahn*. The favourite trick was to put a couple of them in a car, drive them supposedly to a new prison and on the way offer them the chance to take a leak. All were trying to escape or offering resistance, even when the orders for their cremation had been signed before they were dead. The last one, Cookie Long, was executed alone by the *Geheime Staats-Polizei* (Gestapo) at Breslau, 13 April. F/Lt Norman Canton DFC would be liberated by the American 3rd Army and his report on his experiences would close thus: 'During the remainder of my time at Stalag Luft III, I worked on various unsuccessful tunnelling projects.'

A full complement of 9 Squadron was due to go to Brunswick. The target would be marked by their old colleague Bob Lasham, his first in his new role.

The navigation was much better, because we had the ground-surveying radar (H2S). We didn't carry any bombs, not even a little one, only markers. When the master-bomber method came in full time for everybody, we had flares, and then spot fires, which we put on the ground as opposed to a thousand feet up. There wasn't much difference as a PFF pilot. You were still flying at 18,000 feet or so. The bomb aimer had a quite different job, operating the H2S set and dropping his markers by that, not in his normal Perspex cabinet looking through a bomb sight. He was in a warmer place behind the navigator.

Only three of 9 Squadron got away for Brunswick because the fourth in line, piloted by Jack Maule, suffered a partial undercart collapse and swung while taking off, crashing on the edge of the runway and catching fire, but it was a historic raid in other ways. It was a first-time trial for 5 Group's low level Mosquito marking on a German city and it didn't work very well.

The bombers couldn't see the markers through cloud and those dropped by H2S were a long way out.

Mick Maguire: It was our first night with this bomb load, one two thousand pounder and the rest packed with J bombs. I was in the office with Chiefy Harrison, who was earnestly filling in his private operations record book for the night before, his glasses on the end of his nose. Some of the armourers were playing cards. We were finished for the night. The squadron was taking off. So, the door opened. It was Corporal Steel, a very quiet chap, unobtrusive. He said, 'There's an aircraft burning on the runway.' The card school looked up. Chiefy looked over the tops of his glasses. I said, 'Say again?' He said, 'There's an aircraft burning on the runway.' We pelted outside, and I dashed into my superior's office and shouted, 'Aircraft burning on the runway!' and a voice from beneath the desk said 'I know.'

I thought, no help from this quarter so I dashed outside again. I could see the aircrew, running flat out, Jack Maule in the lead by a short head with the last man in his Taylor suit which made him look like a Michelin man, so he was Charlesworth the rear gunner. I counted them, they were all out. We ducked down behind something concrete when one of the electricians came up and tried to go past. Sergeant Gallant grabbed him and asked what the hell, and he said he had to get to the aircraft because he was on fire duty. We pointed out that even the regular firemen with their fire engine were waiting until the bombs went off, so he'd better do the same.

The 2,000lb HE, a smaller version of the cookie, soon exploded and sent a shower of J bombs arcing into the bomb dump. The J bomb was a new type, an incendiary inside a tube of methane, which acted like a giant flamethrower at 1,500°C.

We knew all about these J bombs. We'd had one to pieces and we'd test-fired them, so we knew they weren't going to explode. We had various kinds of fire-fighting gear all around the bomb dump so we just ran there and started putting out the fires, and the fire tender arrived with no water, and the new station CO came up, Group Captain McMullen, in his staff car. 'How's it going?' he said. 'Oh, we're beating the fires out, sir. I've got people all over the dump. Nothing to worry about.' 'Well,' he said, 'you'd better tell that to your immediate superior. He's evacuated the Waffery and the villagers are moving out with their furniture.'

There was a big explosives factory at St Médard-en-Jalles, between Bordeaux and the coast. The Lancasters of 5 Group, 68 of them, went to see to it and some of them bombed, but not 9 Squadron. There was haze over the target and quite a few fires but not, it seemed to the squadron, in the right place. They waited for the master bomber's orders, and waited, and waited. Young had an engine on fire and went home. Ginger Craig flew round and round for almost an hour, so did Horne, Keir, Pooley and others. Recent arrival Ray Cornelius orbited from 02.34 to 03.18, was hit by flak, the port inner was on fire, they put it out with the extinguisher but it was u/s, and they were last home. Everybody did get home but it all had to be done again the next night, 29 April, when only one 9 Squadron crew had to hang about.

Up ahead of the rest was Plowright in J-Johnny as windfinder, whose extra job was to assess strength and direction of the wind over the target so that adjustments could be made to the Mark 14 bombsight.

Norman Wells: We flew up and down, up and down at about 6,000 feet, being shot at, until Lucas (navigator) was happy that he'd got the wind just right, then he passed that to Harry Hannah (w/op), who sent it back to base, who worked out the numbers and transmitted those to all the 5 Group aircraft so they would know what to feed into their bombsights, which calculated accordingly. We did that, then we flew up and down some more, and we flew up and down for sixty-one minutes until the rest arrived.

When they did, hell broke loose. They bombed from between 4,000 and 6,000 feet. Mathers saw 'numerous large explosions typical of gunpowder'. Young said 'the whole area was one large inferno'. Hill saw 'the country lit up for miles around'. Clark bombed at 02.28 and saw 'six very large explosions which lit up the aircraft. After bombing, a large explosion lifted the aircraft and a further tremendous explosion was seen at 02.33.' Nobody lost and the target obliterated. Excellent.

'Everything was coming up,
from high explosive to rotten eggs'
Sq/Ldr Prichard

6

THE FLOWERS THAT BLOOM IN THE SPRING

May 1944 would be a fateful and reformative month for 9 Squadron, in several ways. Keen young men would come and go. Some of the very best would flourish, or die, like the flowers in May.

Dougie Melrose and his men were almost there. Bob Woolf: 'We went on to Syreston where we were converted to the Lancaster in seven lessons, mostly circuits and landings. Four exercises had Dougie flying solo but the star turn was Flying Officer Yackman who took us on two hours of white knuckle rides, showing us combat manoeuvres, how to get by on three engines, what to do when we had no engines at all, and so on.'

1 May: P/O Lake, AKA Puddle, took his crew on their first Op, to Toulouse. There were 402 Lancasters over France that night, and only four were lost.

3 May: P/O Maurice Bunnagar went on his first Op to a German army base at Mailly-le-Camp, depot of 21 Panzer Division and a big centre for tank training. Lou Glover was nearing the end of his tour but he and his crew were caught up on the French rule, three Ops equals one and the end seemed to be getting no nearer. They too went to Mailly, that evening in May.

Frank Belben: The fighters were there, waiting for us, before we got anywhere near the target. It was terrible. You could see aircraft going down all around you in flames, and you'd see when they hit the ground and exploded. Terrible. There were fires burning all over the place and not from bombs, from our aircraft. You had to think, am I next? Then we got to the target and the fighters were there as well.

Norman Wells: The markers had to be put down at two minutes past midnight, because the soldiers in the barracks would all be in bed by then. The time came and went and we saw no markers. Nobody knows quite what happened. There were stories about Cheshire arriving too soon, flying over and coming back late, and more about radios not working. Whatever it was, it was a disaster for us. We smashed up the barracks all right and left the town unharmed even though it was right there next door. I heard that the only French civilians killed were by a Lanc which crashed into their house.

Cheshire the perfectionist may have taken rather longer over his marking than usual but the markers were right. He sent his satisfaction to the Lancaster of the master bomber, Group Captain Laurence Deane DSO, DFC, whose VHF was being jammed by The Bing Crosby Programme or some such, and whose W/T had been set to the wrong frequency. He could not raise any of his pilots. The attackers milled about, awaiting instructions, which gave sufficient time for more nightfighters to scramble from a near-by base. Those aircraft whose skippers had decided to mill a little further away from the target escaped lightly compared to those who stayed above it, where the bombers took a dreadful pounding. Perhaps five weeks on squadron was not sufficient experience to persuade Jim Ineson to move further away from the danger area. In any case, he was among those waiting for orders who were shot down before getting them. Two of his crew got out but he and the rest, all J-Johnny graduates, did not.

> 'Do you wear your tin helmet over the target?'
> F/Lt Watts
> (before his second Dicky flight)

Ken Chamberlain, now a flight lieutenant, was there on the first Op of his second tour. He had been posted to 630 Squadron and was being skippered by a sprog sergeant pilot. 'The fighters got in among us and it was like a shooting gallery. It was (pilot) Sgt Mitchell's first trip and aircraft were dropping out of the sky all around us. He said "If they think they're going to get me they've got another think coming!" Very gung ho, I thought. I said to myself, it's not entirely up to you, my lad.'

The raid got under way when the deputy controller, Sq/Ldr Sparks of 83 Squadron, took over, but out of 346 bombers on that all-Lancaster trip, 42 were lost, including Sparks's, plus one that struggled home but was beyond repair. That part of France through which flow the Marne, the Seine and the Aube, that triangle of Champagne country, had a grandstand fireworks display as bomber after bomber plunged to earth, huge and ghastly chariots on fire. With all the disaster, the Mailly raid was a success by bombing standards. Many buildings were destroyed, ammunition dumps, dozens of tanks, and well over 350 soldiers were killed or injured, a lot of them Panzer men.

Bunnagar came back from Mailly, ready to go again. P/O Hugh Campbell arrived from training school and would have been pleased to learn that the heavy losses at Mailly had forced a rethink. French Ops would henceforth count one on a tour, not a third of one.

6 May: Bunnagar went on a modest raid – 64 Lancs and four marker Mosquitos – to an ammunition dump at Sable-sur-Sarthe. 'A number of big

explosions with debris flying 5,000–6,000 feet in the air. Target was burning well as a/c left and fires were visible for nearly half an hour.' On this day, Melrose and his men at Syreston went up in a Lanc for the first time and did Exercise No 1.

8 May: Melrose made five more exercise flights. Third trip for Bunnagar, similar sized 5 Group raid on an airfield and seaplane base at Lanveoc-Poulmic, near Brest. The Australian Hugh Campbell also went, second Dicky with Mathers. The custom was still to have second Dickies, usually after a few days' acclimatisation on squadron and a couple of cross-countries.

Lanveoc was Norman Wells's twenty-sixth Op and his thirteenth in W4964 J-Johnny. 'Mick Maguire came with us, the armaments officer. For an experiment he'd rigged up an extra gun in the belly of the aircraft, where the under-turret had been in the original design. We had a second Dicky with us as well (Sgt George Langford) so we were quite a party.'

There had indeed been a belly turret with two .303s but it was much too small to house a man, so the guns had to be fired from inside the aircraft by a gunner searching the night sky with a periscope. This was not a great deal of use; the equipment was withdrawn but not the idea of a ventral turret, which might be an answer to *Schrägemusik*. Some squadrons were instructed to have a go at fitting a single point-five-inch gun to be manned inside the aircraft and to fire through a hole in the floor.

Mick Maguire: The idea was a bit late in arriving and there didn't seem to be any special urgency or impetus behind it. Some squadrons never bothered with it at all, and point-five ammo was in short supply. We fitted it to three aircraft, including J-Johnny Walker. I flew with Phil Plowright to test it a few times. The notion suffered with the usual problem of that gun at that time. The breech mechanism left it with one up the spout after it had been fired, and the hot barrel meant that it would pop this round off at any moment. It was disconcerting at first but you got used to it and remembered to keep the thing pointing the right way.

The station commander wanted to know if the new gun was fit to go. I said, there is one thing. I want to go with it. McMullen said, 'What? You want to go on the Operation?' I said yes I did. He said, 'Have you got the time?'

At the briefing, Maguire saw that the target was Lanveoc airfield south of Brest on one of the promontories of the Cap Finistère.

There would be about sixty Lancs there altogether plus some marking aircraft. Our load was eighteen five-hundreds and a cookie. Off we

went, and we got some flak over the Channel Islands. The w/op, Harry Hannah, was not at all keen on having a big hole in the floor of J-Johnny and when he went to the Elsan he clung to the fuselage like a rock climber. Approaching the target there was a lot of light flak then suddenly we were caught by searchlights. I'd got a smoked Perspex screen over my goggles so I wasn't dazzled even though the inside of J-Johnny looked like it had been whitewashed. Phil was on his run and the bombs went, more or less as I fired at the searchlights. He and the mid-upper, Sgt Corr who was right above me, both said, 'Christ, what the hell was that?' and the searchlights went out. Now, I don't think I shot them out although everybody said I did. I think Ron Mathers, who was just behind us, had hit them with his bombs.

Home and at interrogation, Maguire went straight to the armaments table where all the gunners congregated to report any problems. Instead of the usual one man there was a whole collection of armourers, including Chiefy Harrison. 'What are you doing here?' said Maguire. 'Why aren't you in bed?' Chiefy looked up with a tear in his eye, and said, 'I thought, if you'd got killed, I'd have your toolbox.'

Harry Irons, now with 77 Squadron flying the Halifax, had a distinctly hostile attitude to that same belly gun.

We were losing so many to this upward firing gun the fighters had, so a hole was cut in the floor and a free-standing gun put in, a point five, which was supposed to surprise the Germans. They said at briefing, don't worry about your bombing, just make sure you get a fighter underneath to test this new gun. It never worked. It had a very small field of fire but mainly it was so cold, high over Germany, that the crew at the front were frozen. The draught could be at forty-five below coming up through that hole.

(while being attacked by a formation of Messerschmitts,
rear gunner to captain)
'Don't look now, sir, but I think we're being followed'

9 May: P/O Kidd, bomb aimer, who had joined 9 Squadron in March with his skipper, P/O Stafford, transferred temporarily to 59 Base. Mick Maguire was accosted by the squadron Bombing Leader, F/Lt Gilbert 'Dinger' Bell DFC. They discussed Ops, official and unofficial. Maguire was not supposed to go at all; Bell was not obliged to go but, following usual practice, would go as a spare bod if needed. He said he hadn't been for a month, since Marignane. Everybody liked old Dinger. On those nights

when the squadron wasn't operating and an impromptu party developed at the pub, with aircrew buying drinks for groundcrew, Dinger would lead the way home playing percussion on whatever was handy, singing MacNamara's Band.

10 May: P/O Stafford needed a bomb aimer instead of Kidd. Dinger Bell stepped forward. Maguire: 'In The Jolly Sailor that evening he left a pint of beer on the mantlepiece and said he'd be back for it. The Jolly Sailor had that pint of beer on the mantlepiece for a long, long time. He was very popular, Dinger.' They were shot down by a fighter over the rail yards at Lille with all crew killed. The engineer and the mid-upper were both nineteen years old.

George Langford flew his first Op and was not shot down. Plowright flew his twenty-seventh, ditto. Hugh Campbell, who had been with Mathers and seen the searchlights go out over Lanveoc, also went to Lille with his freshmen on their first. Approaching the target they and their Lanc were instantaneously transformed into a flightless fireball and all their lights went out for ever. That was some picnic, Lille, with twelve down out of eighty-five, one in every seven.

> 'This fighting in the air would be absolutely
> fascinating if it wasn't so dangerous'
>
> Anon

11 May: during the day, P/O Hallett arrived at Bardney with his crew. At night, there was an Op to Bourg Leopold, Belgium, where there was an extensive German camp. It was only three and a half hours there and back and defences were not expected to be severe. They were severe enough for Maurice Bunnagar, aged twenty like three others in his crew, after an operational career lasting eight days. A nightfighter found them near Leuven. The moon would be full over the next few nights, so no Ops.

12 May: Exercise No. 7 was five and three-quarter hours' cross-country and practice bombing for the Melrose boys and the skipper passed his heavy bomber training course at average. His efforts and 43 Stirling flying hours were certified by none other than No. 9 Squadron tour-expired veteran, Flying Officer James McCubbin DFC. So, they were ready. All pilots at this stage had had 450 hours or more flying time. Gunners had had 150 hours in the air, the others various amounts between. Melrose had 450 hours and 15 minutes and goodness knows how many classroom hours, plus 70 hours on the Link trainer.

15 May: Flying Officer James Douglas Melrose and crew were posted to Bomber Command No. 5 Group, No. 9 Squadron, RAF Bardney,

Lincolnshire, along with Pilot Officer Leslie Baker and his crew from the same training unit.

17 May: F/O Allinson was similarly posted. These new men were full of hope. Losses would be standard diet in the months to come, sometimes right in front of their eyes, sometimes of men they knew well, sometimes of men they had not had the chance to meet.

The sprogs, the new kids, watched the routine, trying to absorb the way things were done. It would be known by 11.00 if there was an Op that night. Breakfast might be fried bread and tinned tomatoes, or sausages whose ratio of meat to breadcrumb was such that margarine and wartime jam was their best accompaniment. Early breakfaster, squadron adjutant F/O Rushton, whose young son Willy would make his name in comedy, strode forth from the officers' mess every day, folders of papers under his arm, calling 'Shocking breakfast, shocking!' to anyone he saw.

Aileen Walker: 'My first customers every morning were North the weather man, Squadron Leader Summers, he was an older chap with white hair who was the engineering officer, and Rushton. They were there at quarter past eight when the official time was nine.'

Some aircrew would read the DROs, Daily Routine Orders, which announced various squadron matters and listed promotions, postings, and aircrew missing. This was the main way you found out that one of your mates from training had been shot down with another squadron. Some men would be impatient to look at a scrappy piece of paper, usually typed, sometimes handwritten, fixed with drawing pins to the several mess notice boards. Nancy Bower used to pin it in the officers' mess. The paper was grandly called Battle Order and it listed the crews who were to go on Ops. Usually, if your aircraft was serviceable, your crew was available and it wouldn't be your third on the trot, if there was an Op you would most likely be on it so the Battle Order was more confirmation than news headline.

The two flight commanders – A Flight had the top half of the aircraft alphabet, B the bottom half – would go through their lists of serviceable machines and crews before 11.00 so that when the signal came through, Ops tonight, they could decide on the best the squadron could do. Aircrew normally had leave for a week after every five Ops, which sometimes meant spare aircraft to cover for any that were temporarily out of commission.

The crews would go out to their aircraft to run up the engines and check everything, come back to the mess for some lunch and hang around waiting for the briefing to find out where they were going. After briefing, with the target announced, no telephone calls were allowed and no one was to go off the station. People did, of course, even quite eminent people like the bombing leader and the armaments officer. There were lots of holes in the fence and security, like discipline, was not a top priority for aircrew.

Later in the day, it would be bacon and egg and a half pint of a rarity, fresh milk, unless you decided to tempt fate. The system at No. 9 Squadron was that you could have bacon and egg before you went and bacon and egg when you came back, or you could have double bacon and eggs when you came back. You could not opt for double portions before you went. Obviously, if you were lost on the Op, that was one egg to which you had not been entitled.

An independent observer like the station medical officer might have noticed a pattern in the morale of these crews, these men who, whenever they flew, had to obliterate their most basic instinct, that of self-preservation, so they could do their work. Generally speaking, spirits would be at their highest when they knew nothing about it, when they were going on their first few Ops. These flights would be so full of novelty, such an amazing and mind-boggling experience, that most aircrew could cope with their fear while in the air. Fear, if it is to have an effect, needs time and space to work, which it could for hours before take-off. Aircrew on their first Ops (and on their first doses of benzedrine) might feel a frantic kind of excited horror but they didn't usually have the room in their spirits to be genuinely, gnawingly afraid. They were too busy. Flying an Op in a Lancaster was a highly complex business for every crew member and, until they got used to it, there was never a thinking moment other than about the job in hand.

If they lasted five or six Ops, spirits might stay high with relief – if we've got this far, we're going to be all right – or begin to sink as the enormity of their task became increasingly obvious. The novelty had worn off, they had become battle-scarred professionals in a short couple of weeks and, like all veterans, had come to recognise the price their profession had to pay. Perhaps the worst time for morale was around halfway through the tour, when a crew might be fully justified in thinking that their luck was due to run out. Once that dark period was passed, a devil-may-care kind of attitude could take over. The bastards haven't got me yet and they're not going to. Then, before the last few Ops of the tour, a certain dread might creep in. Are the Fates going to let me through, or are they going to let me think I'm through before having the last laugh? For some, running inside all of this was a thread of addiction, to the risk, and to the nerve-jangling exhilaration of doing something about smiting the enemy.

For inactivity, the officers' mess at Bardney was compact but comfortable, basically just another Nissen hut but with a large red-tiled fireplace, a board showing all the targets attacked and the 9 Squadron crest, a bat with wings extended inside a blue circle and a laurel wreath, surmounted by a crown. The motto beneath was *Per Noctem Volamus*, correctly translated as 'Through the night we fly' but with the additional proviso inscribed 'There's always bloody something'.

There was a large and well-stocked bar and waitress-service restaurant under the charge of Squadron Leader Burns, station adjutant.

Aileen Walker: He was the old-fashioned type, RAF since childhood, and he had standards. We were the last squadron in Bomber Command, possibly in the entire RAF, to go over to self-service. He just wouldn't have it.

Nancy Bower: In his view, officers had to be treated in a certain way and they had to have the best of everything. The food, for wartime, was outstandingly good. There was usually a breakfast menu although they might be told the night before if it was kippers or something different.

Aileen Walker: They had their rations like everybody else and the cooks had to do what they could with that. I went on a motorbike with sidecar, with the PMC (President of the Messing Committee) to Waddington to get it. Flight Lieutenant Doig, that was. But they must have had other resources. Anyway, Burns would never have stood for the bread sausages and so on that the other ranks had. We who worked in the officers' mess had a very good fringe benefit because we ate there, and we had a better class of joke to put up with if the menu said potato balls.

The sergeant cook was a chef from a London hotel and he was a dreadful man for jokes. If it was chicken, he used to make us go and ask the officers: 'Do you want stuffing?' I nudged his arm once when he was icing a cake and he said he'd get his own back and he did when I was on night duty. We were waiting for them to come home and I went in the kitchen and he was sitting there plucking a goose. I'd just washed my hair and it was still wet. 'Come and look at this,' he said, and like a fool I did and got my head covered in goosedown. And I had to stand on duty in the mess with a thousand white feathers sticking to my hair.

Another time we were entertaining a load of Yanks and Arthur, the cook, gave me a tray of sausages on sticks and said to take them round. I went in the anteroom, which was where the bar was, and they were half of them drunk, and I had to go round saying 'Chipolata, sir? Chipolata, sir?' and when I got back Arthur said where were the sticks. He wanted the sticks back. I was just a girl, I couldn't stand up to him, so I went back in and crawled about picking up all the sticks.

The sergeants' mess also had a well-stocked bar but was otherwise less well appointed. It had a large room with brown lino on the floor and a brick fireplace but the few armchairs had clearly been donated from spare stock by the local saleroom; otherwise there were wooden folding chairs, old card tables and an even older upright piano.

Most new pilots now coming on the strength were commissioned. It was felt that the skipper of a Lanc should have a rank befitting his role, also that it was potentially awkward to have the captain a mere sergeant when it was quite likely that a member of his crew would be an officer. Still, in the sergeants' mess, not everything had caught up with the new order, although a sergeant pilot lasting a decent length of time, like Plowright, Gradwell, Sheppard or Ryan, would be given his commission, asked if he wanted to settle his officers' mess bill monthly, and given his share of a batman or batwoman. The days were gone when officers automatically found themselves with a personal servant. These batpeople might bring the hut some mugs of hot water to shave in, collect and deliver the washing, keep the coal bucket full and very occasionally polish the shoes. Poached eggs, toast and coffee in bed were strictly for Pinewood Studios.

The sergeants who were members of new crews in May 1944 met gunners in the mess, bomb aimers, wireless operators and so on who were old hands but they also met Flight Sergeant Cornelius, pilot, and his all-sergeant crew, with half a dozen Ops behind them.

May was turning out to be a very merry month for staff recruitment. By the 19th, nine pilot freshers had brought their crews to the university of Bardney. P/O Campbell, 3 May to 10 May, had already gone down and five more would be arriving, making eleven new officer pilots (including the one dead) and three new sergeant pilots altogether, plus full crews.

Maguire was called into the Group Captain's office and shown a signal from HQ 5 Group: Technical officers will not fly on Operations under any circumstances.

I said to McMullen, does this mean I can't fly any more? He said no, it means that your name must not appear on the battle order any more. Next time I went our Nav Leader, Jock Rumbles, who'd been on the Dambusters raid with Munro, said to me 'You flying?' I said I intended to do a few, as many as my day job allowed. He said that he was going to keep on with it and if Group rang up on a particular night for him, the call would be put through to me. I was to tell them that he was in Lincoln collecting his laundry.

It had never been the practice to wear medal ribbons on uniform tunics. When it became so, Jock Rumbles DSO, DFC sewed his on with black knitting wool. He was a surveyor by civilian profession, not a seamstress.

19 May: P/O Worner was another fresh pilot arriving on the strength.

The Handley Page Heyford was a weird, long-nosed, sad-looking creature entirely useless for the war which was about to break out. Standing by in case the September 1938 meeting between Hitler and Chamberlain failed to bring peace in our time, Heyford crews of No. 9 Squadron were briefed to attack targets in the Ruhr, knowing they would not be able to get back. They were issued with passports, money and maps and told they would have to bale out over Holland.

Some people realised the parlous state of the pre-war RAF, even if the British Government did not.

ANOTHER ONE FOR DR. GOEBBELS' LIBRARY OF WAR PICTURES: One of Britain's fleet of mighty war 'planes. This monster of the skies flies aloft at nearly 52 m.p.h. and is declared capable of crossing the Channel. Trained aeronauts are in charge of the machines. The principle of the engine is that of internal combustion. Britain now boasts proudly that she has not one steam-driven air-o'-plane left in the Royal Air Force. Her fleet of the up-to-date machines pictured here is upwards of 40. Each pilot is a Master of Arts and has reached the qualified age of 65.

No. 9 Squadron pilots pictured in front of a Heyford in 1938. Sgt Charles Bowen is first left, back row; P/O Grant is second left seated; P/O Bob Turner is seated far right. All three would feature in their country's first modern air battle. Another name to note is P/O James Smalley, standing third from left.

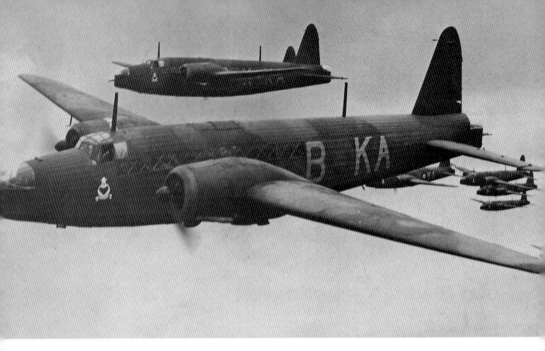

At last, a modern aircraft – Wellingtons of 9 Squadron in the summer of 1939 with old letters KA which changed to WS soon after the war began. L4275 KA/H, centre beyond B, was lost at Brunsbüttel, September 4 1939, with F/Sgt Albion John Turner and all his crew.

Above: The first air battle of the war, Brunsbüttel, September 4 1939, as told by George Davies. The cartoonist seems to have been illustrating only that part of the story featuring Grant's section of three Wellingtons, and forgetting about the two lost out of three in Sq/Ldr Lamb's section.

Left: Aircraftman First Class Charles Driver, the first DFM of the war, was an 18-year-old fitter/rigger in ground crew when he found himself seconded to front gunner in a 9 Squadron Wellington at Wilhelmshaven, December 18 1939. His heroics on that Op might have earned an officer a somewhat higher award

A picture taken by Sgt Wood in F/O Smalley's Wellington, 6 June 1940, shows the potential of the night camera. The observer/bomb aimer dropped photoflash 'bombs' with his ordnance, and the camera shutter was timed to open as they flashed. Here are illuminated two bomb-bursts in a field at Rosières-en-Santerre in the Somme, unopposed by the guns in the farmyard which was a secondary target of opportunity because intense searchlight activity had prevented all twelve of the squadron's aircraft attacking the primary. Towards the end of 1941, the Butt Report's analysis of such photographs would prove just how badly Bomber Command was doing in the early years of the war.

A Line Book entry for the squadron's illustrious adjutant in 1941 shows a lamentable lack of respect for someone, unique in the officers' mess, who had met Hitler. Boothby had also campaigned before the war for a big increase in the strength of the RAF and had been rebuffed by Chamberlain. Coming from the Ministry of Food, where he served under Lord Woolton, to one of our crack operational bomber squadrons, where he served under Wingco Wasse DFC, Bob Boothby responded with his natural cheer, charm and gusto. One day he would be Baron Boothby of Buchan and Rattray Head; meanwhile, the Penelopes of the world had to watch out.

Pilot Sgt McKeen and observer Sgt Bothwell were at Wilhelmshaven, July 9 1942 with ten others and were annoyed that German flak and searchlights on their photograph 'obscured some of the detail'.

Sq/Ldr G S 'Tubby' Fry DFC (left),
flight commander on his second tour
through late 1942 and early 1943,
lived through his war. Another
second-tour man, Wingco Pat Burnet
DFC (right) became squadron CO on
12 April 1943 and was awarded the
DSO in the October. He later became
head of Air Ministry intelligence when
the war was cold and the enemy
Soviet Russia.

P/O James 'Cookie' Long as a new pilot at
training school in 1940 before joining No. 9
Squadron (right), and as a prisoner in Stalag
Luft III before taking part in The Great
Escape (above). Cookie Long was the last of
the fifty escapers to be executed, by the
Gestapo at Breslau, 13 April 1943.

This is what bombing could and would do, from 1943 on. The cities of Bremen and Essen (below) are but two examples of the terrible efficiency of the bombers. By the end of the war, around fifty German cities would have less than half of their buildings left standing.

Sq/Ldr Murray Hobbs DFC and crew, plus a second Dicky F/O Sams, died in ED831 WS/H, 25 June 1943, Gelsenkirchen. Climbing in first is the rear gunner, F/Sgt Bill Slater, before their Op to La Spézia, 23 June.

F/Lt Dicky Bunker DFC and his lucky swagger stick completed a tour in Hampdens with 83 Squadron and another in Lancasters with No. 9. He is pictured in ED700 WS/O-Orange after the third Hamburg raid in July 1943. Ahead of O lay many adventures with a watery end on her 50th Op. Ahead of Dicky Bunker lay 620 Squadron, Arnhem, and 190 Squadron as CO. Wing Commander Richard Henry Bunker DSO, DFC and Bar, would be killed, 20 April 1945, after taking off in a damaged Stirling.

The motto on JA852 WS/L says 'Let's go upstairs'. Alas for P/O Bob
Ord and his victory sign, and his crew of Sgt George Palmer, F/O
Edward Davies, and Sgts Tom Graham, John Wilson, Rowland
Williams and Gordon Fowler, there was nothing funny about
Mannheim, 23 September 1943 when they were all killed in this
Lancaster on only their second Operation.

Taken by the technician unloading the operational camera from their Lancaster,
this shows Sgt Doolan's crew. From the left: Baines – mid upper, Buckley –
bomb aimer, Pratt – engineer, Chappell – w/op, Doolan – pilot, Cramp –
navigator, Robinson – rear gunner. Reginald 'Robbie' Robinson was killed while
they were mining over the Baltic, 8 January 1944. With the whole of the turret
and rear fuselage on fire, 'Chap' Chappell dragged what was left of Robbie back
into the body of the aircraft and Doolan somehow got them home. Harry Irons,
still with Ops to do after Dick Stubbs had finished, volunteered as replacement.

No. 9's first losses of 1944. F/Sgt Geoffrey Ward and crew came on squadron in the summer of 1943 and they were all still together when they died on their twentieth Op, on the way to their sixth Berlin, 2 January 1944. From the left: back row, Ward, F/Sgt George James – bomb aimer, Sgts George Bedwell – w/op, Eric Keene – navigator; front row, Sgts Willard Doran – rear gunner, Norman Dixon – MU gunner, Jack Sutton – flight engineer. Norman Dixon was 19 years old.

F/O Albert Manning and crew, home after Stettin, 5 January 1944, in W4964 WS/J, her 41st Op. From the left: navigator F/O James Hearn, Manning, rear gunner F/Sgt 'Pinky' Hayler, mid-upper gunner Sgt John Zammit, flight engineer Sgt Bill Burkitt, w/op F/Lt A G Newbound standing in for F/Sgt G T M Caines. Just visible behind Manning is Canadian bomb aimer F/Sgt Peter Warywoda. The skipper and most of this crew, near the end of their tour, fell at Frankfurt, 22 March 1944.

Paddy Ervine (centre), debriefing after Stettin, 5 January 1944. Note the plentiful mugs of tea and the authentic Period intelligence officer (right).

Sgt Preston, having avoided Bunnagar's loss, joined Maule for a difficult and dangerous Op to Tours. It was difficult because the target, the rail yards, was in the centre of town and they had to avoid killing French people. It was especially dangerous, like Mailly had been, because the master bomber kept them hanging about. He wouldn't let the next wave bomb until he was quite satisfied that the previous wave hadn't hit anything French civilian.

Mick Maguire: The squadron CO, Porter, said he wanted a practice-bomb carrier in the front end of his bomb bay in place of two five-hundreds. He was going to make two bombing runs, the first with smoke bombs to check the wind. That's the kind of man he was. He was going to stick out his neck and his crew's necks for the sake of the job.

F/Sgt Halshaw went to Tours, second Dicky with Squadron Leader Pooley, P/O Baker went with Clark, Hallett went with Hancock, Allinson with W/Cdr Porter, and Melrose went with P/O Plowright in W4964 WS/J on her sixty-sixth Op.

Plowright had lived through some of the worst times of the war. He'd done six Berlins and was now very near the end of his appointed task. He only had a couple more Ops to do and he would be posted away from the battle.

21 May: the battle order on the mess wall showed that nineteen Lancasters would be on Ops that night. The captains were: Maule, Mathers with Worner second Dicky, Glover, Ryan, Gradwell, Plowright, Clark, Young, Reeve, Lake, Langford, Cornelius, Hill, Hancock, Redfern, and debutants Halshaw and Hallett. Also appearing for the first time were Baker in WS/N and, in WS/Y, Melrose.

The tension began immediately, in everyone who read their names. One crewman would feel less tense as he progressed and did more Ops. In another, the tension would increase as the trips were racked up. For four crews today, the tension was new. This was their first Operation. Here it was. Here was the day they had trained so long and hard for. They had proved satisfactory to their instructors but they could not guess how well they would function under fire.

They already knew about flying three or four miles high, in bitter cold, at night, with nothing but the few words in their intercom headphones to connect them to the living world. Outside the aircraft was the universe of stars. Inside, they were alone with no light but the dim orange glow of the navigator's table lamp hidden behind a curtain, and the faint green luminescence of the pilot's and engineer's instruments. Yes, they knew about that. What they didn't know about was the hundreds of miles of hostile airspace, the sudden, blinding convergence of searchlights, the hammering, all-enveloping torrents of flak, the nightfighters' incessant and determined infiltrations into the bomber stream, the dangers of colliding with your own in a crowd, the even worse dangers of getting lost over Germany.

> 'Are there any wicked women around this district?'
> P/O Bone

They didn't know what it was like to be under sentence of death, sentence suspended for an unknown length of time while taking a series of flights where not one single moment was free of danger. They didn't know what they would feel when they saw another bomber exploding in midair or, ablaze, falling from the same sky they were in. They would very shortly know all about it and, from this point on, the gods would decide. Whether they proved capable as an aircrew team need not necessarily determine whether they survived. Wing Commanders with experienced crews could FTR as well as a sprog crew with a boy wonder as pilot.

For Melrose and his men, the day went by in a nervous and excited blur. Equipment and kit were checked and rechecked, then checked again. Bob Woolf went to the signals briefing, Jimmy Moore to the navigators', Sammy Morris to the bomb aimers', and all of them to the general briefing. The target, Duisburg, and the technical details of the Op were noted, marked, learned and inwardly digested, but goodness knows how. The usual cheery message at the end of the briefings from Wingco Porter – words to the effect that this was to be a vital, nay, supremely important blow at the heart of the enemy, so go to it, lads – may have had a slight impact on the new crews but the experienced ones' thoughts were already elsewhere.

They had become used to the smaller, more precise type of raids that 5 Group had generally been doing of late, but this was different. This was mainforce. They were back among the throng, joining in with five hundred others on a mass attack. Mass attacks usually meant massed defences and, if one felt oneself to be part of an elite, special-purpose unit like 9 Squadron, mass attacks also meant more chance of a collision or some other cock-up.

For Plowright and his men, this was to be the end of their tour. They had expected it to be another French target. Norman Wells: 'When we saw it was back to Germany, we couldn't help but feel a few butterflies. There were no easy Ops but after all those Berlin trips and Stuttgart and Essen and whatnot, you'd pick France if you had a choice, which we hadn't, of course. There was no choice. Duisburg it had to be.'

One crew on their last, four on their first and fourteen at various stages between, ate the traditional egg and bacon. The new crews watched the older hands for clues.

Bob Woolf: When the Battle Order was posted up on the notice board, all those listed for the trip felt the tension, and this would continue to build up right through the briefing, the preparation for the flight and the pre-flight meal. Sometimes the reaction would be instant. Suddenly some fellows would need to go to the toilet in great haste. Others would try to show a forced kind of levity, cracking jokes and laughing too easily. Others would become quiet and withdrawn. Nobody wanted to reveal the fear they felt inside but it was deep in our souls and I know that I always gave a thought to whether this trip would be the one from which there would be no return.

Every man, every single one, felt the same but not a man there would admit it. He would do everything humanly possible to hide it. Some could hide it naturally, even from themselves most of the time. Some wrote a letter and left it in their quarters, to be posted, if.

They knew little about Duisburg except it would be heavily defended. They didn't know that this would be the fourteenth time Lancasters had been there, or that 47 of those Lancs had been lost in the process. Nor, of course, had they any idea that another thirty would go down tonight.

At all times of the day or night on the airfield, there would be engines going, one or two or half a dozen, being revved up and tested, and there would be men using wireless and intercom as they worked on the Lancasters. The only time there was silence was before an Op, for a couple of hours, which gave a signal to two quite different groups of people.

The Germans, who had been listening to the radio traffic, gauging its volume in the hope of guessing the size of the impending raid, would know that the time was nigh. The village children of Bardney would stop whatever they were doing, come to the airfield and get as near to the end of the runway as they could, oblivious to the danger, to be thrilled by the sight and sound of Lancasters roaring away into the sky.

On a normal Ops night with a south-westerly wind, at the north-easterly end of the main runway stood a wooden caravan, a black and white garden shed on wheels with a Perspex dome on top. The ACP (Aerodrome Control Pilot) stood in the dome, with a landline telephone to the control tower and an Aldis lamp that shone red or green. He and his lamp would give the pilots the signal to go; he would write down the identity letters and take-off time, called 'time up', for each aircraft.

Bob Woolf: By the time we were taken out to dispersals the tension had reached a high peak and in the buses there was quite an amount of heavy humour and repartee between crews. Those young WAAFs who drove us out to our aircraft were so considerate and friendly, and they did much to soften the emotional stress of the occasion. So, we clambered aboard and set about checking our equipment once more, leaving nothing to chance. This busy activity was good for our nerves and the familiarity of it was reassuring as we waited for the word Go.

Plenty of time was allowed in case anything was wrong that could be fixed so, usually, when everything tested in good nick, it meant more hanging around, talking, chatting to the ground crew, kicking a ball about or perhaps sitting on the grass, looking at the sky.

They might discuss the films that had been showing lately. Robert Donat and Greer Garson in *Goodbye Mr Chips* would be compared with Betty Grable and Robert Young in *Sweet Rosie O'Grady*, or George Murphy, Joan Leslie and Ronald Reagan in *This is the Army*. One aircrew member might mention his intentions of taking such and such a WAAF to the film tomorrow night, Charles Laughton and Clark Gable in *Mutiny on the Bounty*. His skipper might point out that the WAAF in question was bad luck. She'd already lost three boyfriends killed in action and there was no need to make their own odds any worse than they were already. He'd have to find another WAAF to love, perhaps this one here who had come with the Doc in the blood wagon, or Miss Carriage as it was sometimes called, doling out the wakey-wakey tablets and anti-sicks.

Bob Woolf: As it happened, on our first Op we needed some of our spare hour. I was doing my tests and found that one of the two generators wasn't working. Well, that didn't matter in theory. The Lanc only needed one generator and had the second as back-up. Still, it wasn't the best thing on your first operation. The skipper spoke to the control tower and the Chiefy of the electrical section came out. He checked the instruments and concluded that, yes, it was indeed the case that we only had one generator. The point was, should we go? Dougie asked me what I thought. We both asked the Chiefy what he thought. He assured us that a second generator failure was most unlikely. It was decided. We would go. We would carry our 4,000lb cookie and our load of incendiaries to Duisburg. Doug signed Form 700, to certify that the aircraft had passed into his command in a serviceable condition and Chiefy went his way.

When the Go signal was received, engines began to fill the air with their crackling roar and our Lancaster became alive and vibrated with power as the revs were run up and we rolled onto the perimeter track to join the long line of aircraft moving towards the runway. Having made it so far we felt there was every chance of the Op going ahead and we were desperately hoping that there wouldn't be a scrub. This was an immediate and complete cancellation of the whole Op by Bomber Command, usually indicated by yellow Very lights from the Control Tower.

On this night, 21 May 1944, there was no scrub. Those crackling roars (four times V12 Merlins = 50,000 horsepower + unbelievable racket) got louder as the first big bird stood, restrained by her brakes, shaking, building up the energy she needed to leave the earth behind. From the little black and white chequered caravan with the Perspex dome, the light of an Aldis lamp changed from red to green at 22.36 hours. The roars straight away got fantastically, double-fantastically louder as the pilot, Ernie Redfern, pushed forward the throttles, released the brakes, and the matt-black, cross-shaped, deadly poisonous Gargantua, the finest flying machine of its kind seen in the world, set off along her mile or so of launching ground. The blistering, clamorous engine shouts became so beyond ordinary sound that no unprotected ear could bear them, and the firecrackers flying from the engines made any novice seer and hearer believe that Armageddon had been given shape and form in this great black bird.

Along the road to the air the bird rushed, fifty miles an hour, sixty, stick forward to get the tail up, rudder under tension, pilot in control. Flight engineer Sgt Jones took over the throttles as Redfern asked for full power. Seventy miles an hour, eighty, ninety, stick back, a hundred . . . airborne. Away. There was a gap of a few minutes then another bird made the ear-crashing, sparks-flying rush, Clark at 22.44, then Gradwell at 22.46, Langford at .47, Glover at .48, Hancock at .49, Mathers at .50, Plowright at .51, and another, and another. Nobody said anything. There was no commander sitting at a microphone, issuing instructions. There was no necessity for such a thing. They had the green lamp.

Melrose was ninth away at 22.53. The engines were revved up against the brakes. The green light shone. The brakes were eased and the bird began to roll. Over the intercom came the voice of Ernie Stalley, rear gunner, and for the first time he said what he would always say: 'We off'.

Bob Woolf: We'd found out during training that our skipper had developed a very bad habit. No sooner were we off the ground and climbing than he would fall asleep for about half a minute. We rather hoped he wouldn't do it on Ops. Luckily, Ted (Selfe, flight engineer) was on the ball and kept us going upwards while our captain took his

nap, and was always ready for it. Doug would never believe he did this until one day Sammy (Morris, bomb aimer) broke all the rules and took a camera with us and got a photo of Doug in the land of nod while at the controls of the King's Lancaster.

Following Melrose, one minute behind, was his contemporary Les Baker. The last to go was F/Sgt Cornelius. He was up at 23.05 and the night was empty. In twenty-nine minutes, nineteen birds of prey had flown away and now nineteen examples of the best, hardest-working, most capable bomb-carrying mechanical bird, became nothing but a few specks in the sky. A few slow-moving dark stars were all that remained for the seers and hearers who had witnessed the end of the world in the shape of a black cross. The lights on the runway were turned off. The green lamp was put out. Silence. Nothing. Nothing to be done by those at home except the waiting. Somewhere up there the squadron was circling to gain height and convening with the rest of the bomber stream around a rendezvous, but that was only visible to the radar watchers. That was only known about by those with the maps and the technology in the control rooms, in Britain and Germany.

None of the birds had turned back. Sometimes, a mechanical fault didn't show itself until the Lancaster was in the air. Sometimes, a skipper might be feeling especially nervous going to an exceptionally well-defended target and, of a sudden, a fault would appear which, later, on the ground, under the inspection of the fitters, could not be found. Other times, a skipper or another crew member might feel a phantom illness coming on, or a real illness.

Tonight, all of 9 Squadron's aircraft climbed to the prescribed height, achieved straight and level flight and set the prescribed course. The crews settled in to their routines. In WS/Y, Ted Selfe the flight engineer began logging his oil temperatures and pressures, his fuel readings and all the other complex processes which, being the latest thing and of their time, were delicately poised between superb efficiency and failure. Most if not all the skippers would have switched on George, the automatic pilot. Some would have switched him off again because he wasn't working but they'd all switch him off when they reached height and were flying into ever-increasing danger. If you were attacked by a fighter, the gunner who spotted him wanted you to corkscrew now, not after you'd disengaged George, which only took a few seconds but by then you could be dead.

Bob Woolf: We functioned well on our first trip. We did our various jobs by the book as the skipper liked but, with ten tenths cloud over the target, there was not much to see in the way of results. I somehow

managed to fulfil all my wireless-operating tasks while keeping half my attention on the remaining generator ammeter and the other half on Monica.

Monica was a form of radar meant to pick up enemy fighters and, quite often, she worked. She could not discriminate between RAF and *Luftwaffe* – all aircraft were the same to her – nor could she tell where they were coming from. She could only give their distance. The closer together her pip-pip sounds, the nearer was the aircraft.

It was as well that Bobby Woolf and the others didn't know that Monica had developed into a very attractive lady, *une femme fatale*, in fact. The Germans had devised an instrument called *Flensburg*, which picked up Monica's radar signals and used them to home in on the transmitting aircraft from as much as forty-five miles away. Monica would be retired from active service in September 1944 but, for the moment, bomber crews thought she was an angel of the night, not a mixed blessing.

There was heavy flak over the target but we weren't hit. We had no idea who was hit, or if anybody from 9 Squadron was, alone in our cramped, vulnerable, black metal tube in the black sky. A Lancaster and her crew made an independent fighting unit, operating under strict instructions but, when it came to it, we were alone, depending only on ourselves and our aircraft.

With headphones and helmets, oxygen masks sealed to the face with cream to prevent them freezing to the skin, and a job to concentrate on, bombing was a surprisingly quiet business. The massive amount of engine noise tended to recede into a kind of vibration, a feeling rather than a sound. To the men at the front – bomb aimer, pilot, engineer, navigator – the rear or mid-upper guns made hardly more of a chatter than a WAAF's typewriter. Light flak, looking like waving strings of fairy lights, fizzled out below or zipped up and past without a sound. Heavy flak exploded in black, orange and red balls, also silent unless right beside. A near miss bumped, but quietly. Shrapnel rattled like a knock on the door, if it wasn't near enough to make a hole.

Sammy Morris had already programmed his bombsight's valve-driven computer with the target's height above sea level, the local barometric pressure and the terminal velocity of the bombs. The aircraft's height and airspeed fed into the sight automatically. Sammy just needed the wind speed and direction from Jimmy Moore, the navigator. Sammy had the best bombsight currently available, the Mark 14A, developed at Air Chief Marshal Harris's insistence on two major principles: that an aircraft should have to fly straight and level on the bombing run for the absolute minimum amount of time; and that the bomb aimer should have as few settings or adjustments to make as possible so he could devote his attention to releasing the bombs, pressing the tit, at the right moment.

Bombsight or no, when they were called in to make their run Sammy didn't have much to aim at in all this cloud. There were no markers that they could see, only the glow from the fires already started. Nevertheless, Sammy concentrated utterly on the graticule, the little grid of optically flat glass with the sword of light, point up, down which moved the target. His thumb was on the bomb release, the tit. What was happening outside the aircraft was, for the moment, irrelevant. He instructed Dougie Melrose who, too, was not looking at anything except his instruments. Doug tried to fly the perfect, rock-solid line while he listened to Sammy's voice, 'Left left, steady, right, steady, steady' as the bomb aimer kept the target on the shining blade until it touched the crux of the sword. 'Steady, hold it there . . . bombs gone.' In good visibility they would keep flying straight and level until the photoflash went off. No need to bother with that this time.

As each bomb fell, a small propeller in its tail was driven around by the airflow, which screwed a shaft inside the bomb, which drove forward into the fuse, or pistol as it was called, to arm the bomb by crushing an ampoule of acetone. The strength of the acetone determined the delay of the fuse, by the time it took to weaken an acetate disk which held in check a spring-loaded component called the striker. When the striker broke free, it hit the detonator. Delays could be anything from seconds to hours to seven days.

In the bomb bay, the little propellers were held by a device which was unlocked when the bomb aimer operated his fusing switches. It was thus possible, if thankfully rare, for a bomb to stick, to hang up, with its propeller unlocked and able to rotate in the rushing air while the bomb doors were open. If that happened, whether the aircraft got home or not might depend on the delay in the fuse. If it did get home, the armourers had a similar problem with defusing. Tonight, all of Melrose's bombs fell towards their target noiselessly, unseen, for thousands of feet. Time for home.

Back at Bardney, in the control room, in the watch office, the strain was astringent, growing, in everyone. The flying control officer could feel it, and the recorder WAAF who kept the log, and the R/T WAAFs, in a biggish room which got busier as the time came nearer for the boys to be back. The MO came in, North the Met man, Rushton the squadron adjutant, McMullen the station CO, Porter the squadron CO, everyone anxious within but studiously calm without. The focus of attention was the two girls with their headphones like small black saucers and their telephone mouthpieces standing in front of them on black Bakelite candlestick stems.

They had been there for hours. They did eight-hour shifts in theory, whatever was necessary in practice. The atmosphere, no matter how outwardly calm the participants, was restless, fearful. Nerves were stretched taut. The officers might puff gently on their pipes and wonder if it would rain in the afternoon for the cricket match, but the waiting was not just something you could feel. You could almost see it.

In 51 Base operations room at Waddington they might well have heard, or not, from the flyers, but not in Bardney Flying Control. This would be their first contact of the night. The radios were much better these days. Those early ones, those TR9s, had only had a range of ten or fifteen miles and suffered a lot from interference. This modern kit was crystal clear. By now the boys would be looking for the Boston Stump as they came in over the coast, and they'd follow the River Witham until they saw the oblong tower of the sugar beet factory. Home.

Rosen was 9 Squadron's wireless identification. Thus aircrew would refer to a particular Lancaster as J or W, or J-Johnny or W-William or, over the radio when coming home, as Rosen Johnny or Rosen William.

Pip Beck, R/T WAAF at Bardney, had heard those words many times and remembered the deaths of Anderson Storey and so many others.

You had to be cool and calm. You couldn't start flapping about, and if your boyfriend didn't come back, well, you had to carry on. If you were heartbroken, you had to leave it until afterwards. You couldn't burst into tears and go all hysterical on duty. And nobody did. It was very hard sometimes but you had to get used to it and quick. Off duty, you were more vulnerable. Three of us had little breakdowns one night at a choir practice. A piercing sense of sadness flooded through me. Oh God, what was the matter with us all? I ran for the corridor where I sobbed my heart out.

At a few minutes after three, the first aircraft called in. Phil Plowright had headed for home at top speed. Norman Wells: 'We were determined to be first back and when it was time to call base, Phil dispensed with the usual routine. Instead of the Rosen Johnny over business, he said, 'Johnny Walker, still going strong. Get some in!'

'Hello, Johnny,' said the smiling WAAF. 'Pancake. Over.' They were down at 03.09.

Redfern was next. 'Aerodrome, one thousand. Over,' said the WAAF. He had to join the circuit at a thousand feet until told to land, called pancake. Soon there were several in the circuit, at 1,250, 1,500, 1,750 feet, and the ambulances and fire tenders were there ready, and the WAAFs' voices serene and precise, and the squeak of the chalk on the blackboard as the homecomers were written up, and the waiting seemed to get easier and harder at the same time.

Pip Beck: The routine was always the same. Stack them up, bring them in. You might have a complication if the runway became blocked or there were some other special instructions to make you depart from the script. If someone was very late, we might get a phone call from another aerodrome to say they were down there. We might get a stray from another squadron, with wounded or dead maybe, or a shot-up aircraft, and he would make a Darky call.

I would say, 'Hello Darky, this is Bardney' and we'd find out what the matter was and sort him out accordingly. Whatever it was, there was nothing personal about it. You couldn't. That was just not on.

By 03.52 they were all down except Cornelius and Melrose. Most people were in the interrogation room; McMullen and Porter and a couple of others would stay with their pipes and their small talk, until the chaps were in.

Interrogation reminded everyone of school, except they all had mugs of tea and cigarettes, and the crews looked much too old for school even though most of them had not been left very long. There was something wrong with their faces, the skin around their eyes and mouths seemed to have aged. These young men with old faces sat on one side of a table on a school bench, and the intelligence officers asked them questions. The questions and answers were businesslike and flat. An interview for a position as a bank clerk would have generated more agitation.

It hadn't seemed a particularly successful trip. Unsatisfactory. Frustrating. The marking had been hard to pick or invisible and results had been obscure. In fact, it had been a good raid with a lot of damage done but they didn't know that. Hill had had a fairly exciting time of it. 'On arrival at estimated position of target at 01.14 no markers were seen. Continued on course for two minutes, then attacked by a fighter, first from ahead then two attacks from astern. By this time there were only three minutes left for bombing and no flares had been seen and in view of this and also presence of fighter, bombs were jettisoned and course set for home at 01.20.'

Puddle Lake had got slightly lost and bombed Mönchengladbach, thirty miles to the south west. And Melrose was back at last, which just left Cornelius.

Pip Beck: We might overhear a conversation between the CO and the flying control officer. 'So-and-so's very late. Doesn't look good. If we don't hear something soon, I suppose that's it.' It was a very saddening

thing and there was nothing anyone could do. The aircrews went to bed, they knew what the chances were and the war had to go on. It was no good waiting up and biting your nails. You'd never cope if you did that.

Melrose answered his questions. 'Primary attacked 01.18, 21,000 feet. No markers seen except a presumed dummy. Red glow seen in patches over a large area. Approximately forty miles south of track homeward.'

Plowright's crew were in the mess. Norman Wells: 'We had a few drinks, and later on our flight commander signed my log book, that was F/Lt Mathers, and the CO, Wingco Porter, he signed it and wrote "First operational tour completed: 29 and a third sorties". A third? I don't know which one they were counting as a third.'

Everybody went to bed knowing that the Melrose crew had indeed been the last back. One of their squadron had failed to return, DV295 WS/T. That was Ray Cornelius. That was his kite, T. Nothing further had been heard from this aircraft, as the phrase went, and nothing ever would be.

In the morning, when they got up to look at the battle order, the word was that Cornelius was definitely missing. No messages. He hadn't limped home to land at another base. He was a goner, Raymond Summers Cornelius, husband of Ellen, he and all his sergeants, unless they'd parachuted out. They hadn't. In fact, none of their bodies would ever be found.

Melrose and the others heard the news and, for the first time, felt the standard aircrew feeling. Sorry. Poor chaps. Rotten luck. Glad it wasn't me, and it was time to concentrate on the next thing. Still tired and tense from their first Op, they saw that they were on again tonight. Everyone had his own way of coping. Melrose, the disciplined professional, the stickler, sought refuge in duties and detail but no man escaped the emotional pounding of returning from his first Op, finding out the squadron had lost one and realising he had to go again, with no respite.

That night, 22 May, it was to be Brunswick. The list was very similar to the previous one, nineteen aircraft again, with Wingco Porter coming on one of his frequent occasionals and claiming back his kite WS/Y from Melrose, who was in the old girl W4964 WS/J.

> 'I didn't spend six days in Paris for nothing'
> Sq/Ldr Fordham

Training seemed in the distant past, now that Ops had been experienced. Back then, at crewing up, life-and-death decisions had been made in the most casual way. For no set of reasons that could be analysed, quantified or tabulated, one lot of six men had joined up with Melrose when they – all, some or any single individual – could have joined with Baker, and another lot of six joined with Baker when Melrose was equally available.

Pilot Officer Leslie Baker, aged 22, from Raynes Park, had had the same experience of flying as Melrose. He had his 450 hours in his log book. He'd gone from Tiger Moth to Lancaster like everybody else and his Lancaster for Duisburg and now Brunswick, LM519 WS/N, was a sight newer than Melrose's. Baker's six men were indistinguishable by any known RAF measure from Melrose's six, and Baker likewise was indistinguishable from Melrose. The WAAF who drove them to dispersals that night would not have noticed any difference between the two lots of boys. When the green light flashed, their respective take-offs were not noticeably dissimilar and, even with the age difference, their aircraft were equally and excellently serviceable.

So why was it that Baker was shot down and Melrose was not? Why did the nightfighter pick WS/N to rake with bullets and cannon shells, near Ems, and not WS/J? With Baker, on his second Op, after all that training and anticipation, died the w/op, F/O Joseph McKee known as Paddy, whose wife had had their baby three days before. It could be called a human tragedy, or a waste of resources, or a great pity, or a dreadful bereavement for all the parents, wives and girlfriends. Whatever it was called, it hadn't happened to any of the other 9 Squadron aircraft on a trip which had largely been a waste of time. The master bomber's R/T had gone u/s and it had been cloudy so the 5 Group method didn't work and they'd been bombing by guesswork again, which never felt any good. On this particular night it was no good at all; the population and buildings of Brunswick suffered hardly a scratch although there were lots of new potholes in the surrounding countryside. Still, they were back and ready for the next one and during the day another new pilot had turned up, a very young looking pilot officer called Ray Harris.

When crewing up, Harris had been deeply worried. He was a callow youth, an entire year younger than he should have been. Why, the other skippers were all at least twenty and here he was, barely nineteen. Nobody, he'd thought, would want to fly with him. In the event, he'd had no more difficulties than Melrose, for different reasons.

Harris attracted the easy-going type. 'I found one of my crew at a railway station on a bleak November night. There was quite a crowd of airmen, standing around in overcoats. I said aloud, but to myself, "Nobody will fly with me" and a boy turned to me and said "I will". The boy became our rear gunner, Sandy Sanders.'

Flight engineer Andy Andrews, bomb aimer Harold Parsons known as Jimmy, wireless operator Bill Newman and mid-upper gunner Big Jock

Walker were all lads of an age. Tommy Adair, the only married one, the navigator, was ten years older than everybody else but they were a crew of like spirits.

Spirits in 9 Squadron were slightly brittle. It seemed that a crew was being lost on virtually every Op. If that was going to be the way of it, unless something marvellous happened, none of the May intake would be bothering the battle order typist much after the end of June.

23 May: another Stubbs, Flight Lieutenant D R, pilot, arrived.

25 May: Air Chief Marshal Harris sent a letter to his men.

I have always considered that the strain imposed by sustained Bomber Operations requires that aircrew personnel should enjoy the maximum amount of freedom from restraint and should be relieved, as far as can be done without loss of efficiency, of routine Station duties. This policy, and I can see no reason for changing it, places on Station, Squadron and Flight Commanders the responsibility for ensuring that such privileges are not abused.

Unfortunately, my attention is continually drawn to the lack of discipline prevalent amongst operational aircrew, and to causes of complaint such as irregularities of dress, lack of smartness in bearing and appearance, slackness in saluting and a degree of untidiness in some of their living quarters which practically amounts to squalor. Apart from the bad impression created both inside and outside the Service, such symptoms cannot help but have an adverse effect on the behaviour in the air of the personnel concerned, as conditions of modern warfare, and in particular the gruelling task of Bomber crews, demand instantaneous and unhesitating obedience to orders, combined with a degree of physical and moral stamina which can only result from a high standard of self discipline.

It has become apparent that an attitude, or perhaps I should call it an affectation, which rates the normal obligations of Officers and NCOs in matters of smartness and cleanliness as of negligible importance, or even slightly contemptible, is more or less general amongst aircrew personnel. It is clearly essential that such an attitude, to which most of aircrew shortcomings are attributable, should be eradicated. The junior aircrew members of today are the Flight and Squadron Commanders of tomorrow, and the Station and Base Commanders of the future, and unless they grow with an understanding of and a sincere regard for, the right ideals and best traditions of the Service, our efficiency and our prestige will inevitably decline. The conduct of our aircrews on operations has won, and continues to win, the admiration of the world. It is particularly undesirable, therefore, that their conduct on the ground should fall short of this magnificent standard, and should excite unfavourable comment by the other members of the Royal Air Force, by other Services, or by the general public.

The last thing which I would wish to do would be to impose on aircrew personnel an irksome regime of inspections, parades and 'spit and polish'. I want their special privileges in the way of leave, petrol, extra rations and freedom from routine Station duties to continue and everything possible be done to relieve the strain of operations and to increase their fitness for their primary role. Station, Squadron and Flight Commanders, and even Captains of Aircraft themselves must, however, ensure by leadership, encouragement, education and personal example, that those measures are reinforced by that strength of mind and body which derives from right thinking and right living.

Constant steps must be taken to see that aircrew personnel take sufficient physical exercise to keep them fit, particularly during lulls in operations. They must be educated in matters of general, as well as Service, knowledge. They must be made aware of the achievements, both past and present, of the Royal Air Force, and thus gain pride in their membership of our Service. Finally, they must be reminded that, as aircrews of Bomber Command, they form the spearhead of the national offensive, and as such lay claims to be called a 'crack Corps', but that every 'crack Corps' which has ever existed in any arm of the services in any country, has been distinguished for its all-round efficiency, smartness and esprit-de-corps, just as much as for its valour and fighting skill. Let us see to it that Bomber Command aircrews do not forfeit in the eyes of the world, through ignorance fostered by poor leadership, their full claim to that title.

Whatever the boys thought of the rest of it, there was no doubt that Sir Arthur wrote the truth when he said the junior aircrew members of today were the flight and squadron commanders of tomorrow. At the rate they were going down, anyone surviving until tomorrow and the next day was bound to be promoted. Of course, during the lulls in Operations, they could take physical exercise, if there were any lulls, and they could reduce their shortcomings by tidying their rooms, and reduced shortcomings would surely mean fewer deaths.

> 'But you should see me naked.
> And how. I suit all tastes'
> F/Lt Boothby MP

27 May: Melrose, J-Johnny and the lads went to Nantes, to bomb the

railway yards and buildings. Up 22.58, attacked the target 01.41 at 9,000 feet, down at 03.55. Routine, really, except J was now seventy trips old. The first fifty aircraft, including 9 Squadron's, bombed so accurately that the master bomber sent the rest home.

Ray Harris went second Dicky on that trip with Pilot Officer Forrest. Harry Forrest was a very old hand. He'd been at 9 Squadron since February. His own second Dicky had been to Berlin; his first Op to Leipzig when 46 Lancs were lost. Blowing up the rail junction and workshops at Nantes, no aircraft lost, must have seemed a bit of a jolly to Forrest although, bearing in mind the dead aircrew he'd heard about since his arrival, possibly not to Harris.

> 'Is it true that the Germans are offering
> £500,000 for the capture alive of a certain
> squadron leader from Number Nine?'
>
> Anon

Frank Belben, engineer to Glover, and all the original crew except the w/op, finished their tour with Nantes. As Ray Harris came in, they bowed out. Frank Belben had thirty six Ops in his log book including all those French thirds, and the CO signed it as he did Norman Wells's:

Tour completed, 29 and a third. We couldn't believe it to start with. We never expected to survive. Like most crews, because of the dangerous life we led, we functioned as a unit socially as well as professionally. We'd go to the pub, go into Lincoln to a dance, and sometimes roller skating at Boston rink. Then we'd be back to it and all those meals after Ops when we sat and ate bacon and egg and looked at the empty tables and chairs. Lou Glover got us through. He was an excellent pilot. Good take-offs and landings, obviously, but on Ops his reactions were superb. He reacted on the instant when the gunners shouted to corkscrew. He'd be into the dive before anybody knew what was happening. Some of them weren't so quick and they were ones whose empty chairs we were looking at. Of course, there was no way of knowing, when you crewed up, which sort you'd got. Anyway, everyone was there on the last one, then they gave us seven days leave which was kind of them.

Frank would spend almost all the rest of the war as an instructor, until crews were wanted on a second tour with Tiger Force, Lancasters for the Far East, which never happened, and for Lancasters to take staff officers, MPs and other worthies on aerial tours of defeated Germany, which did.

28 May: Melrose went to Cherbourg, more precisely the German guns at St Martin-de-Varreville. That was Harris's first Op, in LL853 WS/W, with his all-sergeant crew. Up 22.38, attacked 00.26 at 7,500 feet, down 02.05. Also making their debut that night was the crew skippered by Flight Sergeant King.

29 May: another new pilot, P/O Wood, was posted to Bardney with his crew.

30 May: F/O Blackham and P/O Marsh, more pilots and their crews, arrived.

31 May: Marsh went second Dicky with Gradwell to Saumur, a railway junction; target destroyed, no losses. For them, and for all the surviving crews of 9 Squadron at the end of May 1944, it was so far, so good. They knew for certain that in a day or two, or a week, or a couple of months' time they would not all be seeing each other, talking shop, going for a pint, trying to persuade the WAAFs that their intentions were perfectly honourable. They could not all survive but some would, surely.

Pilot Officer Plowright was posted to No. 17 Operational Training Unit. That was one survivor, anyway.

7

FLAMING JUNE, FLAMING D-DAY, FLAMING FRANCE

D-Day, the biggest Op in history, was only a few days away but no one would have known at Bardney and Ray Harris saw his name on the battle order along with fifteen more captains, 3 June. The raid was another 5 Group speciality; there would be approaching one hundred Lancs going to Ferme d'Urville where there was a German signals station. This would be the Harris boys' second Op, again in LL853 WS/W. She was their own aircraft for the time being but, fortunately for Harris and Co at any rate, not for very long.

The raid was out of the text book. Target found without difficulty, clear weather, not much in the way of defences, perfect marking from the Oboe Mosquitos, bombing well concentrated, target destroyed, home with no losses. End of signal station; where do you want us next? Perhaps the Allies were winning the war after all. Perhaps the Germans were starting to give up. Perhaps this bombing business wasn't so bad.

On 4 June, nothing of operational importance occurred. On 5 June, Pilot Officer Kidd, the bomb aimer who had missed being killed with Stafford by one day, came back to the squadron. In Horne's crew, he would find life exciting. Also on this day, Flight Sergeant King, veteran of one Op, received his promotion, noted in the Operations Record Book in standard but quaint fashion since he was already there, as 'P/O C R King posted to 9 Squadron on appointment to commission'. These were minor matters, tiny specks on the big picture of the war. A sergeant became an officer. A chap returned to his old unit. What did that signify, when a fleet of 4,000 ships and boats was waiting to carry many, many thousands of men across the Channel? Tomorrow was D-Day, Operation Overlord. The railway system in France was a wreck and more attacks would be made to render it almost totally useless, and many sorties had been flown to bring about the second condition for a successful invasion: disablement of the armed defences. So as not to give away the real invasion point, at least two targets were bombed on other stretches of coast for every one attacked in Normandy.

Came the day, the deceit continued. Squadrons 218 in Halifaxes and 617 in Lancs feinted right and left of the actual destination for Overlord, dropping vast quantities of Window in a meticulous display of precision flying which simulated on enemy radar an approaching invasion fleet. Most of the rest of Bomber Command mounted, at the last possible moment, its biggest hit of the war so far, against the gun batteries of Normandy.

The battle order WAAF at 9 Squadron still had King down as a Flight Sergeant. He went, as part of this massive force, with Harris and fifteen more from Bardney to Pointe-du-Hoc, near the quiet little Normandy town of St Pierre-du-Mont, marked on the Overlord map as gun batteries which would threaten Allied landing craft. Tomorrow, the US Rangers would be wading through waves and bullets, struggling up Omaha Beach and trying to take that same Pointe-du-Hoc promontory. It was 9 Squadron's task to make sure that they would at least get as far as the beach. Doing the same for all the other units coming ashore, strung along miles and miles of hellish golden sand, more than 1,200 aircraft, including seven hundred Lancasters, attacked the guns at Fontenay, Houlgate, La Pernelle, Longues, Maisey, Merville, Mont Fleury, Ouisterham and St Martin-de-Varevilles as well as Pointe-du-Hoc and St Pierre-du-Mont.

Bob Lasham was pathfinding with 97 Squadron at St Pierre. 'We had our briefing from our CO, Wing Commander Carter DFC, and he told us about this target just on the French coast, "if you can call it a target," he said.' The Wingco had every right to be confident and a little scathing. He could look at his crew and see three DFMs, a DFC and Bar and a DFC, plus his own gong. He had two bomb aimers with him; one was F/O Henry Jeffery who had won his DFM on his first tour, with 9 Squadron. Between them they'd seen and done all that could be. 'Well, we lost two crews, including his and they never found any bodies from it. The rest of us were in and out in no time at all. We didn't know it was D-Day and we were flying home in the dark and the cloud but Harry (Wilson, bomb aimer) called everybody back to see the H2S screen because it was showing the Channel full of ships.'

Over 5,000 tons of bombs were dropped, the most ever in one night, and all but one of the batteries were severely damaged. Only five Lancs altogether went down out of the seven hundred. If 9 Squadron's experience was typical, five was a lucky number. Redfern: 'We had to break off the run to avoid another Lanc which dived at us. Engaged by heavy flak and about seven searchlights. Jettisoned bombs safe to enable aircraft to climb.'

Allinson: 'After descending through cloud as ordered by W/T, orbited to get on correct heading and on approaching target on bombing run was driven off by another Lancaster which appeared from port slightly above.' Horne, Craig, Redfern, Harris, Blackham in WS/J and the others all bombed successfully in the earliest hours of D-Day. This was Ray Harris's fourth and his crew had knitted together as a unit. They took it as it came. Jimmy Parsons, the bomb aimer, felt he was very, very lucky 'because I didn't have much in the way of nerves. A bit of flak here and there didn't bother me, so long as it wasn't right in my face.'

As 9 Squadron flew home that early morning, they saw the armada below, thousands of ships and boats, thousands of white wakes. The first gallants of the Allied armies were already ashore.

Next night it was German army positions at Evel, near Argentan, a small town in the department of Orne, Normandy. This was another thousand-bomber night, helping to clear the way for the Allies' push into France.

> 'I was so low I could feel the heat of the searchlights'
> Sq/Ldr Turner
> 'The flak was so horrible and the puffs so thick
> I had to fly on instruments'
> Sq/Ldr Turner
> (on a daylight)

Most of the 9 Squadron pilots encountered little opposition. They all attacked the target at around 01.15 from between 5,000 and 6,000 feet. There were some hits and some misses, a lot of smoke and not much seen in the way of results. They turned for home.

The raiders were expected back between three o'clock and a quarter to four. At 03.05 Gradwell was first down 'but then I usually was. On the grounds of fuel economy, the instruction said you were to throttle back after crossing the enemy coast on your way home and lose height gradually. I always preferred to put the nose down and get on, and I was ticked off for it by the CO until proper fuel comparisons were made. I showed them that my method used no more petrol than the official one. Anyway, I liked being first back.'

Clark came in five minutes later. Redfern was home at 03.18, then Ryan, then Craig. They were landing almost every minute now, Lake, Melrose, Stubbs, Langford, Marsh, Blackham, Harris. After a few minutes' gap came another cluster; Reeve at 03.37, Horne, Allinson, Hill, Forrest, Wood, Hallett.

Of the twenty aircraft flying from Bardney, nineteen had come back. A-Able was late. According to the government, Bomber Command and Uncle Tom Cobleigh, nineteen home out of twenty was exactly what the ratio should have been. The anxious Flying Control WAAFs and intelligence staff in the operations room, the officer of the watch in the control tower and WS/A's ground crew, well, they would not have agreed. They were not going to shrug their shoulders and say, 'Oh, you know, it's to be expected. It's our turn.'

Pilot Officer King had not been with the squadron long enough for anybody to get on much more than nodding terms. He'd been going in the sergeants' mess for a fortnight and the officers' mess for two days. He and his crew had not become familiar to the rest, had not been absorbed into the station's body corporate. What nobody at Bardney yet knew was that shortly before half past two, a few miles away at Waddington base station, the D/F (direction finding) unit had picked up a very weak signal from Rosen Able, asking for the way home. This was not at all unusual. Even with the Gee box, aircraft got lost. The ground unit tried to get a fix to help out but no acknowledgement came and no further contact could be made.

At Bardney, the weary flyers of 9 Squadron were interrogated and went to bed. The WAAFs waited, and the officers in command, until there was no point in waiting any longer. If King hadn't gone down or landed somewhere by now, he'd be out of petrol. The conclusion had to be reached. One of their aircraft was missing.

It was only twenty miles away. Pilot Officer King was lying dead in the burned out wreckage of his aircraft near Belvoir Castle, by Grantham. Two of his crew's bodies were never found. They hadn't had the chance on their tour of operations to prove the five per cent rule. They had got nowhere near their nineteen. They'd got the chop on their third.

For 9 Squadron, the next few days and the next few raids were relatively uneventful; searchlights, flak, holes in the aircraft, the usual, nothing to write home about. Bomber Command's brief was to support the armies and, in generally cloudy weather which badly hampered the daylight American bombers, they attacked at night, often low to get under the cloud ceiling. At Bardney there was much movement among personnel. New pilots came with their crews; Taylor, Scott, McMurchy, Ron Adams who would earn the nickname Lucky, Woods, and the man at the top changed. Wing Commander Porter, DFC and Bar was one of the RAF's leading exponents of the arts and sciences of bombing. Now he followed Lasham to Pathfinder squadron No. 97 and was replaced by Wing Commander Bazin DFC, another of the same mind when it came to practice and accuracy.

James Michael Bazin, Jimmy, a rather cultured fellow from Newcastle, was a very experienced pilot. He'd begun the war in France, flying Gladiators and then Hurricanes with 607 Squadron, often making half a dozen sorties a day in support of the British Expeditionary Force. He shot down a Heinkel 111 on his first Hurricane day and was shot down himself behind enemy lines but managed to evade capture. In the Battle of Britain, he had ten kills or possibly more and was shot down again, although this time the victorious Me109 only holed Bazin's fuel tank. He glided in to land and was in the air again a couple of days later in the same aircraft, meanwhile having flown several sorties in different Hurricanes. For two

234

years he had posts in operations control and pilot training, joined 49 Squadron on active service in Lancasters for a short while and finally came to Bardney.

His predecessor, Wing Commander Edward Leach Porter DFC, age 33, veteran of the Battle of Berlin and dozens of other Ops, was another who defeated the law of averages by many a country mile. He truly hated the enemy and would bridle if any aircrew called them Jerries. 'They're Huns!' he would exclaim. 'Jerries have a use. You can put one under your bed.' W/Cdr Porter would at last fall to the Germans while laying mines in the Baltic Sea at Stettin Bay, 17 August. Contrary to stories later circulated, he did not refuse to parachute to safety with the rest of his crew saying that he preferred death to capture. His aircraft went down in flames and he and all his much decorated men perished.

Bazin, continuing in the Porter tradition of emphasis on bombing perfection, was to have significant and positive effects on 9 Squadron's destiny but, for the moment, in high June and early July, his first fortnight in charge, starting with some incident-free French railway trips, would gradually turn into a nightmare.

Allied forces were moving, sometimes rapidly, over enemy territory near the bombers' targets and news of ground troops' latest positions was not always bang up-to-date. The aerial attacks also were great in numbers and closely concentrated; it was possible to have too many bombers flying about. Confusion was not the only result; so was cancellation. Between 14 June and 4 July, 9 Squadron attacked seven different targets but were scrubbed after preparing for four more.

If the lights did go up for a scrub, some aircrew would feel a huge hurrah of relief. They wouldn't be killed tonight. Some would feel a deflated, exhausted anti-climax as they realised that all that nervous energy expended during the day had been for nothing and that they'd very probably have to do it all over again tomorrow. They sat around afterwards, listlessly, with no energy or will power left. For most, though, the strain and the 'speed' pills combined to produce a right boys' night out.

Bob Woolf: For me and plenty of others, the mixed feelings of relief and disappointment and the sudden escape of pressure had one result only: an irresistible urge to remove to the mess as fast as possible and get thoroughly hammered. So demoralising could scrubs be that official tolerance of schoolboy antics and riotous behaviour was raised to the highest level. There was one time when the station CO, Group Captain McMullen, had us gather together in the mess bar. He shut the doors and declared 'No man shall leave here tonight until he is well and truly drunk', only he didn't say drunk. Leaping about like wild monkeys,

getting thoroughly sloshed and singing extremely rude songs late into the night had not yet been classified by doctors of the mind but it clearly was an effective therapy. It came naturally and it worked.

As if scrubs were not frustrating enough, there was a recall from an attack on the V-weapon site at Watten after being in the air for an hour.

We were after flying bombs and expecting a hot reception. Whether for this or another reason they gave us an extra gunner to operate the point-five undergun, a Canadian called Sangster. Only three kites had these guns, which we didn't think a great deal of and which usually went unmanned. They caused a lot of humorous remarks in the mess and the thought of Mick Maguire, the armaments officer, actually getting airborne to test out this idea in anger, generated a string of jokes and witticisms.

The Allied armies, fighting their way forward, expected to find strong opposition at Aunay-sur-Odon, in the department of Calvados, where intelligence reports had large concentrations of troops and vehicles. Their request for bombing was met by a quickly organised raid using over two hundred Lancasters of 5 Group, including nineteen from 9 Squadron. Bombing was so accurate that it put the red spotfires out. The target was obliterated.

By this time the Germans had 55 launching sites in France operational for the flying bomb, the V1, the buzz bomb, the doodlebug, and they set off the first volleys in a new form of warfare: death by self-propelled missile. By noon of 16 June, almost 250 doodlebugs had been fired, destroying nine of their own launching sites and a French village and mostly missing London, but by midnight London had taken 73 hits and one bug had doodled all the way into deepest Suffolk before dropping harmlessly into a field.

'You call that thick? I've flown
through fog so thick it took
thirty miles an hour off the airspeed'
F/O Bamford

Hitler came to northern France to see for himself and was immensely proud of the German nation which was able to fight with weapons so advanced. He assigned top priority to production of three thousand V1s a month. The feeling among V1 field commanders was that one hundred a day was nowhere near enough to force a victory in the war, which was the ultimate objective of the V-weapon programme. Hundreds of sorties were being flown against V1 sites, with few Allied losses since Hitler's promised ack-ack guns and fighter squadrons had yet to arrive. Also, the threat of the V2 had not been forgotten. The Allies suspected much and didn't know much. The Americans had suggested it might well be a biological weapon. Until the launch sites could be overrun by ground forces, the only option would be to bomb them.

Melrose and his crew had completed ten Ops in about three weeks. That their careers might be cut short on the count of nine had become a distinct possibility as they flew back over the English shore and the coastal batteries opened up on them. There were several reasons why this could happen. The gunners might not have had correct information about times and heights of aircraft returning. The IFF (Identification Friend or Foe) radar unit in the Lancaster might not have been working. Or there might have been a complete cock-up. Anyway, it was the wireless operator's responsibility.

Bob Woolf: While the skipper took evasive action and he and the rest of us swore mightily at the incompetence, parentage and sexual proclivities of ack-ack gunners everywhere, I checked the IFF. It was working. So I fired off as many Very lights as I could from the signal pistol, fixed in the fuselage above my head, to show the colours of the day but that didn't work. The gunners couldn't see the lights through the cloud.

Thanks to the miracle that was British technology, they could see W4964 WS/J-Johnny Walker on their radar screens. Their blip should have been turned into a distinctive, friendly one by the IFF machine. As it was, Melrose and his men were shaken up and WS/J had a few light bruises but no serious damage was done.

No. 9 Squadron was switched to a mission inside Germany, the regularly visited and constantly repaired synthetic oil refineries near Gelsenkirchen, 21 June. There were two targets, Scholven-Buer and Wesseling; 133 Lancasters and six Mosquitos went to Wesseling, 123 and nine went to Scholven-Buer.

This was in a different league from their recent Ops. They were all dangerous from all kinds of angles but hot targets in the Ruhr, Happy Valley, had everything, including large numbers of nightfighters. Flak would be excessively intense, fired from guns which had a neat white circle painted on their barrels for every Tommy shot down.

Bob Woolf: The flak was very evident, very heavy, very solid, and we all had a few holes here and there. There was no warning before a

sudden burst in fiery red and the rattling sound of shrapnel against the sides of the aircraft. Over a well-defended target there was no let-up of the continual flashes in the bomber stream, producing the inevitable bright cascade of colours when an aircraft was fatally hit and blossomed into a huge ball of flame, gradually falling earthward like some giant firework.

The available strength of 9 Squadron took off, nineteen of them, between 23.00 and 23.30, for Scholven-Buer. Maule turned back after an hour and a half with an electrical fault. Horne had new boy Woods with him as second Dicky, Craig had Adams. The difference between this and the French raids, which were all they had known up to now, became horribly apparent to Harris and his men when they got to the target area. Jim Parsons was Harris's bomb aimer.

In bombing practice over southern England, on the Salisbury ranges, we'd bombed red and green target indicators from 7,000 feet and these were the sort of heights we'd bombed at in France, so we could be super-accurate and avoid hitting our French allies. Over Germany, we were way up there at almost 20,000 feet, as far away as possible from the flak and never mind about allies, there weren't any. At this height, the way the TIs behaved in the bomb sight was quite different. I was looking and I could see the markers but, as we flew towards them, they didn't seem to be moving much. Then I realised I'd picked up on the second target, Wesseling, several miles further on.

Much to the rest of the crew's disgust, this became a dummy run and they had to turn around, not the wisest thing to do in a bomber stream, and come in again to bomb. This was their duty. This was what they were supposed to do. Bob Woolf: 'Our squadron lost one over the target. Another was hit by flak and dived thousands of feet upside down. The pilot ordered the bomb aimer and second Dicky out but couldn't go himself as some of his crew were wounded. He got home on two.'

That was Horne who, as a flight sergeant, had flown his first Op in J-Johnny all that time ago in March and on his third had been coned, hit by flak, attacked by a fighter and had flown while blinded with a u/s rear gunner. Now a wise old man three months on, coming back from the oil refineries, he never knew if it was heavy flak, cannon fire or both which hit him at 01.30 hours. It was probably a fighter but the question seemed rather academic as the aircraft went screaming into a steep dive, the starboard inner engine aflame and fire pouring from the rear turret. Horne told everyone to prepare to jump. His crew, with the exception of second

Dicky and bomb aimer, were original members. Rear gunner Sgt Parkes, who had missed enjoying their earlier adventure over Berlin while unconscious on the rest bed, might have wished for the same release now.

The second Dicky, P/O Woods, did bale out, following the bomb aimer, P/O Kidd through the front hatch. Kidd could have been thinking that his recent death-escape by posting, when he had been saved from Stafford's total loss by a day, had merely been an adjournment by the gods, a deferral of his sentence by six weeks or so. He was right. He was killed; Woods was taken prisoner. The rest were stuck. They'd started together and now it looked a certainty that they would finish together. Both gunners were hurt and out of commission, not that that seemed to matter much. In a power dive, on fire in several places, they could do no more than wait in terror for a few more seconds of life to pass before oblivion. They could only hope that death would be instantaneous.

They had been hit at 17,750 feet. 'Captain finally managed to pull aircraft out of dive at 2,000 feet and flew back to England, landing at Wittering 04.05.' The ORB monthly summary was even more succinct. 'The Captain succeeded in bringing his aircraft back to base.' Which was nothing more than the truth.

The rest of No. 9 began arriving back at Bardney in good time and did their interrogation. Melrose had had his belly gunner again, for the last time, and Sangster would replace Sgt Parkes as Horne's tail ender. Bob Woolf: 'The flak was very close and tossed us around but we were lucky and damage was not so severe. The nightfighters were having a go as well.' Everyone came home with holes in his aircraft except Flying Officer Lorne McMurchy. Eleven days, he'd lasted. For almost three years he'd trained for eleven days of active service. His aircraft, ME704 WS/B, had been on the squadron since March so she'd had a reasonable go, considering. Four of the crew got out and were taken prisoner but, out in Alberta, McMurchy's wife Lucy got the dreaded telegram and so did the parents of rear gunner Donald Redshaw, only eighteen.

Sq/Ldr Turner: 'Have a drink, Angus?'
P/O Taylor: 'Well, if you insist'

More practice was followed by a night raid to Limoges, where the Gnome & Rhône factories were making fine products for the Germans, including engines of various sorts and the star of many subsequent war films, the Wehrmacht motorcycle with sidecar. This was a 5 Group raid, 97 Lancs aimed at the extensive railway yards as well as the factories. Melrose thought that the marking and timing were good and the bombing was well concentrated around the markers. Harris saw a big fire which was still visible seventy miles away. Scott and Redfern saw fires and explosions in the aero-engine factory. Nobody had been lost, they noticed, when they got back, but only just.

Bob Woolf: Johnny Allinson's kite was hit by two five-hundred pound bombs which passed right through his wing but didn't explode. He limped home OK. Lucky chap. We had our own little incident when our brakes failed the check and we diverted to Wittering which was an emergency 'drome with a three-and-a-half-mile grass runway, a bumpy, undulating strip with two roads running across it. This was not entirely what we would have preferred as a landing ground but, of course, Dougie got us down all right.

Allinson's kite was O, ME757. She would mend this time but in August, in full view of everyone, she would dramatically become unmendable.

It was on targets like this that 5 Group developed an advanced and very successful form of offset marking. One specially trained crew would drop a marker at a given distance, say, four hundred yards from an aiming point, and the master bomber/controller would estimate how accurate that was. Several other aircraft would then find winds in the target area and transmit those to the master, who would calculate an average plus an error for the four hundred yards offset. This new, false wind was broadcast to the bombers and fed into their bombsight computers; the bomb aimers lined up on the offset marker knowing that the bombs would actually fall on the target.

The advantages were clear. The marker remained visible, it wasn't likely to be blown out and – this was the new advantage – the master bomber could calculate several different aiming points from the one marker, which was very helpful, for instance, in the case of railway attacks where the targets were long and thin. The disadvantage was that complexity took time. Although results were astonishingly good, the bomber force was sometimes kept waiting while targets were re-marked, winds were found and calculations made, which meant extra opportunities for the enemy.

It was 24 June. The men of 9 Squadron got ready for a night raid. There was, for example, Eddie Halshaw, who had made his debut to Duisburg, the same night as Melrose, Hallett and the late Leslie Baker. Halshaw was a Lancashire lad, 21 years old from Bacup. Harry Rae, with four Ops plus second Dicky behind him, was with Halshaw on the battle order, along with Craig, one of 9 Squadron's most experienced pilots. Ginger Craig had arrived on squadron a few days after Gradwell, way back in February. He'd been one of Maguire's unofficial tour operators and been trusted several times to take rookie pilots for their work-experience trip.

Halshaw would be in W, Ray Harris's old aircraft, with the same crew he'd had for every Op so far plus a belly gunner. They were part of a massive exercise, five hundred Lancs and over 230 other bombers hitting seven different V-bomb sites on the same night. The buzz bombs were becoming a real menace, knocking out railway stations, telephone exchanges, factories and hospitals, cutting power supplies and killing people; well over a thousand by this point.

At Prouville, where 9 Squadron was going, there would be intense opposition from the fighters which packed the Somme/Pas de Calais region. It was a clear night and the searchlights found Craig's WS/H over the French coast at only 12,000 feet. They held her long enough, which wasn't very long, to hit her time and time again with flak. The bombs were jettisoned but it was too late. Down they came at Yvrencheux, a village in the Somme, and in the little churchyard were lain five of the crew including the skipper, P/O Ronald Henry Craig who had, along with Gradwell, Horne and Forrest, formed a sort of old guard of the longer lasting, the grey bearded ones, the old lags as the C-in-C called such men, those who had flown Op after Op after Op since the winter and the Battle of Berlin. For all that, being an old lag with his tour of thirty Ops nearly done, Ginger Craig was still only twenty years old when he died.

Pilot Officer Rae and his crew had had a much shorter career; a fortnight to be exact. Rae had been to Rennes with Forrest, then it had been Aunay, Poitiers, Scholven-Buer, Limoges, bang, exploded in the skies over the Pas de Calais. Only the mid-upper got out.

Maule saw bombs falling on both sets of markers as there were no instructions received about which set was the one to aim for. Some crews were too busy to bomb. Adams was taking his crew on their second Op and they had the port outer engine on fire, one rudder and fin shot away, six feet of port wing and part of rear turret ditto, and cannon shell holes the length of the fuselage. In his report, Adams saw no need for a lot of detail. 'We were coned continuously from the time of crossing the enemy coast. Bomb load jettisoned during combat in target area. The aircraft was damaged. Off track on return after combat, believed crossed English coast off Dungeness, skirting London to west of Reading.' They got home. An eye witness said Adams looked quite drawn and pale. W4380 S-Sugar never flew again, becoming a training frame at No. 4 School of Technical Training, and Adams was henceforth known as Lucky.

At Prouville, P/O Wood, more experienced than the drawn and pale Adams – he'd been on six Ops – also jettisoned his bombs while he was coned by searchlights and shot at by flak, immediately after he'd escaped from 'an encounter with an enemy aircraft', as he phrased it.

Sgt Bob Riches was rear gunner with Larry Marsh:

(Prouville) looked a doddle. An hour and a half each way and only fifteen minutes over France. At the coast we could see TIs burning but we were told to hold, then we were told to bomb, then, with the doors open, we were told to hold again. Flares were dropping everywhere and the whole area was like daylight. They were using a searchlight with a smoky blue beam and it would lock on to a bomber, then six or eight more would do the same and the nightfighters came in, flying up the beams. The bomber crew would be blinded. They'd have no chance. There were aircraft burning and crashing all over the place but, apart from being caught in a searchlight briefly, all we felt was the turbulence of all the aircraft milling around. When we did get the go-ahead to bomb we couldn't find the target so we dropped our load across a searchlight battery and got the hell out.

The Flying Control people at Bardney wouldn't have been too worried at first, when Eddie Halshaw didn't show up. He'd been late before. He'd been the last back by a good half an hour from Brunswick, almost two hours behind the first home. He'd hung around over Nantes for half an hour, waiting for some red spot fires to appear. They hadn't so he'd brought his bombs home.

This time, though, he would not be late back. He'd been on twelve Ops in his career, almost the average expectancy, parallel with Doug Melrose. He'd been second Dicky to Tours, 19 May and on 24 June he was approaching the target when, almost simultaneously, a Lanc went down in flames beside him, a German fighter flashed past and he was caught in searchlights. After a twisting, diving turn to escape, he climbed to bombing height and had another go. Searchlights again picked out LL853 WS/W. With only a few seconds to bombs gone, Halshaw held fast. The bombs went, the aircraft was hit, nothing on the intercom, rear gunner Henry Garrett jumped from his turret and belly gunner William Wilson through his hole in the floor. The mid-upper, Jim Abbott, was there, ready to go the same way, but didn't make it and, with the rest of the crew, smashed into the road that leads from Coulonvillers to Doullens. Wilson and Garratt were taken prisoner. The other six were taken to Coulonvillers Cemetery.

The operational summary in 9 Squadron's ORB says of Prouville: 'Considerable opposition was encountered. Poor marking. Three did not bomb. No results were observed. Three aircraft failed to return.' It's hard to see how it could be put in fewer words.

The trip to Beauvoir, 29 June, was their first daylight for quite a while, striking at flying bomb installations. No marking was seen and nothing was heard of the Controller, no fighters were sighted and a good deal of smoke covered the area. None of the pilots, including Adams back on duty with some colour in his cheeks, thought anything about it worth mentioning.

In June 1944, Dougie Melrose and his crew flew ten Ops, two air tests, two cross-countries returning from diverted landings, one bombing practice and the recalled Op to Watten in Holland, all in WS/J-Johnny. Operationally, that made a total of fifteen for Melrose, fourteen for the crew. It was early days but, noted the great statistician in the sky, they had passed beyond the average thirteen. Harris, a few days behind Melrose in starting, had done nine Ops. Only twenty one to go.

8

THE HOT SUMMER OF 44

1 July, cancelled Op. 2 July, cancelled cricket match – RAF Woodhall (617 and 627 Squadrons) v RAF Bardney. 3 July, cancelled Op, and that was the last uneventful day for a while. The brief for the month was more transport targets to help the invasion, and V-bomb sites, code named No Ball, part of the long standing Operation Crossbow. First up of the No Balls was Creil.

Bob Woolf in his diary was not enthusiastic. 'Target tonight is Creil. It may be sticky, it's a secret target. Short trip, four to five hours. Nightfighters and flak are two of the catches. The third is that we are Joe'd for a suicide squad effort. Five aircraft in the first wave are to fly around and over the target while the others drop their bombs. We are first over the target and last to leave. Bloody lovely. Heaven help us.'

Creil was a small town with some industry and a railway junction, 65 miles from the coast in the department of Oise, north of Paris. Nearby was the village of St Leu d'Esserant where there was a network of caves and natural tunnels which the locals had been using for growing mushrooms. The Germans threw out the mushrooms and the villagers and, seeing a series of bomb-proof shelters ready made, stored in the caves large quantities of V-weapons and associated supplies, more, probably, than at any other site. Here were assembled doodlebugs for taking by road to the launching points. Bombing was not going to wreck the caves altogether but it could bring a lot of rock down to block the entrances and it could make a mess of the immediate area, smashing up the roads and railways and making normal use very difficult.

Earlier in the day, the same target had been attacked by the Lancasters of 617 Squadron carrying Barnes Wallis's superbomb, the 12,000lb Tallboy, two piloted by 9 Squadron alumni, Stout from 1943 and Gingles from way back, a Wellington pilot who'd crashed and burned in September 1941. Now it was a clear, moonlit night with the promise of plenty of fighters about. Railway raids on Orleans and Villeneuve helped spread the fighters more thinly but there were many battles going and coming back.

Melrose, Joe'd for a dicey drop, stayed over the target as ordered to inspect results. That went well. It was the way home which was dicey.

Bob Woolf: One fighter had a crack at us, an Me410 but Ernie (Stalley, rear gunner) gave him a good squirt while we corkscrewed like hell and he broke off and we lost him. Guess we were lucky. There was a lot of nightfighter activity, we learned later, and it was a clear night with a full moon. No cloud cover to help us along and we saw quite a few kites shot down. Nightfighters are deadly sinister because we never know where they are until they move into Monica range or they're spotted by eye. We sometimes see them flash past in the opposite direction or right across our bows, pursuing somebody else. If they do see us, we have to hope the encounter will be a momentary thing and that the darkness will give us a chance of escape, because they outgun us by so much. It's incredible what damage those cannons can do.

There were combats over most of the route. Gradwell didn't have one, not tonight anyway. He'd never been attacked by a nightfighter in all his long career and he'd very nearly finished his tour. Just starting his was F/Sgt Tweddle, destined to become something of a 9 Squadron legend and to be misspelled for ever by the WAAF battle-order typists as Tweedle, who was with Gradwell as one of the last second Dickies to fly.

Nancy Bower: 'Tweddle was married and his wife used to ring up, which was a difficulty most of them didn't have. We weren't allowed of course to say where he was, but we'd say, "He's just not around at the moment", and she knew by that he was flying.'

P/O Marsh's crew had two combats and lived. Having pressed on to bomb on three engines with a u/s bombsight, Marsh flew as erratically as he could away from the target, which meant that the first blast of cannon fire from the Me110 missed them. The German prepared for another attack and Marsh corkscrewed for their lives. As the fighter came in, Sgt Riches in the rear turret and Sgt Marshall in the mid-upper poured bullets into it and its starboard engine began smoking. It peeled off, fell away and crashed. One to the boys in the Lancasters.

The 9 Squadron ORB described the night: 'A successful attack was made on Creil in which fourteen of our aircraft took part. One of these failed to return.' In all, 228 Lancasters took part and fourteen of these failed to return, including LL785 WS/F-Freddie skippered by Ryan, first Op 10 April to Tours, same crew all the way. Pilot Officer Dennis Ryan, 21, like all RAF Ryans of the time, was familiarly called Buck after the fictional detective turned MI5 investigator in his own sixpenny 'world famous comic'. The real, flying Buck Ryan had with him another of the last second Dickies, a Kiwi, F/Lt James Patrick. They were killed on the way home, all eight of them, and became world famous that way.

The success of the attack on the caves at St Leu d'Esserant had to be put beyond doubt; doodlebugs were droning in at more than one hundred a day. Deaths in London had reached 2,500. If the first raid had softened up the target, another should flatten it so 9 Squadron was ordered back, 7 July. Taking part then were 208 Lancs; fourteen went again from Bardney and, with Russ Gradwell, new boy F/Lt Oldacre. Oldacre was different from all the others; he would be 9 Squadron's last second Dicky of the war.

> 'I find that running commentaries
> on the proximity of flak shells which include
> remarks such as "Christ that was close"
> are apt to confuse the pilot'
> Anon

Again, the bombers had fine moonlight to work in and the attack on St Leu, whimsically Anglicised in the squadron ORB as St Len, was spot on. Ex CO W/Cdr Porter was master bomber. The caves, they were sure, had been blocked, rendered u/s, with goodness knows how many souls buried alive.

Wehrmacht Colonel Walter of the special purpose V-weapon army unit, the 65 Corps, was there. 'You could hear a constant rumbling overhead, and began to feel that the very mountain was on the move and might collapse at any moment. It was asking too much of any man's nerves to expect him to hold out in caves like that.'

Through this and other No Ball attacks in the middle fortnight of July, the rate of doodlebugs hitting London was cut in half but on that night over St Leu, there were many eyes glad of the silver disc which illuminated the bombers' targets and against which a Lancaster also silhouetted beautifully. Everybody in 9 Squadron was shot at. They were all damaged, every one. Larry Marsh's gunners, Bob Riches and Sid Marshall, claimed an Me110 down, which was confirmed but that was only one. Rumour had it there had been 150 fighters waiting for them; with that number, they couldn't all be lucky enough to get back to Bardney.

Blackham, one month with 9 Squadron, went down to the west of Paris; all killed except one. Langford fell at Gamaches, between Dieppe and Abbeville; he and two of his crew had got out and were taken prisoner. George Langford, a man with strong opinions and a famous way with the ladies, would not be seeing any more girlfriends for a while. The worst casualty for 9 Squadron was Russ Gradwell. That was three ex J-Johnny pilots in one night.

Gradwell had had his first Op to Leipzig, 19 February, in M-Mike, with Pete Lynch, Tommy Arnold, Atch Atkinson, Jim Price, Bill Best and Les Sutton. Atkinson and Best were Canadians. They'd crewed up feeling they were potential friends and, like most Lancaster crews, had become so.

Russ Gradwell: 'I met my rear gunner, Les Sutton, on the train. Pete Lynch had been an apprentice at A V Roe, building Lancasters, which seemed like an excellent qualification for a flight engineer. We used to say that if all the bits were heaped in a corner of a hangar, give Pete a day or two and a Lanc would roll out.'

Still in M-Mike after almost six months together, they crossed the French coast and straight away saw dogfights all around. The stream of Lancasters with accompanying Mosquitos met a queue of Messerschmitts, Focke-Wulfs, Junkers and Dorniers. German fighters and British heavy bombers pirouetted in the moonlight with the inevitable dying falls in flames. 'There was nothing we could do except plough on and, about halfway between the coast and the target, it came to our turn. We were flying south-east, into the moon. Anyone behind us would have seen the unmistakeable shape of a four-engined bomber against the circle of light, as clearly as they might on an aircraft recognition chart.'

Counting those early French trips as ones rather than thirds, this was Russ Gradwell's 33rd Op, the crew's 32nd. Officially, it was the crew's 29th. They only had one more Op to do and they would be tour expired. They had been everywhere and done everything except this was the first time they had been attacked by a fighter. This, it would appear, was the way fate worked.

Les Sutton had been a gamekeeper in civilian life. He had exceptional night vision; that was his official RAF category, exceptional. The rest of us were marked above average but Les was even better. Suddenly he screeched out 'Corkscrew port, go!'

In all our time together, I'd never heard him say it like this. In fighter affiliation, the practice was 'Rear gunner to pilot.' 'Yes, rear gunner.' 'Prepare to corkscrew. Corkscrew to port, go.' Fortunately for us, Les's eyesight and disregard for formality gave me enough time to begin evasive action before, we thought, being hit too seriously.

That they were being hit was apparent from the smell of cordite. It was extremely tense inside that Lanc, with the only sounds being Gradwell's commentary to his gunners – diving port, rolling, climbing starboard, rolling. The pilot's concentration at such a time was utter, total, obsessive, flying the aircraft in a maneouvre he knew but which he'd never flown under such an imperative before. The gunners meanwhile listened to the commentary and worked out where they were in the sky and, therefore, where the fighter should be.

Gradwell thought he heard someone laugh. If it had been the gods laughing he could have understood; it was one of their better jokes, having you shot down one Op short of your lot.

It sounded very like one of my own crew laughing on the intercom and when I heard it again I interrupted my commentary to ask who the bloody hell it was. Bill Best, the Canadian mid-upper, owned up. His reason was that his hydraulics had been shot away and he was slowly spinning around and around in his turret, out of control. You had to be there; it seemed funny at the time. 'Not to worry, skip,' he said. 'Every time the bastard goes past, I'll give him a burst.' 'Level out!' shouted Les Sutton in the rear turret.

'Level out, skip.' We had complete trust in each other, I had complete trust in Les, so I obeyed his curious order. The reward was the sight of the fighter passing underneath us with the pilot apparently slumped at the controls. It looked like the gunners must have got him. His aircraft had automatically reverted to flying straight and level and would do that until it ran out of fuel, so it was goodbye to him.

The Lanc was flying straight and level too, nobody was injured, and Gradwell decided to go on to the target on the grounds that he would rather be one of two hundred in a bomber stream than on his own flying home. Atch Atkinson, the bomb aimer, called up to say he'd got the markers so Gradwell replied, as always, 'OK, over to you' and took his last search outside before concentrating on the instruments to fly the aircraft inch-perfectly to the bomb aimer's instructions.

My last look around revealed a small fire on the port wing. Let's be rid of the bombs, I thought, and we'll deal with the fire later. Normally, after bombs gone, Atch would keep up his instructions with 'Steady, steady . . . camera gone'. We didn't bother that night. 'Forget the camera,' I said as I turned for home and the navigator called the course. Now we would try to put the fire out. Pete Lynch feathered both port engines and switched all the fuel off on that side. The fire was inside the mainplane, inside the middle of the wing. The fighter must have shot a hole in a tank and a spark from an engine or ack-ack from the ground had set it alight.

Lynch's measures had no effect. While Gradwell strained to keep M-Mike straight on just the two starboard engines, the little flame moved slowly but certainly back across the width of the wing, like an oxyacetylene torch cutting through sheet metal.

Pete said, 'I think we've had it, skip.' He knew every component and he could visualise what was happening inside the wing. The flame was getting near the main spar. If it cut through that, we would be in a one-winged aircraft, so I gave the order to bale out. Pete Lynch went to pick up three parachutes and gave one each to second Dicky Oldacre and me. Atch unshipped the escape hatch and dived out, followed by Oldacre, Pete and Tommy (Arnold, navigator). Bill Best was still going round and round in his turret although not laughing so much by this time. He reached down to grab the stirrup he used to haul himself in and out of his position and jammed it into the turret mechanism.

With that stopped he dropped down into the fuselage, missing by the very narrowest squeak dropping a great deal further, through the hole in the floor that none of them had realised was part of their damage, and he hadn't got his parachute on yet. Price the w/op kept his helmet and intercom on and met the two gunners at the rear door. He called the skip to say they'd gone and he was going, which left the pilot.

I had to use full right rudder and full stick to keep her in line against the pulling power of the two starboard engines. George the autopilot wouldn't have been any use. He wasn't strong enough to do this job, so I had to climb down from my platform onto the cockpit floor, standing on one leg, keeping one hand on the stick and one foot up on the rudder bar. I knew what would happen when I let go. The aircraft would take a huge diving turn to port and on into a spinning power dive and I would be stuck in the cockpit, pinned to the wall by centrifugal force.

He would not have been comforted by the thought that, if there was any justice in the world, he would be awarded the posthumous Victoria Cross like P/O Leslie Manser had been for doing exactly this in a Manchester after the 'Thousand Plan' Cologne raid.

If Gradwell was not to be dragged swiftly and terrifyingly to certain death he would have to achieve another first on this night of first times for everything. He would have to let go of the controls with his hand and foot and at the same instant dive from the cockpit down through the bomb aimer's hatch. He was, he thought, not really cut out to be a circus act or a Hollywood stunt man but there was no point in messing about. Do it. Go. He went.

Next thing I knew, I was swinging from my parachute, descending on a glorious moonlit night towards a forest. And, like so many bomber crew whose only parachute jump was their first parachute jump, I couldn't remember pulling the rip cord. I had no real idea how I came to be there, swinging gently in the French July air, and I had no idea how I could avoid being speared and slashed by the trees I was going to hit, or how I would reach the forest floor if I became suspended by chute and ropes in the tree tops. I needn't have worried. I landed in a heap on the ground, stowed away my chute and Mae West, realised I was in enemy territory on my own and began imagining a German soldier behind every tree.

Second Dicky Oldacre, a few miles away, had hidden his parachute and flying kit in some brambles and was walking away from where he thought their Lanc had crashed. In varying circumstances, the rest of Gradwell's crew were experiencing much the same feelings as their skipper, except for Sergeant James Thomas Price, wireless operator, aged 21. His parachute hadn't opened and he was lying dead in the same forest. His body would not be found until February 1945.

Gradwell set off towards the north-west where the front line was. He knew he was somewhere north of Paris (in fact, near Beauvais in Oise, hardly fifteen miles back from the target), probably fifty or sixty miles from the English Channel coast. Progress was very slow, with much bumping into trees, stumbling about and falling over, until he found a path which led him to a track which took him onto a country lane. After walking along for three-quarters of a mile he heard a vehicle. He dived into the ditch and peered nervously at the steel helmets of the passengers in the truck which came up and past.

When they'd gone, I carried on for another half mile, expecting to hear vehicles, marching boots or shouted challenges in German. I came to a village; there were shots being fired. I took off down a side road and turned into a cornfield. I walked with great care through the ripe corn so I didn't leave a trail and, strangely considering my circumstances, I also didn't want to spoil any of the crop by flattening it. My thoughts turned to the common sense which so far seemed to be lacking in my plan. If Jerry was out looking for me, surely it would be better to hide until he'd moved well on? So I lay down in the corn and fell asleep.

Walter Oldacre had walked through the night. Having no better ideas he kept going, using his escape-kit compass to head south-east towards Paris. At about six o'clock on a breathless, brilliant, cloudless sunny morning he found a hiding place and fell gratefully asleep.

Half an hour later his skipper was woken by a group of Typhoon fighters flying very low. Resigned to a long, hot day with no food or water, he got up but had only taken a few steps when he heard the clatter of a reaping machine being pulled by two horses. The choice was plain. He could stay in the corn as the reaper went around in ever decreasing circles until it found him in the middle with the rats and rabbits, or he could walk out and greet whoever was harvesting today.

I was very proud of the fact that I was that rare thing among aircrew, a man who could speak French, but I'd never tested it in a French cornfield before. 'Hey, Messieurs. Je suis Royal Air Force,' was the best I could manage and it didn't seem to be good enough. The two French farm workers looked blank. I pointed to the wings on my uniform and the letters RAF. 'Ah!' they cried, '*vous êtes* Royal Air Force.'

Clearly, Russ Gradwell's French accent was in need of some homework. A young couple turned up, on an early morning stroll down the lane, and the resulting chatter between them and the two men often featured parts of the French verb *cacher*, to hide. The English assumed things were going his way and so they were.

I was taken to a farm, a very big farm, and word had gone ahead of me because formed up outside the farmhouse were a dozen or more people, all anxious to shake hands and kiss both cheeks with the brave English flyer. As I worked my way down the line, I really did wonder at it all. If the Germans had arrived they'd have shot the lot of them. Anyway, with formalities complete and protocol satisfied, everyone went back to their work except for Madame Carron, the farmer's wife. Inside the house, she wanted to know if I was hungry. RAF procedure on an escape was to accept food only if you were desperate, because the French were themselves desperately short. So I said, 'Non, non merci, je suis bien.'
Madame Carron gave me a nod and a smile and went down the cellar steps. She came back with the biggest steak I had ever seen, which she began to fry in about half-a-pound of farm butter on top of the wood-burning stove. While that was doing, she produced a gorgeous white loaf, more butter and a bottle of red wine. I hadn't seen white bread since the war broke out and I had a year's ration of butter in front of me.

Somehow, out of politeness, he managed to demolish it, plus the wine, plus the steak which, at home, would have been expected to feed a family of four for a fortnight. He sat back with a sigh of contentment, appreciation and entente cordiale. The smiling Madame Carron placed a large bowl of strawberries on the table with a jug of fresh cream. Cream was illegal in Britain.

A strange incident followed, when I was subjected to a close but wordless inspection by a small boy. I felt that my authenticity was being questioned so I placed my packet of Player's cigarettes on the table top. The boy examined this, seemed satisfied and left, still without a word, to be replaced as validator by an elderly lady, Madame Ravel, who was clearly not to do with farming but rather a gentlewoman, nobility maybe.

She spoke good English and had been to school in England, in Richmond, Surrey of which Gradwell's knowledge was limited having driven through it once with his parents before the war. Madame was happy to hear instead about Gradwell's home town, Llandudno, and the Great Orme, and Mostyn Street and anything else he could bring to mind.

She didn't say but he felt that Llandudno had been among her visited places and that he was passing the exam. 'I am sure you are an officer in the Royal Air Force,' she announced. 'I will fetch assistance.'

Losses or not, there was still a war on and W/Cdr Bazin was determined that his squadron, No. 9, would perform to the utmost. It was the second week in July and whole days were devoted to a very extensive practice bombing programme – and there was more practice, of school French. Gradwell was making progress. Two men had arrived after Madame Ravel, introduced themselves as Maigret and Thibou, and asked for the names of the rest of Gradwell's crew.

One took a camera from his pocket and photographed me. Apparently the Germans had recently changed the pattern of French ID cards so the pictures we carried in our escape kits were no longer any use. The French patriots were being supplied directly with ID card blank originals by the same printer who produced them for the occupying forces, and with official stamps by a lady who worked as a cleaner at German headquarters.

Oldacre had walked through the night again. If he'd kept going in the same direction he would have come to Creil but he too was about to change from outdoor to indoor fugitive. 'I hid in a haycock and at about 16.00 hours a farmer walked by alone. I hailed him and he returned a little later with another helper who brought me civilian clothes and took me to the police station at Bresles.' This was back the way he had come, near Beauvais, and he stayed there four days. Word was given and Messieurs Thibout and Maigret told Gradwell that they had found six altogether. Gradwell became Roger l'Anglais, which Thibout and Maigret thought frightfully witty since he came from Wales, but which Gradwell simply thought frightful.

At Bardney, Ops were cancelled but not the practice. On 12 July, twelve aircraft went to Culmont-Chalindrey, a railway target in the Haute-Marne. A dozen squadrons were there and the pilots of 9 Squadron, all of whom followed the controller's orders, complained bitterly about some of the others. Horne: 'Other crews were bombing without instructions from the master bomber and their photo flashes greatly impeded those who were trying to make a correct attack.' Melrose: 'Controller's instructions not adhered to by many crews.' Maule: 'Many aircraft bombed without instructions.' Perhaps Canadian Bill Hallett had no time for the same thoughts. The Germans certainly made a correct attack on him and all his crew.

Bad weather meant a homeward diversion for Melrose, to Balderton, near Newark, an American glider base.

Bob Woolf: It was always a delight to be diverted to American aerodromes because the breakfast we received was so much richer and more selective than anything the RAF could provide. Imagine, as many eggs as we could wish for, and a variety of food that otherwise we could only dream about. This was all served up with a warm welcome from the American personnel who always showed a great interest in us fellows and our Lancaster. When we landed and Doug opened the bomb doors, one Yank looked up in awe and shouted 'Goddam, it's a flying bomb bay!'

'How did you approach the target? Sideways?'
Intelligence officer at interrogation

After another railyard trip to Villeneuve St Georges, it was German army targets at Caen, a dawn raid, 18 July, up at about 04.00, down at about 07.30. Allied armies were struggling to break through strong enemy positions and a thousand bombers were sent to pave the way by hitting half-a-dozen fortified villages around the town. Large numbers of tanks and other vehicles were destroyed and those that were left could hardly move for bomb craters. Many, many German soldiers were killed and wounded and the Allies found hundreds wandering about, dazed with shock and unable to resist capture.

This was F/O Garlick's first Op, and F/O Morrison's in WS/J-Johnny, and F/Lt Relton's. Relton was 34 years old; Garlick was 20. These three were the first 9 Squadron pilots to go on Ops without having had a second Dicky flight. The loss, as then believed, of Oldacre and Gradwell would be the last of a new pilot with an old hand.

Aileen Walker: The telephone rang in the officers' mess and it was the CO. 'Wing Commander Bazin here. Can you get Morrison for me?' I looked about and couldn't see him. "Where's Eddie Morrison," I said. Somebody piped up 'He's in the windsock.' That's how naive I was and they knew it. 'Sorry, sir,' I said. 'Flying Officer Morrison isn't here but you'll find him in the windsock.'

On another occasion, a certain senior officer rang and asked to speak to one of the WAAFs. I could hear the conversation. He said, 'Slip into something loose and we'll go mushrooming.' I asked her, 'what are you going mushrooming for at this time of year?'

In a force of about a hundred, 9 Squadron took off that night for the railway junction at Revigny-sur-Ornain on the Champagne/Lorraine border, making two Ops in one day for the Dickyless Three, Garlick, Morrison and Relton, also Tweddle, Camsell, Dunne and Adams, and for some of the aircraft, such as ME833 WS/Z which was given to a man with six weeks' worth of grey hairs, Leslie Wood. Two previous attacks on Revigny had resulted in no fatal damage done except to seventeen Lancasters.

The German fighters were in the air, ready, as the bombers crossed the coast. 'Lucky' Adams corkscrewed his way to the target and corkscrewed his way back under more or less constant attack while he and his crew saw what seemed like dozens of aircraft falling in flames. It was testimony to the ability of a Lancaster to take punishment that they got home.

Leslie Wood was one of the May intake, like Melrose and Harris. He'd flown his second Dicky with Forrest plus eight Ops over France, been on a spot of leave and taken off at 23.01 for Revigny. On that terrible night the railway was cut but a great many tours of Operations were ended prematurely. Enemy fighters had one of their best bags ever and almost a quarter of the force went down. Adams and his men were right; they had seen dozens, two dozens. No. 9 Squadron lost Z on her way home. Wood's navigator, F/Sgt Oates, was taken prisoner. The rest were taken to the graveyard as were so many more who were lost in the cause of Revigny junction. Of the fifteen pilots and crews arriving at 9 Squadron in the month of May, eight had been lost by mid-July and the other seven were roughly halfway through their tours.

Courtrai, or Kortrijk, over the border into Belgium, offered another key railway target linking Germany and occupied Holland with northern France. The official report of the Courtrai raid, 20/21 July, said that the rail junctions and yards were devastated. It was a straightforward trip for some. Adams even did two camera runs over the target to make sure it was thoroughly pasted. Also devastated were ten Lancs, including PD205

WS/H. F/O Graham Garlick and crew, on their third, were killed as they smashed into the ground about four miles west of the target.

The Melrose men were returning from leave. Bob Woolf had taken a bus from Lincoln to Bardney and was sweating in the hot afternoon sun as he started the long walk from village to airfield.

With my suitcase in one hand and my RAF greatcoat over the other arm I was making slow progress and I quite failed to notice the RAF staff car coming towards me from the direction of the aerodrome. To my shock and horror, as it went past, I saw the pennant on the bonnet which told me that inside the car was Air Commodore Hesketh, CO of 51 Base (Waddington, Bardney and Skellingthorpe) and therefore our most senior officer.

And I hadn't raised a salute! I glanced over my shoulder to see the car turn around and come back my way. It drew alongside, the rear door opened, and there was the Air Commodore. I was standing stiffly to attention and trying to salute with both hands. The great man leaned over and said 'Get in, son.' I climbed in, luggage and all, wondering if I was to be executed privately or out on the runway in front of the entire squadron, but the Air Commodore simply questioned me about my Ops, my pilot and so on. When we reached the aerodrome, the big boss opened the door and motioned me out. I stood to attention, threw the best salute of my life and tried to stammer some words of thanks for the lift. He smiled and said, as he drove away, 'Think nothing of it, son. King George's car, King George's petrol. Bloody good firm to work for, what?'

The first raid on Kiel for well over a year, 23 July, and the first big raid on a German city for two months, had six-hundred-plus Lancs and Halifaxes.

Bob Woolf: We'd dropped our bombs when suddenly we flipped upside down, and J-Johnny fell in a long spiral, and we remembered something similar happening to Horne at Scholven-Buer. We all thought we were goners, of course, except we had Doug and Ted, and they likewise managed to pull us out of it somehow and we levelled out flying low over Germany. Just where in Germany we didn't know, and the boys to tell us were somewhat hampered by an accident to a tin can that we used to save us from venturing all the way to the Elsan at the back of the aircraft. The can had spilled during our rapid descent and saturated our Gee box and radio, so they were no help. The front half of J-Johnny was filled with Window flying about, and Jimmy Moore had lost his navigation chart.

The regulation was that you had to empty your pockets of all private stuff before a flight but Jimmy had a three-page letter, from his family in Australia, in his battledress pocket. He stuck these pages to his table with drawing pins and, from memory, sketched out the area of Europe we were in and the various appropriate latitudes and longitudes, as far as he could. From this he worked out an approximate direction for home and, pointed in the general direction, we reached the English coast. At Bardney, in interrogation, the intelligence officer said 'Where's your chart, Moore?' and none of us would ever forget the look on that officer's face as Jim sheepishly presented him with a three-page letter from Australia. And we never did find that chart and never knew how it escaped from our aircraft.

Flying Officer Melrose had become Flight Lieutenant Melrose, leading A Flight of 9 Squadron. That was what could happen to you in two months. If you lived for that length of time, you could go from new bug to being in charge of half a squadron. Ray Harris, equally good as a pilot and bomber but a very different sort of personality, would not have wanted to be put in charge of a flight, ever, and the heirarchy might have agreed with him.

They were off to Saint Cyr-l'École, not far from Paris, at the bottom of the garden of the palace of Versailles, where there was an aerodrome and signals station. There would also be large numbers of ack-ack guns and a *staffel* or two of fighters. Never mind. If you thought like that, you'd never get on the bloody aircraft. It would be Melrose's twentieth Op, the crew's nineteenth, the magic numbers. It was the closest they had ever been to Paris.

Bob Woolf: After operating in the dark for so long it was a thrilling thing to see the beautiful sky above and the cloud formations below, and to look over a formation of so many of our bombers was a comforting experience as we headed for the target. Very accurate flak but only a moderate amount. We had a near miss when two bombs fell past us and a piece of flak knocked a fair hole in the fuselage as it came through between Jimmy Moore and me. A sobering thought.

Later, in recognition of their colonial cousins' near miss, the ground crew painted a kangaroo on J-Johnny.

Givors was yet another French railway target, in the south this time, on the Rhône below Lyon.

Bob Woolf: Givors was an eight-and-three-quarter hour trip (26 July) in extremely poor weather. We were in electrical storms continually and the whole aircraft was alive with St Elmo's Fire. There were static

sparks everywhere and the exterior of J-Johnny was covered with blue flames. Aerials, guns and wings were brilliantly alight. The props were just four circles of flame. Visibility was almost zero though enough for us to see three aircraft hit by flak and go down very close to us. There were hailstones. Rain poured into the aircraft making the floor awash with water. In such foul weather there would be no fighters about so the master bomber gave the order to turn on navigation lights. Immediately the surrounding sky was filled with red, green and white lights showing just how close and heavily populated the bomber stream was. It was terrifying. Surprisingly, we later learned that the attack had been quite successful. Not surprisingly, the hailstones had stripped the paint off our aircraft.

Never mind. Harry Forrest, who had had his mid-upper killed over Nürnburg back in March, who had taken Ray Harris for his first ride over enemy territory, Harry had done it. Tour complete. He could have some leave now, and a posting to a conversion unit and a DFC in November when they got around to it.

The aircraft Woolf saw fall were from 619 and 83 Squadrons. Five were lost altogether and in one of them was Flight Lieutenant Jock Gilmour DFM, once observer to Douglas and then Tiny Cooling, all those long days ago flying Wellingtons from Honington. He'd been with 207 Squadron since then, added wireless operating to his trades and now was flying with the Pathfinders, 83 Squadron, when he was killed at Givors in a crew with five DFCs and a DSO between them.

Stuttgart featured in a rare return to the area-bombing tactics of the pre-invasion war. This city of half a million people had had plenty of attention from Bomber Command but it was still there, nestling in its valleys. It was the publishing capital of southern Germany; much more importantly, it still had Daimler-Benz making aero engines, trucks and tanks, the VKF ball bearing plant and Bosch making spark plugs and other electrical equipment. On the way back, Lucky Adams and his men sang *Happy Birthday* over the intercom to their w/op, Jack Faucheux, whose twentieth it was. Glaswegian Charles Scott's was the only crew to be attacked by a fighter – they were in J-Johnny, seemingly immune on her 93rd – but other squadrons were not so invisible to the enemy and forty were shot down, mostly on the way to the target.

Flight Lieutenant Brian Moorhead DFC, late of Anderson Storey's original Wellington crew and then rear gunner with Dick Stubbs, was in a Lanc of 463 RAAF Squadron. He wasn't Australian; he was their gunnery leader. He filled in for the regular man with a 20-year-old skipper and that crew, like Stuttgart, was put to the torch.

When Lieutenant Shuff of the USAAF landed his B17 Flying Fortress at Bardney on the morning of 29 July, there was some excitement among the Melrose men. They were off for a couple of days' holiday, or a General Liaison Visit, to an American bombardment group.

Bob Woolf: We spent a very interesting two days, escorted by American aircrew throughout, being shown the whole routine and exchanging information on equipment, bombing techniques and crew functions. We went to their briefing for a mission and saw all the procedures. Quite a contrast to what we were used to. We went to a concert at night by Captain Glenn Miller's army band and enjoyed stuffing ourselves with American grub. They seemed to have more of everything than us. They even made going home a bit special. The pilot of our Fortress took us down to zero feet and buzzed our aerodrome, very thrilling, but when we headed straight for the control tower we could see the occupants making for the door, and there was a lot of fuss afterwards about 'those crazy Yanks'.

For 9 Squadron it was back to daylights and a trip to Cahagnes, in support of advancing crazy Yanks in Normandy only to be recalled, which caused F/O Macintosh, on his third Op in J-Johnny on her 94th, to jettison his bombs. His inexperience almost led to the end of them both when he ordered this flying far too low. The shrapnel from the explosion riddled the aircraft and put her out of action for almost a fortnight.

Ten aircraft attacked Joigny La Roche (31 July) and 'concentrated bombing was carried out'. The whole target area appeared to be hit. A further four aircraft were detailed for an attack on Rilly-la-Montagne. Of these, one failed to return.

F/O Worner took off at 17.30, followed by Bazin, Harris and Redfern, and joined a concentration of about one hundred to bomb the approaches to a railway tunnel used as a warehouse for V-weapon supplies. LM453 WS/E was fatally hit by flak. The local French saw the doomed Lanc heading for their village of Piusieulx, in a starboard curving dive with half its cockpit missing. At the last moment, the pilot somehow managed to drag her round to port to crash in open fields. That pilot, Charles Edward Michael Worner, known as Jack after the actor or Tubby after himself, had been a long laster. They were a May intake crew, two aged nineteen, two twenty, flown sixteen Ops, and their rewards were cemetery plots at Clichy.

At the end of July, Melrose had done 21 Ops. Like Worner's had been, the crew were old lags after a couple of months. During their time on 9 Squadron, fourteen aircraft and crews had disappeared. Captains Baker,

King, McMurchy, Craig, Halshaw, Rae, Ryan, Langford, Blackham, Gradwell, Hallet, Wood, Garlick and now Tubby Worner, all gone, and Doug Melrose was still there. Roll on August.

Three modestly defended French raids began the month and that was it for F/O Horne, shot up and wounded over Berlin in March on his third trip, who pulled his aircraft out of a screaming dive after being attacked at Scholven-Buer in June, who had suffered all the ordinary hazards of war over and over again, had earned his training unit posting and DFC, if you please, sir, and Bar.

Harris, Melrose and the rest went to Trossy, 3 August, another V-bomb target. It was Ray Harris's birthday; on his 18th Op he was twenty years old. Trossy St Maxim was only a mile from St Leu d'Esserant and was believed to be a fuel supply depot. This was a big daylight raid and the flak was intense. Some skippers, perhaps inexperienced, tried too hard to avoid the flak and crashed into other bombers.

Bob Woolf: We took off at 11.45 on a beautiful day with pretty cloud formations and bombed rocket installations near Paris from 17,500 feet. Flak was very accurate but not too thick. We saw one kite go down, hit by falling bombs. This packing in close on the run-up to bomb is deadly. They should stagger the formations more. Two hundred Lancs weaving in and out can be a nuisance. It's bad enough without all that.

Adams had a collision happen right next to him and decided to dive below the confusion. The risk of being bombed out seemed less than the flak, exploding precisely at formation height, and the daft weavings of green skippers. Adams was in WS/R, not destined for the final dive. Back in 1943 she'd been McCubbin's, when they'd shot down a fighter and had bullet holes too numerous to count, and P/O Lyon's and then P/O Siddle's. At this time in her life she was normally Puddle Lake's aircraft. He'd done 20 Ops in her. EE136 Spirit of Russia would end her days in undignified flames, not in battle but as a firefighting exercise on the ground.

Bob Woolf: 'F/O Ron Reeves, our only Aussie pilot, finished his tour so we were all off to Bardney to celebrate. We put Ted (Selfe) and Bert (Hoyle) to bed at 03.30, well drunk and very happy.'

4 August was a significant date for 9 Squadron. For the first time, they flew with 617 (Dambusters) Squadron only, 27 of them together, to hit a precision target in daylight. Normally, 617 would have had the Tallboy deep-penetration bomb but there was a shortage so everyone had normal thousand pounders. The target was Étaples, a small port on the Canche estuary near Calais which was significant militarily only for its railway

bridge. If the bridge could be downed, a main line of supply to anti-invasion forces would be cut. Redfern said he hit the bridge, Bazin also, and Scott, and Taylor. Camsell thought he hit it and Macintosh saw the bridge destroyed. When the smoke cleared, it was still there.

Bob Woolf: We had one touchy moment when a piece of flak hit our left windscreen, shattering it and spraying particles over Doug and Ted. Ted had a few cuts and his eyes were affected by flying fragments. I happened to have given Doug a good pair of sunglasses and he was wearing these in the bright sunlight and they probably saved him from worse injury. Of course, if the flak had been two inches to the left it would have taken his head off. Doug kept the aircraft stable and under control. No doubt about it, the boys handled the situation with a minimum of fuss. A good show.

Next day, 9 Squadron went back again, fourteen of them on their own this time, and did the job. Jim Parsons, Ray Harris's bomb aimer, witnessed it: 'On the run-up to the target I saw two bombs hit the bridge. When I released my stick, I saw my first bomb hit. We were bombing from 10,000 feet. The PRU took a picture the next day and we'd breached it in several places. This was with the Mark 14A bombsight, the 'old-fashioned bombsight used to hit cities', as an expert from a certain other squadron put it, as opposed to SABS presumably.'

Stabilised Automatic Bomb Sight, Mark 2A, was used exclusively in wartime by 617 Squadron, the unit which had been formed for the dambusters raid and was thereafter trained for 'the precision bombing of selected targets'. Being stabilised meant that the sight automatically compensated for some of the minor aircraft movements which were inevitable on a bombing run, making the bomb aimer's job that much easier. Earlier models of this bombsight had been in service as far back as February then withdrawn, and the improved 2A remained a complicated and temperamental piece of kit.

From a crew's point of view, its main drawback was the amount of straight and level flying you had to do on your bombing run. To be sure that the best was obtained from the equipment, the aircraft had to maintain position for around twelve miles, five minutes, which gave the enemy many more chances of a better shot.

Both types of sight, SABS and Mark 14, had computer boxes to make calculations about windspeed, height and other factors, although the Mark 14 especially was reliant on accurate wind-finding over the target. With SABS, fully trained and highly skilled crews should have been able to achieve an average error of 80 yards from 20,000 feet. With the Mark 14A, similar crews should have expected an average error of 150 yards from 20,000 feet. This might have implied that SABS was a better bombsight but, like most things, it was ultimately down to the human element. Even in the safety of the bombing ranges, where crews could do as much straight and level flying as they liked, the SABS-equipped squadron did not always win the Camrose Trophy, the prize for best results in 5 Group competition. There were many, many influences on accurate bombing and the sight was only one of them.

Maule saw five bombs hit the northern end of the bridge which SABS-aided crews had failed to hit yesterday. Redfern thought at least two aircraft put their sticks of bombs along it and Melrose saw one stick right on it. F/O Lake had other things on his mind. 'Target not attacked as when on bombing run a steep turn to port had to be made to avoid bombs dropped by another Lancaster from not more than 100 feet above. This Lancaster had previously crossed three times.' Lake knew who it was; not one of the aldermen like Maule, Redfern or Melrose. One of the new boys had got overexcited.

Bob Woolf: Much to our pleasure we had successful results with our attack. Having flown in conjunction with No. 617 Squadron, the Dambusters, who missed the target, we are feeling rather full of ourselves at present. There wasn't much opposition, peculiarly enough, and only our squadron on it. I was Deputy Controller; everything went bang on and fortunately the wireless was good. Up to today, this squadron has operated on fifteen days out of seventeen. Some of the chaps, armourers and so on, haven't been to bed for three days. Ground crew never receive the recognition they deserve.

It was Friday and no bed since Tuesday for those men but, by the nature of things, their special brand of heroism remained largely unsung. Ken McClure was in signals ground crew at Bardney.

A bicycle was an absolute necessity. Our living quarters were a long way from our workshops and even further from the dispersals. A lot of the everyday repair and maintenance work was done at the dispersals by men who hardly knew what leave was and for whom a seven-day week was normal. We had to work whatever hours were required to get the aircraft operational on time. Fourteen hours a day was not exceptional although a standard day was probably 08.00 to 18.00, but on top of that we still had to fit in our station duties like airfield guard and firewatch. We had three of what you might call bottom lines. Time of take-off, time of return, and the special views of a given crew on

'their' aircraft. Some crews, and some members of crews, were very fussy and were forever checking their own positions. If the skipper had a different opinion from the official one on how, what and when to test, we had to follow the skipper.

Often without the proper spares and official tools, ground crew's one aim in life was to keep their Latin motto for ever holy: *Ubendum wemendum*. A fitter looked after the engines and a rigger kept the aircraft shipshape and clean, with everything in its place. These two belonged to one aircraft and one aircraft belonged to them. The other trades – signals, electrician, armourer – worked across a flight which was usually half, sometimes a third of a squadron, with a flight sergeant in charge of each trade who was known as Chiefy. Once settled into their flights, they felt the same kind of possessive loyalty for their own aircraft as did the fitters and riggers and had a certain rivalry with the other flight.

Each aircraft had an aircraft manager, a sergeant who was usually the engine fitter/mechanic. In his dispersal hut he kept the much revered Form 700, the aircraft's maintenance log, which had to be signed by representatives of all the trades each time the aircraft was to fly, passing her over to the pilot and crew in serviceable order. If the erk responsible for the wireless telegraphy, for example, was not satisfied with the aircraft, he would not sign Form 700 and the aircraft would not fly, no matter what the Wing Commander, the Group Captain or anybody else said.

A ground crew worked on their aircraft perhaps for a long time, perhaps for not so long, until she failed to return and they were given another one to look after. Of course, if it was a long time, a crew became very attached to their aircraft and very jealous of her virtue, and they expected whichever aircrew had her that night to take good care of her.

Some skippers would take an intense interest and be out there during the day, at the dispersals, usually with their flight engineers, talking to the ones who worked in all weathers and at all hours. Their conversations would be technical and practical, about what they were testing and how certain things had shown up last time. Such skippers were never content with the amount of knowledge they had. They always wanted to know more. Another skipper would believe that the ground crew knew all about it and didn't need any help from him. He would trust them completely and didn't see that he could improve matters beyond reporting any faults, any more than they could improve his flying or his chances of seeing them again.

The technology was as advanced as it could be, with wartime pressures rarely allowing reliability to be built in, but everything had to be driven, operated, controlled, worked, retuned, checked, calibrated, and possibly mended in the air. It was a constant process. There was no computer

F/Lt Charles Newton (centre, back row), the first of W4964's long-term skippers, flew sixteen Ops in J-Jig as she was then, starting as a sergeant. Here he is in February 1944, tour expired, with all his original aircrew who first flew together 3 July 1943 as Sgts J Turner, P Hall, E J Duck, J Ryan, W J Wilkinson and R McFerran, also the groundcrew of their last aircraft WS/Z LM445, which flew twenty Ops before going down at Munich with Sq/Ldr Gilmour DFC, 25 April 1944.

Many aircrew considered photographs bad luck and would avoid them, especially the new-crew pictures. Ralph Hawksworth the mid-upper gunner is standing far right and Joe Marshall, rear gunner, is sitting right. Pilot Ray Cornelius is sitting centre. The others are Fred Violett, 19-year-old flight engineer (probably far left), Alex Porter, bomb aimer, next to him, then Jim Gledhill, navigator. Les Chappell, w/op, is probably sitting left. Their first Op was to Schweinfurt, 26 April 1944. Their last was to Duisburg, 19 May.

Sgt Ralph James Hawksworth, aged 19 from Sheffield, had this picture taken for his mum and dad, Elsie and Fred.

Pilot Doug Melrose takes his habitual catnap shortly after take-off.

Doug Melrose and crew with a Flying Fortress on their July 1944 liaison visit to an American airbase. From the left: Ted Selfe - engineer, Bert Hoyle – mid-upper Melrose, Bob Woolf – w/op, Sammy Morris – bomb aimer, Ernie Stalley – rear gunner, Jimmy Moore – navigator.

E-Easy with, for some reason, her nosepaint tomatoes and, 31 July 1944, away with her English aviators at Rilly-la-Montagne. 'During the attack, she was hit by enemy anti-aircraft fire. The machine, which had lost pieces of its cockpit, was on a starboard heading towards the village of Puisieulx. As it reached the village, at very low altitude the aircraft turned to port, exploding in open fields. We shall not forget these seven English flyers who, knowing their last moment had arrived, acted to save our people.'

All that remained of 'I'm Easy' – Charles Worner's Lancaster LM453 WS/E in the fields of Puisieulx, one of Champagne's grand cru villages.

/Lt Edward Relton and crew as
ME757 WS/O is made ready on a
ummer's day in 1944. They flew
aylights or early evening ops in
) on 7, 9, 10 and 11 August, and
n such a day were all killed at
rest, 13 August.

Corporal Frank Hawkins posed for a newspaper photographer standing beneath a Tallboy, not something he'd normally do. With him is LAC Sid Hodson. Note the simple chain mechanism for bomb release.

In the middle is Kenny Burr w/op with F/O Taylor in PB289 WS/B. Also represented are the Soviet navy and the Yagodnik Glorious October Charwomen's Collective. Taylor's aircraft was among the first to bomb the *Tirpitz* and the crew reported seeing what appeared to be a hit and indeed turned out so, by Melrose and crew.

Official 5 Group plot of bombfall on the first *Tirpitz* raid. Pryor in 617's KC/U and Fawke in KC/J had near misses. T/9 was actually WS/P, F/O Jones, the 9 Squadron near miss. The only hit of the day was F/Lt Melrose of 9 Squadron in WS/J.

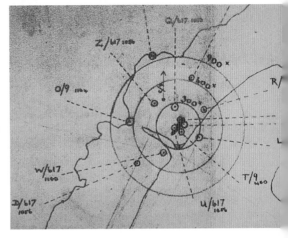

This picture was taken in July 1944. Coming home from Münster aqueduct, September, six of those in were killed. From the left back row, Sgt Jack Simkin engineer, F/Sgt Louis Harding (father of the comedian Mike Harding) navigator, F/Sgt Langley bomb aimer, was the only POW, Sgt Les Hambly – rear gunner; front row, Sgt Maurice Hayward – w/op F/Lt Charles Scott – pilot Sgt Frank Saunders – MU gunner.

MK. NBR.	LTR:	CAPTAIN.	SOR.	F/ENGINEER.
NO. 9 SQUADRON.				
"A" FLIGHT:-				
3. JB. 146.	"A".	F/O. SCOTT(S)	3.	SGT. BAKER.
JB. 289.	"B"	F/O. FOLLETT(S)	2.	SGT. FLANAGAN.
LM. 548.	"J"	F/O. BUCKLEY(S)	1.	SGT. DAVES.
NF. 937.	"E"	F/O. ARNDELL(S)	4.	SGT. JONES.
1. ED.,213.	"F"	F/O. READ(S)	--	SGT. WHITE.
ED. 596.	"H"	F/O. REAKS(S)	--	SGT. SCOTT.
3. W. 4964.	"J"	F/O. REDFERN(S)	35.	SGT. WILLIAMS.
1. LL. 845.	"L"	F/O. JEEVES(S)	3.	SGT. HIGGINS.
LM. 745.	"M"	F/O. MARSH(S)	12.	SGT. HARRISON.
SPARE.				
		F/O. WILLIAMS(S)	7.	SGT. LEWIS.
"B" FLIGHT				
1. NF. 929.	"P"	F/L. CAMSELL(S)	19.	SGT. ANDREWS.
1. LM. 220.	"Y"	F/O. AYRTON(S)	3.	SGT. HUDDLESTONE.
3. EL. 136.	"R"	F/O. WATERS.(S)	1.	SGT. BOOTH.
LM. 736.	"S"	F/O. COSTER(S)	2.	SGT. PINNING.
3. LM. 448.	"T"	F/O. REES.(S)	4.	SGT. MAYHEW.
1. ED. 198.	"W"	F/O. HARKER(S)	2.	SGT. WHITWORTH.
PB. 594.	"D"	F/O. DAVIES(S)	1.	SGT. RICE.
LM. 713.	"Z"	F/O. NEWTON(S)	3.	SGT. GREGORY.
3. LM. 715.	"O"	F/O. JAMES(S)	--	SGT. POCOCK.

Battle order, 5 October 1944. Cyril Redfern will take WS/J on her 106th. Redfern was on his 36th but he was not the senior man. That was F/O Williams's engineer Sticky Lewis, who had started at Berlin, 2 December 1943, with Plowright. Next skipper to Redfern in experience was F/Lt Camsell, nineteen Ops; most of the rest were between none and four.

Tirpitz party, Officers' Mess, Bardney.

Pilots of 9 Squadron, from left: McDonnell, the American Ed Stowell, Keeley, Laws. As with the Melrose crew's Standard Flying Nine, this Austin Seven had been adapted by groundcrew to run on aviation spirit.

Harry Watkins (right) was a popular chap with a tale to tell. He'd been a Butlins redcoat, a freedom fighter with the Finns, a Russian POW and now he was a bomber pilot.

PB368 WS/A failed to make her tenth Op. This was Buckley's Lanc after a very short flight on New Year's Day 1945.

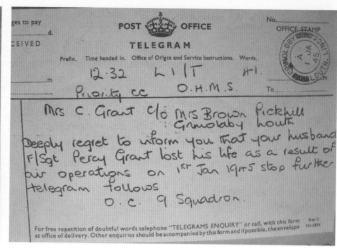

Not so lucky was the crew of NG252 R-Robert. Percy Grant, American Cliff Newton's navigator in the New Year's Day crash, recently promoted to Pilot Officer, was 30, here with his wife Constance and their young son. This is the dreaded telegram she received (right).

F/O Jeffs, pilot, Sgt Higgins, flight engineer and WO2 Fisher, bomb aimer, with Tallboys. These were in the last crew to fly WS/J-Johnny and almost the last of J's old boys to be killed.

VE Day at RAF Bardney. For us the war is over.

automation beyond what could be achieved with a few diode and triode valves in the bombsight, no solid state electronics of any kind, and some equipment was the equivalent of highly strung. Damp, a drop of oil, somebody brushing against it; it didn't take much to disable a piece of vital kit. The amplifier on the intercom, for instance, a two-valve unit with a dry battery and a wet accumulator, needed inspecting almost by the hour and its failure was a prime cause of aircraft returning early.

You could get a fault report first thing and it would look fixable but it wouldn't fix. If there was a flap on, you could be working on it all day, with the engines running up to give you power while they were refuelling and loading the bombs. The crew could arrive and you'd still be at it, desperate to get her airborne, and they might even taxi to the runway with you still on board. Of course, the worst thing that could happen then was a scrub, and it did happen.

F/O Sweeney: 'Why did it take you an hour longer than everybody else? It was light enough to map read.'
P/O Cooper: 'Oh, we never map read. We always steer a course.'

August was going to be a bad month for former 9 Squadron men. The first to go, at Mare de Magne, was Reg Blaydon, now Flying Officer, evader from Vichy France with Stuart Parkes in 1941. Parkes was up to Squadron Leader DSO and he too would not see the end of August.

The day-to-day life on the squadron had something in common with an ordinary job, as perceived by those at the bottom of the ladder, looking up and wondering how on earth certain people ever got to be managers. From Bob Woolf's point of view, all the normal laws of the universe seemed to apply to the working week; Murphy's, Sod's, and so on.

7 August, Monday. Take off was a hell of a rush. We weren't on until the last moment then everyone had to tear around to get off on time. The target was Lorient but, as we were on our bombing run, group cancelled the Op so we had to come home, every aircraft dropping a couple of bombs to make a safe landing weight.

8 August, Tuesday. Had the same kind of panic today as is usually found with these daylight tactical targets. Panic this morning, then we were on and off all day, and finally it was all scrubbed just as we were about to go out in the buses. It's a bad show. We get so hot and perspiring with all the rush and bother and then it's freezing cold when we get up high. The build-up of tension and then the deflation is hard to take.

9 August, Wednesday. Arose at 01.00. Take-off scrubbed, back to

bed. Up again, mad rush to take off at 07.00. Target was La Pallice on west coast of France. Trip went OK, not too much flak, over six hours in the air. Signals were a shambles due to badly planned briefing but no damage done. This was another joint Op with 617 who attacked the U-boat pens with Tallboys while 9 Squadron hit the oil storage with conventional bombs.

10 August, Thursday. Our crew not on the battle order. Sammy (Morris, bomb aimer) went as spare bod with Sq/Ldr Pooley. F/O Morrison came home sick having got over halfway there, to the oil depot at Bordeaux. His crew has the world's biggest bomb aimer, F/Sgt Westrope. He is a professional wrestler and must be 19 or 20 stone. Our a/c J-Johnny became serviceable today and we went up for an air test. J has been repaired after some clot took her on Ops and nearly blew her out of the sky. He had to jettison his bombs which he did from a ridiculously low height and the shrapnel nearly wrecked our beloved plane coming very close to one hundred trips.

11 August, Friday. Givors again, we didn't go. Apparently it was a piece of cake with hardly any flak.

12 August, Saturday. No war today so we went to Bardney village, that is to say The Jolly Sailor and The Black Horse. Five of us came home after closing time in our little car which we call The Twitcher, some hanging out of the sliding roof. We were honoured to have our very own motorcycle escort in the shape of Sq/Ldr Harry Pooley and one F/Lt J D Melrose, on their 'Flight Commanders' Machines'.

The Twitcher was a 1936 Standard Flying Nine, nine horsepower. After four years of wartime shortages this vehicle had been in a sorry state but was restored to roadworthiness by J-Johnny's groundcrew. Most of the spare parts were of RAF origin, down to the doped fabric used to rejuvenate the sliding roof. The dashboard reminded you of a Lancaster crossed with a Tiger Moth and the engine was modified to run on aviation spirit, kindly diverted into our tank at dispersal, so it smelled like a Lancaster as well. Somebody nicknamed it The Twitcher on the grounds that anyone driving it would immediately develop a nervous tic like we all got from too many Ops.

Dougie Melrose was not satisfied with his Flight Commander's Machine. He had his eye on Mick Maguire's.

I had a Matchless 350cc with leg guards and Doug Melrose had a 500cc Beezer. He preferred the looks of mine and said he was going to swap with me. I said like hell you are. He said, 'I'm a Flight Commander.' I said stuff the flight commander. I'm the armourer and I'll blow you up next time you go on Ops. So Dougie said he would race me round the perimeter track and the winner would have the choice of machines. I couldn't see what was in it for me but I rode round that track a hundred times a week. I'd no fear of losing to Mr Melrose. We set off in front of Flying Control and by the time I got to the end of the main runway, Dougie was nowhere near. I stopped to look and there he was, halfway along the track, stranded. His spark plug lead had come off and the silly sod had tried to put it back on from the saddle, while the wheels were still going round, so he got a severe electric shock. I rode slowly back to find him rubbing his arm and looking decidedly fed up. You all right? I said, and Dougie replied 'You can keep your bloody Matchless.'

More sergeant pilots were joining 9 Squadron. Keeley went to Lorient on his first, Begg was on his fifth in eight days, and the American F/Sgt Ed Stowell went to La Pallice, Bordeaux and Givors. They would all be officers by the end of the month, which at least meant they had a few more shillings a day.

Nancy Bower: Keeley was a very popular chap, and he was another of the cheeky ones like Ray Harris. There were many different types, it was no indicator of whether they'd last or not. You could have the anything-goes sort like Keeley and Harris, or the top-drawer officer like Melrose, but they got the same results.

Aileen Walker: The MO at this time was called Napier, and he came to me one day with a plateful of Crooke's cod-liver-oil capsules. I was to stand by the big table which was on the left of the door as you came in, with all the cups and saucers and tea urns on it, and I was to give a capsule every day to every member of aircrew who came in for breakfast. Ray Harris said, 'What are they for, Aileen?' in a very cheeky way, and half of the officers wouldn't have them. So I used to take them away, and I had them. I was fighting fit, I can tell you.

Nancy Bower: That was just breakfast. The big thing was a Dining In Night. Squadron Leader Burns would decide when there was to be one and all the officers had to attend. Sometimes there would be men who'd been promoted that day, and we'd end up sewing the new badges of rank on their uniforms. It was absolutely best dress and best behaviour, and no women, only us. It was quite an atmosphere, and very hard not to clatter the cups when you were serving the coffee. One time there was a band in the corner, playing very quietly, and there was celery on the tables. Every officer except Burns got hold of a stick and started conducting the band. I'm not sure the squadron leader thought it quite the thing.

It was Brest again, 13 August. Melrose was deputy controller on their part of the raid, the objective being to sink a tanker which the Germans were going to use to block the harbour. 'Ship was easily seen and hit many times. Burning well as aircraft left and down at the stern.' Melrose saw four sticks hit the stern of the ship. Ray Harris saw something else too. It was Relton in O, flying right alongside.

Some of them said he was hit by flak. My own bomb aimer, Jim Parsons said it was flak, but I saw him at 16,000 feet being hit by bombs dropped by another Lanc flying above us. They could have hit me but they hit him, and there was no doubting the result. The nose was gone and half the starboard wing was missing. They tipped over and went straight in, into the shore by the harbour. Nobody could have survived.

F/Lt Edward Harry Maxwell Relton, age 34, was on his 12th Op. His wife was staying in Bardney village. They had been married one week.

The other precision target for the day had been an old battle cruiser *Gueydon*, which was the responsibility of 617 Squadron and was also intended for scuttling to block the harbour. The German army was trapped on the Brest peninsula but still fighting hard to prevent the Allies from taking the port, which would then be able to accept shipping direct from the USA and greatly increase supplies to the invasion forces. General Patton had issued his famous order 'Take Brest' on 1 August. Brest, like the other U-boat bases, had been classified as *Festung* (fortress, to be held at all costs) and the Americans wouldn't get in until 18 September, for the loss of 10,000 men. By then, the docks would have been smashed by air raids and artillery and the front line would be five hundred miles away.

Mick Maguire had hitched a lift to Brest and noticed a curious thing about one of the 617 Lancs.

When we got back I rang a pal at 617 and asked him if he knew who was flying as rear gunner in this particular aircraft with the gun pointing sideways, and he started laughing. Why did I want to know? So I told him, the rear turret was on the beam and the doors were open. He said it was a sergeant cook from the officers' mess. Everybody had thought it would be an easy Op so this fellow had pleaded to be allowed to go. Anyway, luckily for the officers' dinners, he didn't jump.

14 August and the whole of 617 was assigned to the *Gueydon*, still there obviously, and 9 Squadron was given another old warship to destroy for the same reason, the *Clémenceau*. Other squadrons were there too,

including No. 97 with Bob Lasham, carrying armour piercing bombs rather than markers.

I had S-Sugar at 9 Squadron and S-Sugar at 97, but on this day she wasn't serviceable. There was always a rogue aircraft in every squadron, always suffering with faults, and the ground crew hated it and would say, 'Oh skipper, bring her back Cat A/C', which meant write the aircraft off but preferably not yourselves with it. That was the one we had, and we got badly shot up with anti-aircraft fire. Reg Powell (mid-upper) had a lot of facial injuries which scarred him for life, and the aircraft had ninety holes and, as instructed, was classified Category A/C.

Also at Brest was 61 Squadron, 9's sister squadron based nearby at Skellingthorpe and, unnoticed by anyone in particular, a Lancaster with a crew on their first Op, QR/F-Freddie, pilot the young Australian Sgt Loneon, navigator Sgt Henry Wilson. This crew would not be together long and, after a rare adventure, Tug Wilson would move to Bardney and join Dougie Melrose when Jimmy Moore, already the oldest member of aircrew on the 'drome, decided against a second tour.

Bob Woolf: 'Bombing was not as accurate as yesterday's. Don't know how 617 got on. I think Group is pitting 617 against 9 to see who is best. We often say a rhyme at Bardney. "Six one seven shoot the line, Got their gen from Number Nine". Flak was worse today and just as precise. We all had holes in our aircraft.'

Attacking in daylight at moderate height with a clear sky allowed the German gunners to plot the bombing run's height, speed and direction so they could put up a box barrage. 'In order to bomb, each Lancaster had to fly straight through the box and we were sitting ducks with the inevitable large amount of damage to every aircraft. It was a very scary effort.'

Another pilot called Scott joined No. 9, so there would be three aircrew Scotts for a while. There had been five but two of that name had been killed with Relton. The newest Scott, a Scotsman and imaginatively nicknamed Scotty, had a crew with a 17-year-old w/op, Sgt Tollast, and a poetical bomb aimer, Sergeant Jim Brookbank. They went to Givors, Tollast had his 18th birthday, and here they were at Brest. They had just finished their bombing run when a salvo of ack-ack hit them, killing the w/op instantly and very nearly killing the rest of them.

Jim Brookbank: The piece of flak which gouged a groove in Scotty's head was only a few fractions of an inch from slicing it right off, and it took him a few moments to regain control as the Lanc dropped several

thousand feet. The skipper was concerned about Johnny (Tollast) so he decided to land at a nearby airfield. I assured my captain that there was nothing to be done, our friend was dead, and I pointed out that coming in to land at an enemy airfield would differ in no noticeable way to the defending gunners from coming in to bomb it. We would be shot to pieces.

The rest of the crew heartily concurred. Democracy and common sense prevailed and they set off back to Blighty, aiming for the nearest aerodrome at Exeter.

When an instruction to steer ten degrees to starboard was met with a steer ten degrees to port, we realised that Scotty's headwound was perhaps worse than it looked. We had no wireless so I fired off a couple of Very lights above the airfield, red distress flares, the sight of which brought the local blood wagon racing down the runway. Scotty landed on the grass, the undercart stayed put and all, apart from poor Johnny, was well.

> 'My instructor was only happy when flying upside down.
> Do you know that I've covered the whole
> of the north of England on my back?'
> Anon

Ray Harris and a dozen more went to a night-fighter base in Holland, Gilze Rijen, part of a raid of over one hundred Lancs, part of a co-ordinated effort against military airfields, and part of the preparations for a new bomber offensive against Germany. Harris went in first; the rest of the squadron all bombed within one and a half minutes. The base was obliterated. The runways were hit and the whole airfield was plastered with bombs. The woods around the airfield were set on fire. Taylor was on this in J-Johnny, and the American Ed Stowell, and it was the first Op for another, less favourably fated transatlantic, the quiet man from Michigan, Clifford Newton who would have a spectacular end in January.

They were back to U-boat pens at La Pallice, 16 August, with 617 Squadron whose Tallboy bombs had penetrated the massively thick concrete roofs on previous raids. Although the damage had been considerable, the real disaster for the Germans lay in the shattering of their belief in the pens as impregnable, bomb proof, free from the worry of aerial attack.

Bob Woolf: We made our thirtieth trip that night, to La Pallice. Target

was covered by cloud. We were Controllers and luckily everything went OK. We led the formation with Dougie giving directions over the R/T and me confirming the details with my ever-reliable Morse key. We also had a radio link with our base so we could pass on a recall or whatever from Bomber Command. They painted our tailfins white for the occasion, so that the Germans knew who was in charge. There was a fair amount of flak but not as accurate as our last two trips to Brest. J-Johnny's 96th.* What a great aeroplane we had.

*Actually, 98th.

They went to La Pallice yet again with 617, Tallboys for the pens, 9 Squadron including Camsell in J-Johnny for the oil storage. Everyone seemed to get what they wanted, holes in the roofs, the surrounding district made into a moonscape and home soon after five. The E-boat pens at Ijmuiden had Camsell in J-Johnny again, on her century trip although it was not so counted at the time, and saw Tallboys hit the pens and his own squadron's bombs score direct hits on the support facilities. The squadron must have got quite excited. The day before had been their first practice with the Tallboy.

There was a moderate 5 Group raid on 25 August, without 9 Squadron, to Darmstadt; less than two hundred Lancs. The master bomber had to go home early leaving his two deputies in charge who were both shot down. One was a former 9 Squadron man from 1941 who had been awarded the DSO for showing 'unswerving determination, courage and skill in the face of powerful defences. Squadron Leader Parkes has completed very many operations and his devotion to duty has been unfailing.'

The new emphasis on Germany was prioritised thus: oil installations, railways and vehicle factories, cities in general if the other types of target were not practicable. Beside all this ran the support of the ground forces and keeping the V-weapons in check, plus any special targets which might be considered imperative from time to time. C-in-C Harris believed that Germany would implode if city bombing was resumed at full power, making a high-casualty invasion unnecessary. Other service chiefs wanted the oil and the transport knocked out so that the invasion would be easier. The compromise meant that neither philosophy was fully tested.

The emphasis was changing at 9 Squadron too. By late August everyone in the squadron, and 5 Group for that matter, knew that the Bardney boys had been judged most accurate squadron. There was a monthly practice bombing competition with results shown on a Bombing Ladder, like the ones customary in tennis and squash clubs. Every squadron in 5 Group flew at 10,000 feet and dropped smoke bombs and the results were published in 5 Group News. Customarily at or near the top of the ladder was No. 9, which was therefore selected to become the other half of the RAF's only pair of Tallboy squadrons.

Upkeep, the bouncing bomb used against the dams, had not made the transference to other kinds of target and Barnes Wallis had come up with the more orthodox Tallboy design, streamlined, rocket-shaped, which would break the sound barrier but clearly looked like a bomb and which was dropped in standard fashion. Rather than rely on direct hits, this bomb was meant to penetrate deep into the ground beside the target and explode below, causing a miniature earthquake which would bring the target down. RAF strategists had always had other uses in mind, for example the roofs of U-boat and E-boat pens and the massive concrete fortresses of the German secret weapons programme, and its first use by 617 Squadron on a railway tunnel at Saumur in early June had seemed to prove the point, that it could knock holes in the tops of things as well as blow them up from beneath.

Dennis Nolan was a 9 Squadron bomb aimer, with Buckley. 'The Tallboy was a wonderful weapon, a beautiful piece of kit. It was painted, and it was polished. It had a finish on it like a new car. The last thing the armourers did when they'd got the grab arms around it was to give it a buff up. When it dropped it was horizontal, of course, then it would slowly dip its nose and start to rotate, to spin on its own axis, and you knew it was going to cause havoc.'

Only 9 and 617 were believed capable of using this fearsome weapon to its full potential and only 9 and 617 would ever drop it. Practising began in earnest. No. 9 were out day and night, at Wainfleet and Epperstone. There were experiments to see how fuel economy could be maximised, which combinations of propeller pitch and throttle settings would yield the most miles per gallon when fully loaded and more than fully loaded. Clearly there was to be a very special mission indeed, a long way away. The build-up to the first *Tirpitz* raid had begun.

> 'I was flying so low that when
> I pulled the nose up to climb
> I almost drowned the rear gunner'
> P/O Pink

9

HOLIDAYS ABROAD

In France, the Resistance had brought Russ Gradwell's Atch Atkinson to keep bombaimer Gradwell company, but there was quite a deal of traffic past the farm, including refugees from Paris begging food. Somewhere quieter was preferable and so the two of them were moved to a hunting lodge a few fields away and then, in a covered cart, through the town of Auneuil to the tiny village of Villiers St Barthélemy where Marcel and Germaine Dubois had a three-roomed cottage. Marcel had been taken prisoner at the Maginot line, escaped, broke his leg in the process, had it fixed by a local doctor and walked home to Paris.

The couple had taken cover at Villiers. He worked on the land and she, having been a Paris milliner of the film-star class, took in sewing. They managed, and they shared what they had with the airmen who did what they could in return, chopping wood, pressing the cider apples, going out to the woods at dawn in search of snails and mushrooms. This carried on for six weeks and still Russ Gradwell and Atch's presence in the village was a complete secret. Even the people next door didn't know, nor did they know that Maigret and Thibou had moved four more airmen, Gradwell's crew minus Price and Oldacre, into another house in the village. The lads had a reunion every Sunday.

Oldacre: 'About 25 August, a German staff HQ moved into the house and I went to live with the chief of the Resistance of that village and I remained there until Allied troops arrived. During the last week I helped the Resistance to collect arms and ammunition dropped by parachute and I instructed several Frenchmen in the use of automatic arms.'

29 August, 189 Lancasters of 5 Group raided Königsberg, also called Kaliningrad depending on which nation had possession at the time, Germany or Russia. Königsberg was a substantial and ancient university city and garrison, population 370,000, the old capital of East Prussia becoming a major industrial centre and railway junction with a deep canal leading to the Frisches Haff and thence to the Bay of Gdansk and the Baltic Sea. It was always highly disputed territory and the air force of the Soviet Union attacked it regularly. For the RAF it was an eleven-hour trip.

At the briefing, they were given a choice. They were to fly home over a small section of occupied Denmark but they could elect to do so at 20,000 feet, thus being more difficult to hit from the ground but staying in the enemy's territory and arc of sights for longer; or they could hedge-hop flat out at 2,000 feet in which case they could hope to be gone before the flak woke up and the fighters would not be expecting them to be that low. Of course, if the anti-aircraft crews did spot them, they would be a relatively easy target. The Aussie Sgt Loneon, Tug Wilson and crew had done six Ops in two weeks with 61 Squadron. Their choice was to go low.

There was some flak around the target area but they never felt a bump. Finch the bomb aimer was satisfied with their run, bombs were gone and, with large parts of Königsberg wrecked, it was home time.

Tug Wilson: The route home was sea all the way except for the Denmark part coming up and our mood was cheerful as we crossed the Danish coast near Ålborg. As navigator, I did wonder why we had not been routed a few miles further north, to keep to the sea and avoid enemy territory altogether, but orders were orders. Well, we'd been over Denmark hardly more than two minutes when there was a terrific thump and the aircraft lurched sharply to port.

Our starboard inner was on fire, really on fire. Our mid-upper, Sgt Longhurst, saw the flames leap and begin to threaten the tailplane. It had been a good shot. We weren't flying through masses of flak. It had been a deliberately aimed, precision job, a pot shot. The Germans must have been tracking us on radar. We'd had no warning, no range-finding shells, just the one bang.

Loneon pushed the graviner button for the starboard inner. This activated a stream of carbon tetrachloride, dry cleaning fluid, from a pair of bottles strapped to the engine. It was supposed to put the fire out and sometimes it did, but by the time he had the aircraft back on an even keel and Harris the engineer had the starboard inner prop feathered, the fire was raging. Given a few minutes, the starboard wing and tailplane would be blazing and that would be that. The ORB WAAF would be typing 'Nothing further was heard from this aircraft.'

Loneon on the intercom offered a choice of ditching in the sea or parachuting onto dry land. The answers were prompt, unanimous and briefly expressed. Tug Wilson announced a change of course to due south, down the centre of Denmark; it was obvious to everyone that PB436 QR/D-Dog would never trouble the scorers again. They scrambled nervously for their parachutes and clipped them on but the thought of what they had to do next made them hesitate.

Tug Wilson: Our skipper shouted his order into the intercom to jump, 'Abracadabra, jump, jump,' plus something about Pommie bastards. The gunners went from the side door. Bomb aimer, flight engineer and wireless operator jumped from the front hatch. I sat for a second or two on the edge of the hatch then rolled out into nothing. Finally Loneon, who had been struggling to hold the aircraft level, jumped as well. None of us had ever done it before, nor even had a go at anything approximating. Parachute training for RAF Bomber Command aircrew in 1944 consisted of showing us (a) how to clip on the chute and (b) where the rip cord was.

Two thousand feet wasn't all that high for a parachute jump but it was probably high enough for complete beginners, who would also be happier that they had the dawn to light their way down to the quiet countryside rather than be dropping blindly earthwards on, say, a moonless night in the rain towards goodness knows what in the Ruhr. At a quarter past four on a fine summer's morning, the intrepid parachutists could admire the sun rising over Denmark, where the bacon comes from.

The navigator and the pilot were still in the air when their lovely, hardly used Lancaster, having spent a mere forty hours flying on tests and three Ops, hit the ground and blew up into small pieces. The two men hit the ground a few moments later, quite a distance from each other.

Wilson: I was in a field of cabbages, which didn't offer me much cover but I made half a fist of hiding my chute between the rows. I'd no time to dig a hole. The chute would be found, so I thought I'd better make sure I wasn't anywhere near when they found it. At the edge of the field was a ditch. I jumped in and threw off my Mae West and pushed it into the mud, and scraped some more mud over it.

Ever so carefully I peeped over the top of the ditch, and I was straight back down into it when I heard shots. The firing seemed some way away. The Germans were shooting the other crew members. So, that made my own instructions clear. Unless I wanted to be shot, I had better get the bloody hell out of there.

Running in the ditch was hard work. Here was a fence and a bit of a wood, a copse. He climbed over, fell exhausted into the undergrowth, and reviewed the situation.

I had my standard issue escape money, in Deutchmarks naturally. Nobody would think to issue us with Danish kroner, simply because we happened to be flying over Denmark. I had my photograph, for use in forging identity papers. I had my escape kit, obviously designed by an ex boy scout with its water sterilising tablets and length of fishing line with a hook. There was a compass and maps, except there was no map of Denmark, and a hacksaw blade. The main use for the hacksaw blade was not to saw through prison bars but to cut off the tops of flying boots so they looked more like ordinary shoes.

The escape lectures we'd had in training were still fresh in my mind. I'd only heard them a few weeks before. First, they said, get away from your aircraft. I'd done that all right, not that there was much aircraft left to get away from. Second, hide your parachute and Mae West. Well, I'd more or less done that. Third, contact the Resistance movement. What? Come again?

Wilson searched his memory for some tiny, glistening gem of information from the lectures about how that might be done but nothing appropriate sprang to mind. Time passed in his hideout in the bushes but there was no sign of the Resistance. There was a farmhouse but it wasn't flying a banner saying HQ Royal Danish Popular Front for the Resistance of German Aggression. On the other hand, neither were there any signs of the *Wehrmacht*. It looked very like an ordinary working farm, working an ordinary day.

Dusk was falling. A man who seemed to be the senior character on the farm came out for his last look around. He was an oldish chap, someone who had seen all kinds of fashions go by while the farming stayed the same. As soon as this serene, untroubled man strolled near the hideyhole, Wilson the English flyer, or Man from Mars or Archangel Gabriel as he may as well have been, stood up.

The old fellow's jaw dropped and he took a pace back. Then he took a pace forward and peered. Here was a youth of about twenty, he would say, dressed in pale blue, covered in mud and jabbering in tongues while pointing to himself and a piece of embroidery with a wing on it. Perhaps the youth was indeed an angel.

When the said pale blue youth began doing wavy hand movements and throaty engine noises, followed by Yeeee-ow! noises and Boooff! noises, the farmer thought it was time to seek assistance from the rest of his family. Kindly and politely, he shoo'd Wilson into the trees, making it clear that angels should keep quiet and out of sight for the moment. He went back into the farmhouse and came out again, with a large piece of sacking. He wrapped this around Wilson and took the boy to his home.

After much pantomime, it was established that I was Tug Wilson, Royal Air Force, and they were Mr and Mrs Kjær, Danish farmers, and this was their son. They were by a place called Valgård, near Farsö. I would indeed like something to eat, and there were no Germans stationed near by. At least, there was nobody stationed near by who goose-stepped up and down farmhouse kitchens with his right hand extended aloft while two fingers of his left held his nose up.

It became clear that the supper was not the limit of the Kjærs' compassion. They would have been in no doubt about the penalty for discovery. It was the firing squad or worse. Even so, they were prepared to shelter me for as long as it took. My bed was to be among the straw in the barn, with underfloor heating provided by the cattle below, but before that I had to be inspected by the local veterinary, Mr Sonne. Mr Sonne spoke some English and knew about the crash. He seemed to think that I was genuine enough.

Wilson spent his first full day in the straw, wondering what on earth was going to happen but feeling as safe as could be, given the circumstances. Farming life went on, beneath and around and Mr Kjær brought him some lunch; black bread and boiled bacon. By early evening, with the recuperative properties of youth, Wilson was fully prepared for whatever surprises might come next.

The farmer arrived among the cattle, gesturing for me to come down the ladder. We went together into the house. I was shown to a chair and the wireless was switched on to the BBC six o'clock news. At the sound of the familiar announcer's voice, my thoughts were transported to another kitchen, in a modest family house on Somerset Avenue, number 23, in Welling, Kent. My mother, father and elder sister Alice would be listening to the wireless too, while they were having their tea.

Tug Wilson was partly right. His family didn't want any tea but they were listening to the wireless, in the vain hope that something might be said which would throw a little more light on the telegram they had received the previous day. Sent at 12.56 p.m. on 30 August, it had been received at Bexleyheath at 2.14 p.m. It said:

= DEEPLY REGRET TO INFORM YOU THAT YOUR SON 1398593 SGT H W WILSON IS REPORTED MISSING AFTER AIR OPERATIONS ON 29-30 AUGUST 44 STOP ANY FURTHER INFORMATION RECEIVED WILL BE COMMUNICATED TO YOU IMMEDIATELY PENDING RECEIPT OF WRITTEN NOTIFICATION FROM THE AIR MINISTRY NO INFORMATION SHOULD BE GIVEN TO THE PRESS = 61 ADJUTANT

Of course, Wilson knew the procedure. He didn't know how quickly the

61 Squadron adjutant would move. He guessed it wouldn't be long, bearing in mind the rarity of aircrew reappearing after getting the chop. If an aircraft was posted missing and, as usual, there were no witnesses to what had happened to it, the crew were missing too. They were not yet killed in action but to most parents, sisters, brothers, girlfriends, wives, it came to the same thing. They would hope, naturally, and they might even believe, but the forces of reason said that missing in a bomber generally meant dead.

After the news, Mrs Kjær showed me the sink and the tap and gave me a towel. While I washed, she dished up a meal. Boiled bacon, with potatoes this time. We ate in silence but not an awkward silence. We knew we couldn't communicate across the language barrier and Mr and Mrs Kjær were too polite to talk between themselves in Danish in front of their guest. I did feel awkward but not about that. I felt very, very awkward as long as I was in that house. If I was discovered in the barn, the Kjærs could claim they didn't know I was there. Sitting at their table, sharing their food, there could be only one result from the dreaded sound of rifle butt on door.

With the meal over and the requirements of hospitality served, Wilson could go back to his straw and resume his wait. The Kjærs were so calm about it all he guessed that there was something to wait for. It came that night, when Mr Sonne turned up with his daughter Else and his assistant Hald, all speaking English. They had bits of the exploded wireless set from the Lancaster. They did their best to interrogate Wilson but were clearly rank amateurs at the job. It became obvious that, while they could never have found out if Wilson was a German plant, there to expose Resistance members, equally Wilson could never have deceived them. They told him that the other crew members were all alive and prisoners of war (in fact, Loneon was still free).

There was some animated conversation in Danish between young Kjær and Mr Sonne, pointing at me and discussing me as if they were trying to decide if I was a porker or a baconer, or perhaps not yet fit for either. I deduced that these two, the leaders, must be active Resistance members, in which case they would be on the radio to London for confirmation of my identity. Mr Sonne explained that his own son had been among a group of eighteen Resistance members taken by the Germans. All of them had been shot 'while attempting to escape'. This was why Else was here, home on compassionate leave from her hospital in Copenhagen where she was a nurse. Sonne, the brave man, said he thought I was about the same build as his son had been and that the clothes still hanging in the cupboard would do very well.

Tug was about to become a Dane as Russ Gradwell and Atch Atkinson, accomplished French-looking men by this time, were setting off on their dawn snail and mushroom raid with Marcel when a truck came along full of German soldiers. Two NCOs jumped down and, pistols threatening, demanded in French to know what the three of them were doing out before curfew was up. Atch, who didn't speak French but had grasped what was going on, instinctively looked at his Bulova watch. The other two froze in horror. If the Germans noticed the watch they would ask some very awkward questions. Where did a French peasant, apparently a deaf and dumb one, get the Swiss watch favoured by the wealthy and those concerned with perfectly accurate time-keeping such as Allied aircrew, who would be shot as spies if not in uniform? For whatever reason, the Germans could not be bothered to make anything of it and with a *Raus!* and a wave of their guns sent the three on their way. Sauntering as fast as they could, they rounded the corner and scarpered.

Russ Gradwell: Mushrooms and snails were still to be got so we continued our mission by another route but, returning by the way we always used, coming out of the woods onto a main road, we were dumbfounded to find German army vehicles parked as far as the eye could see. The soldiers were lounging about in the sun having their breakfast. Marcel took the lead, Atch came next and I, with my French now fluent after many tutorials with Madame Dubois, brought up the rear.

This was the German army in retreat. They didn't care about three poor Frenchies carrying some rubbish out of the woods in their shirts. Nobody spoke to anybody as we three threaded our way politely through men and vehicles, but the experience was quite enough for us. Two narrow scrapes in a day was pushing it. The third would surely see us taken. We were discussing this burning topic over our own breakfast, mushrooms, when two Germans walked past the window, then two more. It ended up with about fifty of them billeting themselves in the barn next door.

Two days passed without incident. On the third morning, Atch the Canadian farmer's boy, who had lost his father and was quite used to helping around the house, was giving Germaine a hand in the room they used as kitchen, diner and parlour. Russ was making the bed in the airmen's room with the door to the street open, to get some air in. The room darkened suddenly.

I turned to find a large German soldier in the doorway with a couple of eggs in each hand. He wanted me to make an omelette for him. I waved at him to say, stay where you are, and went into the kitchen, smuggled Atch into the Dubois' bedroom and persuaded Germaine to cook the eggs, on her condition that the soldier didn't eat them on the premises. I went to the window, called the man over and passed the eggs to Germaine. We stood there, enemies divided by a kitchen wall, although only one of us knew the whole of it, and conversed as best we could. My French was a lot better than his. He was a typical conscript squaddie. He didn't want a war. He didn't want to kill anybody or be killed for the Fatherland. All he wanted was to get back to Dresden, to his wife, his family and his rose garden.

His wish came nearer next day when machine gun fire was heard, the Germans disappeared and the British replaced them in the street. Atch was taken to the village square to listen to the new soldiers' conversation. It had to be checked because it had become quite usual practice for Germans to appear in Allied uniforms, wait for the Resistance to appear out of the woodwork to welcome them, and shoot. The Canadian's reassurance that the British accents were authentic was enough for the villagers and the church bells rang out.

Russ Gradwell and Marcel walked towards the village centre. Everyone called out 'Les Anglais sont ici,' and Marcel would introduce Russ saying the English had been here for over six weeks, actuellement. With that, bottles and glasses had to be produced and both men were quite squiffy by the time they reached the square, hardly caring if it was les Anglais, les Allemagnes, les Russes or the Queen of Sheba they were going to meet.

The British reconnaissance unit told them to stay where they were until the infantry came through in force. Before that happened, Maigret and Thibou in a large and sumptuous motor car came to pick the six of them up and take them to the epitome of luxury, the château where dwelled Madame Ravel.

The table was set for a magnificent luncheon with different wines in their own glasses to accompany each course. At the end came brandy, real Cognac which we hadn't seen for years, and real coffee. Real coffee, made from coffee beans. We couldn't have been more impressed if she'd taken us out to look at the lake and walked across it.

Madame Ravel had spent the equivalent in francs of £35 to buy that coffee on the black market. £35 was ten weeks' wages for a working man.

The next day, amid many tears and kisses, we said our goodbyes and thankyous and hitched a lift to start our journey home, which included passage through areas where fighting had been fierce. In some places, the German bodies had been bulldozed to one side to open the road. In others, they still aimed their guns from their foxholes but could not see anything to shoot and never would. Once back in Blighty we found that, of course, we had been listed as missing and immediately sent off telegrams to our relatives, who had assumed, because there had been no news on the BBC of capture for all this time, that we had been killed.

The two Canadians, Atkinson and Best, were repatriated and the other four were given the glad tidings that, although they were one trip short, they were counted as tour expired. Even better, being successful evaders, they could transfer wherever they wanted. 'I asked if I could be CO of the radar station on the Great Orme.' This, apparently, would not present a problem.

No, really, they wanted to stay together, but the only place gunners were required was in Bomber Command, which would surely mean they would be split up. Les Sutton, rear gunner, proclaimed himself the fly in the ointment and opted for airfield controller at Beaulieu. It was a shortish cycle ride from his home in Ringwood. The other three joined Transport Command and were posted to 242 Squadron and the Middle East, flying the York, the wide-bodied version of the Lancaster.

I assumed temporary command of a flight of ten crews. When the permanent officer arrived to take over the flight, it turned out to be a certain Squadron Leader Micky Martin, DSO and Bar, DFC and two Bars, ex 617 Squadron Dambuster, who insisted on doing his second Dicky as per proper procedure, so he went with me to Colombo, capital of Ceylon (Sri Lanka). We had a fault with the aircraft so, when we got back, Pete Lynch and I stayed to discuss this with the ground crew while Micky Martin went up to flight control.

Everyone sprang to attention when he walked in, saluting such a highly decorated officer. A WAAF got out the flight record and asked him to sign here. 'Oh no,' he said. 'I'm just the second pilot.' Gradwell walked in and sensed an atmosphere, which disappeared as soon as he said he was the skipper.

'What was all that about?' I asked Martin outside. He laughed. 'Well, I told them I was only the second pilot, so they were jumpy. They must have thought the pilot was going to be at least an Air Vice Marshal.'

After a week in his Danish barn, with bacon and black bread for lunch every day – Wilson had almost run out of black-bread hiding places – and

279

visits from Else and the others every evening, there came news that Loneon had contacted the Resistance and was being looked after. It was time for the next stage. Wilson said goodbye to his courageous friends, the Kjærs. Tears fell, kisses were exchanged, hands were shaken firmly and promises made in two languages before Wilson mounted a bicycle, accompanied by Else and Hald, and set off for a house in Farsö.

In civilian clothes now, I was liable to be shot as a spy. I only hoped that if we met a German soldier, it would not be one who spoke Danish. My new identity card, using my escape-kit picture, showed me to be Jens Christian Hansen, born 11.10.1924 in Nodagir. It was beautifully produced, worn and used to perfection and overstamped by the police apparently in October 1943. This would be fine, so long as I wasn't asked what I did, where I lived or if I agreed that the weather was excellent for the time of year.

At the house, Loneon was waiting. They had little time for tale swapping although Loneon was desperate to tell Wilson that one of the places he'd stayed in had been the hunting lodge of King Kristian, no less, although he hadn't actually met the King who was under house arrest at his palace.

A car arrived to take us away. They drove us out of town, far, far into the country, to meet a police car. Cheerily and with much jesting in Danish, we were placed under arrest by Constables Nielsen and Pietersen. They explained to us, the prisoners, that we were burglars, going for trial in Copenhagen. 'Only a couple of common burglars, but you never know with these criminal types.' This was thought to be a huge joke by the policemen and they kept repeating it in variations between themselves, roaring with laughter. Loneon and I thought we would never understand the Scandinavian sense of humour.

Hospitality in Copenhagen reached new heights. People were thrilled to meet the English (and Australian) heroes and vied with each other for the privilege of being shot should they be found in association.

By day we were shown the sights, even though there were Germans everywhere. The Danes constantly reminded us not to do anything English such as looking the wrong way when crossing the road. By night we were kept inside, often by serious Resistance fighters who never opened the door without a gun in their hand. A squadron of Mosquitos had raided the diesel engine factory in Copenhagen quite a while before, January 1943, but everyone we met had their own story

to tell of the great excitement, and they were all eager to encourage the English to bomb their home town more often.

One dark night, the two fugitives were collected by a very dubious looking fellow, a swarthy type who might have been an arms smuggler or a Mafia hit-man if those professions had not seemed too tame. He ushered the Englishes into his large, shining, black saloon car. Perhaps, they thought, they were VIP guests being taken to meet the head of organised crime in Scandinavia.

To our complete astonishment, this character turned on a siren and put the headlights on full beam. He drove as if in hot pursuit, tyres squealing, engine blasting, screeching around bends and flying down straights. He could not have been more noticeable. We couldn't believe it was happening. Anyway, after a few minutes of this, with his foot hard down and one finger on the wheel, he turned to us, sitting terrified in the back seat, and let us into a little secret. 'Not my car,' he said. 'Gestapo. I steal him. Nobody try to stop us.'

This confidence was followed by huge guffaws. What a wizard wheeze, he thought, to spirit a couple of spies away in a luxury car stolen from an enormously powerful and totally ruthless gang of official murderers and torturers. Wilson and Loneon once more failed to see the funny side of the Norseman and were much relieved to arrive at the dock gates, which opened up for them. The car came to a skidding halt beside a ship. Their swarthy chauffeur showed them up the gangplank and the party were welcomed aboard by the Swedish captain.

Aquavit being an essential component of running escaped enemies of Germany into neutral countries, many toasts were proposed, seconded and thirded before the two centres of attraction were allowed to retire for the night. Their chauffeur, unaffected by enough aquavit to render senseless an entire rugby league team, said his goodbyes and left, presumably to return the Gestapo car so that it might be refuelled, polished and maintained in peak condition, ready for when he needed it again.

We were allowed on deck the next morning, to watch the approach of the Swedish coast, and a small motor boat came alongside. The big ship hove to, we said thank you to the captain and his crew, and soon we and the motor boat were docking in Malmö. The British consul gave us £10 each. All that was left for us was a train ride to Stockholm, a trip to Scotland in the bomb bay of a Mosquito, and a lift back to our station at Skellingthorpe where, following tradition, we found the

ladies who had packed our parachutes and gave them ten shillings. Then I was interrogated and given three weeks' survivor's leave, finishing on 5 October. I said to the WAAF, can't you make it more because I'm twenty-one on the tenth. She said she couldn't give me more than three weeks officially, but she could misread the calendar and put fifteen instead of five.

10

'I WANT YOU TO SINK THE *TIRPITZ*'

The awe-inspiring battleship *Tirpitz*, sister ship to the *Bismarck*, was a weapon of mass destruction before that phrase was ever coined. She had eight fifteen-inch guns, twelve six-inch, sixteen four-inch, eight quad torpedo tubes and a huge number of anti-aircraft guns. She could steam at over thirty knots, had a range of 9,000 miles at nineteen knots, was manned by 2,400 crew and would alter the balance of power wherever she went.

Any conventional naval engagement would bring heavy losses to the attackers and she was designed to resist all forms of aerial attack, by bomb or torpedo, known about at that time.

> Sq/Ldr Patterson: 'If you're fat in
> any aircraft, it's damned difficult to get out'
> F/Lt Wills: 'You're telling me. I tried,
> I couldn't cope, and I had to bring the damned thing home'

Tirpitz was launched at Wilhelmshaven, 1 April 1939 in the presence of Adolf Hitler by Frau von Hassel, a granddaughter of Alfred P Freidrich von Tirpitz (1849–1930), father of the German navy and architect of U-boat strategy. Sea trials were completed by February 1940 and *Tirpitz* was commissioned early in 1941, whereupon she became a constant cause of violent mental exercise in the British government although she hardly went to sea. A considerable proportion of British naval resources was always deployed, watching and waiting, in case *Tirpitz* should sail. There was continuous reconnaisance and espionage activity to establish whether she was at anchor and the convoy programme of aid to Russia was always liable to be interrupted by the menace of *Tirpitz* if not by *Tirpitz* herself.

Pressure increased constantly on Churchill and the British, from Stalin and the Russians and Roosevelt and the Americans, to do something about it. Churchill ordered *Tirpitz* must be destroyed and, over the months which turned into years, more than thirty attempts were made by over seven hundred British, Russian and American aircraft and midget submarines, causing some damage but not enough. By September 1943 the battleship was in Kaafjord, an offshoot of Altenfjord in the very north of Norway, thoroughly protected by her own armour and armoury, plus anti-submarine booms and nets, shore batteries of anti-aircraft guns, permanently installed smokescreen gear and nearby squadrons of fighter aircraft. In Kaafjord she was also out of range of heavy bombers flying from the UK.

Sir Arthur Harris later told the short story of how the job of sinking *Tirpitz* was passed to him. Harris's view was that such a mission could only be the result of a mating between a red herring and a wild goose.

Churchill rang me and said, 'I want you to sink the *Tirpitz*.' I said, 'Why bother, Prime Minister? She's not doing any harm where she is.' Churchill replied 'I want you to sink the *Tirpitz*.' So I sent the boys out and they sank the *Tirpitz*.

The boys in question were those of Nos. 9 and 617 Squadrons, and sending them out was not quite so simple as Harris implied. The northern winter was coming and with it the darkness which would postpone the job into the next year, making it more likely that the Germans would commit *Tirpitz* to battle as the Allies took charge of the war. If the boys were to be sent, it would have to be soon, and September was a poor month for bombing weather in those parts. They would go with the Tallboy bomb, the only bomb which could slice through *Tirpitz*'s armour plate.

Kaafjord was too far, even for Lancasters modified well beyond specification. Overload tanks could be installed in the fuselage. To save weight, the mid-upper turret could be removed. With six-ton bomb and full tanks, the all-up weight of the Tallboy Lancasters would be 70,000lb which was 5,000lb over the specified maximum for take-off.

Assuming they could get off the ground, a conventional approach by two squadrons of Lancs from across the North Sea would mean an early warning for the target. The smokescreen and the fighters would be up to meet them. If these problems were solved, there remained the little local difficulty of actually hitting the bullseye. Both 9 and 617 Squadrons were practising hard, every day and night for what was to them still a mystery mission, but the secret target, big as she was, wouldn't look so big from three or four miles high. She was hugely powerful and heavily armoured. A high-level attack would be necessary. This would give aircrew a better chance of survival against intensive shelling and the bomb enough time to build up armour-piercing speed. Of course, the higher you flew, the tinier the ship looked in the bombsight.

Kaafjord was only six hundred miles or so from Archangel. The plot was therefore hatched to send the boys to Russia. The two squadrons would fly to Scotland and top up on fuel, fly beyond the Arctic Circle at night, bomb *Tirpitz* soon after dawn, then carry on to an airfield near Archangel, a journey of well over two thousand miles altogether. They would recuperate in Russia, patch up their Lancs, and fly home.

On 8 September, this plan was outlined to the two squadrons. Some of the Lancasters would be detailed to take the new, untried Johnny Walker mine, an ingenious, idiosyncratic and oh-so-British secret weapon. Johnny Walker was a self-powered, roaming mine which was supposed to keep looking until it found its target. Lancaster crews didn't like it because its self-power was a bottle of compressed hydrogen. Crews were under instruction to jettison their mines if they came under fighter or flak attack, which made them wonder what might happen in a dodgy landing or other out-of-the-ordinary, mine-jolting circumstance.

The mine had a parachute and an arming pin, both deployed by a fixed line as the weapon left the aircraft. It was extremely difficult to drop accurately but, in theory, this didn't matter too much. When it hit the water and detached its chute, it sank to fifty or sixty feet then, using its compressed hydrogen system, rose up again. If it didn't hit anything, for example the underside of *Tirpitz*, it sank again and 'walked' thirty feet to the side. To which side was anybody's guess. Up it rose again. If it missed again, it did another sink, walk and rise, wandering around at random until its gas ran out whereupon it exploded, thus preventing German mine designers from finding it and having a good laugh. The Johnny Walker mine could only be deployed in deep water, like you had in a fjord but didn't have in normal harbours, canals and so on where the shipping tend to be. It had never been used operationally before the *Tirpitz* raid. This was the novelty mine's chance to prove itself. Hopes among aircrew were not high.

Mick Maguire: 'If by some remote chance one of them had hit *Tirpitz*, the armour plating would have shrugged it off. It had a very small charge. I thought they were a bloody waste of time and it would have been far better to have had all the Lancs carrying Tallboys.'

In the event, weather changed the main plan. There was no point flying all the way to Kaafjord then finding cloud obscuring the target. Cloud was forecast, September was a cloudy month, so the revised scheme was to go straight to Russia, missing out Scotland, and wait there for the few hours of clear weather which must surely come along. This decision was passed to 9 and 617 Squadrons around the middle of the day, 11 September. Orders were to put together an overnight bag and take off at 17.00, land soon after dawn at an airfield on an island called Yagodnik in the river Dvina, and be prepared to attack *Tirpitz* in the afternoon if the weather was right.

The task force initially consisted of twelve Lancs from each squadron with Tallboys and six from each with twelve Johnny Walker mines apiece, but 617 sent two extra Tallboy aircraft. Two unarmed B24 Liberators of 511 Squadron, Transport Command carried the ground crews and the officer in charge of the Op, Bardney station commander Group Captain McMullen and his staff for the operational HQ. There was also a Lancaster of 463 Squadron armed with cameras and a film crew, plus a Mosquito of 540 Squadron for reconnaissance and additional photographic duties. Altogether, there were almost three hundred RAF personnel headed for Russia and the Arctic Circle. Mission: sink the *Tirpitz*.

The Liberators set off first from Bardney – they alone were going to Lossiemouth to top up with fuel before turning for Russia – then eighteen operational Lancasters led by Wing Commander Bazin, plus the camera Lanc. Puddle Lake's Tallboy, Russia-bound, worked loose in the bomb bay of his usual aircraft, WS/R Spirit of Russia, and he had to jettison and come home. Meanwhile, twenty Lancs of 617 Squadron took off from Woodhall Spa, led by Wing Commander Tait.

Ernie Stalley, Melrose's rear gunner, wrote in his log book that this was the longest flight ever undertaken by Bomber Command fully loaded with bombs and fuel. It would also turn out to be the Operation to which the greatest variety of other superlatives could be applied: most chaotic and most flea-bitten, for instance, and most aircraft lost without interference from the enemy. It would also qualify for most memorable; nobody on it would ever forget it.

The British forecast said cloud above 1,500 feet and visibility six miles at Archangel. The Russian forecast said that for the last hour or two hundred miles of their epic journey the Lancs would be in ten tenths cloud down to a few hundred feet, with heavy rain squalls. The Russian forecast was the correct one but it had not been made available to the two squadrons. The hosts were astounded when their guests started arriving in such atrocious conditions. The guests were, many of them, equally astounded that they managed to arrive at all.

The weather made it impossible to relate map to ground and the maps were hopeless anyway, army maps from the First World War which showed the White Sea coast but missed such helpful little details as towns and railways. Even if they had had decent maps, the countryside, when they could see it, was against the aircrews. Someone who had lived there all his life might have recognised the subtle differences between one small lake and a thousand others, one seemingly infinite stretch of pine forest and another, or this marshy wasteland and that marshy wasteland. The crews of the RAF in the worst possible flying weather had no chance. It was a situation which threatened disaster, possibly complete disaster, before they came anywhere near *Tirpitz*.

Bob Woolf: We encountered extremely bad weather on route and for the last hour of the flight cloud was down to three hundred feet combined with rain. None of the promised radio aids were available and the navigating was done by means of dead reckoning and map reading. Jimmy and Sammy did a wonderful job and Doug flew so well considering the poor weather. We ultimately landed at Yagodnik after 10.25 hours in the air. A very exhausting time in a tin tube.

Adams had one engine overheat which burst into flames when he was about seventy-five miles from the Norwegian coast. They extinguished the blaze and feathered the prop. It would have made sense to jettison his Tallboy and go home, but the crew agreed to fly on and they landed safely at Yagodnik, a grass field, marked out, with a windsock at the end and a brass band to play them in. The band struck up as each Lancaster arrived but, when one aircraft swung rather dangerously on landing, the band stopped oompah-ing and ran in all directions, dropping their red welcoming banner. Melrose immediately liberated the banner from Stalinist oppression, thanked the Union of Soviet Socialist Republics for their kind gift to the officers' mess of 9 Squadron, Bomber Command and headed for his billet, an old paddle steamer moored by the river bank.

Over the doorway was another banner, fixed this time, saying 'Welcome to the Glorious Flyers of the Royal Air Force'. Inside, waiting for the tired western airmen, was a small but fit army of eastern bed bugs, huge ones, with enormous appetites. Almost everyone was bitten, Adams so badly that he needed treatment from the MO. Among the few who escaped was Adams's rear gunner, Fred Whitfield, who was never without a bottle of TCP. He rubbed himself all over with this universal medicament and proved conclusively that Russian bed bugs did not like it.

> 'It's a funny thing but every time the airmen
> have their ears syringed by the doc,
> we have lemon curd for tea'
> F/Lt Wills

Everyone complained that the radio navigation aids had not been available but the Russians did have their beacons turned on. The crews had been briefed with the wrong call sign, confusing the Cyrillic letter B (sounded as V) with the Roman one but that hardly mattered since they worked on an incompatible system.

No navaids, the filthy weather and nothing left in the tank induced thirteen of the thirty-eight Lancaster crews to go astray. Ray Harris, like the others, was relying on his navigator's dead reckoning.

We were far, far out of range of the Gee box, the wind was uncertain and visibility was dreadful, so anything like accuracy from Tommy (Adair, navigator) would have been much appreciated. I have to say my mind was not entirely on my flying. Before we took off for Yagodnik, I'd had a letter from my mother saying my brother, in the army, had gone missing presumed killed.

His worries were interrupted when Adair's calculation that they were now flying over the Russia/Finland border was confirmed by the anti-aircraft guns of their Russian allies opening up, enthusiastically but without result.

When dead reckoning said we were over Archangel we went down low and saw the ships, the harbour and the town. The problem now was to find the airfield. We stooged around and were delighted to see an airfield with aircraft, including a Lancaster, which must have been the right airfield because we hadn't been told about any others around there.

In fact there were several around there, and this was Kegostrov, not Yagodnik. Bomb aimer Jimmy Parsons saw another Lancaster obviously intending to land, so Ray got into line.

Parsons: There were flares going up, which could have been meant to tell us we were coming in across the wind, which we were, or this was the wrong airfield, or what. Well, Ray just kept going and almost scraped a few scattering Russian guards off the top of the perimeter wall as we roared in and landed about halfway along the grass runway. I told Ray on the intercom that we were taxiing directly for a small building, a sentry post perhaps, so to turn to port, although there wasn't much airfield left before the farmland started.

Braking hard, Harris almost pulled NF985 WS/E, a brand new Lancaster on her first Op, to a near halt. She was rolling along at little over walking pace when her wheels dropped into a ditch. Slowly but inevitably, impelled by momentum and the forward weight of the Tallboy in her bomb bay, the great bird lifted her tail and bent her head, gracefully burying her nose in the soft soil of the local garrison's rows of potatoes.

Parsons, in the nose, now partially underground, had no idea what other damage had been caused. He only knew he was caught by the foot and couldn't get out. The rest of the crew made their way up the aircraft to the side door, looked out, and saw a drop of twenty feet. They didn't fancy that, even into soft soil, so they came back down again and climbed out through the pilot's hatch. Jimmy Parsons, with no assistance whatever from his friends and colleagues, managed to free his foot from his flying boot and followed them out into the Russian day.

While this was happening, Sq/Ldr 'Duke' Wyness of 617 came in as close to the near boundary as possible, only to find his brakes had no effect on the wet grass. He smashed into a fence on the far boundary and wrecked his undercarriage. As was often the case in pubs and messes, such stories could seem too dull in the retelling, even though Wyness was carrying twelve temperamental JW mines, and it would not be long before he was swerving like a racing driver to avoid a mystery riderless horse which chose that moment to gallop across the path of a Lancaster bomber.

Taylor in WS/B was down soon after, followed by another four Lancs and a Liberator. So low on fuel that he didn't have enough left to take off again, was F/O Tweddle in WS/U. That problem would be solved by laborious hand-filling with cans of petrol from Wyness's wrecked kite, although the Russians did eventually produce a small bowser with some fuel in it which they said was the hundred octane stuff the Lancaster's Merlins were used to.

> (Flying Officer X, on leave)
> 'Damn it! And blast it!'
> (small daughter)
> 'Daddy, remember you are in the Air Force.
> Or do they say things like that?'

F/O Keeley made five runs back and forth from Archangel trying to find Yagodnik. The cloud was down to fifty feet and his fuel was fast running out so he jettisoned his dozen JWs in the river and crash-landed with his wheels up among marsh and scrub. F/O Laws was slightly luckier. He found a runway made of wood but it was wet and too short for a Lancaster. The starboard wheel went into a drain at the end of it and the resulting lurch fractured the wing. He kept his JWs on board.

F/Lt Camsell was virtually out of fuel when he saw a town which had a landing strip beside it. Coming in to land on the parish runway of Belomorsk, both his starboard engines began spluttering at about one hundred feet and conked out completely at fifty feet. Without the power to make the start of the landing strip he'd been aiming for, he dropped too soon and hit a pile of mud and stones which broke off his undercarriage. The Lanc skidded along on its belly and reached the landing strip that way.

The last aircraft of the adventure landed in a muddy but approximately flat place, at 07.45 with a sick flight engineer. Skipper Morrison in WS/Q was making a decent go of it until one wheel dropped into a soft spot and snapped off. Nobody had ever heard of Chubalo-Navolsk but they had to leave their u/s Lancaster there in a field with twelve JW mines in the bomb bay.

That morning, by a marvel, nineteen Lancasters had landed safely at Yagodnik. Dunne had been first down for 9 Squadron in WS/C, at 05.05, along with 617's Pryor. Scott of 9 Squadron in WS/V must have been flying on the smell of petrol only by 06.20 when his navigator F/Sgt Harding guided him in. F/Lt Buckham, 463's photographer, and ten others had landed at Kegostrov. Otherwise the score was: two at Vascova of which one was wrecked (category E) and one was stuck in a bog. The two at Onega could be made serviceable. Four were Es at Belomorsk, Chubalo-Novolsk, Molotovsk and Talagi, all outlying and outlandish places even by local standards. The Russians sent out search parties for the crashed crews except for Keeley and his Johnny Walker mine-loaded WS/H at Talagi, which was considered far enough into the wilderness to justify dropping a parachutist in. Somehow over the next day, 13 September, all the crews were assembled, present, correct and unharmed, at Yagodnik.

Not a single one of the Lancasters had been fit to operate as planned on the day they landed. The crews were exhausted and scattered in any case but every aircraft needed work doing to it and, because of the late change of plan, ground crews and spare parts were not already there as they should have been but were in the Liberators, one of which was at Kegostrov. Two Lancs needed an engine change, one had extensive flak damage, one had a burned out exhaust valve. One had its nose in a potato patch, there were broken ailerons, cowlings, fuel tanks. Even the noble lady J needed minor adjustments. As if that were not enough, the refuelling arrangements were quite inadequate for this number of hungry big birds. Tanks said to contain 3,500 gallons were found to hold 350, and it would take sixteen or more hours before all the aircraft were filled.

For the next two days, frantic efforts were made to collect, repair and refit as many Lancasters as possible, robbing the Category E kites for spares. It was decided that Harris's could be rendered serviceable but first she had to be tipped back onto the level and the Russians devised a novel method for this. They built a haystack under her tail for a cushion, and dozens of 'menskies' climbed up and sat where they could on the very tail end of the aircraft. She came down under their weight to rest on the haystack, which was gradually taken apart so that, gently and entirely without mechanical aids, she could be returned to her proper, dignified position.

RAF ground crews, with Russian mechanics and sheet-metal workers, laboured continuously for almost 48 hours until they were ordered to take a rest. They allowed themselves four hours sleep then went back to their aircraft, which were dispersed in a line a mile long, in the cold and the rain, with no transport to carry anyone anywhere.

Ray Harris and his men were not quartered in the riverboat but in a kind of underground Nissen hut. The Potato Patch Boys soon found that the already legendary strain of bugs inhabiting the boat was also fully adapted to life on land. Rapacious as they were, the bugs didn't dare bite the Russian army batwoman, a quite elderly lady in the uniform of the marines, who pressed RAF uniforms using her own ironing technique, taking a mouthful of water and spraying it on the cloth as she went.

The stove's clay chimney stuck up above ground and was visible from the outside lavatory where seating arrangements were primitive, plentiful and restful. Two of Harris's men were sitting there taking pot shots at the chimney with their Smith & Wesson .38 service revolvers when, out of their sight, the elderly lady marine came along with two full buckets of water on a yoke.

Jimmy Parsons: 'I was standing in the doorway of our quarters, looking out, when a shot was fired and, to my horror, the woman went down. I ran over to her. She wouldn't let me touch her but I could tell she wasn't dead, anyway.' Parsons had not been in Russia long but he had quickly worked out what the local priorities were. 'I shouted to the two in the midden to go and get the vodka we had in our hut, and I waved at a nearby Russian to come and help. It turned out to be a false alarm. She'd heard the shot and felt something, but the something was a chip of clay off the chimney. Not knowing that you are never killed by the shot you hear, she had given herself up for dead. A couple of vodkas revived her.'

Not all aircrew were so able to supply their own entertainment. Some had to be provided and in this connection the Russians took their responsibilities seriously. Hospitality was a matter of life, death and honour and, not having a great deal in the way of facilities on the base, full use was made of the little they did have. The Soviets of those days knew how to make massively boring films which, without English subtitles, signally failed to impress the eager RAF audience used to frothier and more amusing productions. Other cultural events similarly did little for Anglo-Soviet relations and even the dance was something of a failure, the Russian girls seemingly being under instructions to socialise in general but not in particular for any length of time.

The mess dinner was, by contrast, a riot. During and following a meal of raw fish, borshch and roast meat – possibly yak, possibly not – there were many toasts, in vodka and a red wine carefully selected to complement the yak, to King George, General Secretary Stalin, President Roosevelt, Prime Minister Churchill, the Royal Air Force, the Red Air Force, Bomber Command, 5 Group, 9 Squadron, 617 Squadron, Yagodnik aerodrome, the Avro Lancaster, Barnes Wallis, and to the runway tarmac which was arriving tomorrow or possibly the next day.

On the Thursday, the proposed attack on *Tirpitz* was scrubbed at 04.00. It was the weather again. Such holidays could not last and soon there was a war on for definite. Operation Paravane was about to come to a point. 15 September, all available Lancasters were to attack the battleship, ten of 9 Squadron and seventeen of 617 Squadron, twenty altogether with Tallboys and the rest with Johnny Walker mines.

Force A, the Tallboy aircraft, began taking off at 09.30 local time, 617 Squadron first. All were up and on their way soon after ten. Gp/Capt McMullen's report:

> Force A was to be disposed in a height band of 14,000–18,000 feet and attack in four waves of five aircraft in line abreast, each wave occupying 1,000 feet in height with a distance between waves of a few hundred yards . . . (At a) point 140 miles due south of the target . . . the three 9 Squadron wind finders were to be three minutes ahead . . . approximately 60 miles from the target Force A was to lose 2,000 feet to gain speed, this distance being considered the limit of surprise.
>
> The operation proceeded as planned until the final run up to the target, when a large alteration of course was necessary as (the Force) was several miles west of track. On the run up a small amount of low cloud drifted over the fjord which, together with the smoke screen, prevented some crews from bombing on their first run. Two 9 Squadron aircraft (C & V) had their bombs hung up and did several runs.

Most of the Tallboy aircraft came in more or less directly astern of the battleship which, to the bomb aimers, looked the size of half a Swan Vesta. Not only were they three miles or so above her, but they also had to hit from an aircraft flying at about two hundred miles an hour and they would have to release their bombs a mile and a half in advance. Over the target something like 25 seconds later, flying much more slowly than the bomb was falling, on a clear day they would have been able to see if their own near-supersonic speck of a bomb had hit the matchstick. Clarity was in short supply as the Germans put up their smokescreens and filled the air with a barrage of flak and shellfire, including the heavy artillery, the fifteen-inch guns. *Tirpitz*, the bomber crews saw, could defend herself very well indeed.

As it was, they bombed from various heights and all within thirteen minutes, sometimes aiming for a piece of the ship they could see, sometimes for her gun flashes in the midst of the smoke. Not surprisingly, some bombs fell in the water.

WS/J, F/Lt Melrose, bombed at 10.55 from 14,900 feet. 'Stern of ship seen in sights. Five Tallboys seen to burst between ship and boom.'

WS/U, F/O Tweddle; 10.56, 15,800 ft. 'A large column of brown smoke rising from target.'

WS/L, Sq/Ldr Pooley; 10.57, 14,000 ft. 'Three bursts seen; one looked as if it might be a possible hit.'

WS/B, F/O Taylor; 10.57, 12,500 ft. 'Two Tallboys seen to explode, one of which seemed close to the ship.'

WS/P, F/O Jones; 11.00, 12,500 ft. '(own) Results not seen. One plume of smoke seen at estimated position of ship.'

WS/O, W/Cdr Bazin; 11.04, 15,000 ft. 'Smoke started at 10.55.'

WS/C, F/O Dunne. 'Hung up, Tallboy returned to base.'

WS/V, F/O Scott. 'Target not attacked. Tallboy would not release in spite of making four runs over target. It eventually fell off through bomb doors.'

The other two 9 Squadron aircraft had Johnny Walker mines. The record shows that Melrose's W4964 WS/J was first to drop, followed a minute later by Tweddle and five of 617 Squadron: Tait in KC/D, Howard in M, Kell in Q, 9 Squadron old boy Geoff Stout in R, and Pryor in U, who were fractionally ahead of Oram in KC/Z and Sq/Ldr Pooley in Lonesome Lola.

Tait never saw Melrose and Melrose said that, regardless of the official timings, one of his crew saw Tait bomb a few seconds before J-Johnny. None of the 617 pilots reported a hit of their own, only some near misses. The general opinion was that there had been one or perhaps two good hits. Several crews were convinced that one hit was obtained with a Tallboy and that five or six fell very close.

Intelligence confirmed it as one hit and three near misses and the 5 Group official plot of calculated strike position of Tallboy bombs showed that, of the first bombers, Tait had fallen short by 700 yards, Oram was 450 yards to port, Stout had overshot by about 350 yards and Pooley was 300 yards to starboard on dry land. Howard was nearer, less than 300 yards off the port bow. Pryor and his bomb aimer, P/O Hoyland, missed by a whisker. The sound of their Tallboy, dropped at 10.56, piercing the sea and exploding just off the starboard side must have echoed and amplified the terrible shock and much louder, slightly earlier bang of the single hitting bomb smashing through the foredeck, dropped at 10.55 by F/Lt Dougie Melrose, bomb aimer F/O Sammy Morris.

Altogether, four were pretty well on target, including Fawke in KC/J.

The chart shows WS/T bombing at 11.00 and near-missing, but WS/T was the American pilot Ed Stowell carrying mines. The only 9 Squadron aircraft to bomb at 11.00 was WS/P, F/O Jones, so it has to be assumed that P goes for T as a clerical error on the chart. Some of the mines fell in the fjord. Some fell on the land. None hit the target before or after walking.

That anybody came anywhere near was a marvellous tribute to the determination and sheer flying abilities of these crews. Every Lancaster on the Op was hit by flak and/or developed mechanical faults from 'Starboard inner banging' to 'Monica u/s' to 'No oxygen', except for WS/O and the old centurion WS/J-Johnny Walker. Without enemy fighters it had not been as hazardous a trip as they might have expected. Even so, to get there they had flown thousands of miles through rain and freezing air, they had been unable to rest properly because of man-eating fleas and they had been subjected to huge quantities of Russian hospitality. They still hit *Tirpitz*.

It was time to go home to Bardney and Woodhall Spa as soon as the aircraft could be fixed. Meanwhile a little celebration had been arranged. While Russian baths and entertainments were set up for the ground crews on the Friday evening, something slightly more Bacchanalian was in store for the airmen. There is one common language understood by all service personnel, especially the glorious comrades of the Royal and Red air forces, and that is the one spoken after much alcohol has been consumed. The premier event in this respect was clearly going to be the special stage show and luncheon to be given at an hotel in Archangel on the Saturday.

Alas for those crews with easily repairable aircraft. They were scheduled to fly home on Saturday night so getting sloshed beforehand was not permitted; 9 Squadron crews with captains Melrose, Bazin, Taylor, Tweddle, Jones and Macintosh had to miss out. That still left plenty of fully serviceable crews from both squadrons to embark on a river boat for the fifteen miles or so to Archangel, including Ray Harris who was in high spirits after receiving news that his brother was a POW, not killed.

Whatever they had expected, they could not have imagined the fact of Archangel (Arkhangelsk). Come the winter and the vast harbour would be frozen over and the days would be three hours long, but for now it was a frontier town, beside the sea and an infinite mudflat, yet still managing to have a certain charm. Fitting in with the general tone, it was obvious that this particular hotel and auditorium had been adjudged suitable for entertaining, wining and dining the Royal Air Force largely because of a lack of suitability in the other options, if there were any.

After the show, a Russian opera, had been endured heroically, the bottles were got out and a sincere effort was made by the hosts to be as generously sociable as they possibly could. Here was a high moral obligation and they were going to fulfil it, come what may. Harris's happy state of mind, plus the fact that he'd had hardly anything to eat since he got there, perhaps contributed to his early departure from the party for a brief spell of post-vodka care in the Russian naval hospital. The others enjoyed their vodka, the potato soup, the vodka, the fish, the vodka, the black bread, the vodka, the blinis, the vodka and the vodka.

A long time later, the party arrived back at the boat in giggles and loose gaggles, accompanied by the young ladies who had been detailed for social duties and who stayed on the quayside while the airmen boarded their ship. The river was covered with disc ice, independent circular ice floes like white lily pads, originating far upstream as rough breakages off the solid block and formed into rounds in the currents as they floated down. One flyer thought that these looked very like stepping stones which could take him back from the departing boat to one particular girl who, he had decided, was in need of further goodbyes. He jumped onto a disc which immediately capsized and threw him in. With all aboard again, inter-squadron rivalry soon developed into throwing each other's hats into the water. The Russians in boats behind patiently picked the hats out and handed them back.

Next morning, there was nothing left to do but go home. Everyone was looking forward mightily to seeing what effect there had been on their bank accounts of the ten roubles per day special allowance added to their pay.

Ray Harris: There seemed to be no end to the supply of free vodka so we wondered how we might get some of it home. The word was that a supply of condoms had been thoughtfully brought to Russia by the medical officer, in case we boys should find ourselves unable to resist the seductive charms of the local talent, such as our very own elderly fourteen-stone steam iron. We made some discrete enquiries which resulted in the condoms being requisitioned for vital military purposes. We filled them with the free vodka ready to fly them back to Bardney, hoping that variations in air pressure would not strain the rubber unduly. Our aircraft wasn't fixed yet so when we went on the Monday, we took Sq/Ldr Williams's WS/N, engine repaired at last, and besides the condoms we had twelve Johnny Walker mines.

News was already through that one of the aircraft which left on the Saturday night, 617's KC/V, had gone missing. With their aircraft written off, Sq/Ldr Wyness's crew had had to hitch lifts. Two of them were Levy's passengers. Everyone in the aircraft was killed, all nine of them. Why ten graves should be dug by the villagers of Nesbyen was always a mystery. No RAF personnel were unaccounted for and no local people were reported missing but an extra skull was reportedly found and certainly a tombstone was set up to an unknown British airman.

For days after the raid, reports from Norwegian intelligence and intercepted German coded messages gave differing versions of the damage caused during Operation Paravane. In summary it seemed that the one hit had drilled through the foredeck at an angle and come out of the ship's hull near the waterline, before exploding some distance away. Had it exploded inside the ship it might well have sunk her.

On *Tirpitz* the officer commanding heavy gun range calculation was Lt Willibald Völsing.

What we had expected happened on 15 September. Twenty-five four-engined Lancasters, so-called 'Flying Fortresses' (sic) were announced over the PA system by our own observation posts (on the mountains). We opened up with our 38cm guns at 25km. The attack was thus interrupted because they had expected no firing at that range. A direct hit caused the fore part of the ship severe damage. From that time we could only operate three nautical miles from the coast, ie *Tirpitz* was no longer any use on the high seas. During this raid, on the spit of land where we lay an unexploded bomb had dropped* – nine metres long. When we saw this six tonne bomb, it was obvious that a direct hit from a bomb of this size would mean the end of our ship.
*This was probably Sq/Ldr Pooley's bomb, which seemed to have been the only one to hit dry land near the ship.

Tirpitz was far more badly damaged than her attackers realised or the Germans would admit, except to themselves. A huge quantity of sea water, 1,500 tons, had flooded into a hole big enough to sail a boat through. Eventually, bomb aimer Morris and pilot Melrose would receive the DFC for their feat in hitting the target although it was not realised at the time that the crew of WS/J had achieved all that was required. They hadn't sunk *Tirpitz* but now there was no need to. *Tirpitz* had been reclassified by the Germans as u/s for war. Admiral Dönitz and a group of senior naval officers decided only a week after the raid that *Tirpitz* was no longer fit for duty. She would need to sail to the Fatherland for repairs and could only manage slow speeds, less than ten knots, which would be a highly dangerous journey for her. Even then, it would be June 1945 before she could be ready to fight again, so it was thought that she could cause more short-term disruption to the Allied cause by doing the same as she had so far: hanging around in the fjords. As long as the Allies didn't find out what a mess she was in, they would continue to hop about in anxiety and tie up large resources in case their fears were realised.

Bomber Command, therefore, was bound to mount at least one more attack on *Tirpitz*, in which case, said certain RAF officers, lessons would have to be learned from The Russian Experience:

Flight engineers could easily acquire more knowledge of daily inspections, refuelling etc. at base stations. This would assist and save time when on detachment. Some engineers (in Russia) were an asset, while many were a liability. Very few crews are capable and willing to maintain their aircraft and to safeguard their personal flying gear under the conditions existing at Yagodnik. The comparative luxury and organised treatment they receive at home does not train them to be self reliant and to use their initiative. If heavy bombers are ever to leave this country to operate from primitive bases in other countries, it is obvious that efficiency will suffer unless aircrew personnel are trained to appreciate that they have responsibilities on the ground as well as in the air.

Quite so, sir. Luxury treatment. Absolutely, sir. Totally agree.

There was one last toast and one final speech to be made before this first *Tirpitz* episode could be closed. The makers of Johnny Walker whisky might not have wanted to be associated with the eponymous joke mines but they had seen the reports in the papers about W4964 WS/J-Johnny Walker the Lancaster, making her century trip with Doug Melrose and Co. They wrote a congratulatory letter, saying they had taken the liberty of forwarding a case of one dozen bottles of Black Label. Some liberty, thought the air and ground crews.

Not noted at the time but a fact nonetheless, it was W4964's 102nd trip. Traditionally this Op has been given as the 100th possibly because one Op has her listed as W4946, a Lancaster already lost with 467 Squadron, or another as W4963 which was in the Middle East. Despite the numbering errors, these were W4964 Ops and counting both gets us to 101. Unlike aircrew, DNCOs and other aborted missions counted as trips for aircraft, for obvious mechanical reasons. The Watten recall is not shown in the squadron ORB but only in aircrew logs, and so has never been counted before: 102.

> (while pouring tea)
> 'Here am I, completely domesticated and
> the perfect lover. My wife doesn't know how lucky she is'
> F/Lt Perry

Normal squadron service was resumed, 23 September. Full control of Bomber Command was back with C-in-C Harris after his summer of following Eisenhower's demands. Although army support work would still be on the roster and 9 Squadron would be closely involved where great precision was needed, the overall emphasis swung back to the industries of Germany. Some other things had changed, too. The *Luftwaffe* was no longer the power it was and, with the resources of Fighter Command much more at his disposal, Harris could order daylight raids with strong escorts. All the other risks remained, of course, and the flak was still there. You could never forget the flak.

First up was an evening raid, take off at seven, back at one. Melrose led A flight to aqueducts near Münster on the Dortmund-Ems Canal. It would be the last time that all the original crew flew together and the last time they flew in the beloved aeroplane. Their tour would be officially complete. Melrose would be up to 32 including 24 in J-Johnny, Bob Woolf 30, Sammy Morris 32, the others 31. After this one, they could pack it in.

The canal was of the highest importance to the Germans and they had seen Bomber Command drain it several times. It would be breached again tonight, by a force including twelve of No. 9 (six with Tallboys), while eleven Tallboy aircraft of 617, the squadron which had lost six Lancasters out of nine there only a year before, went to the aqueduct at Ladbergen. Another ninety or so of other 5 Group squadrons went with 1,000lb bombs. A warm welcome was guaranteed; the Germans expected the bombers all the time and were ready.

WS/W, Adams's *Tirpitz* aircraft, was back, skippered by the American Ed Stowell. Melrose, Tweddle, Taylor and Scott were the other ex *Tirpitz* captains and these, plus Laws in Lonesome Lola, carried the Tallboys.

Mick Maguire: We still had manual winches to wind these things up and when I had my first go at it, I couldn't turn the handle. Gallant was laughing his head off and said Joe Johnson would do it. Joe was an ex-blacksmith.

Bob Woolf: There was a panic to get airborne. We didn't have enough Tallboys on the station so we and three other crews went to Woodhall Spa (617 Squadron) to pick up our bombs and go to the briefing, which was a shambles as far as I was concerned with no gen at all for wireless. It was throwing it down as we took off and things got worse over the Channel as we saw two kites go down together. They must have collided. We saw the yellow ball of flame slowly falling, leaving a streak of fire hundreds of feet long, before being scattered in a bright glow along the coastline.

Melrose found ten tenths cloud over the aqueduct target and it was still thick when he took them down to 7,000 feet. He flew around for ten minutes but it was hopeless so he brought his Tallboy home. They were expensive things, Tallboy bombs. You were not allowed to waste them, even if landing with one was a hazard.

For the Melrose boys, that was it. They had achieved where so many had failed, a tour of bomber Ops, and they were all of four months older than when they started. That was one way of measuring their achievement. They had stayed alive for four months. Time for merriment and a good stretch of leave. Let the others fly the next few.

The canal banks were another primary target on this night for the aircraft with 1,000lb bombs. Jim Buckley and crew were on their first Op, with bomb aimer Dennis Nolan.

We saw about six-tenths cloud and they went ahead and marked it, so we went right down below the cloud, green as grass we were, looking around at all the pretty colours. When we got back and went into interrogation, I said it hadn't been as bad as I expected. I wasn't as frightened as I thought I would be, then when we talked to the other crews they were saying 'What a nightmare', 'Christ that was bloody rough.'

Bloody rough it was, for Rees on his second, attacked by a fighter, hit by flak, home on three, and even rougher for F/Lt Charles Scott and his crew, with Tallboy in LL901 WS/V. They had recovered from their Russian exertions and were restored to normal squadron routine after the adventure of a lifetime. They failed to return from Münster. They did not bring their Tallboy home. Their lifetime was finished as they crashed in Gelderland. They were a week or two short. They had only managed three and a half months. Scott had 28 Ops, F/Sgt Harding and the rest of the crew 27, and V-Victor wanted one for her half century. Scott had come on squadron with Taylor, McMurchy, Woods and Adams. Taylor and Adams were still there.

Geoff Stout, late of 9 Squadron, now of 617, had been to the aqueduct but hadn't bombed and was carrying his Tallboy home to Woodhall Spa when a nightfighter got in an unanswerable volley of shells. Three engines were u/s and the bomb bay was on fire. F/Lt Geoffrey Stevenson Stout DFC, who had second Dickied half a war ago, April 1943, with Bill Meyer and Murray Hobbs, held his aircraft as steady as he could while his crew, some of them wounded, parachuted out. Four men survived. The aircraft crashed at Lochem, roughly halfway between target and coast, and Geoff Stout was still in it.

Jim Brookbank: Our skipper Scotty, F/O W Scott, wounded at Brest, was still convalescing. He, and all of us, were posted as killed instead of

F/Lt C B Scott. When the Service Police came to clear up our quarters and started taking our stuff, it was a stroke of luck that some of us dead men were there or the telegrams would surely have gone out to the wrong crew's families. A few days after that I was walking down Lincoln High Street and a lad I knew from training in Canada came up to me and asked me what I was doing there, seeing as I was dead according to the 5 Group news sheet.

26 September, Karlsruhe. For Ray Harris, Karlsruhe represented nothing more than another night, another trip, except it was his 29th. For the New Zealander Dave Coster, it was his first. For J-Johnny, in the hands of F/O Arndell, it was her 104th. For Scotty and his men, it was their first one back after Brest and the death of Johnny Tollast.

Jim Brookbank: We were a sprog crew and the mark of a sprog crew was not knowing what to expect. This was our first over Germany and we approached it with our usual optimism. We had our replacement wireless operator, Mossie the Aussie (Pilot Officer Mossenson). He'd come into our hut when I was the only one there and introduced himself in his special Australian way. I said that he should be warned, we killed off our wireless operators. He said that was all right, he'd killed off his entire crew.* Mossie had his burns very visible still, including a purple band across his forehead. He told the story that when he got out after his crash, he'd tried to clamber back into the aircraft and the firefighters stopped him, thinking he was bent on rescuing dead men. In fact, he'd forgotten his hat and wanted to get it. That's what a crash could do to you, and then as soon as they classified you physically fit, you were flying again at night over Germany.

*F/O Mossenson had been the only survivor in a June crash at Catfoss, an OTU airfield near Driffield, East Riding, of a Waddington crew, 467 Squadron, returning from Rennes.

They were going for the railways and the engineering factories at Karlsruhe, taking off after 01.00 and expecting to be home at about 07.45. It was cloudy. They dropped their bombs on the glow of fires already started. Adams hadn't got very far on the way home when his mid-upper, Frank Stebbings spotted an Me410 coming in very fast on his starboard side. The gunner ordered corkscrew starboard and swung his guns, as did Fred Whitfield in the rear turret. Exactly according to the book, the German aircraft sped over the top of them as they dived. Frank and Fred poured bullets into him and he broke away in flames. Nothing better, thought Fred and Frank.

6 October, Bremen, the last and most successful of more than thirty attacks on this city. It was a clear, moonlit night and around 250 Lancasters destroyed approximately 5,000 houses and fifty factories, including some of Focke-Wulf and Siemens, for the loss of five aircraft. J-Johnny was driven there and back on her 107th and last journey by F/O Jeffs: 'fires were seen covering large area between the river and the marshalling yard'.

It was retirement at last for an old girl more painted up than a dowager duchess, with medal ribbons – four DFMs and three DFCs earned by crew – a searchlight to denote Mick Maguire's shooting, various stripes for hurts received, more medal ribbons, a Russian star, two kangaroos, a swastika for a fighter shot down and a chevron to denote a year's active service. Not many Lancasters got that one. W4964 WS/J-Johnny Walker was going strong no more. She had been one of over seventy Lancasters delivered to 9 Squadron in 1943. Apart from a single aircraft which had been transferred to other duties, all of those 70-odd, every one of them, had been lost except for J-Johnny and her near equal, EE136 WS/R Spirit of Russia with 93 Ops. Most of the seventy Lancasters had failed to return; a few had ditched or crashed. W4964 had done eleven Berlins, all four Hamburgs, Peenemünde, all the Ruhr targets, *Tirpitz* . . . she'd outlasted them all, plus a great many of the 1944 new ones, and she'd outlasted many of the men who had flown in her.

Around 220 different airmen flew in WS/J. None were killed while doing so and only a very few were wounded, but about a hundred died in other aircraft. Crews with skippers Herbert Wood, George Saxton, the Canadian Gordon Graham, Gilbert Hall, Reg Knight, Tom Gill, Geoff Ward, Australian John Syme, Denis Froud, Albert Manning, James Ineson, Wingco Porter, Peter Blackham and Charles Scott – men who were lost while WS/J flew on – also George Langford, who did his second Dicky in J, and Ernie Redfern and Alf Jeffs, who flew on but would not reach the end.

There were the skippers who finished their tours before she did; Aldersley, Reid, Pearce, Newton who flew sixteen in J, Horne, Plowright who flew eighteen in J, Clark, and the ones who kept on going after her; Morrison, Macintosh, Tweddle, Pooley, Taylor, Camsell, Arndell and Dougie Melrose, who was champion J skipper with 24.

W4964 was allowed to keep her mid-upper turret, her kangaroo patches and her decorations won during her long and gallant flying life, and she was pensioned off to a new career, dull but safe, as a Ground Instructional Airframe. Spirit of Russia transferred to 189 Squadron and another sixteen Ops before she was allowed to rest. The other magnificent veteran, LL845 Lonesome Lola was almost a year younger than J-Johnny, having arrived in mid-March 1944. She would battle on to the end and finish with 97 Ops.

A series of watery daylight targets followed for 9 Squadron; Dutch sea walls to be breached and a dam to be bust. The sea walls proved easier than the dam and were part of the plan to bomb the Germans out of their fortress at Walcheren Island. They were on the run everywhere else but here, at the mouth of the Scheldt, the route into Antwerp. The city was already in Allied hands but could not be used for urgently needed supplies because the Germans controlled the estuary from Walcheren, most of which was below sea level. Macintosh definitely hit the dyke at Vlissingen (Flushing) from around 6,000 feet, Redfern saw water coming through it, Harris hit it with all of his bombs, which he felt was appropriate for a skipper who'd done the four months stretch and thirty Ops.

No. 9 Squadron was now seen as a specialist outfit for whom special targets could be reserved. When they did join in mainforce raids, they usually carried 12,000lb bombs although not always the Tallboy. There was also a 12,000lb blast bomb meant to devastate a wide area rather than penetrate and knock down a small but tough target, which they would carry to Munich (twice), Heilbronn, Essen, Dortmund and Würzburg. This bomb, very ugly compared to the Tallboy, was made in three sections bolted together, with a drum-type tail like the cookie.

Mick Maguire: As armourers we didn't much like the twelve thousand HC.* We could use the Tallboy trolleys and winches to load it but it was an awkward sod. I spent a whole night sitting on one, winding it up and down into the bomb bay, filing away at the G attachment, which was a big forged grab originally meant for the cookie but which we'd modified to take the extra weight. When eventually I got it to fit and it went click and it was in, I fell off the bomb onto the ground and saw them fire a light from the tower to say the Op was a scrub.

Denis Nolan: As well as the Tallboy we had the 12,000 pound cookie, the HC bomb, which used to roll and tumble and corkscrew and do all sorts of funny things on the way down. It had all the aerodynamic qualities of a London bus.

*HC, high capacity bombs, also called blockbusters, had thin casings so that the maximum possible weight of explosive could cause the biggest blast. Medium capacity bombs, like Tallboy, the standard 1,000-pounder and others, carried less explosive proportionately but had strong casings designed for maximum penetration.

15 October, eighteen Lancasters of 9 Squadron went to the Sorpe Dam, escorted by almost sixty Mustangs including 315 Squadron, the Poles who, in January, would figure prominently by default in the histories of 9 and 617 Squadrons. The Sorpe was the one in the great 617 Squadron

Dambusters raid which was left to last, not usefully damaged and kept the Ruhr supplied with water while the breached Möhne dam was rebuilt. At the time of the Dambusters raid, the Germans had speculated on what might have happened had the second dam on the list been the Sorpe rather than the Eder, the breach of which didn't affect the Ruhr.

All the skippers on that famous moonlit night had been very experienced; most were so on 9 Squadron's morning effort, but not all. Two aircraft were jostled by others over the target and as a result were unable to make an attack. No definite breach of the dam was seen to have occurred although several hits were registered.

Laws, an experienced pilot on squadron since July, was overtaken by another aircraft. 'I was driven off course to starboard and came over target on wrong heading, so bomb was not dropped.' Redfern had the narrowest escape. He missed having a Tallboy through his wing by the very thinnest of toothskin. 'Target not attacked as aircraft directly above dropped bomb as own bomb aimer was about to get aiming point in the graticule. Turned own aircraft to starboard to avoid bomb which fell just ahead of port wing. Request made for another run but leader instructed to rejoin formation.'

There were nine hits and near misses, with one direct hit on the very crest of the dam, smack in the middle. Accurate though the bombing was and in trying circumstances, the dam was proof against the Tallboy, being a thousand feet thick at its base with its concrete centre reinforced and protected by many, many feet of earth and rubble. Perhaps, had the Germans kept the water level as high as it had been pre-Dambusters, the extra pressure would have made a breach. More likely, the Sorpe would have stood however many bombs hit it, bouncing, spinning or otherwise.

On the same day *Tirpitz*, her every move watched by Norwegian spies, steamed very slowly down the coast to Tromsø where she anchored off Haaköy island, to be a floating gun battery against the expected Allied invasion of Norway. The spies reported extensive damage to her forward hull. Her low speed, plus a huge escort of more than fifty warships, might have convinced an independent mind that she was hors de combat, no longer an independent fighting force. A more enticing thought was that she had sailed herself into range. No need for Russian adventures now. Lancasters with a few further modifications could reach her from Scotland.

After two days of bombing practice the truth was revealed, as if they hadn't guessed. They were going to fly to Scotland, and then it was *Tirpitz* again. Dougie Melrose was in J-Jane, a new aircraft and he, Ray Harris in W-William and 38 other Lancs of 9 and 617 Squadrons flew to Lossiemouth and Kinloss from Bardney and Woodhall Spa and, on 29 October, set off on Operation Obviate, to attack *Tirpitz*, a 2,400-mile, twelve-hour round trip flying over the spectacularly beautiful Norwegian landscape in glorious weather.

Egil Lindberg was a Norwegian Resistance radio operator, a meteorologist at Tromsø put out of work by the Germans who had their own weathermen. He regularly sent covert signals to London and was a close observer of the battleship.

The situation in Tromsø was hectic, to say the least. Russian troops had crossed the Norwegian border and the German army, retreating from Finland, adopted a scorched-earth policy. The result was 15,000 German soldiers in Tromsø and many thousands of new refugees every day. Then, when *Tirpitz* arrived, everybody knew something extra-ordinary was going to happen.

Lt Willibald Völsing: In Tromsøfjord we discovered quite different geographical conditions. Here there were no mountains close at hand. Rather, for a distance of some thirty kilometres around, everything was open, so it was no longer any use to have land-based observers. On 29 October a sailor on watch at the ship's foremost observation post sighted the enemy approaching at a range of 70km. The Captain awarded him the Iron Cross on the spot. We had enough time to make ready and go to action stations on that day.

Egil Lindberg: The air-raid siren went off and the Lancaster bomber squadrons came sailing in above the town from the east. The Germans immediately struck up with their anti-aircraft guns and there was a deafening noise. Shell fragments rained down upon the town. You could see the planes dive into the clouds and out, while the anti-aircraft shells exploded around them.

Wing Commander Bazin led 9 Squadron in and bombed at 08.54. He thought the ship seemed to be beached at one end. Squadron Leader Williams at 08.55 had the centre of the ship in the bombsight. Light and heavy flak were moderate to intense from shore batteries, flak ships and *Tirpitz* herself, also firing her heavy guns from aft. Lt Völsing: 'Our salvoes gave us cover and the British had to scatter.'

Dunne's bomb aimer, F/O Philpott, reported at 08.55 that flak had blown a hole in his compartment; they carried on the run and he pressed the tit at 08.56. Williams's rear gunner, Sgt Watt, saw a direct hit on the bows followed by a big explosion and a column of brown smoke. Jones bombed at 08.58 and had his cupola smashed by flak at 09.00. 'Pilot sustained facial injuries. Bomb aimer thought target pranged.' Several other pilots saw the brown smoke and a hit on the bows.

About to start the bombing run a few miles from the ship, where the flak was thick and accurate, Adams's rear gunner Whitfield reported he'd been hit in the foot but not badly, so the skipper told him to hang on until he could send the engineer Larry Brown to help. A few moments later, Whitfield came on again. He hadn't been hit after all. His heated slipper had fused and burned a small hole in his foot. The skipper briefly expressed his deepest regrets that the gunner should have to suffer the discomfort of one u/s slipper and hoped very much that no further inconveniences would occur. Meanwhile, there were large flak holes in the starboard tanks and petrol flowed in rivers before they self-sealed.

Lt Völsing: 'A near miss caused an influx of 8,000 cubic metres of water but we did not list because of compensating currents in the fjord. Several Lancasters were shot down or lost on their way home. Even an attack by four-engined aircraft can be fought off if there is enough warning.'

Morrison did five runs, Taylor three and Harris two. He didn't mind doing two. He was one of the last to bomb 'and we didn't sink it either', but this was his 31st Op. He and now all his men were tour completed. In jocular mood they set off for home.

We hadn't got very far when a message came in on the VHF. It was a 617 Squadron pilot, an Australian, Carey in E. He'd been hit in two engines, lost a lot of petrol and was sending out a Mayday to anybody who might be listening. I picked it up and told Carey that the best thing he could do would be to head for Sweden and try and get down there, and that was the last anyone heard until, eventually, word came through that the crew were safe after landing in a Swedish bog.

Adams, diverted to Sumburgh in Shetland, was flying on empty long before he got there, with all the crew except himself cut off from the oxygen supply. As he touched down, all four of his engines died. In Jones's aircraft, the bomb aimer took over from the wounded pilot and flew the Lancaster back to Scotland where Jones managed the landing himself.

Most of the 617 Squadron crews had also seen hits and smoke but, when it all cleared and reconnaissance pictures could be studied, *Tirpitz* was still there, apparently unharmed. The Lancasters had had one bomb each and all the bombs were dropped, and only Carey didn't return, which hardly counts as scattering, being driven off and several shot down, but the damned ship was still afloat. Sure that another, third attack would come, the Germans got on with the job of saving *Tirpitz* by the only method open. Lt Völsing: 'We now set about encasing the ship in sand so as to make her unsinkable.' They built up the sea bed beneath her.

Bomber Command's orders, from the very top, said to sink *Tirpitz*. Not render her u/s, not turn her into scrap, but sink her. It was becoming as much psychological warfare as anything. The negative effect on German morale of sinking the mighty *Tirpitz* could hardly be underestimated. The value of her staying there, defiant and indestructible, was opposingly great. If she was to be sunk, increasingly shallow water was not the only problem. The days were very short and getting shorter. So far, two squadrons had been twice in the daylight and hit the target with a single bomb between them. How many night trips would it take?

Every day they practised. Considering the weather conditions and the few daylight hours, if they got one more shot at it they would have to make sure. Somebody, some pilot and bomb aimer combination, in 9 Squadron or 617, absolutely had to stick a Tallboy right on the money. Off they went again up to Scotland.

John Runnacles, a sergeant at 9 Squadron when he started as a Wellington second pilot in the autumn of 1940, was now a flight lieutenant Lancaster skipper with 97 Squadron pathfinders. After a few Ops of his second tour, he'd telephoned Ken Chamberlain to tell him how he wished he had agreed to volunteer for the Lysander idea, because he was sure he would never get through this. Chamberlain did get through his twenty, as a mainforce second tour then was, and was posted to 106 Squadron as a navigation analysis officer, but Runnacles had seen the future. On a night exercise, training over France with a new but not very successful navigation aid called Loran, 11 November 1944, he and his crew disappeared into a marsh and were posted to the Runnymede Memorial.

The dark early morning of 12 November was exceptionally wintry and those responsible for de-icing the aircraft did not get up soon enough. In any case, some Lancasters were refreezing as fast as they were defrosted and it was snowing. To his great frustration, Doug Melrose, commanding B Flight, was among those who couldn't take off, likewise W/Cdr Bazin, OC the squadron. With two of the top men grounded, Sq/Ldr Williams moved up from commanding A Flight to take charge of all of 9 Squadron including the veteran Puddle Lake who had the even more venerable F/Sgt Parkes, Horne's old rear gunner, holding the tail for him.

Doug Tweddle was a pilot with a special reputation for skill and finesse. With him on this trip, called Operation Catechism, was Buckley's bomb aimer, Dennis Nolan.

A long period of boredom on the way in was interrupted by flying over a flak ship at 2,000 feet in one of the big fjords. We were low, ready to hop over the mountains at the last minute and down into Swedish territory, keeping out of sight of the radar. That ship didn't half open up. It was only thirty seconds but it was a very hairy thirty seconds. Anyway, we rendezvous'd over a lake, twenty minutes south of

Tromsøfjord. We were on dead reckoning and I was supposed to help the navigator by map-referencing from what I could see. Well, when dawn broke and I did see it, it was a whole series of pointy mountain tops covered in snow, and a load of little valleys all filled with white mist. No distinguishing features whatsoever. We'd just got it sorted when a Lancaster up ahead started shooting off Very lights. It was Tait (W/Cdr Willy Tait, 617 Squadron), saying, 'Here I am, chaps, pull in behind.' So 617 sorted themselves out behind Tait and we got behind Bill Williams.

Lt Völsing was in position on *Tirpitz* as range finder for the heavy guns. 'The alarm was given and in forty seconds the guns were cleared for action. The Commandant spoke words of encouragement and optimism and held out the prospect of support from squadrons of fighter aircraft. Since we had so far survived without outside help, this time the optimism was all the greater.' The fighters were FW190s of *9 Staffel, Jagdgeschwader 5* (coincidentally, No. 9 Squadron, 5 Group) but the support never got beyond the prospect stage.

As the leading Lancasters cleared the last peak, crews were astounded and delighted to find that the fjord they wanted seemed to be the only one in Norway with no white mist and there, in front of them, tiny but perfectly visible, was *Tirpitz*.

Egil Lindberg: It was an unusual day for the time of year. The sky was bright and there was not a breath of wind.

Lt Völsing: Electronic range calculation was in its infancy and never were the calculations so far out as on that day. The first gunnery officer repeatedly ordered the heavy guns to open fire, but there was no data and so the automatic firing devices could not be used. We fired too late and overshot.

Dennis Nolan: On the run up I spotted the ship from some distance and there were gouts of flame coming from it. They'd opened up with their main armament at maximum elevation, to try and frighten us off, I suppose. Then suddenly in front of us was the biggest burst of flak you've ever seen in your life.

W/Cdr Tait led the attack and his bomb, the first to fall, was almost certainly a direct hit on the ship.

Egil Lindberg: I and some other Norwegians were (watching) from the weather office, on top of the island of Tromsø, while the huge bombs were dropped in a circle around the ship. As the bombs burst, our own windows were blown from their fastenings and panes were shattered, and from the sea columns of water rose several hundred feet into the air.

Lt Völsing: There was no longer any distinguishing between our firing and the enemy's bombs.

Coster in WS/T had not even begun his bombing run when he was hit by heavy flak. The pilot and F/Sgt Boag, the bomb aimer were concentrating on their immediate priority, the target, as was Jim Pinning, flight engineer.

The rear gunner Taffy Jones came over the intercom. 'Jim,' he said. 'Your starboard outer's on fire.' We followed the routine: open the radiator wide, dive and try and blow it out. Didn't work, close the throttle, feather the prop, press the extinguisher button, and it went out. Other flak damage had petrol leaking badly and the starboard inner was running rough. I assessed the fuel situation. We were not going to get home.

F/Lt Bruce Buckham DSO, DFC was captain of the 463 Squadron camera Lancaster:

We descended to about 2,000 feet and the bombers were right overhead doing perfect bombing runs, bomb doors gaped open and the glistening Tallboys suspended. Now they were released and to us they appeared to travel in a graceful curve like a high diver. (I thought) the first two were near misses and then Pow! a hit which was followed by two more in as many seconds. There was a tremendous explosion on board and *Tirpitz* appeared to try to heave herself out of the water.

Egil Lindberg: The anti-aircraft fire of *Tirpitz* soon became more tame. Only the aftermost guns were still firing angrily. Some minutes later the guns fell silent and a tremendous mass of smoke rose from the ship and we assumed there had been an explosion of the boilers or magazines. When the smoke lifted and lay like a dark cloud in the sky, we could see the battleship stripped of masts and towers, as if she was part-finished in the shipyard.

Johann Tröger was a signaller, aged 22, who had been blown into the fjord by a direct hit on the bridge.

The ship seemed to leap out of the water when the magazine went up, making a huge hole through the side. There were men everywhere in the water. It was bitterly cold and there was black smoke billowing over everything, then another bomb hit the waterline alongside. The suction pulled the ship sideways and she stayed there for what seemed a very long time but water was pouring in through the hole and suddenly she keeled over and slid bow first into the harbour sand.

Bruce Buckham: (Eventually) we decided to call it a day, when our rear gunner Eric Gierch called out, 'I think she's turning over.' We flew in at fifty feet and watched with baited breath as *Tirpitz* heeled over to port, ever so slowly. We could see German sailors swimming, diving, jumping and there must have been sixty men clinging to her side.

Tröger was among those picked up by a motor torpedo boat.

We were crowded on deck when a single aircraft came back and circled overhead at very low level. I said to the man next to me, 'There you are. They've come back to make sure we're really finished and take a picture of us.'

Lt Völsing: A few minutes after the action started, the ship began listing and in about 45 seconds was over at right angles to port. The ship turned some more and stayed there. Now we were standing on what had been the ceiling. There was only a dim glow from the emergency lighting. Water was swirling and bubbling from every corner. It was as if we were in a whirlpool below a waterfall which could swallow us up at any moment. Communications failed completely. The officers in charge could not free themselves; they were shut in behind the plating. I reached the forward radio room where fifty or sixty men lay dead, then I got to the main steering room where I stayed with fourteen men alive. There was no water here but there was gurgling all around us. We were prepared for the worst. The ship had capsized at about 09.00 and the emergency lighting failed at about 15.00. We had no sense of time passing, surrounded by darkness and a grave-like silence in which every man gave way to his own thoughts.

Where had the fighters been all this time? For once, the Germans were inefficient. At the nearby fighter base at Bardufoss, the FW190s were scrambled to attack enemy aircraft in the east but were ordered to wait on the ground for the commander. There didn't seem to be a commander so one of the more experienced pilots among a fairly raw lot, Heinz Orlowski, took off and the rest followed.

We saw anti-aircraft fire in the Tromsø area and set course for it, not knowing why anyone would want to raid the fjord because the fighter base had not been informed about *Tirpitz* being there. On the way, we met two Me109s flying in the opposite direction. I assumed that one of them must contain the commander, so I wheeled around and the rest did the same and we flew back with the Messerschmitts to land at Bardufoss. By this time, flights of four-engined aircraft had been reported as coming and going high over Tromsø but it was too late for us to catch them.

The pilots of 9 *Staffel* and the commanding officers of *Jagdgeschwader* 5 had missed the show. It was lack of communications, but they were still blamed in some quarters for the sinking of *Tirpitz*.

Ashore at the fjord, the half-frozen sailors were dried out, warmed up and sent back on rescue duties.

Tröger: We spent from ten at night until four the next afternoon, cutting into the two-inch steel. It was hard and wintry work but in one case I saw 45 men climb out of a hole we cut.
Egil Lindberg: Only a few hundred men were saved. About a hundred dead bodies drifted ashore; the rest remained inside the ship. There was a great enthusiasm in Tromsø over the successful attack and the joy manifested itself loudly, which resulted in quite a number of arrests among the civilians by the Gestapo.

There was a great enthusiasm in Britain too, with congratulatory messages to both squadrons from the King, the Prime Minister, the War Cabinet, the Admiralty, the Russians, President Roosevelt and all the biggest brass hats in the RAF. The very top man, Air Chief Marshal Sir Charles Portal, Chief of Air Staff, wrote privately to Sir Arthur Harris.

I have just heard of the splendid achievement of 9 and 617 Squadrons in sinking *Tirpitz*. Please pass to them my warmest congratulations and an expression of unbounded admiration which I feel for their skill, courage and perseverance now so happily crowned with full success. Apart from the effect on the war at sea of the permanent removal of the most powerful unit of the German Navy this exploit will fill the German Nation with dismay at a critical time and will enhance the fame of Bomber Command and the Royal Air Force throughout the world.

The two squadrons were pleased with the praise and the fame but were more immediately concerned not to be filled with dismay at a critical time, and so would enhance the bar takings in the mess. The parties at Bardney and Woodhall Spa were most memorable, except hardly anyone could remember. Of course, 9 Squadron had lost Coster.

Jim Pinning: We didn't have any proper maps but we knew where Sweden was. Our plan was to fly down the Norwegian coast and turn left, and it went wrong from the start. We flew over an aerodrome and they sent up a load of flak which did some more damage, then we ran into German fighters. One came in from the starboard quarter, my side, and Coster corkscrewed for our lives on two and a half engines. Sounds impossible but he did it. Taffy (RG) was firing, I saw some smoke and the fighter gave up. Whether he was out of ammo, or hit, I don't know. It may be that just at that point we crossed into Swedish airspace, and the Germans would not violate that on any account.

We were flying over dense pine forests alternating with snowy peaks, the cloud was low and it was getting dark. There was hardly any petrol left and there seemed no end to trees and mountains, mountains and trees.

They didn't know it but, as well as petrol, they were running out of Sweden. Ahead of them to starboard was the sea, the Gulf of Bothnia. Straight in front was the dangerously confused situation in Finland where the Finns, having been on the German side, were trying to come to terms with their Russian invaders.

Then we saw a bare patch. We went down to have a look and it turned out to be an island in a river. Coster took her in on our two and a bit engines, undercart up, bellyflop, knowing he only had one shot at it. Good pilot, Coster.

They landed at Vandnasberget, on the River Kalix, hardly thirty miles from the Finnish border, in northern Sweden or southern Lapland.

The aircraft half filled with slush as we ploughed along but we were all fine, and the locals took us in and gave us some reindeer meat or whatever it was, and some hot water to wash in.

There were many *post mortes*, bomb plottings and analyses of the final *Tirpitz* raid, all of which disagreed with the men who were there, but the consensus was that the leader of the Op made the first hit. Errors of two hundred yards were accepted in such plottings since they relied on data given by the pilots – time of bomb release, aircraft speed and height – but, as with the plot for the first attack in September, there seemed no reason to doubt the central premise. Just as Melrose and his crew dealt the blow that time, so did Tait and his men on this fine November morning. Other 617 pilots claimed hits and very near misses.

For 9 Squadron, Lake's rear gunner F/Sgt Parkes saw their own bomb which he considered hit the ship as a big explosion and fire followed immediately. Tweddle saw a large explosion at the same time. Stowell saw his own bomb fall approximately at the centre of the port side, before he was hit in the tail by flak. Newton didn't hit *Tirpitz* but he did have a shoot-out with two E-boats ten minutes after he bombed and his rear gunner, Sgt Stevens, put one of them out of action.

Whatever the claims and witness accounts, there were only two direct hits on the battleship, almost certainly Tait's and one other from 617 Squadron. It was enough. *Tirpitz* was a kill. She was finished, at last, after all those attempts, but she hadn't sunk immediately, after the direct hits. The tradition grew that 617 Squadron had put the holes in the ship and 9 Squadron had blasted all that extra sand and gravel away from the sea bottom so that she could turn over. It was certainly the case that 9 Squadron bombed after 617 and had the smoke from previous hits obscuring their bombing. They also had an error built in to their bombsights; the wind at the target was different from the wind they were working on. It looked from the plot as if Marsh put his bomb close to the ship, whereas some of his 9 Squadron colleagues were a great deal less accurate. Perhaps if Bazin and Melrose had been there to share the burden of leadership, things might have been different.

The ineffective and timid fighting career of *Tirpitz* was concluded when she keeled over on her side and lay there, a useless steel island and giant coffin. Among the dead – figures varied from 971 to 1,204 – were the captain and most of the senior officers, trapped in their heavily armour-plated command post with massively thick doors which, twisted by the explosions, could not be opened.

The squadron scribe at Bardney summed up in near biblical style.

As is now known, this operation was completely successful, and was no doubt the outstanding operation of the month, and when it became known at the station great jubilation was evident amongst the ground crews, the extra work called for being thought well worth while.

Jim Pinning: We expected we'd be arrested by the Swedish police but before that the local schoolmaster and his wife had us round for dinner and wine, a lot of wine, and then we were interned at an army camp for two nights. They took us to Stockholm, put us up in an hotel, gave us full civilian kit, suit, socks, shoes, shirts, coat, hat, gloves, the lot, and we just wandered around the city. Nobody bothered about us, except we often noticed one particular policeman who, we were told, had German sympathies. We were issued with ration coupons and it wasn't like back home where, if you could afford it, you could go into a smart hotel and get a meal without coupons. In Sweden, it was always coupons everywhere you went. The British assistant military attaché looked after us very well and when it came to our time to go home he was choked. 'Well done, chaps,' he said. 'You got *Tirpitz* by the balls.'

As with all men who had been shot down and interned, they would be offered the choice of something peaceful or back to Ops. They would choose Bardney and be greeted with 'Where the hell have you lot been for three weeks?'

At head office there was proof that, in the RAF as well as in so many other firms, there was no pleasing some people. There may have been great jubilation evident at Bardney, Woodhall Spa and the high corridors, but not here.

A study of the plot (of the third *Tirpitz* raid) reveals a highly unsatisfactory bombing pattern. It will be noted that the Mean Point of Impact is some 300 yards offset from the target . . . It is obviously uneconomical to attack these small targets with a bombing pattern so widely dispersed.

This was written by Air Commodore Elworthy, Senior Air Staff Officer, 5 Group, the same Samuel Charles Elworthy DSO DFC who had once been 9 Squadron's station CO, future Chief of the Defence Staff.

Melrose's crew had completed their tour in the accepted sense. They could have called it a day but only navigator Jimmy Moore did. He was much older than the rest and perhaps that bit wiser. He was posted to a non-combat job and was replaced by Tug Wilson, now a pilot officer. 'Doug Melrose used to take quite a bit of stick in the mess because he was a little short chap who insisted on growing this huge, droopy, bushy moustache which was a bit out of RAF fashion by then. They used to call him the man with the rug in his mouth. He was a bloody good pilot, whatever.' Melrose had been promoted to squadron leader with a new daily pay rate of one pound, ten shillings and tenpence, a rise above flight lieutenant of one shilling and one penny *per diem*. To count it more meaningfully, that was two pints of bitter and a box of matches.

Losses on recent raids had not been as severe as usual but the figure was back to normal, 4 December, Heilbronn. Only a fifth of the town was left after a few minutes' supremely efficient bombing started a firestorm, but thirteen Lancasters failed to return. That the figure was not fifteen was entirely a matter of luck. Vincent Peace was mid-upper gunner with Reaks.

The whole area was already well ablaze but before we could set ourselves for our bombing run, the Master Bomber ordered a rerun on a different marker and at a lower altitude, which let loose several minutes of complete mayhem. There were Lancasters flying in all directions, clearly visible in the bright glow from the fires below. We seemed to be not much above the roof tops. I'm convinced that had I fired my guns downwards, quite a lot of firemen would have fallen off their ladders. We dropped our bombs and climbed with all speed out of the blazing, flak-infested area, when another Lancaster passed a few feet above us, almost on the same heading. If I could have stood up in my turret and reached out, I could have touched his tail wheel.

As if that wasn't enough good fortune for one night, Peace also encountered *Schrägemusik* for the first time and didn't know what it was.

Only a few seconds had gone by after this very near miss when I reported to the skipper that there was a string of multi-coloured balls arching over us, coming from starboard down and looping up and across to port. A few more moments went by after this excitement when I lost all power to my turret. Nothing would work. The guns wouldn't fire and my heated jacket stopped heating. It was minus 30° Centigrade outside and soon it was about that inside as well. I was still frozen at the interrogation, when they told us that the pretty coloured balls were from a nightfighter with an upward firing gun.

'Before arriving at that hotel,
I had led a very sheltered life'
F/O Skinner

The French evader F/Lt Oldacre turned up at Bardney, a complete stranger to almost everyone. He'd been the last second Dicky and only the old guard like Melrose and Harris knew at first hand what a second Dicky was. The enemy territory into which he'd parachuted was no longer in enemy hands. Number 9 was a specialist squadron now, with 12,000lb bombs. Who did you say you were?

Apart from two fruitless trips to the Urft dam, the next few days were a mixture of aerial frustration with scrubs and earthly pleasures with gongs. Nine DFCs and one DFM were awarded with immediate effect for the last *Tirpitz* raid, which was the correct ratio. Non-commissioned aircrew of the time would always point out that you had to be nine times as brave to get a DFM as a DFC. Munich, 17 December, was a positive relief. The squadron was now putting up 23 Lancs on one raid, eighteen with 12,000lb HC bombs and five with cookies and clusters, compared with six

Wellingtons carrying 1,500 lb between them at the start of the war. Lancaster NN722 WS/Q-Queenie was badly damaged in this raid but she would be repaired by 2 January at a cost of £107 6s 5d for materials and over 550 man-hours of labour.

In 1924, Gdynia had been a little Polish fishing village on the Baltic near Danzig. Ten years later it had become one of the biggest harbours in Europe and now it sheltered the German battleship *Lutzow*.

Jim Brookbank: At the bomb aimers' briefing, as with any other, the first thing we did was look at the map on the wall to see where the target was. That day, as the bomb aimers came in one by one, every one of them moaned about how far it was. I was pacing up and down and lighting a cigarette when Dunne's man, Philpott, naturally known as Tosspots, pointed at me and said to the assembled throng, 'Look at him, he's got The Twitch,' and before I could reply, someone else turned round and said, 'What of it, haven't you?' And somebody else said, 'Tosspots, you've bloody got The Twitch worse than any of us.'

While 218 other Lancs of 5 Group attacked the port, the *Tirpitz* boys had the ship with ten thousand-pounders each but there was no glory this time. Some saw the target, some saw only cloud. Rees had heavy flak damage and nobody saw any results. Scott was attacked by a Ju88.

Jim Brookbank: Jeep (Jepson, rear gunner) was banging away and, as the drill was, had his oxygen mask open to the side so that his microphone would pick up everything that was going on and we could all hear the guns. Jeep said his tracer was bouncing off the Junkers, then he said it was breaking away starboard down. My drill then was to depress the guns in the front turret to starboard and just blast away, in the hope that the enemy would fly through the bullets. I didn't see him, he didn't hit us, and for ever after we told Jeep that it had been a Mosquito he'd been firing at.
Tug Wilson: When we were attacked by a fighter and Ernie shouted corkscrew, Doug would throw the ship about and get us out of it and then come over on the intercom, all calm, and say 'What course, Tug?' What course? He'd just had us all over the sky and my instruments were all over the floor and he's asking what course. I'd say just keep going where you're going and when I've found my stuff in every corner of this bloody aircraft I'll try and work something out.

It was foggy at home and only four got down there while the rest mainly diverted to Langar in the Vale of Belvoir, between Newark and Melton

Mowbray. This would prove highly inconvenient. The crews could come back by road but bad weather prevented the aircraft and it would be 1945 before they were all available for selection.

Christmas Day was relatively warm; only six degrees of frost compared with nine the day before and twelve on Boxing Day. It was still twelve below when five went in a force of 67 to attack a warship fleet in Oslofjord near Moss. No. 9 was detailed to attack the flagship; Camsell was first in and scored a direct hit. Stowell saw hits too and when Keeley turned in for his second run, only one gun on the ship was still firing and that soon stopped.

Another year of war was over. Maybe when they got their Lancasters back from Langar they could help finish the damned thing.

11

THE NEW YEAR, THOMPSON VC AND BATTLES OVER BERGEN

For off-duty aircrew, every night was party night. Eat, drink and be merry, for tomorrow we die. Even so, there was a special atmosphere about New Year's Eve, 1944. Most people hoped and many expected that this year coming would be the last of the war in Europe.

Those crews of ten Lancasters whose names were on the battle order for a New Year's Day 07.45 take-off had to keep to a modest few beers and get to bed in good time. Their alarm clock, a Service Policeman, would be shaking them at 03.00 and asking them to sign his clipboard to confirm that they had indeed been woken.

Bomber Command was now an extremely effective and powerful force. Butch Harris was not alone in thinking that, if the invasion faltered or was repelled, the RAF on its own could render Germany incapable of further resistance. Von Rundstedt had opened his counter-attack in the Ardennes in mid-December, greatly aided at first by a long period of bad flying weather, fog and low cloud. A year before, the *Wehrmacht* Field Marshal Keitel had said that the strength of the Allies lay chiefly in their air force, and von Rundstedt knew that his hopes of turning back the invaders rested to an extent on the luck of the weather.

By the end of the month his luck had run out. Bomber attacks on roads and railways had prevented or decisively slowed troop movements and were a key factor in the swift breakdown of the Ardennes counter-offensive. Panther and Tiger tanks were brilliant fighting machines but bombing had brought tank production to a level far below what was wanted. Fuel was desperately short, because of the raids on refineries and synthetic oil plants, so that many of the tanks never got to the battlefield or were very restricted in what they could do if they did arrive.

Attacks on the means of production and distribution remained a high priority and the Dortmund-Ems canal once again appeared at the top of the list. So essential was it to the German system that every possible resource was always put into repairing it. It seemed that no matter what the bombers did, the Germans and their slave labour could nullify their efforts in short order and get the ships floating again along this vital highway of war.

New Year's Eve had been another very cold night. As usual in the Nissen huts, the coke stoves had been stoked up and given full draught until they were glowing red and, as usual, they had gone out soon afterwards. The men who liked a glass of water by their beds found it frozen over in the morning. Only those who wore their inner flying suits or other such insulation over their pyjamas could lie in their beds without shivering.

It was perishing, frosty and black dark as the crews were taken to their dispersals and it was still dark when Kiwi F/O Harry Denton, captain of U-Uncle, was first up. At 07.47, American Cliff Newton surged down the runway in R-Robert and took off. Immediately filling his place at the end of the runway was Australian F/O Buckley in A-Able. He and his flight engineer, Sergeant Ken Dawes, began their usual last-minute checks. At the moment they were expecting a green from the caravan, there was a huge Wooomph! and a great flash of fire, some distance away. Everyone thought some poor sod at Woodhall had gone in. Woodhall Spa, base for 617 Squadron, was six or seven miles away. The explosion was much nearer home. Once in the air, Newton's engines had cut and the Lancaster, powerless when it needed power the most, had crashed into a field. The pilot and five of his crew, including the gunners who had done for the E-boat on the *Tirpitz* raid, were killed in the fire; the Canadian rear gunner, Bob Stevens, had recently married his English girl Margaret. Another founder member, the bomb aimer, P/O Paddy Flynn, was thrown clear and escaped with injuries.

Unaware of all this, Buckley still waited for his green but got a red. They sat, and they sat, and they sat. It seemed like half an hour although it was hardly ten minutes before the green came. The Lanc rolled forward, faster and faster. The navigator, F/O Shutler, called the airspeed, the tail was up, the engineer had the throttles, on the point of leaving the ground . . . red lights came on from both port engines. Denis Nolan was the bomb aimer.

At the same instant the aircraft gave a mighty lurch as she hit the ground and the pilot shouted 'Cut!' Ken instantly did that realising, like we all did, that we had been only a couple of seconds away from an almighty prang. If we had been a foot or two higher in the air it would have been a wingtip which grounded, not the undercarriage, and we would have been cartwheeling down the runway, spilling bombs and bodies everywhere.

As it was we were still almost at airspeed, veering sharply to port and flitting across the grass. The Lancaster was a great aircraft for flying. Just as she had to be reined in hard on landing, so she was keen to get up there when she was moving fast enough. As the speed dropped, the ride got bumpier, from near-hover to jolting and banging along. Another Lancaster was at dispersal with her nav lights on. We watched

them and they watched us in mutual horror, as A-Able bore down on their stationary aircraft with nobody able to do a thing about it.

The gap between wingtips was later judged by measuring tyre marks in the grass. It was no more than six feet. In Lancaster terms, that was half a whisker and Buckley and Co were still doing about 60mph in a very large vehicle, completely out of control.

At the edge of the airfield ran the stream. It had originally been in an inconvenient place so, when RAF Bardney was built, a steam shovel dug a new watercourse and piled the soil up on the airfield side. The pile was about three feet high and it made a nice launching ramp for the speeding Lanc.

We hit the ramp, tore our wheels off, waffled through the air for quite a few yards and hit the young pine trees of the plantation rather higher up their trunks than would otherwise have been the case. The trees bent, instead of making a barrier of posts, as we tore into them ripping off Perspex and other bits and pieces but we didn't get the explosion we were expecting. Finally we stopped.

I'd seen the clearview panel next to me snatched off by a tree so I climbed through it, onto the wing. Next problem was, where could I go? It was dark and we were in the trees. I could hear the w/op, F/Sgt Moore and the mid-upper, Sgt Round, behind me. They were leaping for safety, convinced that she was about to blow. There was an overpowering smell of petrol and the exhaust stubs of the engines were glowing red hot.

The rear gunner, Sgt Copperwaite was trapped. Nothing would open for him. Skipper Buckley, powerful, well built, was heaving the engineer through broken Perspex, and Dawes was shouting like mad because his leg was broken. They were one man missing, who must have been that chap Copperwaite making muffled cries and banging on his turret. Buckley and Nolan went back inside the aircraft, grabbed the axes, came out again, chopped the turret free and waited for help, which was a while coming. All resources were at the scene of Newton's crash. The cause of failure in both aircraft was never finally resolved but frozen water in the fuel seemed the most likely possibility.

Eventually Scott had his green and set off to catch Denton, followed by Jeffs, Wiley, Macdonald, Oldacre at last flying his first Op, and Reaks. For Reaks in D, this was his ninth Op, all with exactly the same crew, among whose characters was the bomb aimer, Warrant Officer Edward Percy Bates, age 31, son of Sir Percy Bates of Neston, fourth baronet and

Chairman of the Cunard shipping line. Nicknamed 'The Master' behind his back, noted for not going to the pub and instead spending almost all his free time playing chess with the same wireless mechanic, W/O Bates was also famous for his car, a vast American job of the sort seen in gangster films. Wing Commander Bazin had to ask him not to park it in front of the station offices because it was embarrassing for the Wingco when he rode up on his bicycle.

'I know a few other things beside navigation, you know'
F/O Creswell

Vincent Peace was in D's mid-upper turret.

We were so late taking off that Reaks asked Frank (Alton, navigator) for a more direct route to the target. We flew over Belgium and Holland alone, not something we or anybody liked to do, even though the whole of Belgium and about half of Holland were now in Allied hands. We thought we were in for a nasty moment when I spotted a squadron of FW190s. By the time I'd told the skipper and brought my guns to bear, I'd realised they were American Thunderbolts.

Denton was over the target. His crew included a gentle giant of a Scotsman as wireless operator, F/Sgt George Thompson. Thompson, always wireless mad, had been through a year of the war on ground stations in the Middle East; he came home to train as aircrew and at last was posted to 9 Squadron at the end of October 1944. This Op was his fifth.

Flying through curtains of ack-ack shells, Denton made his run. Bombs gone, job done, watch them fall, then bang, bang, bang. One shell hit them amidships, forward of the mid-upper turret and behind the main wing spar, ripped a great hole in the fuselage, set the aircraft on fire and filled it with smoke. Another hit the starboard inner engine and set it on fire too. Yet another hit the front turret and smashed its way through the cockpit canopy, or maybe, it was more than three shells. Denton had no idea how many. All he knew was that the intercom was u/s and the freezing wind, blowing a double gale through the newly disappeared nose of the aircraft, had cleared the smoke, revealed the horrendous damage and was fanning the flames into fury.

The bomb aimer, F/O Ron Goebel, thought he was quite lucky. He hadn't had time to get from his bomb-release position to his front-turret guns. If the shells had struck a few minutes later, he would have been dead. Denton now thought they were being attacked by fighters. His gunners were firing back. If they were ordering a corkscrew he couldn't hear them, not that he would have had much hope of corkscrewing or completing any other violent manoeuvre. They were sinking, slowly but surely, towards the ground.

Two parachutes had been shot and torn open so that removed the choice of abandoning the aircraft. The best thing he and his engineer could do was to concentrate simply on keeping U-Uncle flying for as long as possible, at least until they were away from enemy territory.

George Thompson knew that they were not being attacked by fighters. The gunfire Denton could hear was his own ammunition going off in the heat of the fire. Bullets were exploding everywhere and Ernie Potts lay dead or unconscious in his mid-upper turret. Thompson didn't know about the other crew members' parachutes being destroyed so, in his mind, leaving his post meant he would not be able to hear any order to jump. Despite that, he got up and, hunched over, headed back down the fuselage and climbed over the main spar, into the flames.

It was difficult enough crawling around a Lancaster when it was stationary. There were obstacles everywhere and no movement was exactly free. It was ten times worse when your space was lit by fire, ventilated by a freezing hurricane and set with traps like exploding machine gun bullets and a gaping hole big enough to drop through. Thompson struggled his way around the hole – it would be much harder coming back, carrying somebody – and reached the mid-upper turret and the lifeless dummy that was Potts. The gunner was spark out but not dead. George Thompson, the big Jock, ploughman's son from Glencraig in the Kingdom of Fife, used to all weathers although not used to being freeze-dried while being roasted alive, pulled the gunner out of his blazing turret and, against the force of the wind, half carried and half threaded him past the hole to the rest bed, a spot where there was solidity and no fire, at least, no fire in the aircraft. There was fire in Potts's clothes.

Thompson was already badly burned. His face and legs were giving him hell, much of his flying gear had been scorched away but Potts's personal fire had to be put out. Lancasters had blankets as standard equipment but U-Uncle's blankets were burning worse than Potts's uniform. Thompson had nothing to use except his hands, so he used them. Denton and the others were not aware of any of this. Everybody was concentrating on trying to keep the aircraft where it was meant to be, in the air.

Peter Reaks in D-Dog caught up with the other bombers over the target and amid concentrated flak started his run. Behind him but at precisely the correct height, three shells exploded. The gunners saw this and told the skipper but he refused to do anything. To dive or climb was the obvious move, but no. They were on their bombing run. That's why they were at Ladbergen.

The German gunners noted their very near miss and made their adjustments. As Bates called bombs gone there was a bang and a flash in the front of the aircraft and a loud scream from the pilot. He managed to cry 'Bale out' before the Lancaster went into a steep dive. Somehow the navigator had avoided serious injury while around him the bomb aimer, pilot, flight engineer and wireless operator had been killed. He climbed up the steeply diving aircraft to the door at the rear, followed by the mid-upper, Vincent Peace. Geoff Bamforth, the rear gunner, coming from the opposite direction, had to hang on to prevent himself tumbling down into the flames.

Vincent Peace: We three jumped into the German morning. It was around 11.15 and I had no idea what to expect. Possibly the Germans would shoot us on the way down. Possibly we would be treated according to the Geneva Convention, like we'd been told we would be. Possibly the German civilians might not accord with Geneva. In any case, I knew the rest of the boys had not survived because I watched our Lancaster go past me in flames and smash into the ground.

In U-Uncle, looking up from his task, now completed as far as it could be, George Thompson saw that the rear turret was aflame too. The gunner, Sgt Price, was lying helpless, overcome by flames and fumes, unable to do anything for himself about his inevitable and unbearably painful death by burning. Thompson's own pain would have been unbearable to almost all men but it didn't stop him making his way aft for a second time, forcing himself to slide down the ramp into the rear turret and, for a second time, dragging a heavy, smouldering, semi-conscious man, to all intents and purposes a dead body, from his battle position to some sort of relative comfort and, for the second time, with hands already burned beyond repair, beating out the fires in the man's clothes.

That done, Thompson's military training told him that the skipper must be informed. The skipper must know that he had no mid-upper or rear gunner to defend them. Gripping the sides of the fuselage to get past the holes, Thompson was putting burned flesh onto searingly hot metal but he had to get forward. He must make a report to the captain and not only about the gunners. The captain had no wireless operator either. There was no possibility of those burned hands working a wireless set. Unknown to George Thompson, some of the burning wasn't from the flames. Incredibly, inside that fiery furnace, the wind was giving him frostbite as he staggered and groped his way to the cockpit.

Denton, his friend Denton, the New Zealand country boy who had been to the Thompson family home a number of times, did not recognise him. The aircraft was a burned black wreck and so was this man, swaying behind the pilot, trying to say something above the wind and the engines. When a few words did get through, Denton realised who it was. This filthy, frayed, blackened being who looked like he'd been tied up with Joan of Arc at the stake, was his pal George.

Denton took in the news about the gunners without emotion. It was one disaster on top of another, and the sight of all those German fighters flying past the other way didn't help matters. They took no notice of the doomed Lanc. They had no ammunition left after strafing some Allied positions. In pursuit of the Germans came Spitfires. They felt obliged to lend a hand to their comrades and tried to guide Denton towards the nearest airfield. No airfield, though, could be near enough. After three-quarters of an hour of flying what seemed like half an aircraft, with three engines and more hole than skin, Denton knew they'd had it with proper landings. He felt he'd about had it too, with the frostbite he'd suffered.

The attitude of the aircraft was all wrong. She was tail down. She had virtually no Perspex in her front and the inrushing wind was causing enormous drag. She was flying along as if permanently about to stall and the pilot was having trouble seeing anything other than sky. Never mind airfields, anywhere would have to do and it would have to do this instant. This part of Holland was held by the Allies and very pleasant it was, with its villages and flat fields.

Denton was about to choose a field when a Spitfire flashed across his nose. He looked and saw the power cables the Spit pilot was warning him about. In among his efforts to climb over, the aircraft really did stall and she flopped down outside the village of Heesch, not far from Nijmegen. Denton disembarked using the quickest route, straight through the front where his Perspex should have been. U-Uncle, God, what a mess she looked. How she'd stayed up in the air for five minutes, let alone 45, he could not imagine. Thompson got out, too, to congratulate his skipper on a good landing. Unusually for a pilot with so few Ops clocked up, Denton's landing and his flying would earn him the DFC.

Help arrived. Ron Goebel, with nothing worse than frostbite, was sent back to Blighty and the rest were taken to hospital in Eindhoven. Sergeant Potts never recovered consciousness and died of his dreadful burns. Sergeant Price made a good recovery from his ordeal and owed his life to Flight Sergeant Thompson. The doctors wanted to fly Thompson home to a specialised burns unit but it didn't happen. He stayed at a military hospital in Brussels, caught pneumonia and there, three weeks later, far from home, he died.

The award of the Victoria Cross calls for the highest standard of personal bravery. The many brave deeds of recipients of this coveted

award during this and other wars are faithfully recorded and I consider the actions of Flight Sergeant Thompson fully merit the inclusion of his name among this illustrious and distinguished company.

Flight Sergeant Thompson in this instance acted in excess of the normal demands of duty and quite beyond that which any individual might expect of another. He has set an example of which the Service, his parents and his comrades may all be justly proud. I do therefore most strongly recommend the posthumous award of the Victoria Cross.

A Hesketh, Air Commodore, AOC No 51 Base, Waddington.

Thus four 9 Squadron Lancasters were written off on the morning of New Year's Day 1945. On the afternoon raid to Gravenhorst, all eight aircraft came home again and two days later Buckley was found a new flight engineer to replace the one with the broken leg. He took his crew up in C-Charlie on a cross-country to get their collective nerve back.

News was through that three of Reaks's crew were captured.

Vincent Peace: I was sitting in the snow with a sprained ankle, beside a field gate, smoking a cigarette, when a *Luftwaffe* corporal turned up on a bicycle. 'You all right?' he said, in perfect English. I said I'd never felt better, so he said to come along with him. He helped me fold up my parachute, put it on his cycle pannier and, as I hobbled along, told me about the marvellous time he'd had while he was a student at the University of Hull. We walked past several anti-aircraft emplacements whose gunners waved a cheery greeting, and we came to a hut where I was interviewed by a junior army officer. When I gave my name, rank and number, as per instructions, the German smiled. 'Peace?' he said. 'We have been waiting a long time for you.'

Waiting to go to the U-boat pens at Bergen were Melrose and Harris. For both of them, it would be the 34th trip, into their second tours as previously classified although now the rules had been changed to allow a straight run at 45 Ops with the same squadron and no question of a second tour. Bergen would be the 40th for Ernie Redfern.

It would be a joint daylight effort by 9 Squadron and 617 Squadron, with Tallboys. Local fighter stations were equipped with the Me210 and Me410 but these, Intelligence at Bardney said, would be snowbound. Harris was designated one of the wind-finders and so needed to be first over the target. Intelligence at Woodhall Spa had a different opinion on fighters. Here, the officer said that there were two FW190 squadrons based at Herdla, north of Bergen and strong fighter opposition could be expected. Nobody told 9 Squadron.

On the sunny morning of 12 January, they took off from 08.30 onwards. The aim was to bomb at 13.00 and be home in time for tea. A fighter escort of Mustangs, thirteen aircraft of No. 315 (Polish) Squadron under Squadron Leader Anders plus two Mosquitos of 169 were to pick up the four flights of bombers near Peterhead and stay with them over the target.

Three hours drummed along over the North Sea on a sparkling clear day. Ray Harris: 'I'd caught a glimpse of them (fighter escort) on the flight over but I hadn't seen a sign of them since', and here was Harris, looking down on the U-boat pens. There was plenty of flak, both the light and the heavy kinds. It was especially unnerving on daylights seeing the patterns of the heavy flak exploding so clearly, those innocent looking puffs of smoke which could blow your wing off. Harris would much rather he couldn't see such things. On night raids you got the chop and that was that, no warning. He didn't really want to see his own doom approaching in a neat, German arrangement of smoke puffs.

I flew in a wide triangle while Doc (Young, navigator) calculated the precise wind speed and direction and Bill Brownlie transmitted the data to the rest of 9 Squadron so they could set up their bomb sights. As the others began arriving, a few little clouds were starting to drift across, eighteen thousand feet below, and there was some haze but the bombing conditions were good. I was early so I asked Fauquier (617 Squadron, master bomber that day) for permission to bomb. Jimmy (Parsons, bomb aimer) stood out for his single-minded approach to his work, even among that good company, and he began calling the run which was perfect.

Bomb gone was just after 13.01 at 17,600 feet. Parsons was happy and, if he was happy, they all were. The usual surge upwards from the suddenly lightened aircraft confirmed the good news and the crew watched as the huge bomb fell, spinning faster and faster as it accelerated to the speed of sound. With two thousand feet to go, a scudding cloud hid its last moments. Parsons thought he'd hit but their photograph would probably say very little. Success or failure, not known. Oh well. Call it a day. There was nothing more they could do except break out the cigarettes and head for Lincolnshire. Smoking was strictly forbidden at all times while flying and every crew observed the rule on the way out. On the way back, quite a few had a little ritual after, say, bombs gone, or enemy coast behind them. The ritual on Willing Winnie, as soon as home was turned for, was signalled by Doc Young. He pulled back the curtain which enclosed his private office and opened a small flat tin which contained that most famous product of Messrs W D & H O Wills, the Wild Woodbine. Also in the tin, way ahead of fashion, were some menthol tablets. Doc's second duty was to light and hand to the pilot The Captain's Woodbine, among the world's first menthol cigarettes.

Harris: I had two exceptional gunners with me that day, the squadron gunnery leader Bill Gabriel and his deputy Mac Williams. 'Four Mustangs approaching, skip, starboard bow,' came from Bill Gabriel in the rear turret, on the intercom. I thought, what's the use of a fighter escort now? We'd bombed, we were leaving the coast behind. They would surely have been better employed protecting our aircraft which were still going round and round over the U-boat pens. I'd almost finished my Woodbine and, as always, I was scanning the sky. I couldn't see the Mustangs. I thought they must have swung round from the bow and be coming up behind.

Blasphemies and obscenities burst simultaneously through the intercom from Bill Gabriel and Mac Williams, the mid-upper. The much closer look the fighters were now allowing showed them to be, not Mustangs, but Focke-Wulf 190s. They both shouted 'Corkscrew starboard!' just as a salvo of cannon shells crashed into them, so that's what Harris did.

Ray Harris stood his aircraft on her right wingtip, dived, and turned to the right at the same time. The German pilot who had fired the first burst, Heinz Orlowski, he who had missed the attack on *Tirpitz* in Tromsøfjord, had never seen a Lancaster before. 'I had to admire the way it flew for such a big, big aircraft.' He could also have admired his own shooting, since his first volley had put Bill Gabriel's rear turret out of action.

Harris: 'Like all the others in the Lanc and in any other aircraft that ever was attacked, I was terrified. No matter how well trained we were, no matter how battle hardened, being shot at was the most frightening thing.'

It also concentrated the mind and Harris found himself having a few cool thoughts among the frantic, panic-stricken manoeuvres. He reserved one special thought for the intelligence officer at the briefing who had said there would be no German fighters.

'Corkscrew port, port, go!' Mac was screaming into the intercom while he fired off four or five short bursts. I did as bidden, with as much effect and urgency as I could, but we took another lot of cannon shells. Mac came on with some more good news. He couldn't rotate his turret. The hydraulics had gone. 'What about you, Bill?' I said. But he didn't reply.

Harris threw the aircraft into another half roll. Losing a colleague, a mate, was one thing. Losing a rear turret and four Brownings when your mid-upper wasn't working surely meant the chop for all of them. This latest blast from the fighters must have cut the rest of the hydraulics and virtually disarmed the Lancaster. If there had been a chance before, it had gone now. They were a lumbering, bovine lump, cut off from the rest of the herd, and they had four hungry cheetahs biting into them. All Harris could do was corkscrew and corkscrew again and hope that Williams, and Parsons in the front turret, could get the odd shot in as the foe flashed past. The front turret was also only operable by hand and very nearly without a man to operate it.

Jimmy Parsons: I'd been uncoupling my intercom so I could move from my bomb-aimer's position to my other job, which was manning the forward pair of guns, when suddenly we were going very fast downhill. It was like being in an express lift in a skyscraper, or weightless in space. The thing went down and left me where I was, with a gap between me and where I'd been, which was fortunate because, where I had been, holes appeared simultaneously in both sides of the nose section and a pipe, fractured, started spilling pink hydraulic fluid. With my intercom unplugged I hadn't heard anything about corkscrews, so I thought the skipper was wounded or worse, our aircraft was fatally injured from many more cannon shells than the one which had missed me, and we were spiralling headlong for the drink. I was putting on my chute, wishing I'd learned to swim, when I thought I'd better check with the skipper before I undid the escape hatch in the floor.

He looked up and saw two white-faced, gesticulating idiots. The pilot was trying to turn his Lancaster inside out while waving to his bomb aimer, and the engineer was waving too, while frantically checking and rechecking his instruments as if that might somehow influence the engines to keep going at full bore. Plugging in his intercom, Parsons thought that he shouldn't abandon ship yet and perhaps a gunner up front might be appropriate.

Corkscrew port! Corkscrew starboard! The shouts were still coming from the mid-upper turret and the occasional shot was still being fired off from the Brownings. This was a grossly one-sided contest. The Lancaster was trying to down four FW190s with a few stray .303-inch machine-gun bullets, while the fighters each hammered the Lanc with cannon shells at forty rounds a second.

Harris: I reckoned we'd been hit by ten, a dozen, maybe more of those bursts of cannon shells when Bill came on at last. 'Hello, skip,' he said. 'Rear gunner here. Sorry about that. Buggers cut my oxygen supply.

Got the pearly grey mists for a bit there.' So, that was all right, then his voice changed. 'Bloody hell,' he said, 'here they come again. Prepare to corkscrew starboard. Go!' We tried, but she was handling badly. The trim tabs on the ailerons had gone. Well, they were still there, some of them, but I couldn't move them. Neither the hand trims nor the servo trims would work.

Harris needed all the flying performance he could get and here he was being asked to run the two-twenty yards in pit boots. In a brief interlude of stability, Harris was astounded to see an FW190 come up on his port wingtip. He could see the pilot clearly. The *Luftwaffe* hunter, Orlowski gave him a weird kind of a grin and a nod, which seemed to say 'Well done, Tommy. Very well done. But we have played with you long enough, I think. Goodbye.'

'"Up yours, mate," I said to him, and I slid open my side window and fired my service revolver as he peeled away. I knew it wouldn't do any good but I thought it might make me feel better.'

Very well, Maker of the Universe, Guardian of the Righteous. This was the moment. Prayers were said in all quarters of His Britannic Majesty's Lancaster PD198 WS/W-William, AKA Willing Winnie, as the four fighters regrouped for the kill. Ray Harris felt his hope slip away. He had tried everything. If there were any more tricks in or out of the book, he didn't know them.

Over Bergen, the escorting Polish pilots had turned up and were becoming anxious about the amount of flak to which their bombers were being subjected and thought they had better do something about it. Possibly they didn't realise how long the raid might go on and how long the Lancs could be hanging around trying to bomb in the smoke and haze. Possibly they had had the same briefing as 9 Squadron: no fighters expected. In any case, they concluded that there was nothing more productive they could do than shoot up the ack-ack, so down they went.

This might have been jolly good fun for the light brigade but not so much for the heavy mob, which was beginning to feel collectively nervous about a large number of tiny dots in the sky, speeding towards them with ferocious intent. The dots were FW190s of *9 Staffel* and *12 Staffel*, *Jagdgeschwader 5*.

Down below, the Mustang pilots were having a great time, killing Germans and taking revenge for their national tragedies of 1939. Not surprisingly, having forgotten their original purpose and now going hammer and tongs at the enemy, the Poles didn't notice that their British colleagues were under threat many thousands of feet above. Several of the Lancaster skippers ordered Very lights to be fired from the signal pistol, which was fixed aft of the astrodome, angled backwards, behind the wireless operator's position. The idea was that a red flare might catch the Poles' attention. Even if the ploy worked, the Mustangs still had a long way to climb before they could be any use against the German fighters.

Keeley saw two Lancasters being attacked and said the fighter escort did not go to their assistance. Five FW190s, no less, picked on WS/G-George, skippered by F/Lt Larry Marsh. They must have thought they couldn't fail when they came in from behind for their first attack at 16,000 feet. F/Sgt Riches and Sgt Marshall, Marsh's gunners, did not agree and had the most concentrated eighteen minutes of their lives. They had shot down that Me110 over St Leu d'Esserant but this was something else again. Marsh: 'We were attacked by five FW190s who peeled off in turn and the attacks went on consistently from 13.09 to 13.27. We ended up at 900 feet with 360mph on the clock after corkscrewing continuously. After seeing the fighter escort at the concentration (assembly point, Scottish coast) we never saw them again except for one which stood off and watched us near the end of the attacks.'

Despite many, many German hits, Riches and Marshall had kept them at bay, Marsh had shaken them off and WS/G was on her way home. Marsh was awarded the DFC, Riches the DFM.

F/O Harper in WS/S was attacked by two of the Germans and had a similarly difficult time escaping their attentions. His ORB account could not be more economical. 'Unable to assess bombing due to combat.'

Another, single German fighter settled in some distance behind his Tommy, ignoring the rear gunner's efforts as his thumb tightened on the firing button and his huge black target settled nicely into the centre of his sights. He hardly noticed the red Very light shooting out, being caught in slipstream and smacking straight into his engine. The FW190 was powered by a radial engine, partly open to the elements behind the propeller, unlike its brethren such as the Me109, the Spitfire and the Hurricane, whose in-line engines were enclosed in a long, streamlined nose. Once the Very light lodged itself in among the cylinders, it set fire to the fuel. The pilot could smell burning, then he could feel it and in seconds he was consumed by it. Mystified but satisfied, the Lancaster crew watched as the enemy fell helplessly down in a plume of smoke.

The bomb aimers of 9 Squadron seemed to be having a good day. F/Lt Dunne saw his own bomb hit the target and explode. Sq/Ldr Williams saw his own bomb hit. Dennis Nolan, Buckley's bomb aimer, was sure they'd hit it too, by which time the target was like a dreadful kind of fountain display. As a Tallboy exploded, smoke and dust shot up hundreds of feet through the hole. Before long this aerial debris, combined with bright sunlight, was making bombing difficult and Lancs were coming in from all directions and heights. There seemed to be aircraft everywhere, including FW190s.

Sammy Morris was not content with his first run so Melrose went around again in Q-Queenie. The second was no good either. On the third, at 17,000 feet, Morris at last said the words they all loved to hear, bomb gone. It was hell, but it was worth it when you scored a direct hit, which they did this time, when you knew that 12,000 pounds of bomb had smashed through concrete six yards thick and caused goodness knows what havoc in the U-boat pens below. Melrose's job was done and he got out of it as fast as he could, watching a Lancaster going down as he turned away. Marsh saw the same as Melrose. 'One Lancaster was seen to be shot down on fire and to go straight into the sea.'

Dennis Nolan saw disaster befall the same Lanc but there was a more dramatic edge from his point of view.

Our Lancaster and another were flying on a similar course but the other was about two thousand feet lower, and we could see three more aircraft, which were FW190s. They stooged about while we watched them make up their minds. They were choosing. The sods were selecting which bomber to go for, us or him. They chose him. He corkscrewed and appeared to be getting free when one of his engines caught fire, and then another. That Lanc hit the sea in a way which clearly said to us, watching from above, that there would be no survivors but the fighters carried on shooting into the burning wreckage until they had no ammunition left. They couldn't attack any more Lancasters, such as ours for example, so they flew away. I thought that here were three of the best fighter aircraft of the war, operated by three of the worst or least experienced pilots.

The Lancaster that was seen to be shot down was NG257 WS/N, Redfern's. He had joined the squadron as a Flight Sergeant in early May 1944, been promoted to Flying Officer in the July and awarded the DFC. He'd flown some routine missions, like everybody and, like everybody, had been to some of the most perilous places. Unlike so many, he had lasted a long time before becoming a dead old man of 22.

'Here they come, skip.' There was doom in the message from the mid-upper turret and not without reason. Willing Winnie was so badly shot about that she would probably fall out of the sky anyway, without more encouragement from the *Luftwaffe*. Ray Harris felt yet another volley of cannon shells somehow find something solid to hit. The whole crew assumed this must be the final attack. They'd had it. Life had been good, and terrifying, while it lasted. A Focke-Wulf 190 was capable of well over

400mph, that Harris knew. A Lancaster could do 260mph in level flight, unladen with a following breeze but it was specified to do 360mph in a steep dive. If that was the official specified speed, maybe, just maybe, it could do rather more and maybe, just maybe, these particular Germans didn't like flying with their feet touching the water.

He pushed the stick forward. Maurice Mellors, the flight engineer, was now standing behind him, gripping the back of his seat in a futile gesture of solidarity. Rushing towards them at hundreds of miles an hour was the bright, blue, hard ocean. From only 4,000 feet they dived, almost at right angles to the sea. Everything in the aircraft that could scream, screamed. Everything that could rattle, shake, vibrate, shudder or in any other way threaten to fall apart, did so. Mac Williams, his voice well disguised by the thought of imminent vertical ditching at high speed, had something more to say.

Harris: There we were, breaking the downhill speed record, and Mac came on the intercom. 'They're going,' he said. I thought he meant some more component parts were about to fall off the aircraft. 'What's going?' I said, a bit sharp. 'The one nineties,' he said. 'They're in line formation. Heading for home. Thank Christ for that.' Well, we could only assume they'd run out of shells. Four of them. They'd used the bloody lot up, shooting at us, and we were still flying. Or they could have been up to their fuel limit. Who cared why? We were just delighted they'd gone.

That danger, then, was over. Fifteen attacks altogether had not been enough to down the great black bird. The other, now more pressing need was to get the bird out of her dive. Willing Winnie was living up to her name. She was showing her crew how fast she could go.

Without the trim tabs, I didn't have the physical strength to pull her up alone. 'For Christ's sake, Maurice,' I said. He was standing right behind me. Maurice Mellors was a big Manchester copper who reckoned he could handle most things but it took all he had, combined with all I had, to pull Winnie's nose up. We levelled off at a thousand feet. We'd lost eleven thousand feet since we were first attacked. Time to review the situation, but Bill Gabriel suddenly spoke up. 'Skip, if you can, I could do with some help,' was what he said, and he hadn't said anything for quite a while. I sent Jimmy to see what was what.

Jimmy Parsons went to the rear turret to find a badly injured man. In one of the attacks on his smashed-up turret, Bill had been hit in the head and leg. There was blood everywhere. It was flowing out of him. While the Lancaster struggled onwards, with Harris and Mellors taking stock of their plight, Parsons had a struggle of his own, to get the desperately hurt gunner up the ramp, over the main spar and onto the rest bed where he could give him morphine and try and do something about the bleeding.

Such first aid would be pointless if they couldn't get home, and that glorious event was looking increasingly unlikely. They had three and a half engines with, by a miracle, only the port outer not doing a proper job, but all the damage to flying surfaces and controls meant that any serious climbing or, indeed, any serious manoeuvring at all, was out of the question.

The best we could do was maintain level flight at a thousand feet. By trial and error, we worked out that our stalling speed was a hundred and sixty miles an hour instead of the usual ninety-five. So, we had a flight plan of sorts. Level at a thousand, and one sixty or faster. Anything else and we'd be in the drink.

What then? What about landing, at maybe 60mph quicker than usual? What about the undercarriage? It normally worked on hydraulic power. He'd never tried lowering it on compressed air alone. What did it say in the book? He hadn't read the book for goodness knows how long. Something like the undercarriage can be lowered by compressed air from a special bottle or bottles. Let's hope the bottle or bottles haven't been hit. What else did it say? Leakage of air pressure can cause the undercarriage to collapse. Where was the nearest, widest and, above all, longest runway? RAF Carnaby, outside Bridlington in the East Riding. 'Doc, we want to go to Carnaby. Is it left, right or straight on from here?'

With his course set, there was nothing more to say. Jimmy kept a grip on Bill Gabriel. Mac, Maurice and Bill Brownlie could do no more than pray that Winnie stayed Willing. Doc watched Ray's steering like he'd never watched it before. He didn't want one unnecessary inch to be flown. Ray held that battered, exhausted, crippled aircraft in the sky long enough to make Carnaby a proposition.

Hello Carnaby, hello Carnaby, this is Rosen William. I have wounded on board and am coming in to land. I regret this may cause damage to your runway as I don't think the undercart is going to work and I can't drop below one sixty without stalling.

Very, very carefully, and from as far away as possible, Ray Harris lined them up for the runway. They could see the fire engines and ambulances rushing about. Harris remembered his marks on Assessment of Ability as a Pilot during his training, on Tiger Moths, Harvards, Ansons, Oxfords, Wellingtons and Stirlings. He'd been given average on them all, except for one course which was marked as low average. Well, he'd show the bastards. With another prayer, to the god of aircraft parts, he told Maurice Mellors to blow the undercarriage down. Harris: 'We could hardly believe it but we heard and felt it operate with a gratifying, solid clunk. Two green lights came on. We had wheels. I gave the order. "Safety positions."'

This was Harris's final order of the Op. Everyone except him and poor Bill Gabriel crouched down like it said in the manual, while Doc contrived to crouch and still keep his eye on the airspeed indicator. Harris, the pilot judged to have average skills, who had corkscrewed and dived his way beyond the attacks of four enemy aircraft, each of them twice as fast as a Lancaster and many times as nimble, settled to make the finest landing of his life, at the highest speed of his life. It was at 16.04, well in time for tea, and nobody else felt the tyres touch the tarmac.

'It's all right, Doc,' I said. 'You can stop calling the airspeed. We're down.'

Bill Gabriel was taken to hospital at Driffield where his shrapnel was removed and his wounds repaired by, of all people, a German prisoner-of-war doctor. 'We had debated about (a) whether to go with our old mate Bill in the ambulance, or (b) whether to go to a public house in order to drink large quantities of beer. It must have been the shortest debate in history.' A WAAF happened to mention that there was a really good little pub in the village of Lissett, five or six miles away. She would take them, and pick them up at closing time, that is, if they wanted.

> 'All these daylights. I can't see in the daytime'
> Sq/Ldr Wasse

Both of Harris's gunners received the DFC for the Bergen trip. Harris had been awarded his DFC a few weeks before and was recommended for a DSO for Bergen, but never got it. There were 1,200 holes in Lancaster WS/W, Willing Winnie.

Nobody would forget Bergen but, from some points of view, the raid had been a mess. The Mustang fighter escort hadn't performed. The two Mosquitos had had dust-ups with the FW190s but hadn't really been able to help the Lancasters. There had been sad and bad losses to both squadrons and the bombing results could have been much better. Although 9 Squadron's Harris, Melrose, Buckley, Williams and Dunne all believed they'd scored, later surveys showed that there had been two direct Tallboy hits on the pens between them, and two near misses. One 617 Squadron

Tallboy accidentally sank a moving minesweeper and another damaged a stationary 3,000-ton tramp steamer.

There was a report that a Mustang had gone down but all eleven returned, so it must have been a FW190, the one felled by the Very light. The Lancaster crews knew that their losses – Redfern and his crew killed on his 40th, 617's Ross and his crew, Pryor and his, and three of Iveson's crew – were at least partly ascribable to the Poles. While the FW190 pilots up that day were pleased to report Lancasters being downed, not one of them reported seeing a Mustang, and the Polish squadron leader made no mention of FW190s. The flyers of 617 Squadron might also have questioned the efficiency of their officers on the ground; orders had not been issued about refitting their mid-upper turrets after the last *Tirpitz* raid, two months before, so they fought their air battles a gunner short.

When Harris got back to Bardney from Carnaby, the first person he saw was Ernie Redfern's wife, Frances.

12

THE LAST TALLBOY

13 January, ORB: 'Cloudy with continuous moderate rain and drizzle at first, becoming intermittent after dawn and ceasing during the late afternoon. Very slight ground frost. Nothing of importance to record. F/O E E Redfern pilot, F/O P O Hull air bomber, posted to war casualty.' Actually, it was Ernest Cyril Redfern, not E E, and it was Owen Percy Hull, not P O. Still, Redfern would not be the last to die of those who had flown W4964 WS/J.

The weather for the rest of January was wintry with snow, at one point reaching up to a foot deep and 28°F of frost. They managed some training and a couple of raids to distant synthetic oil works, and a few days off.

With February came the thaw. They loaded up with Tallboys, eighteen of them, and set off for the E-boat pens at Ijmuiden, in German-occupied Holland, which were thought to harbour midget subs. The Germans did indeed have such a weapon, a one-man U-boat which, unfortunately for the one man, tended also to operate only one way. Windfinding was no good, there were no hits except on Follett's and Williams's aircraft, Jones saw a Tallboy flash past him and Macintosh met a mainforce Lancaster, on the way to a night date in Germany, which just missed him with five bombs including a cookie.

Now began a series of attacks on railway viaducts and bridges. Priorities had been assigned and Nos. 9 and 617 were given the brief. The Altenbeken viaduct, by the town of Paderborn in Westphalia, had always been on the list of desirable precision targets. It carried one of the two railway routes from Dortmund and the Ruhr/Rheinland beyond, to Hannover and thence to Berlin and, since the Dortmund-Ems had taken such damage, was ever more important along with its brother in arms-transport, Bielefeld.

Altenbeken was an ancient structure, part of the golden age of railway building, about five hundred yards long by forty yards high but, from the bombers' point of view, only the width needed to carry two railway tracks. Melrose's Op 35 featured eighteen Lancs of 9 Squadron on a solo raid with Tallboys, 6 February.

Bob Woolf: We were up for Altenbeken at 07.50 in O, perfectly good

Lanc but nothing would ever replace J-Johnny. At the French coast a mass of RAF Mustangs joined us as escorts and then our Gee box caught fire, which we quickly put out with hand-held extinguishers but things were quite smoky for a while. There was heavy cloud on the way and over the target so we could not bomb and had to bring our Tallboy home, except there was fog at home so we were diverted to Woodbridge. They had a marvellous system there of pipes around the perimeter which burned oil, generating a mass of heated air over the runway and the approach funnel which cleared the fog away. Aircraft were often diverted to Woodbridge when there was fog at their own 'dromes. The system was called FIDO, which stood for Fog, Instant Dispersal Of.

Jim Brookbank: Jimmy Bazin had this slow, drawn-out way of speaking, a posh drawl you might say. When he was leading the Op on a daylight, his rear gunner would be given the job of spotting whether everyone else was flying as per procedure, usually two lines astern. So the gunner would say, 'They're stretched out a bit, sir, I can hardly see the last one, just a dot in the distance.' Then this voice would come over the R/T, 'Close the gaggle, will you?' If you held your nose and said it at one-third speed, that was him. He had this attitude that we were flying on an Op, we were going to be the best at the job, and the enemy was just a nuisance getting in the way. There was never any let-up in the training and practice bombing, no let-up at all. You would think you had the afternoon off and suddenly you were off to Wainfleet. Bazin made us very conscious of the bombing ladder and one time when the squadron was top of 5 Group and took the Camrose Trophy off 617, I knew that our crew was top of our squadron's ladder, which I calculated made me, a mere sergeant, the best bomb aimer in 5 Group, and so much for Nolan and Tosspots and the other officer bomb aimers. Well, I reckoned so anyhow.

Bob Woolf: If there was no raid to go on, no necessity to risk your life that night, and no official training or there was a raid but you were not on the list, strictly speaking there was little for aircrew to do. You could do what you liked. You could go into town, have a game of snooker in the mess, go for a walk, read a book, whatever. Or, if you had a stickler for a skipper, like we had, he might arrange a few extra drills for you. Worst of all, he might want you to do dinghy drill. You might appreciate how valuable such practice was and what a help it would be in an emergency, but you looked at the other crews heading off to the pub and thought why did I pick Dougie Melrose? He used to emerge from the flight office, wearing that quiet smile which made your stomach sink and which said 'flight testing', so we'd cast a final, jealous look at the disappearing backs of our mates as he strolled over and said, 'Right ho, you lot. It's time to jive with Jesus.'

Those happy chaps would be off to The Jolly Sailor, The Black Horse or The Railway in Bardney, or maybe to the Snakepit (as they called The Saracen's Head in Lincoln) and similar establishments, if there were any similar establishments to the Snakepit, a notorious haunt of waifs, strays, vagabonds, ladies of the night, and airmen. They might travel as far as Nottingham where there were fewer aircrew competing for the girls.

Jim Brookbank: We were in Lincoln one night, a mixed little group of us ending up together in one of the pubs, led by a certain flight looey. The pubs shut at ten and the last bus went at ten, so there was always an element of uncertainty about getting home. We were milling about outside the railway station, wondering what to do, when said officer decided he'd take charge. He telephoned our aerodrome and spoke to the duty officer along the following lines, putting on an Oxford accent because he was from one of the Dominions. 'Wing Commander Keelhouse here, need a car, Lincoln station, myself and a couple of the chaps, what?' The car duly turned up, our leader for the night signed the WAAF driver's chit with something or other, and we never heard any more about it.

Aileen Walker: There was one night when a whole table of officers, ten of them, didn't get out. There was a bus into Lincoln and they just had their dessert to eat. It was raspberry tart. I was carrying probably six dishes of it when I slipped on the floor and threw the lot over them. It looked like they had blood on their collars so the bus went without them.

Jim Brookbank: We were in The White Hart hotel in Lincoln, up near the cathedral. Perched on a tall stool was a very good looking blonde with her nylon-clad legs on display, a long cigarette holder and a fascinating air. She was certainly fascinating one of our group, a pilot officer, and she appeared fascinated enough by him until a flying officer upstaged him. She was entirely concentrating on the new chap when a flight looey muscled in and now he was the bees' knees. We weren't watching this so much as what one of our flight commanders was doing, standing there at the bar, apparently unconcerned, with his raincoat on. Anyway, he let the flight looey get thoroughly comfortable with this girl then said, 'My, it's warm in here' and took his mac off revealing his recently acquired squadron leader's uniform. 'Care for a drink, miss?' he said.

'Since I've been on leave
I suppose nobody has hit the target'
F/O Whitehead

Oldacre and his crew were briefed, alone, to take LL845 Lonesome Lola on a raid which would become infamous, 13 February 1945. Stalin's armies were across Germany's eastern borders and Berlin wasn't far away, while the other Allies were pushing in from the west. There was huge pressure on the RAF and the USAAF to mount some major diversionary raids, the plan being to cause such havoc in civilian Germany that the war would become untenable. Codenamed Operation Thunderclap, it was devised and approved by Churchill, Roosevelt, Stalin, the War Cabinet and the Air Ministry. The three leaders met at Yalta and the button was ready to be pressed. The target decided upon was Dresden.

With over 600,000 population, swelled with thousands of refugees, Dresden was the largest industrial city not previously attacked but a precision raid so far from home was possible now that there were Gee and Oboe ground stations on the western German borders. Dresden's railway and other communications links and choke points gave the city even more qualifications as the ideal target. The Americans would go in first, in daylight, followed by a 5 Group attack using their low-level marking technique, followed by a five hundred-plus Lancaster raid with PFF doing the marking.

The plan went wrong immediately. The weather prevented the Americans from going. Oldacre had his own little piece of excitement. 'Directly after bombing, action had to be taken to avoid another Lancaster and detailed observation of results was therefore not possible. Glow of fires seen from 200 miles.'

Such fires as 5 Group had started were nothing compared to what followed. The cloud disappeared and 1,800 tons of bombs were dropped with awful accuracy. It was another Hamburg, in bombing results and in the effect on German morale. The Americans went the next day, and the next. The war should have ended after Hamburg; how it could continue after Dresden only Hitler knew. The key figures in the plan congratulated each other on a total success; later, they would distance themselves from the destruction they had ordered.

Altenbeken called and seventeen went in daylight, and again they could not bomb.

Bob Woolf: We took a lot of flak, all the way from the battle line to the target. When we got to the viaduct there was ten tenths cloud again. Almost everybody had holes in the aircraft when we came back yet

again with our Tallboys, and on the way we lost our good friend F/Lt Johnny Dunne DFC and saw his Lanc go straight down from 12,000 feet with an engine in flames. Nobody baled out.

Jim Brookbank: We all saw it, all the squadron, and everybody in our aircraft and I'm sure everybody in every other aircraft was shouting jump, jump, jump you fools! But nobody did. They were hit by flak, a single shot on the way back from bombing. We were in a loose gaggle, very loose, kind of scattered about the sky, and one little German flak gun had one pot shot and that was it. They went down rather slowly, not a screaming dive. They couldn't all have been killed because the Lanc wasn't a mess all over. A mystery, that one, and the end of old Tosspots Philpott.

The Australian Johnny Dunne had been with the squadron since 7 July 1944 and had shared in most of the big adventures. His Tallboy had hung up on the first Tirpitz raid; they gave him the DFC after he'd flown home from a midair collision over Paris which left him with serious flying bits missing from his Lanc.

After a few odd jobs it was 22 February before they could have another crack at that viaduct.

Bob Woolf: We were due to take off at 09.45 but endured three one-hour delays before getting airborne at 12.40. With fighter escort the trip was uneventful and the flak was not much trouble. The bombing was most successful and Dougie claimed a direct hit. Result: viaduct out of action. The first span at the eastern end was down and at the other, northern end the first span was u/s with part of the pier destroyed. Our only bother came when we got back to Bardney, where the visibility was bad and Flying Control for once was messing things up. How there was no collision over our aerodrome I do not know. We were all very lucky.

Warrant Officer Harry Irons was now flying with 158 Squadron, Halifaxes, as spare bod. 'My last one was Mainz, 27 February, and they gave me the DFC. I should have tried for a commission much earlier. I could have been a gunnery leader and a flight lieutenant at least, but I was young and foolish.'

The Dortmund-Ems canal had been rendered u/s almost continuously by repeated attacks, despite the Germans' frantic efforts to repair it. Almost was not enough and the aqueduct at Ladbergen was selected as an opportunity for the coup de grâce. Over two hundred Lancs including twenty of 9 Squadron with Tallboys, plus ten marking Mosquitos, waited all through a day of postponements before taking off on the night of 3 March. The results were two massive breaches and the end of the canal problem. There was no water in it.

The timing of 9 Squadron's raid did them a favour. They got home before the Germans.

Bob Woolf: We'd been on leave and were coming back from the pub, very pleased with ourselves, walking along the concrete path to our hut. Everybody had come home from the Ladbergen Op around midnight or a bit later but soon after the last aircraft landed a group of Ju88 intruders attacked. One roared directly overhead, very low and clearly defined against the light night sky. Full of Dutch courage, we shook our fists at the beast and gave him the full benefit of our extensive knowledge of different ways of saying go away, you nasty person. To our horror and astonishment, he did a split-arse turn and seemed to come straight back at us. We did our own version of the manoeuvre and dashed into the nearest shelter, which was the toilet block. A Lancaster crew all trying to get through the door at once created the kind of comic log-jam you see in the films, and we were still in it after our adversary had whizzed past without bothering to stop, whereupon we bravely came out again.

They bombed and strafed most of the nearby 'dromes including Waddington and it was uncanny to see them silhouetted against the moonlit cloud base and sometimes in the moonlight itself, diving and climbing. Each dive had the yellow-white streaks of cannon fire or ended with the sharp crump of a medium bomb. The wireless said that there were sixty bandits over our region that night. They eventually came back and attacked us too at Bardney but no defence was put up against them by our side.

Mick Maguire: We'd come out of interrogation and there was an aircraft flying our circuit with its wingtip lights on. I'd heard enough German engines to know it wasn't one of ours and anyway he was flying the circuit the wrong way around. There'd been some bombs dropped on Waddington and it seemed to me that this pilot hadn't realised he was flying over another aerodrome. I dived into the nearest gun emplacement and lined him up. He was so low I could see his numbers. I was about to pick him out of the sky when a voice came from the squawk box. 'Don't shoot at him, Maguire. He doesn't know we're here.' It was McMullen. I said, 'He's a sitting duck!' McMullen said not to shoot because then he'd be after us. He stooged about, shot up something in the village, then he must have seen our runways because he came back very fast and low and dropped some butterfly bombs (anti-personnel mines). For the next few nights we had the covers off the guns ready in case they came back. It was quite common at that time, night raids. Their speciality was to hang about around the practice ranges hoping to catch the OTU crews unawares, which they did. We lost quite a few that way.

Bob Woolf: They were a menace to our bombers returning from Ops. They would hope to arrive at a 'drome when the aircraft were in their landing pattern. When a crew was absorbed in making a safe landing, tired after a long flight, a big Lanc was an easy target for a short burst of cannon fire. The word was on that particular night that eight of the raiders had been shot down, including 'ours', but that we'd lost fifteen plus the damage on the ground.

This was Operation Gisela, a kind of last hurrah by the *Luftwaffe*. Everybody they could muster and fuel up had intruded all along the eastern side of England, waiting for the bombers to come home. Once their presence was known, incoming aircraft were warned and diverted to aerodromes beyond the threat. Nevertheless, at least twenty were shot down who would otherwise have expected to land safely, mission completed. Of the twenty, three were OTU crews on night cross-countries.

The chief town of the island of Rügen, Sassnitz, was a fishing port and seaside resort for the people of Pomerania. Now there were warships and big merchant vessels pushing the herring boats aside and 9 Squadron was equipped with Tallboys. Bob Woolf hitched a lift with Ray Harris, 6 March.

I wanted to try flying with other crews, to see how the experience compared with what I'd known all my operational life, but Jimmy Bazin or Dougie always seemed to find a reason why I couldn't go. I finally got away with F/Lt Ray Harris and the first thing was how strange to hear different voices over the intercom, something I hadn't experienced since my days in Hampdens in Canada. We flew across Sweden whose neutrality allowed us to look down on fully illuminated cities and towns, so colourful, so brilliant, like diamonds on velvet. The Swedes obligingly fired off a fair amount of light flak to show their neutrality but aimed it at 9,000 feet, well below our height. There was a lot of light flak over the target too, and not much heavy stuff, but the bomber stream was very dense and we had two near misses with other Lancasters. One was a Lanc losing height right above us. I was in the astrodome and saw him, with no time to do anything except shout 'Dive, Ray, dive!' His response was so immediate we dropped like a stone and I was thrown upwards, bashing my head on the dome which added greatly to the star count.

The target was well lit with red and yellow TIs and these, with the colours of the flak, made quite a display reflected on the scattered cloud. Just to finish off a rather special night, we had a chase by a FW190 which Ray lost in the clouds. His reflexes are superb and he is a very good pilot indeed and his crew work well together. It was a privilege to be with them and nice to find out there are teams as good as us.

There was some cloud about, ships were weighing anchor and zigzagging out to the open sea but there was some success. After Laws had bombed, Keeley saw a destroyer stopped and issuing black smoke. Oldacre thought he hit a liner. Harris near-missed a merchant ship. Coster was beaten twice by the clouds so he dropped his Tallboy on the docks and caused a great explosion. Results were three ships sunk and parts of the town and docklands wrecked. It is a comment on the state of the *Luftwaffe* nightfighters at this late stage of the war that Young found his rear turret u/s 'on being airborne and throughout trip'. There would have been a few older heads shaking in disbelief at a skipper who would go on an Op without a rear turret.

In other respects too the world had turned upside down. All those night raids on Essen in the early years of the war produced virtually no rewards and now, 11 March 1945, a thousand bombers could go there in daylight and drop more than four and a half thousand tons of bombs through clouds, aimed by sky markers from Oboe Mosquitos. The order for 9 Squadron to take part was sudden and unexpected; they'd become used to their specialist, precision role and were to join the mainforce on, to them, an old-style area bombing raid. Even so, they were still specialised, carrying the 12,000lb light case HC blockbuster, the massive blast bomb. This raid brought Krupp to a final halt. Essen hardly produced a thing between now and the American army arriving.

Next day it was very much the same except beneath the clouds lay Dortmund. In round numbers, 1,100 aircraft including 750 Lancs with 5,000 tons of bombs (fourteen of No. 9 had the five-ton HC), attacked a single target. It was a record which would never be broken. Production in Dortmund stopped dead. Melrose saw 'smoke causing cloud to billow over a circular area with a diameter of seven miles'.

Bob Woolf: the sky seemed filled with aircraft. Dense cloud covered the target so we bombed on PFF sky markers. Packed in close formation, Ernie watched in appalled disgust as a batch of bright yellow 1,000 pounders flashed past our starboard tailfin. Such a disturbing sight, so obvious in daylight, made us all wonder how often

this must have happened on night Ops, and how often that was the explanation for the red balls of fire in the darkness that meant another bomber going down.

The Arnsberg viaduct was the next hard, slim responsibility. It was clearly vital to jam the German army's ability to move about but it was extremely difficult to hit these targets. Bielefeld viaduct hadn't yet been knocked down. It would take six raids by 617 Squadron and, at the finish, a near miss with the gigantic Grand Slam 22,000lb bomb in the last of a long series of raids over the whole of the war, and Bielefeld was a double, two viaducts together so in theory it was easier to hit. That is to say, if two cotton threads together are very much easier to hit than one.

Arnsberg viaduct was a fairly short and curving thread, only seven spans, and seventeen of 9 Squadron, all with Tallboys, went to try and cut it.

Bob Woolf: We found a thick layer of mist so we couldn't see to bomb and had to bring the beast home, where we found even more mist. Landing became a highly hazardous procedure. Doug overshot the runway twice and had to pull us up with the Tallboy not helping, so he made his next approach so low it was almost minus feet. Talk about picking daisies from the 'drome. Anyway, he got us down and what do you know, next day we were off again.

Melrose led the squadron on his fortieth Op, seventeen Lancs again. Harry Watkins claimed a direct hit, Ed Stowell saw a direct hit and Melrose thought the fourth bomb seemed to hit, and there were some favourable comments on the leadership. The viaduct, however, stood firm.

Bob Woolf: Our aircraft controlled the Op, which was made difficult when my radio receiver went u/s. With some tinkering around and a lot of luck we managed to get it working, so communication was maintained, and I had a lot of fun firing off Very lights to tell everybody when it was time to change course.

Watkins had come from 61 Squadron, Skellingthorpe. He told stories from his days as a Butlin's Redcoat, how he learned to fly and fought in the Finnish air force against the Russian invasion in 1939/40, how he was captured, escaped on a boat, was captured again, taken far to the east, escaped again and got into Persia. There was the time a bomb took away his rear turret with the gunner in it. Harry Watkins had been everywhere and was liked by everyone.

The squadron scribe noted some young men who had been nowhere yet.

'One crew arrived today from No 5 Lancaster Finishing School, Syerston. Captain F/O B S Woolstencroft.'

The squadron went again to Arnsberg the following day, this time with Cockshott and Calder of 617 in the Lancasters modified to carry Grand Slam. Visibility was poor and it was difficult to get a satisfactory run. They went in twice as a squadron but only three bombed, including Cockshott, then they ran in again individually. Macintosh saw 'eastern end of viaduct collapsed from previous attack and a crater at the mouth of the tunnel' which he'd probably made himself on yesterday's raid.

In WS/T, F/Lt Jones was having difficulties. 'Port inner u/s, could not be feathered. Crew ordered to fix parachutes and shortly afterwards oil flowing from behind the prop caught fire. Engine was doing 3,400 revs and aircraft was difficult to handle so I gave the order to jump. The wireless operator (P/O R L Birch) and MU gunner (Sgt R Glover) did not hear. The others carried out the order after which the fire went out and I countermanded the order.'

F/Lt Tweddle heard on VHF that T was in trouble and saw four parachutes open. 'Sat in ahead of T and led to join with mainforce track up the Rhine (mainforce was raiding Bottrop and Castrop-Rauxel in a formation largely of Halifaxes). Reduced speed to 140mph. Permission obtained from leader to stay after reaching friendly territory. T expressed wish to land at the first available airfield.' They set for Rivelles, found Gosselies, and Tweddle landed to check that it was suitable for a Lancaster to land on.

'I wouldn't mind low flying, if there was no flak'
P/O Thomas

Bob Woolf: We were off again to another viaduct at Vlotho and our crew was leading the squadron as before. All went well this time; no radio problems. We had a fighter escort of Mustangs but the bother came from the ground, from very accurate heavy flak, which meant Doug had to work hard weaving his way. Some of our aircraft were hit but not too badly.

The bridge, near Minden, took the railway over the river Weser and Melrose, bombing first, overshot it by several hundred yards but sank a barge with his Tallboy. Somebody did better because one span was sent askew and the next bridge, Nienburg, between Bremen and Hannover, also crossing the Weser, was damaged too. Yet another Weser bridge was at Bremen. During the Op, as F/O Scott reported diplomatically, 'someone had VHF transmitter on over Holland'. Scott was alone in making this official report although an anonymous witness, possibly a certain poetical bomb aimer, had the story unofficially.

There we were, flying in two parallel gaggles in broad daylight, seriously intending to attack Bremen. We should have rendezvous'd with our Mustang fighter escort but they didn't show. Our leader gave it as his considered opinion that we should press on, chaps. Being more frightened of him than we were of the enemy, we dutifully pressed on. At this point, the said leader's Gee box packed up. Unperturbed, he established his whereabouts by consulting with the deputy leader on R/T in plain language. There followed the most unbelievable exchange of information. Latitude and longitude were bandied about, with turning points and our time over target. We imagined the *Luftwaffe* scrambling over the entire area. In fact, all that happened was the flak guns were even more ready for us than usual.

Fears of the *Luftwaffe* were becoming groundless. The German fighter force was not what it was, when eighty Lancs could go to a major city in daylight and bomb uninterrupted. Even without the distraction of enemy fighters, neither mainforce nor 9 Squadron could knock the bridge down this time, and there was always the flak.

Jim Brookbank: When we dropped the bomb we peeled off to starboard as we had to do, because of the situation of the target and the way we were attacking it. The Germans soon had this worked out and were ready for us. We took four flak hits at once, all superficial damage luckily, except one that hit me. As far as I knew, I had one foot fewer than before. I couldn't feel it at all. Scotty checked around, everybody OK, and I mumbled something about my foot and he sent Booster (Baker, flight engineer) to look. Nurse Booster attacked my flying boot in much the same way as a rugby forward tackles an opposing halfback. He pulled my stocking off and I was expecting a right mess, but there was nothing except a nasty bruise on my little toe. The flak piece had travelled down my leg, punctured my boot, hit my toe a glancing blow and lodged there. My captain asked me to bring the toe up to the flight deck where he promised to lacerate it with his escape knife and then I'd have a war wound.

Tug Wilson had flown several extra trips, with Keeley and Jeffs for instance, and now he took another with Waters to Bad Oeynhausen. South of Minden, it was actually two bridges side by side. Rees saw four Tallboys which appeared to burst either on or very near the bridge.

Follett had been out of the gaggle windfinding and rejoined with six minutes to go to the attack when he was set upon by one of the new jet fighters, an Me262. The starboard wing was badly damaged but fortunately the engines were all right. The bomb was jettisoned and Follett got them home. The fighter escort of Mustangs pounced on the jet and shot him down. There were other jets too but after some skirmishing with the Mustangs they flew away.

Tug Wilson: We were in N and the flak got us three times on our Tallboy run, and twice again while we were diving away. I was sitting with my feet in the hole ready to bale out and I said to Waters, 'Is this where I get a bar on my caterpillar.' I was a member of the Caterpillar Club for my parachute jump in Denmark and I thought I was going to have to do it all over again. Waters just said, 'Hold on a minute, Tug.'

The flak at the target was fierce and accurate but both bridges were downed. Waters was hit in both main tanks, the port inner was u/s, the bomb aimer's panel was smashed and neither gun turret was working. Tug Wilson climbed back to his desk and navigated them to Seething.

It was an American base and the Yanks were deeply impressed with our aircraft. They couldn't believe such an old wreck could fly, and that was the end of WS/N. She went for scrap later. Dougie Melrose had to come and pick us up and while we were waiting the Yanks came back from a raid in their Liberators. They weren't quite as orderly as we were. We landed with a gap between the aircraft. They came in nose to tail and if they couldn't stop they ran into each other. More scrap.

The new month would be the last of the war. It should have been pieces of cake all the way but bombing was ever a hazardous trade. They went to Molbis, a town near Leipzig where there was benzol manufacture. For a change, 9 Squadron had a standard mixed load of bombs and, with other 5 Group squadrons, had to battle against unexpectedly strong winds. An enormous explosion was seen at 23.10 and that was the end of the benzol plant. The night would also see the end of a crew who had been on squadron since September. They were in a brand new Lanc on her first op, HK788 WS/E. 'Aircraft missing. No signals or messages received.' There hadn't been time. The aircraft burst into flames as they flew homewards and went in immediately, near Wantage, and they buried them all at Oxford. Alf Jeffs and his crew had taken W4964 WS/J-Johnny Walker on her final and 107th trip and were almost the last of WS/J's century of graduates to die.

Next day, NG235 WS/H took off on her 24th. One of the crew had done forty and more Ops; the other six hadn't done any. Going with six complete sprogs to an oil refinery at Lützkendorf was a flight engineer whose first had been 2 December 1943 with Phil Plowright, Norman Wells and the rest, to Berlin. He'd looked after J-Johnny Walker's engines many times. Lützkendorf? What could happen at Lützkendorf?

The Germans had very little oil left. *Luftwaffe* fighters had had no stocks issued lately. Destruction of this plant would just about finish all prospects of them ever getting any more. It was a 5 Group raid including eighteen of 9 Squadron carrying Tallboys. Buckley was first up; the new pilot, 21-year-old Australian Bernard Woolstencroft, was the twelfth at 18.26. It was a long way, eight and a half hours there and back. The winds were stronger than forecast but the bombing was excellent. There would be no more oil coming from Lützkendorf and 9 Squadron was home around 03.00, except for one.

The rear gunner Sgt Williams lived through the crash and became a prisoner for a few weeks. The rest did not, including Sticky Lewis, still only a sergeant as he had been in 1943. He had been made up to flight sergeant several times but always got busted down again for some indiscretion, generally linked with a few pints too many in The Jolly Sailor. His was an odd case. He'd done his tour, no need to be there, not officially on a second tour but seemingly unable to give up flying Ops. That was something he had in common with the famous greats like Cheshire and Gibson, but Sticky Lewis wasn't famous. He was there when they wanted him, a slight, smallish, often solitary figure with nothing very remarkable about him. The squadron commanders were happy to have a thoroughly experienced, battle-hardened flight engineer to call on when they were short and, for the last time, they were short and he went with Woolstencroft, and the Lancaster strayed near Berlin. This was the final loss for 9 Squadron in World War Two. There would be a couple of almosts and nearlys but this was the last, a crew fresh from training, six hopeful lads wanting to do something before it ended, and an old lag who'd done plenty.

Tug Wilson: I'd had a letter forwarded to me by the Air Ministry, which was from my helpers in Denmark giving an address I could write to. They obviously wanted to know if I'd got home all right. I worded my reply very carefully so it would look real enough to any censor but didn't actually say anything. The simple fact of it was the message. Next thing, I had notice that on 10 April 1945 I was to be court martialled for 'attempting to communicate with countries under enemy control'. They must have run my letter through the Enigma machine and found an uncrackable code. It was a sensation at Bardney. I was stopped from going on Ops, presumably in case I baled out to give a hand to the German war effort, and all sorts of learned friends came up from London to see if I should be sent to The Tower. An officer from Waddington defended me and common sense prevailed. I was found not guilty, allowed to go back on Ops, but the £10 I'd had from the British consul in Malmö was docked off my wages.

Considering everything they'd been through, 9 Squadron might have hoped to end with a glorious flourish but it was more of an anticlimax. The islet of Heligoland, a rock a mile long, had been home to Norse gods, an early Christian shrine, and it had a very decent beach. It overlooked the straits leading to the rivers Elbe and Weser and with powerful guns commanded those waters. Traditionally, Bomber Command flew round it on the way to somewhere else. Now it was in the way of finishing the war and almost a thousand bombers of mainforce squadrons wrecked everything except the big guns. Next day, the big guns were allocated to 9 and 617.

Bob Woolf: 'After much running around we took off at 15.00 in Q-Queenie for the Heligoland gun emplacements. It was a quiet trip and quite unsuccessful.' There were sixteen of 9 Squadron, led by Doug Melrose and twenty of 617, all with Tallboys aiming at three different targets, supposedly in a co-ordinated fashion. Melrose: 'Tallboy fused 25 seconds. Two bursts seen, one an undershoot into the sea, the other to starboard of target. Fighter escort not picked up. Force had to be taken up 1,000 feet owing to No. 617 Squadron running in at same time. Delay in attacking was due to (a) non-appearance of escort and (b) to information from No. 617 Squadron that target was obscured temporarily by cloud, necessitating an orbit.'

Ray Harris was caught in the slipstream of another Lanc on his bombing run and was so tossed about he couldn't bomb, so brought it home. Scott was there with Jim Brookbank and they bombed all right, and Buckley with Denis Nolan, and Coster with Jim Pinning. They saw mixed results, scattered on one target, concentrated on another. Bob Woolf: 'The previous day they had so chopped and churned the place that our 12,000 pounders seemed a bit of a waste of time. Anyway, we were down at 19.20 and off to the pub.'

On the last day of the air war in Europe, 25 April 1945, a force including some 360 Lancs attacked Hitler's holiday cottage at Berchtesgaden, probably the only holiday cottage ever to have several miles of tunnels for air-raid shelters. The Op was viewed by many aircrew as a PR exercise, a

needless risk and a potential waste of good men. Others thought killing
Hitler a great idea except, unbeknown to them, he wasn't in. He was in
Berlin, trying to win the war with imaginary armies and a few boy scouts.
Apart from the barracks of SS stationed there for occasional visits by the
Führer and his entourage, the target was of no military significance.

Bomb aiming would be difficult on a small target in mountain country
and, when they got there, snow made it even more difficult. Ken Dagnall
was with skipper Balme leading a mainforce gaggle: 'The planning was
absolutely atrocious. They hadn't taken proper account of the mountains
and we couldn't get a proper run. We were on top of the target before we
knew it.'

Precedence was usually given to 617 in joint Ops; their SABS bombsight
made them more dependent on an unsmoked visual ID of the target. On
this one, the plan was for No. 9 Squadron to lead, with Melrose in charge,
and they would go in first and lowest with their Tallboys following the
marking of PFF Mosquitos. Following on would be 617 and the rest. There
was confusion over the target indicators and with radio communication;
some crews heard the master bomber, some heard American fighter escorts,
some heard nothing useful at all.

The marking was no good and so it had to be done again. Even so, a few
of the mainforce squadrons were overeager and bombed before the second
lot of markers went down. The Op had already gone wrong for F/O
Williams; a good hour before they got there, 'bomb was selected and fused
at 07.39 and it immediately dropped off the aircraft and burst in a large
wood on the west bank of the Rhine'. Arndell: 'Did not attack because of
late identification of run-in and interference from other aircraft. Instructed
not to make second run.' Watkins: 'Caught in slipstream as bomb left
aircraft. Raid marred by higher squadrons crowding above first and lowest
squadrons thus spoiling the bombing runs.' Follett: 'Results not observed
owing to avoiding action from other aircraft.'

Most of this was missed by *News Chronicle* reporter Vernon Brown;
missed, or thought inappropriate to mention in his paper next morning. He
was with Larry Marsh in WS/G.

**Dawn came and we saw the Rhine. We made rendezvous with our
escort of US Mustang fighters emerging from the sunrise like a cloud of
midges. In one great formation we flew into the Bavarian Alps. As we
approached Berchtesgaden the 'Eagle's Nest' could clearly be seen. Six
of our Lancasters headed towards it. I saw their bombs fall as we flew
alongside to drop our load. It was horrific. Into this scene below, which
had the prettiness of a Victorian picture post card, burst the 12,000lb
earthquake bombs. Our 'plane rocked. Below, the ground spewed**

rocks and earth and bricks, and trees were uprooted and thrown like straws into the sky. I saw thirty bombs go down, there may have been more . . . the force of the explosions tossed our 'plane upwards.

Two bombers went down on this Op, only two, both Lancs, with most of the crews surviving and four killed, only four for a PR stunt. It could so easily have been more. Everybody wanted to get in on the act and whether through misplaced enthusiasm, carelessness or confusion, the last raid of 9 Squadron's war very nearly became the end of life's line for Doug Melrose and his men.

Bob Woolf: It was a fine day and the stream of bombers seemed to stretch from one horizon to the other. We had a clear sight of the target and the military establishment at the foot of the mountains but seeing it and hitting it were two different things. We went on our bombing run with 617 above us. One of their aircraft was directly on us, on top of us, and Doug asked me to watch him from the astrodome. Sammy was calling his bombing instructions, we were moments from release time, and I saw the 617 aircraft had his bomb doors open. I watched in utter horror as the bomb was released and began its curving flight. It was heading absolutely straight for us. I had no alternative, even though we were on our run. 'Starboard, skip, a touch starboard,' I shouted. The bomb missed our port wingtip by nothing at all. I could read the word Torpex on it as it went past, the name for the explosive inside it. Well, the run up was spoiled and we couldn't make another, so we brought our Tallboy home for the last time.

Operations Record Book, No. 9 Squadron, 8 May 1945: 'Intermittent thundery rain. Thunder storms at dusk. One aircraft detailed for cross-country. VE (Victory in Europe) Day.'

'There was a gale blowing and my aircraft
was going backwards so fast I was afraid
to land in case I stuck the tailskid in the ground'
P/O Maude-Roxby

POSTSCRIPT

7,377 Lancasters had been built by the end of the war, of which 3,349 had been lost on operations. In round numbers, RAF Bomber Command lost 9,000 aircraft while flying 300,000 sorties and dropping one million tons of bombs and mines. The busiest months were August 1944 (20,659 sorties) and March 1945 (21,341). The quietest was November 1939 with nineteen. About 90 per cent of the bombing effort happened after February 1942 and Harris's appointment. Of the seventy German cities attacked, only twenty or so were left with better than half their buildings standing.

Von Rundstedt, commander of the last great German offensive against the invading Allies, said:

> **Air power was the first decisive factor in Germany's defeat. Lack of petrol and oil was the second, and the destruction of railways the third. The principal other factor was the smashing of the home industrial areas by bombing.**

He might have saved himself a few words. The second, third and other factors were all part of the first.

The precise number of Bomber Command aircrew, groundcrew and support personnel lost as a result of enemy action is not known but, including flying accidents, out of the 125,000 aircrew who served, 55,000 were killed and another 18,000 wounded and/or taken prisoner.

Number 9 Squadron flew approximately 6,000 sorties. During the 2,500 in Wellingtons, over 100 aircraft were lost. During the 3,500 in Lancasters, approaching 200 aircraft were lost, one of the largest totals of Lancasters lost by a single squadron.

C-in-C Air Chief Marshal Sir Arthur T Harris:

We are ending this war on the threshold of tremendous scientific developments – radar, jet propulsion, rockets and atomic bombing are all as yet in their infancy. Another war, if it comes, will be vastly different from the one which has just drawn to a close. While, therefore, it is true to say that the heavy bomber did more than any other single weapon to win this war, it will not hold the same place in the next.

Certainly not that type of bomber. In the few years of World War Two, the arts and sciences of bombing – by eye, with conventional explosives, from petrol-powered aircraft – had developed from almost useless to almost perfect, to the zenith of its possibilities only to be rendered obsolete almost immediately. 18 May 1951, the prototype of the Vickers Valiant, the first of the V-bomber jets, flew in expectation of carrying an atomic bomb at the speed of sound at 50,000 feet.

Lancaster W4964 WS/J was eventually broken up for scrap and a farmer acquired the centre section of the fuselage. He closed off the two ends with planks and used it as a shed. Later, someone recognised what it was and today the last remnant of the heroic old girl can be seen in Newark Air Museum, Lincolnshire.

Dougie Melrose stayed in the RAF and flew just about every aircraft type, including Canberra jet bombers carrying atomic weapons. He retired, came out of it to transform Luton Airport from a collection of huts into an international hub, retired, came out of it again to run Belfast Airport, and retired. He lived near Harleston, on the Norfolk/Suffolk border, where he and the author often had a pint or two together at The Cherry Tree. He died while on a birdwatching holiday in Spain with his wife Doreen.

APPENDIX

RAF Bardney

There were scores of operational squadrons and dozens of airfields on the Lincolnshire flatlands. Most aerodromes had been built in a hurry in 1942/43 and usually to a standard pattern in which, as with aircraft design of the period, comfort of personnel came a long, long way behind function. RAF Bardney was a community of two and a half thousand, rather more than the village from which it took its name. The airfield had the normal three runways making a kind of capital letter A. The main runway, like the much extended crosspiece of the A, lay south-west/north-east, ready for the prevailing wind. Aircraft generally took off into a south-westerly breeze, roared over the village of Bardney a few moments later, then swung around to the north towards Lincoln before heading for the rendezvous point and mainland Europe. When they came home, they looked if they could for the Bardney sugar-beet factory for their landmark, circled the airfield and landed in the same direction, into the wind. The two other runways, the angled sides of the A, were shorter and just in case the wind changed. With six points of the compass covered, there wouldn't be many days when the wind direction made things impossible.

Around the perimeter ran a winding road wide enough for a Lancaster to taxi along, and off this were strung the dispersals, single aircraft parking places widely spread to make an enemy attack less damaging. The south side of the perimeter which ran in the same direction as the main runway had fewer dispersals but had the squat, square control tower, the flight offices, locker room, briefing room and other necessaries beside it. At the top of the A were the snaking roadways, explosion-deflecting earthworks, hard standings and fusing sheds of the bomb dump. Built to store 500 tons of bombs, it was as far away as possible from most of the living quarters although airman and sergeant armourers slept near their charges.

The standard hotel room was a Nissen hut. Lt Colonel Peter Nissen clearly had only the bare necessities in mind when he designed his basic form of accommodation, made of a concrete floor with a tunnel of corrugated iron over it, bricked up at the ends. At Bardney, these were mainly over on the other side of the Horncastle road. Men and women were kept well apart and, in their various combinations of rank, crew and trade, lived seven or eight to a hut, in clusters of four huts, which shared a toilet block. Baths and showers, which sometimes had hot water and sometimes didn't, were in a separate but equally draughty building near the messes, Officers', Sergeants' and Airmen's.

Well, it was better than Yagodnik.

ROLL OF HONOUR

This is intended to be a complete listing for aircrew of RAF Number 9 Squadron in World War Two. Where possible we have also included those who went on from No. 9 to other squadrons, plus those non-aircrew 9 Squadron members whose details could be traced. Every piece of information has been checked through at least two sources; we have tried our best to ensure there are no errors.

Losses are UK citizens from 9 Squadron unless otherwise stated. Citizens of Commonwealth countries, the Republic of Ireland and of the USA are noted wherever possible. Up to September 1942, aircraft are Wellingtons unless otherwise stated, and Lancasters thereafter.

The names of crew are listed in the conventional order of the Operational Record Book. For Wellington crews this order gradually changed, from (a) pilot, second pilot, observer, two wireless-operator/air-gunners and sometimes an extra gunner; to (b) pilot, second pilot, observer, wireless operator, front gunner, rear gunner. From May 1942, a five-man crew became usual, with no second pilot.

For the Lancaster the order was settled: pilot, flight engineer, navigator, bomb aimer, wireless operator, mid-upper gunner, rear gunner.

Aircrew with no known graves are commemorated on the Runnymede Memorial.

The date of death is given as the date on which the Operation began. The place of death is given as the operational target except where another place is known.

With the addition of personal information from the Commonwealth War Graves Commission, it is hoped that this makes a unique, as well as an accurate, record.

1939
4 September, Brunsbüttel.
L4275 KA/H.
Flight Sergeant Albion John Turner. Buried at Sage War Cemetery.
Sergeant Donald Edward Jarvis, aged 24, from Chatham. Sage War Cemetery.

Sgt Bertie Greville Walton, 20, Leamington Spa. Commemorated at Runnymede.

Aircraftman Second Class Kenneth George Day, 20, Shrewsbury. Becklingen War Cemetery.

Aircraftman First Class George Thomas Brocking. Runnymede.

L4268. Crew commemorated at Runnymede.

F/Sgt Ian Edward Maitland Borley, 30, Weston-super-Mare.

F/Sgt George Miller, 27, Portobello.

Corporal George William Park, 23, Redmire.

Leading Aircraftman Harry Dore, 19, Edinburgh.

AC2 Robert Henderson, 25, Blyth.

Sgt Alexander Oliver Heslop, 23, Wolsingham, was in one of the above aircraft but it is not known which. Runnymede.

8 September, Berners Heath.

L4320 KA/ZB. Four crew buried at All Saints Churchyard, Honington.

Pilot Officer Harold Rosofsky.

P/O Bruce Innes Clifford-Jones, 22, New Plymouth, New Zealand.

AC1 Hugh M McGreevy, 23, Hamilton.

AC1 Thomas Purdie, 24, Glasgow.

AC2 William Charles Hilsdon, 20, Kidlington. On attachment from 215 (training) Squadron. St James's Churchyard, Cowley.

30 October. Midair collision.

L4288 KA/A. Three crew buried at All Saints Churchyard, Honington.

Squadron Leader Lennox Stanley Lamb, 29, husband of Sheila Brady, Wellington, New Zealand.

Flying Officer Peter Edward Torkington-Leech, 26, husband of Alice Elizabeth, Heidelberg, Transvaal.

Sgt Cyril Arthur Bryant. St Andrew's Churchyard, Billingborough.

LAC Stanley Hawkins, 24, Gateshead.

AC1 Edward Grant, 23, Newcastle-upon-Tyne. Byker and Heaton Cemetery.

L4363. Two crew buried at All Saints Churchyard, Honington.

F/O John Frank Chandler.

P/O Colin Charles Cameron, 22, Canterbury, New Zealand.

AC2 Walter James Chapman, 19, Dagenham. SS Peter and Paul Churchyard, Dagenham.

AC2 Leonard George Dicks, 18, Swansea. Cwmgelly Cemetery.

18 December, Wilhelmshaven.
N2983.
LAC Walter Lilley, wop/AG, 21, Kippax. Runnymede.

N2941. Four crew commemorated at Runnymede.
F/O Douglas Bellamy Allison.
F/O Douglas Charles Ephraim Bailey, 25, Wallington.
Sgt John Archibald Brister, 19, Leytonstone. Becklingen War Cemetery.
Sgt Joseph Buglasi Adamson Turnbull.
Cpl Reginald Thomas Black, 20, husband of Doris, Langham (Essex).
LAC Albert George Goodenough. Becklingen War Cemetery.

N2939 WS/H. Crew commemorated at Runnymede.
F/O John Thomas Irvine Challes.
P/O Alistair Hugh Richmond Bourne.
Sgt Frank Michael Mason, 20, Surbiton.
Sgt Thomas Henry English.
LAC Gurth Ernest Cox.
AC1 Alexander Telfer.

N2940. Crew commemorated at Runnymede.
P/O Eric Francis Lines, 24, Brighton.
F/Sgt Alfred Kitto Fearnside, 25, Nanstallon.
AC1 Edward Malcolm George Polhill, 19, Frinton.
LAC Alex Morrison Dickie, 21, Macduff.
AC2 Clifford Walker.

N2872. Crew commemorated at Runnymede.
Sq/Ldr Archibald John Guthrie, 28, husband of Barbara Alice, Tamworth.
F/O John Edgar Atkinson, 21.
Sgt Harold Walter Tyrrel.
LAC Thomas Leo Marlin, 21, Blyth.
Sgt Bertie Joseph Pickess, 21, Edmonton.
LAC Josias Melville Fletcher Key.

1940
8 March, Weybridge.
N3017. Three crew buried at Brookwood Military Cemetary.
Flight Lieutenant Edward Reginald Berrill. Brookwood Military Cemetery.
F/O William John Macrae DFC, 26, Regina, Saskatchewan.
Sgt Cornelius Thomas Murphy, 20, Cork. St Finbarr's Cemetery, Cork.
Cpl Roy Jackson, 23, Sheffield.

AC1 Leonard Leopold James Mackenzie, 19, Barnes.

12 April, North Sea.
P2520 WS/U. Crew commemorated at Runnymede.
Sgt Charles Ronald Bowen, 27, husband of Marjory, Louth.
Sgt William Lockie Balmer, 27, husband of Dorothy Enid.
Sgt James Dougal Aitchison, 25, Eyemouth.
LAC Ralph John Lamb, 27, husband of Kate Vera, Haverhill.
LAC John Lenton Wilkin, 19, South Duffield.
AC1 Percy Frank Ricketts, 22, Belvedere.

7 May, Honington.
AC1 Frederick Gordon Settle, 23, Bolton. Heaton Cemetery.

29 May, Honington.
AC2 William Eric Middleton, Selby. Selby Cemetery.

5 June, Duisburg.
P9232 WS/M. Two crew buried at Geervliet Protestant Churchyard.
Sq/Ldr George Ernest Peacock DFC, pilot, 26, Spennymoor.
Sgt Ronald Charles Hargrave DFM, wop/AG, 25, Sutton Coldfield.

13 June, northern France.
L7787 WS/J. Crew buried at Drosay Churchyard, Seine-Maritime.
Sgt Robert Hewitt, 24, husband of Helen Annie, Glasgow.
Sgt Frank Richard Edwards, 21, Taplow.
Sgt Leonard Wingate Routledge, 22, Wembley.
Sgt Selwyn Frederick Youngson, 22, Inverness.
Sgt Frederick Donald Hardy, 19, Nazeing.
Sgt Cecil Bertram Kircher, 27, Didcot.

19 June, North Sea.
N2897 WS/P. Crew commemorated at Runnymede.
P/O Francis Charles Joseph Butler, 25.
Sgt Raymond Graham Elliott, 24, Hove.
Sgt Charles Naylor, 20, Fulwood.
Sgt Alan Thomas Legg.
Sgt Kevin Barry Brennan, 19, Chester-le-Street.
Sgt Ian Maywood McCulloch, 23, Galashiels.

5 July, Hamburg.
L7786 WS/X.
Sgt Robert Beattie Murgatroyd, 24, Blackpool. All Saints Churchyard,
Honington.

19 July, Wismar.
L7795 WS/G. Five crew commemorated at Runnymede.
Sq/Ldr John Blackwell Sinclair Monypenny, 28, husband of Eveline Maud,
Barkway.
F/Lt Douglas Davidson Middleton, 26, husband of Olwen, Axminster.
Sgt Fred Watson, 24, Newcastle-on-Tyne.
Sgt Walter Robert Cowell, 20, Downham Market.
Sgt Merle Gott, 23, Leeds.
P/O Harold Frederick Archdale Lees, 32, Dartford. Kiel War Cemetery.

22 July, Honington.
P9205.
P/O Peter Roderick Bawtree Wanklyn, pilot, 26. St Michael's Churchyard,
Harbledown.
Sgt Denis Bennett, second pilot, 25, husband of Joan, Wallasey. Guildford
Cemetery.

19 August, Honington air raid.
Possibly not a complete list. Three buried at All Saints Churchyard,
Honington.
AC2 George William Leslie Dudley, 20, Chelmarsh. St Peter's Churchyard,
Chelmarsh.
AC2 Frank Alan Crawford Holdaway, 25, Worcester Park.
AC2 Richard Glynne Jones, 25, Oxford.
AC2 Frederick Leonard Larkin, 23, Kilburn. Willesden New Cemetery.
LAC John Edward Parish, 27, husband of Ada, Bury St Edmunds.

28 September, Cologne.
T2505 WS/W. Five crew buried at Schoonselhof Cemetery, Antwerp.
(Sgt C W Oliver POW)
Sgt Kenneth Bruce Gladwin, 20, Boreham Wood.
Sgt Leonard William Hardy, 27, husband of Mary Isobel, Leicester.
Sgt Jack Woods, 20, Balby.
Sgt Edward John Milsom, 23, Cathays.
Sgt Sidney George Brooker, 26, husband of Mary Catherine, Burnham
(Buckinghamshire).

T2472 WS/G.
F/Lt Anthony Howard Caldicott Cox, pilot. St Catherine's New Churchyard, Merstham.

1 October, Berlin.
R3282 WS/G. Crew commemorated at Runnymede.
F/Lt Charles Douglas Fox, 25, London.
Sgt Ronald Edwin Thompson.
Sgt Donald Bannerman Fleming, 26, Larkhall.
Sgt John Devine Robertson.
Sgt Reginald Philip Sweett, 23, Plymouth.
Sgt Charles Hugh le Blanc Newbery, 22, Canterbury, New Zealand.

7 October, Honington.
Sgt John Davies Cross, 26, Pontardulais. All Saints Churchyard, Pontardawe.
LAC Kenneth Painter, 21, Southampton. All Saints Churchyard, Honington.
LAC Kenneth George Wheeler, 23, Cambridge. Cambridge City Cemetery.

14 October, Magdeburg.
T2464 WS/K. Crew buried at Berlin War Cemetery.
Sq/Ldr John Olding Hinks, 29, Croydon.
P/O Guy Paul Wentworth Austin, 26, Roundebosche, Cape Province.
Sgt Albert Edgar Skidmore.
Sgt Colin Hay, 23, Glasgow.
Sgt Eric Nield.
P/O John Edward Bartlett, 29, husband of Anne.

28 October, Honington.
LAC Thomas Arthur Snell, Grimsby. St Michael's Churchyard, Little Coates.

7 December, Düsseldorf.
R3220. Crew buried at Ostend Communal Cemetery.
F/Lt Desmond Geoffrey Stanley, 23, Lismore, Co Waterford.
Sgt Robert Coates Parker.
Sgt John James Coulsham Nanson.
Sgt Anthony Arthur Rogers, 26, Manchester.
Sgt Joseph Alan Grocott, 20, Waltham Abbey.
Sgt William Humphrey Pontin, 20, Pontnewydd.

21 December, Venice.
L7799 WS-D.
Sgt Robert Norman Harrison. Hendon Cemetery.
Sgt James Frederick Gapp, 23, Le Havre. St Mary Cray Cemetery.
Sgt Leslie William Nichols, 32, husband of Marjorie, Ashford (Kent). Willesborough Cemetery.
Sgt Maurice Holker, 19, Bolton. St Mary Churchyard, Deane.
Sgt John Docker, 30, husband of Anne, Carlisle. Upperby Cemetery, Carlisle.
Sgt William Riley, 21, Mumbles. Oystermouth Cemetery, Swansea.

1941
1 March, Cologne.
R1288 WS/D. Five crew commemorated at Runnymede.
F/O Hugh Gavin Lydford Lawson, 21.
Sgt James Noel Murray, Dunmurry, Co Antrim.
Sgt John Nevil Huddlestone, 20, Hexham.
Sgt Alfred Ernest Waters, 21, Kirk Ella.
Sgt Eric Routledge, 24, husband of Evelyn, Rawmarsh.
Sgt Douglas Alfred Thomas Heslop, 21, Cardiff. Patrington Cemetery.

12 March, Bremen.
N2744 WS/U. Four crew buried at Reichswald Forest War Cemetery.
Sgt Bernard Preston Hall, 19, Marylebone.
(Sgt J R Brown POW)
Sgt William James Manger, 24, Crawley.
Sgt William Leslie Smith.
Sgt John William Hammond, Barnsley.
(Sgt E Collins POW)

9 April, Berlin.
T2473 WS/M. Crew buried at Reichswald Forest War Cemetery.
P/O George Guy Sharp, 29, husband of Jeanette Claire.
P/O John Norman Fisher, 22, Lytham St Annes.
P/O Richard Cardew Rendle, 24, Bude.
Sgt Joseph Anderson, 21, Larkhall.
Sgt Cyril Bruce Parris.
P/O Walter Patrick Strickland, 31.

17 April, Berlin.
T2900 WS/L. Crew commemorated at Runnymede.
Sgt Robert Donald Cowan Stark, 20, Stirling.

Sgt Frank Weldon Baker, Wakefield.
Sgt John William Nightingarl.
Sgt George Gibb.
Sgt John Ernest Johnson, husband of Florence Susanah, Northampton.
Sgt Harry Franklin Hurt, 20, Retford.

N2745 WS/O. Two crew buried at Rheinberg War Cemetery.
Sgt Gordon Ernest Heaysman, pilot, 21, Three Bridges.
Sgt Grant John Mavor, observer, Winnipeg, Manitoba.

16 May, Honington after Boulogne.
R1267 WS/Y.
Sgt Leslie B Mitchell, pilot, 22, Nottingham. Arnold Cemetery.

9 June, Belgian coast.
R1758.
Wing Commander Roy George Claringbould Arnold, pilot, 30, husband of
Vera Constance, Daventry. Blankenberge Town Cemetery.

T2620 WS/G. Three crew commemorated at Runnymede.
F/O Douglas Ferguson Lamb DFC.
Sgt John Claude Partington, 20, Buenos Aires. Flushing Northern
Cemetery.
F/Sgt Dennis John Mansfield. Adegem Canadian War Cemetery.
Sgt David Alfred Humphrey, 19, Woodley.
Sgt Ronald Seward Bunce, 22, husband of Barbara Britton, Boscombe.
(Sgt W A Eccles POW)

7 July, Cologne.
R1040. Crew buried at Jonkerbos War Cemetery.
P/O Douglas James Jamieson, 26, husband of Jessie Moore, Canterbury,
New Zealand.
Sgt Wilfrid George Jesson, 27, Canterbury, New Zealand.
P/O Grossett Keith Coates, Canada.
Sgt Norman Walter Harding, 23, Dartford.
Sgt Cyril George Blandon, 30, Hammersmith.
Sgt John Stanley Burnside.

8 July, Honington.
AC1 John Mackay Macdonald, 24, husband of Daisy. Tomnahurich
Cemetery, Inverness.

8 July, Münster.
T2973 WS/S. Crew buried at Rheinberg War Cemetery.
Sgt Bernard George Pitt, 21, husband of Marjorie, Hull.
Sgt John Arthur Grady, 19, Rongotea, New Zealand.
Sgt Henry Thomas Barrett, 22, Stanford-le-Hope.
Sgt Fred Gilby, 21, Hull.
Sgt Marvin Edson Burtis, Canada.
Sgt Douglas Ray Rawlings.

10 July, Cologne.
W5729 WS/J. Three crew buried at Pihen-les-Guines Communal Cemetery.
Sgt Stanley Cyril Retter, 21, Ottery St Mary.
Sgt Hugh Thomas Martland Ainscough, 20, Bournemouth.
Sgt James Edward Drew, 23, husband of Jeanne, Windsor, Ontario.
    Longueness Souvenir Cemetery.
(Sgt J Pryde POW)
Sgt Wilfrid John Tidey, 19, Leicester.
(Sgt D R Greig POW)

12 August, Keil.
R1513. Four crew buried at Becklingen War Cemetery.
F/Lt Kenneth Rhodes Ball, 22, Manchester.
Sgt Sidney Wintersgill, 21, Orrell.
Sgt Edward Cullen, 20. Runnymede.
Sgt Cyril Harry Chandler, 20, Cambridge.
Sgt Arthur Thomas Hatton, 20, Winnipeg, Manitoba. Runnymede.
Sgt Thomas Edward McGeragle, Canada.

Hannover.
R1341 WS/Z. Crew buried at Becklingen War Cemetery.
Sgt Eric Lewin, 24, Halifax.
Sgt Don Smith, 23, Ottawa, Ontario.
Sgt John Archdale Lennard, 23.
F/Sgt Charles William Albert Wells, 20, Gorleston.
Sgt Hugh Forster Barron, 21, Whickham.
Sgt Ronald Ramsay Passmore, 22, Hawke's Bay, New Zealand.

19 August, Keil.
R1455 WS/D. Crew buried at Tonder Cemetery.
Sgt Cecil Thomas Everitt, 23, husband of Edith, Ealing.
Sgt Patrick John Brady.
Sgt Henry Bruce Stirling Johnston, 21, Putney.

Sgt Thomas Whalley.
Sgt Thomas Armstrong, 20, Willington Quay.
Sgt Herbert Edward Temple.

7 September, Berlin.
Z8845. Crew buried at Opsterland General Cemetery.
Sgt Jack Cyril Saich DFM, 20, Great Easton.
Sgt Robert Arthur Banks, 21, Wilmslow.
Sgt Walter Basil Lowe DFM, 28, husband of Peggy, Blackpool.
Sgt William Ronald Balls, 20, Great Yarmouth.
Sgt Eric Trott, 20, Sheffield.
Sgt Alan Scotland McDonald, 27, husband of Jean, Dalry.

26 September, Rushford after Emden.
X3222.
Sgt Harry William White, 29, second pilot, Northampton. Abington
    Churchyard.
P/O John Baldwin Thompson, 19, observer, Victoria, British Columbia.
    Honington Churchyard.
Sgt Raymond George Lifford, gunner, 19, Hanwell. Brookwood Military
    Cemetery.

28 September, Genoa.
R1279 WS/L. Crew buried at Milan War Cemetery.
F/Sgt Walter Stanley Kitson DFM.
P/O John Roy Freeland, 23, Quebec.
Sgt Ronald Gordon Gove, 25, Hillside (Angus).
Sgt John Richard Palmer, 25, Berkhamsted.
Sgt James Williamson Lee, 21, Bishop Auckland.
Sgt John Alfred McLean, 21, Plumstead.

4 October, Edgehill.
R1146, 21 OTU.
P/O John Edward Anthony H Fairfax DFM, 21, Leeds. Lawnswood
    Cemetery, Leeds.

9 November, Hamburg.
X3280. Four crew commemorated at Runnymede.
P/O Hugh Vincent Wilgar-Robinson, 30, Belfast. Vlieland General
    Cemetery.
Sgt Robert Bamber Fielding, 27, Blackpool.
Sgt Reginald Burchell How, 25, husband of Mary Una, Ipswich.

Sgt George Herbert Dartnall. Lemvig Cemetery.
Sgt Kenneth Quick, 21, Port Talbot.
F/Sgt William Smithson, 24, Dewsbury.

27 November, Herne Bay after Düsseldorf.
X3287.
Sgt Gerald Gordon Armstrong, second pilot, 23, Macoun, Saskatchewan.
  Aylesham Cemetery.
Sgt Peter William Bilsborough, rear gunner, 21, Shipley. Hirst Wood
  Church, Shipley.

28 December, Düsseldorf.
Z1907, 57 Squadron.
W/O Thomas Purdy DFM, pilot, 28, husband of Ellen May, South Shields.
  Eindhoven Woensel General Cemetery.

1942
5 January, Honington after Brest.
X3388.
Sgt Charles William Mills, rear gunner, 21, Diptford Downs. St Andrew's
  Churchyard, Harberton.

19 January, Thetford.
X3370 WS/D. Three crew buried at All Saints Churchyard, Honington.
Sgt Robert Douglas Telling, pilot.
F/Lt Philip Henry Cresswell, Gee instructor, 25, Wellington, New Zealand.
P/O Harry Lionel Tarbitten DFC, observer, 25, Hull. Hull Northern
  Cemetery.
Sgt John Amphlett, observer, 24, Clent.
Sgt Thomas Frederick Greenwood, observer. Hale Carr Cemetery, Morecambe.
Sgt Thomas George Banks, w/op, 26, Godalming. Brookwood Military
  Cemetery.
Sgt Robert Smiles Aitchison, rear gunner, 21, Sidlesham. St Mary's
  Churchyard, Sidlesham.

15 February, Clacton.
X3398.
Sgt John William Dalgliesh, pilot, 23, Mauchline. Mauchline Cemetery.
Sgt Frederick Ernest Coulson, observer, 21, Portsmouth. Milton Cemetery,
  Portsmouth.
Sgt William Hutchinson, w/op, 34, Newcastle-on-Tyne. All Saints
  Churchyard, Honington.

Sgt Hedley Brown, gunner, 20, St Endellion. St Endellienta's Churchyard, St Endellion.

Captain George Rupert Buck, gunner, Royal Artillery, 35, husband of Joyce. Clacton Cemetery.

8 March, Essen.
X3411. Crew commemorated at Runnymede.
Sgt Robert James Tristem Lovell, 19, Southend-on-Sea.
P/O Thomas William Warwick Woodford, 21, Handsworth.
(P/O R P Hoult rescued from the sea)
Sgt William Leslie Cooke, 21, Leigh-on-Sea.
Sgt William Henry Bowers, 27, Dagenham.
Sgt Douglas William Peacey.

X3641. Crew commemorated at Runnymede.
Sgt Joseph Doughty, 20, Chadderton.
P/O Thomas George Hubert Gulliver, 31, husband of Dorothy.
P/O Cyril Douglas Waddingham DFC, 26, Tottenham.
Sgt Ewen Ritchie Stirling, 21, Dundee.
Sgt Derek Shergold Drury Welch.
Sgt James Heslop.

Stirling N3673, 15 Squadron.
F/Lt George William Nicholson, pilot. Appeldoorn General Cemetery.

9 March, Harleston (Norfolk) after Essen.
X3643.
Sgt James Cartwright, 26, Stockport. Stockport Crematorium.
Sgt John Andrew Rogers, 26, Chopwell. St John's Churchyard, Chopwell.
Warrant Officer Terence De Valera Dignan, 21, Liverpool. All Saints Churchyard, Honington.
Sgt Albert Edward Singerton, 21, husband of Gladys Ruby, Barking. Rippleside Cemetery, Barking.
Sgt Thomas Hunter Errington, 19, South Shields. Harton Cemetery, South Shields.
Sgt David Stanley Nicholas, 27, Trealaw. Rhondda Cemetery.

5 April, Cologne.
X3415. Crew buried at Rheinburg War Cemetery.
P/O Paul Rigby Sinclair Brooke, 29.
Sgt Edward Frank Collins, 27, husband of Phyllis Elsie, Dursley.
Sgt Ronald Jacques, 28, husband of Olga, Millthrop.

Sgt Phillip John Coleman, 21, Old Buckenham.
Sgt Cyril Victor Maddock, 20, Plymouth.
Sgt Arthur Naylor.

10 April, Essen.
X3702. Crew buried at Rheinburg War Cemetery.
F/O Alistair Mactaggart, 26, Port Ellen, Islay.
Sgt Jack Walker.
Sgt Laurence David Orbuck, 20, Melbourne, Victoria.
Sgt Roger Owen Francis.
Sgt Stephen Elmes, 21, Birmingham.
Sgt Henry Maxwell Tapley.

12 April, Essen.
X3722. Five crew buried at Reichswald Forest War Cemetery.
Sgt Frederick Davidson DFM, 26, Crook.
Sgt Cyril John Riley-Hawkins.
Sgt Thomas Ralph Mildon, 25, husband of Bettina Kathleen, Deal.
Sgt Carl Vincent Williams, 24, Chirk.
Sgt Denis Riddel Burn, 23, Rake.
(Sgt H James POW)

22 April, Cologne.
X3358.
P/O Henry Alfred Schumm, navigator, 27, Middlesbrough. Rheinburg War
  Cemetery.

X3638. Three crew buried at Bergen-op-Zoom War Cemetery.
Sgt Owen Cicero Charles Barnes, pilot, 30, Southampton.
Sgt Robert Harvey Armstrong, second pilot.
P/O Henry Brener, observer, 28, husband of Mary, Nottingham.

X3759. Five crew buried at All Saints Churchyard, Honington.
Sgt Warren Thompson Ramey, Milwaukee, Wisconsin.
Sgt John Monteith Hubbert, 32, St Catherine's, Ontario.
Sgt John Whiteside Jasper, 27, Henderson, New Zealand.
F/Sgt J Sebberas, 20, Toronto, Ontario.
Sgt Eric Edwin Eglinton, 21, Birmingham.

25 April, Rostock.
X3649 WS/D.
Sgt John Wilfred Watson, wop/AG, 23, Linton-on-Ouse. Newton-upon-

Ouse Churchyard.

X3226, WS/B. Crew commemorated at Runnymede.
Sq/Ldr Douglas Holbrook Holmes AFC, 31, Langley Mill.
Sgt Philip William Clement Flannery, 20, Greenford.
F/Sgt William Burns Richmond, 22, West Hartlepool.
F/Sgt James North, 20, Bradford.
F/Sgt Richard Ballantyne, 28, husband of Margaret, Falkirk.
F/Sgt Walter Lock, 26, husband of Barbara, Leeds.

28 April, Kiel.
X3716. Crew buried at Aabenraa Cemetery.
Sgt George Kellock Sampson, 23, Lochore.
Sgt Leslie Raymond Silver, 20, husband of Evelyn Ann, Woodford Green.
Sgt Ronald Keith Ayres, 21, husband of Clara Florence, Walton-on-Thames.
Sgt Kenneth William Stevens, 21, husband of Irene Alice, Mansfield Woodhouse.
Sgt Alfred William Mount, 19, Ashstead.
Sgt Harold Richard Harrison, 27, husband of Irene Ada, Shirley.

15 May, Great Belt.
Z1615 WS/H.
Sgt Albert Gruchy, gunner, Newfoundland. Svino Cemetery.

17 May, Boulogne.
X3276. Crew commemorated at Runnymede.
Sgt Hugh Nicholas Wanostrocht.
Sgt Raymond Colvin, 20, Spalding.
Sgt Robin Jack Fraser, 21, Dedworth Green.
Sgt Matthew Bates.
Sgt Peter John Lascelles Hoyle.

30 May, Cologne.
*BJ674. Crew buried at Eindhoven Woensel General Cemetery.
F/O Michael Ryland Hodges, 19, Crouch End.
F/Sgt Thomas Joseph Hartnett, Canada.
F/Sgt Thomas Edgar Newby, 30, husband of Phyllis Muriel, Cardiff.
F/Sgt Charles Noel Douglas Stewart.
Sgt Henry Leopold Jones, 26, husband of Mabel Janet, Glasgow.
*BJ = Wellington adapted to carry 4000 lb bomb.

X3469.
Sgt Kenneth Richard Pexman, gunner, 21, husband of Mabel Isobel, Scunthorpe. Schoonselhof Cemetery.

N2894. Central Gunnery School.
F/Sgt John McKenzie McLean, gunner, 22, husband of Edna Mary. Apeldoorn General Cemetery.

11 June, minelaying.
X3695 WS/V. Crew commemorated at Runnymede.
Sgt Harvey Holmes, Bury.
P/O Victor William Saul, 22, Addlestone.
Sgt Alexander Swiderski, Canada.
Sgt James Rutherford, 20.
Sgt Frank Crawford Evans, 20, Windermere.

20 June, Emden.
X3713 WS/J. Crew buried at Leens General Cemetery, De Marne, Groningen.
W/Cdr Leslie Vidal James DFC, 25, husband of Marianne, Bournemouth.
F/Sgt Arthur Dunham Adair, 26, Fairlight, Saskatchewan.
P/O John David Baxter DFM.
Sgt Jack Brown, 21, Leeds.
P/O Alfred Victor Brooks, 22, Chatham.

23 June, Wantage after St Nazaire.
X3423 WS/X. Three crew buried at Brookwood Military Cemetery.
Sgt John Daniel Kingdon, 30, husband of Dora Howard, Carmarthen. Pontypridd Crematorium.
F/Sgt George Allen Morley, 26, Kapuskasing, Ontario.
Sgt Archibald Bernard MacDonell, 23, Alexandria, Ontario.
Sgt Frederick Henry Eubank, 29, Hagersville, Ontario.
(Sgt George injured)

23 July, Duisburg.
Z1577. Two crew buried at Reichswald Forest War Cemetery.
F/O Henry Ernest Brown, pilot, 26, husband of Phyllis Violet, Bramber.
F/Sgt Alfred Frank Chilvers Ratcliff, wop/AG, 26, Toronto, Ontario. Died 6 August of his injuries.

28 July, Hamburg.
X3475 WS/P. Crew buried at Becklingen War Cemetery.

P/O James Doran Mullins, 21, Halifax, Nova Scotia.
P/O George Albert Cooper, 21, Niagara Falls, Ontario.
P/O Maurice Walter Groves, 22, Kingston Hill.
P/O Robert Oswald Cordall, 25, Endon.
Sgt Edward James Henry Gurr, 25, Montreal, Quebec.
Sgt John Cyril Highfield, 25, Nottingham.

X3606 WS/M. Four crew buried at Becklingen War Cemetery.
Sq/Ldr Harry Ledger.
P/O Gerard McKee Beech, Canada.
P/O John Eric Coleman, 21, husband of Dora, Esher.
F/Sgt Jack Robert Ludkin.
(F/Sgt D A Hunter POW)

X3456. Four crew commemorated at Runnymede.
Sgt Henry John Hannaford, 28, Nottingham.
Sgt Eric Jesse King, 27, Heathfield.
Sgt George Lionel Ferry, 33, Gateshead.
Sgt James Arthur Elmslie, Canada.
Sgt William Switzer Warren, Gorey, Co Wexford. Kiel War Cemetery.

31 July, Düsseldorf.
BJ878. Crew buried at Reichswald Forest War Cemetery.
P/O Reginald Ernest Sidney Pink.
W/O2 George Edward Ford, 25, Canada.
Sgt Archibald Edward McIlveen, Canada.
Sgt John Hannaby, Canada.
Sgt Peter John Henry Donelan, 20, Darley Dale.

BJ876. Four crew buried at Heverlee War Cemetery.
Sgt William Thomas George Hall, 21, Ashton Gate.
Sgt Wilfred Victor Clarke, 29, husband of Anna, Winnipeg, Manitoba.
(Sgt H Levy POW)
Sgt Alistair Bruce Martin, 24, Charlottetown, Prince Edward Island.
Sgt Robert George Miller, 21, South Ockendon.

All records below are Lancaster crews except where stated. * = also flew as
    Wellington crew with No. 9 Squadron.

16 September, Essen.

W4186 WS/S. Crew commemorated at Runnymede.
P/O Leslie James Musselwhite*, 31, husband of Doris Rosina, Hampstead.
Sgt James Hall, 33, husband of Edith Marjorie, Liverpool.
Sgt William Hunt.
Sgt William Oliver Snow, 23, Ontario.
Sgt Robert Semple Morton, 21, Newmilns.
Sgt Stanley Victor Miles, 20, Dagenham.
F/Sgt Maurice Emanuel Buechler.

W4765 WS/T. Crew buried at Reichswald Forest War Cemetery.
Sgt Kenneth Beresford Hobbs*.
Sgt George Dennison.
Sgt Dennis Winstone Constance*, 22, husband of Edith Joyce, Leeds.
Sgt Thomas Harold Kidd*.
Sgt Maurice Hull*, 21, Frosterley.
Sgt Dan Oliver Richard Dawson, 21, Hull.
Sgt Allen Hartwell Jones*.

19 September, Munich.
W4184 WS/A. Six crew buried at Dürnbach War Cemetery.
P/O Lewis Boyd Haward, 28, Surbiton.
Sgt Frank Hamer, 23, husband of Marjorie, Moulton.
W/O Joseph Camillus McDonald*, 28, Montreal, Quebec.
W/O Harold Jason Thurston*, 22.
P/O Howard Houston Burton*, 32.
(Sgt M L Douglas* POW)
Sgt Ewart Wright.

23 September, Wismar.
R5907 WS/M. Crew buried at Berlin War Cemetery.
P/O Cyril James McKeen*, 21, Inglewood, New Zealand.
Sgt James John Watson, 23, Dublin.
Sgt Albert James Jarvis Brooks*, 21, Wokingham.
Sgt George Brothwell*, 29, husband of Alice, Sheffield.
Sgt Albert Victor Riggs*, 26, Tullamore.
Sgt Terence Eugene Donnelly*, 33, husband of Lily, Watford.
Sgt Henry Thomas Ramsden.

W4230 WS/P. Five crew commemorated at Runnymede.
F/Sgt Owen Beamish White*, 21, New Zealand.
Sgt Geoffrey William Ardern Higson, 28, husband of Marjorie Kendal,
   Manchester. Svino Churchyard.

F/O Harry Francis Burton Smith*, 25, Wellington, New Zealand.

Sgt John Wallace Henry*, 26, husband of Aileen, Canterbury, New Zealand. Svino Churchyard.

F/Sgt James Alexander Beaton*.

Sgt James Cornwall Gray, 25, New Zealand.

Sgt Noel Henry Crozier*, 21, Hawke's Bay, New Zealand.

29 September, Limfjorden.

W4237 WS/W. Crew buried at Old Garrison Cemetery, Poznan.

Sgt Laurance Walter Goalen*, 20, East Cowes.

Sgt James Victor Redshaw, 26, Hull.

Sgt Donald Patrick Shanley, 20, Slough.

Sgt Alan Gilbert Boughtwood, 29, Billericay.

Sgt David Bruce Paton, 35, husband of Mary Howorth, Tilford.

Sgt Vincent Joseph Louis Lebano*, 24, husband of Denise Marie Rita, Montreal, Quebec.

Sgt John Edwin Watts.

7 November, Waddington after Genoa.

W4265 WS/L. Four crew buried at Newport Cemetery, Lincoln.

P/O Arthur Joseph Macdonald*.

Sgt John William Bowes, 21, Durham. St Mary's Churchyard, Denton.

W/O Donald Leonard Grimes*, husband of Arras, London, Ontario.

W/O Douglas Dunbar Low*, 25, Owen Sound, Ontario.

Sgt Nichol Curd*, 22, New Penshaw. All Saints Churchyard, Penshaw.

Sgt Raymond Gwilym Gwyn Anthony, 26, husband of Margaret Eileen, Mountain Ash. Maesyrarian Cemetery, Mountain Ash.

Sgt Robert Charles Perchard*, 21, Jersey.

R5916 WS/R.

F/O Kenneth Alexander Mackenzie* DFC, 30, husband of Vera Jane, Toronto, Ontario. Newport Cemetery, Lincoln.

Sgt James John Taaffe, 20, Malvern. Great Malvern Cemetery.

Sgt Arthur Reuben Billington*, 20, Pontypridd. Glyntaff Cemetery, Pontypridd.

Sgt Kenneth Thomas John Adams*, 21, husband of Olive, Monmouth. SS Philip and James Churchyard, Penmaen.

Sgt Roy Ernest Werren*, 22, Herne Hill. Tooting Cemetery, Lambeth.

Sgt David John Wicks, 21, husband of Jean, Norwich. Rose Hill Cemetery, Oxford.

Sgt Herbert Richard Willacy*, 27, husband of Muriel, Heckmondwyke. Heckmondwyke Cemetery.

9 December, Turin.
W4764 WS/K. Crew buried at Marolles-sur-Seine Communal Cemetery.
W/O Lawrence Henry Jordan, Canada.
Sgt Leslie Frederick Walter Jones, 31, husband of Elvira, Cardiff.
Sgt Eric Charles Percy Newton, 29, husband of Betty Marie, Barnstaple.
Sgt Allan William Albert Robinson, 20, Croydon.
Sgt Kevin Fenton Neville, 24, Newfoundland.
Sgt Walter Maurice Rimscha.
Sgt Henry John Warburton, 19, Burton-on-Trent.

17 December, Cloppenburg.
ED349 WS/S. Six crew POW.
F/Sgt William Harvey Penn, mid-upper gunner. Sage War Cemetery.

17 December, Diepholz.
W4155 WS/D. Five crew buried at Rheinberg War Cemetery.
Sgt Colin Frederick Allen, 25, Killara, New South Wales.
Sgt Charles Henry Nadin, 31, husband of Elsie, Manchester.
F/O Laurence George Newman, Anerley.
(Sgt H V Brown POW)
Sgt Charles William Dickens, 28, husband of Ivy, Shepherd's Bush.
(Sgt J M T O'Neill POW)
F/Lt Charles Guthrie Shields Bain*.

20 December, midair collision with W4259 near Lincoln.
W4182 WS/B.
P/O Leslie Charles Hazell*, 32, husband of Marjorie Violet, Ilford. Barkingside Cemetery, Ilford.
Sgt Edward Arthur Gardiner, 23, Dover. St James Cemetery, Dover.
Sgt William Thomas Miller*, 33, husband of Margaret, Liverpool. Holy Trinity Churchyard, Wavertree.
Sgt Hubert Thomas Tatley*, 30, husband of Ivy, Mansfield. Nottingham Road Cemetery, Mansfield.
Sgt Charles Harry Sidney Brooks, 27, husband of Winifred Mabel, Lewisham. Hither Green Cemetery.
Sgt Emrys Frederick Sharples, 27, husband of Gwendolin Maud, Chelmsford. Writtle Road Cemetery, Chelmsford.
Sgt Eric Wilson Walker*, 32, husband of Phyllis, Stanningley. Bowling Cemetery, Bradford.

Duisburg.

ED347 WS/N. Crew buried at Oosterhuit Protestant Cemetery, Noord-Brabant.

Sgt John William Tyreman, 26, husband of Dorothy Vera, South Cerney.

Sgt John Sykes, 30, Bradford.

F/O James William Lynes.

Sgt Harold Burrows Stokes, 34, husband of Dorothy Helena Elsie, Rochester.

Sgt Harry George Ford, 20, Bexhill-on-Sea.

Sgt James Hill, 30, husband of Norah, Manchester.

Sgt George Clive Wing, 18, Hampton.

21 December, Munich.

W4185 WS/G. Six crew buried at Oberschleissheim Churchyard.†

P/O Edward Fenwicke-Clennell DFC.

(Sgt P M Slater POW)

F/Sgt Jack Passmore Warren, 25, Leeds.

P/O Robert Guy Clarkson, Canada.

P/O John Alexander Wilson Moffat DFC, 22.

F/Sgt John Frederick Edwards, 27, Portage La Prairie, Manitoba.

Sgt Jack Hilton Baker.

†Six of only ten of Bomber Command left in German civilian cemeteries, not moved after the war to one of the four military cemeteries.

1943

3 January, Essen.

W4840 WS/B. Four crew buried at Rheden (Heiderust) General Cemetery, Gelderland.

F/Lt Douglas Herbert Scott Lonsdale DFC, 31, husband of Patricia Westcott, Westham (Sussex).

Sgt Albert Thomas Riley, 22, Norbury.

F/O Kenneth Read Smith, Victoria, British Columbia. Groesbeek Canadian War Cemetery.

Sgt James Ivor Morris, 22, Kidderminster.

W/O Robert Richmond Moore, 20, Duncan, British Columbia. Groesbeek Canadian War Cemetery.

Sgt Arthur Douglas Smitherman, 21, Tunbridge Wells.

F/Sgt Robert Lloyd Dickie, 23, Duncan, British Columbia. Groesbeek Canadian War Cemetery.

8 January, Baltic Sea.

ED308 WS/R.

Sgt Reginald Warren Robinson, rear gunner, 21, Brixton. Lambeth Cemetery.

W4159 WS/Y. Crew buried at Vorden General Cemetery, Gelderland.
W/O Alan Dick Foote.
Sgt Maxwell Wilson Stephenson, 23, Bishop Auckland.
Sgt Munro McKenzie, 19, Watford.
Sgt William Thomas McLennan, 30, husband of Sarah, Aberdeen.
Sgt George Mitchell.
Sgt Patrick George Brogan, 19, Eltham.
Sgt Robert Wardrop.

13 January, Essen.
W4843 WS/K. Crew commemorated at Runnymede.
Sgt Geoffrey Lyons, 22, Sale.
Sgt Bernard Simmons, 21, Walton-le-Dale.
Sgt Richard Lawrence Chitty, Thornton Heath.
Sgt Harold Cowlishaw, 30, Sheffield.
Sgt Sidney Coates, 27, Wingate.
Sgt Arthur Joseph Kenny, Canada.
Sgt Alun Rees, 19, Trimsaran.

17 January, Berlin.
W4379 WS/A. Two crew buried at Berlin War Cemetery.
F/Sgt John Eldon Galbraith, navigator.
Sgt Joe Herbert Wejies de Silva, mid-upper gunner.

ED436 WS/G. Crew commemorated at Runnymede.
Sgt John George Bruce Chilvers, 23, Axminster.
Sgt Leslie Whiteside, 29, husband of Elsie, Bolton.
Sgt Bernard Naylor, 20, Huthwaite.
Sgt Andrew McCabe, 21, Newmilns.
F/O Charles Broadbent Haslam, 21, Cardston, Alberta.
Sgt Thomas William Jones, 22, Fazakerley.
F/Sgt Florian Mercier Lacasse, 22, Ottawa, Ontario.

W4761 WS/P. Crew buried at Hamburg Cemetery.
F/O Anderson Storey, Jamaica Plain, Massachusetts.
Sgt Harold Claude Griffin.
F/O Gordon Hunt McMillan, Hornchurch.
F/Sgt Ralph Calasanctis Morris, 23, Grand Falls, Newfoundland.
Sgt Robert Francis Matthews, 20, Grand Falls, Newfoundland.

Sgt Frederick William Cater, 27, husband of Elizabeth, Ilford.
Sgt Albert Clavey Spear, 28, Cardiff.

W4157 WS/V. Crew commemorated at Runnymede.
P/O Trevor Leslie Gibson, 24, husband of G E, Kingsford, New South Wales.
F/O Eric William Mitchell Jacombs, second pilot, 27, husband of Frances Mary, Auckland, New Zealand.
Sgt Stanley Wescombe, 29, Liverpool.
F/O Cyril Garnett Tilson, 24, Southampton.
F/Sgt Bernard Kenneth Skinner, 28, York.
Sgt Harry Goodwin Jenkins.
Sgt John William Robinson Broadley.
W/O Francis Arthur Webb.

29 January, near Boston.
ED503. Five crew commemorated at Runnymede.
F/Lt Robert Frood Lind.
Sgt John Doran.
P/O Charles Wilfred Hurman Cocks, 34, husband of Doris May, New Barnet.
Sgt Thomas Joseph Henry, 30, husband of Winifred, Darwen.
Sgt Donald Arthur Brown.
Sgt Thomas Wishart, 25, husband of Jean, Dalkeith. Dalkeith New Cemetery.

30 January, Hamburg.
ED477 WS/O. Six crew buried at Rheinberg War Cemetery.
F/Sgt Jack Findlay Thomas, 26, Wollongong, New South Wales. Sage War Cemetery.
Sgt Stanley Frederick McLean, 22, Walthamstow.
Sgt John Murtagh.
Sgt Bryan Milton Swallow, 21, Sheffield.
Sgt William John Veysey, 23, Nelson, New Zealand.
Sgt Alfred Walter Hover.
F/Sgt Laurence Alfred Morgan, 33, husband of Noreen Grace Rebecca, Geelong West, Victoria.

Hawnby after Hamburg.
ED481 WS/M. Three crew buried at Dishforth Cemetery.
W/O Frank Goheen Nelson, 24, Wilkinsburg, Pennsylvania.
Sgt McKeen Allan, 33, Northport, Nova Scotia.

Sgt George Francis Done, 21, Northwich. Northwich Cemetery.

Sgt Allan Arthur Frederick Williams, 26, Whitstable. Seasalter Churchyard.

Sgt Henry Summers Jones, 21, Sutton Coldfield. Sutton Coldfield Cemetery.

Sgt Arthur William Butcher, 19, Upper Tysoe. Tysoe Church Cemetery.

Sgt Walter George Murton, 21, Cape Town, Western Cape.

4 February, Scopwick.

ED496 WS/P. Four crew commemorated at Runnymede.

Sgt Charles Richard Land, 36, husband of Margaret Maud, Taverham. All Saints Churchyard, Weston Longville.

Sgt Ronald Jack Packer.

Sgt Hugh Francis Gullery, 33, husband of Elizabeth, Belfast.

Sgt Joseph Thomas Levesque, Riviere du Loup, Quebec.

Sgt Francis Victor McGonigal, 21.

(two crew did not fly)

18 February, Wilhelmshaven.

ED492 WS/W. Four crew buried at Sage War Cemetery.

Sgt Ernest John Walter Davis, pilot, 24, husband of Eileen Rachel, Hayes.

Sgt James Storey Aird, navigator, 33, husband of Karen Maria, North Shields.

Sgt Ralph William Darlington, mid-upper gunner, 19, Manchester.

Sgt Thomas Alfred Berwick, rear gunner.

25 February, Nürnburg.

ED495 WS/Y. Two crew buried at Dürnbach War Cemetery.

F/O Joseph Arthur Mitchell AFM, pilot, 32, husband of Joan Agnes, Salisbury.

F/O Victor Charles Sherring, rear gunner, 32, husband of Edith Amelia, Newport (Monmouthshire).

ED520 WS/T. Crew commemorated at Runnymede.

W/O Donald Campbell Hunter, 22, Edmonton, Alberta.

Sgt Richard Ayerst Matthews, 23, Largs.

Sgt Stanley Frederick Essen, 31, husband of Thelma, Palmers Green.

Sgt Donald Carstairs McIntyre.

W/O2 Lloyd Adolf Bernick, Canada.

Sgt Edward Wilkins, 34, husband of Dora Rose, Hitchin.

Sgt Arthur Clarence Blaber, 31, husband of Doris Catherine, Brighton.

27 February, Elsham.
W4857 PM/V, 103 Squadron.
F/Lt Richard Noel Stubbs* DFM, DFC, pilot, 22, Stone. Hull Crematorium.

1 March, Berlin.
ED490 WS/J.
Sgt Edward Stephen Smithson, flight engineer, 22, Romford. Chadwell Heath Cemetery, Dagenham.
P/O Leslie Hoyle Geach, bomb aimer, 31, husband of Lorna S, Cheltenham. Newport Cemetery, Lincoln.
Sgt Kenneth Edwin William Matthews, rear gunner. Morden Cemetery, Battersea.

12 March, Cromwell.
R5556, 1661 HCU.
F/Lt James Cowan* DFC, pilot, 30, Hastings, New Zealand.

13 March, Gdynia.
ED494 WS/G. Crew commemorated at Runnymede.
F/Sgt Howard Clark Lewis, Ann Arbor, Michigan.
Sgt Douglas Cowie, 23, Aberdeen.
Sgt Raymond Leon Laycock, 27, Wennington.
Sgt John Ian Mitchell, 20, Oxhey.
Sgt Reginald Charles Hitchcock, 29, husband of Norah, Dorking.
Sgt Richard Frederick Cunningham, South Bank.
Sgt John Hitchin Howorth.

3 April, Essen.
ED694 WS/Y. Crew buried at Eindhoven (Woensel) General Cemetery.
P/O William Hallewell Swire, 20, Halifax.
Sgt George Robert Gilbert, 20, Hednesford.
Sgt Eric William Cook, 29, husband of Phyllis E M, Abridge.
Sgt Gerwyn Howell Evans, 21, husband of Amy Margaret, Penycae.
Sgt Ronald Douglas Francis, Highbridge.
Sgt Walter Watts.
F/Sgt Roy Reginald Feeley.

ED479 WS/Z. Crew buried at Reichswald Forest War Cemetery.
Sq/Ldr Geoffrey William Jones Jarrett, 34, Kenilworth.
Sgt Harold Precious.
P/O George Smith, 22, Carlisle.
P/O Andrew Greville Seymour, 29.

Sgt Ivor Francis, 27, husband of Elizabeth Mary, Mountain Ash.
P/O George Raynor Dale.
Sgt Jack Miles, 25, New Hanover, Natal.

4 April, Kiel.
ED696 WS/T. Crew buried at Hamburg Cemetery.
F/Sgt John Harvey Courtney Walsh, 22, Bulawayo, Southern Rhodesia.
Sgt Herbert Llewelyn Jones.
P/O Ronald Edward Raven, 23, Woodford Green.
F/O Kennedy Emslie Fraser, 19, Harrogate.
W/O2 Thomas Wilfred Telfer, Canada.
F/O Stuart Melbourne Hobson.
Sgt Eric Sharpe Wood.

6 April, Mildenhall.
ED662 WS/P. Two crew buried at St John Churchyard, Beck Row.
Sgt Arthur England Ingram, Bilton. St Peter's Churchyard, Bilton-in-
    Holderness.
Sgt Alan James McCoy, 22, Biggin Hill.
Sgt Frank Worrall, 22, Barnsley. Barnsley Cemetery.
Sgt Gordon Boyd Walker, 19, Newton Mearns. Mearns Cemetery.
Sgt Alfred Henry Page, 21, Stockton-on-Tees. Oxbridge Lane Cemetery,
    Stockton.
Sgt Henry Wells, 20, Cardiff. Cathays Cemetery, Cardiff.
P/O James Frederick Leleu, 33, husband of Adele, Cuffley.
Lt George Philip Johnson, Royal Artillery, 29, husband of Nancy, Finchley.
    Marylebone Cemetery.

9 April, Duisburg.
ED502 WS/V. Crew buried at Oudewater Protestant Cemetery.
W/O Arthur Miles White, 23, Waikato, New Zealand.
Sgt Norman Percy Tutt, 22, Ashford (Kent).
F/O Hector Robertson, 25, Aberdeen.
P/O Graham John Gibbings, 20, Salisbury, Southern Rhodesia.
Sgt William Arthur Barker, 32, Cromer.
Sgt William Roy Jakeway, 19, Barnet.
F/O Newton Bird.

ED806 WS/L. Crew buried at Uden War Cemetery.
P/O Arthur Frederick Paramore, 24, husband of M S, Fishponds.
Sgt Thomas Hughes, 21, Glasgow.
P/O Eric Hesketh, 29, Farnworth.

Sgt Alan Maxwell Coulthard, 22, Liverpool.
Sgt Ronald Douglas Benning, 21, Shoeburyness.
Sgt David Henry Mactier, 34, Port William.
Sgt Ronald Douglas Wood, 26, Newcastle-upon-Tyne.

ED566 WS/J. Crew commemorated at Runnymede.
Sgt Arthur Roy Hobbs, 22, husband of Gladys Mary, Boultham.
Sgt Richard Henry Thomas, 20, Abernant.
Sgt Sidney John Argent, 22, husband of Pat, Grays.
Sgt Arthur Robert Hollinshead Thompson, 34, husband of Anne, Carrigrohane, Co Cork.
W/O2 William John Reid, 21, Lethbridge, Alberta.
Sgt Dennis Norman Bysouth, 23, Cricklewood.
W/O2 Harold Logan Huether, 21, Canada.

10 April, Frankfurt.
ED501 WS/R. Six crew buried at Rheinburg War Cemetery.
W/Cdr Kenneth Brooke Farley Smith DSO, 30, husband of Esme Doris, Brockenhurst.
Sgt William Thomson, 22, husband of Grace, Deepdale.
F/O Arnold James Turner, 27, Anston.
F/O Bernard James Smith, 27, Spalding.
Sgt Gordon Arthur Taylor, 22, Hastings, New Zealand. Runnymede.
Sgt Louis Stanley Fiddes, 21, Barnet.
P/O Roy Victor Charles Pleasance, 22, Tilbury.

22 April, Gulf of Gascony.
ED799 WS/G. Crew commemorated at Runnymede.
P/O Ralph Brown, husband of Nora, Bishop Auckland.
Sgt Robert Albert Storey, 23, husband of Toni Mary, Southampton.
F/O Basil Carey.
F/Lt Ronald Yarwood Higginson DFM, 22, husband of Margaret, Prestwich.
Sgt Harold Jenkins, husband of Annie, Gateshead.
Sgt Ralph James Mitchell Cox, 21, husband of Phyllis, Kilburn.
Sgt Joseph Arthur Bland, 25, husband of Ruth Irene, Southern Rhodesia.

30 April, Essen.
ED838 WS/R. Crew commemorated at Runnymede.
P/O George Albert Nunez, 32, husband of Olive Adella, St Joseph, Trinidad.
Sgt Cecil Howard Collins, husband of Muriel, Friern Barnet.

Sgt Alvery Beard, 21, Thorpe Hesley.
Sgt Edward Francis Doolittle, Liverpool.
Sgt Reginald Arthur Knapman, 31, Guildford.
Sgt Jack Bayliss, 23, Brockmoor.
Sgt Dennis Robert Barber, 23, Dorking.

13 May, Pilsen.
ED589 WS/O. Five crew commemorated at Runnymede.
Sgt George Henry Saxton, Carlisle.
Sgt Douglas Claude Ferris, 22, Southsea.
Sgt Wallace Reginald Macdonald, Canada.
Sgt Roger Marshall Morris, 22, husband of Isabella.
Sgt John Reddish.
Sgt John Charles Owen, 24, Rhos-on-Sea. Wonseradeel Protestant Churchyard.
Sgt James Buntin. Wonseradeel Protestant Churchyard.

25 May, Düsseldorf.
ED834 WS/Z. Crew buried at Vlissingen Northern Cemetery.
F/O Harold Walter Woodhouse, 32.
Sgt Leslie John Daker, 30, husband of Daisy Rosamund, King's Norton.
Sgt James Brownlie Corbett, 21, Bellshill.
Sgt Harold John Warren, 22, Woking.
Sgt William Smith, 22, husband of Edna Pearl, Gorton.
Sgt Albert Glyn Coffin, 19, Chester.
Sgt Edgar Leslie Matthews, 20, Sheffield.

12 June, Bochum.
ED558, WS/N. Two crew buried at Bergh (Zeddam) Protestant Cemetery.
W/O Herbert Edward Wood, 26, pilot, Barnetby.
W/O2 Herbert George Watson, 19, rear gunner, Lethbridge, Alberta.

14 June, Oberhausen.
LM329 WS/Q. Crew buried at Uden War Cemetery.
Sgt John Evans, 20, London.
Sgt Vincent George Louvaine Smith, 28, husband of Mary, Staffordshire.
Sgt Robert Borthwick, 31.
Sgt Vincent John Tarr, second navigator.
Sgt Alan Wilson Waite, 22, Liverpool.
F/Sgt Walter James Chapple, 32, Forest Gate.
Sgt Herbert Ivor Ashdown, 19, Cardiff.
Sgt Derek Walter Brough, 20, Dartford.

16 June, Cologne.
ED487 WS/D. Four crew buried at Schoonselhof (Antwerp) Cemetery.
(Sgt J A Aldersley POW)
Sgt Patrick Hall.
Sgt Denis Webster, 20, Loughton.
(Sgt H Popplestone POW)
(Sgt C J Sinclair POW)
Sgt Herbert Francis Poynter, 19, Islington.
Sgt David Gerald Tremblay, 27, Elm Creek, Manitoba.

22 June, Mülheim.
ED699 WS/L. Five crew buried at Rheinburg War Cemetery.
P/O Kenneth Denness, 20, Speen (Berkshire). Reichswald Forest War
   Cemetery.
Sgt Cyril Hunt, 31, husband of Nancy Maxine, Whitwell (Derbyshire).
Sgt Albert George Bryan, 27, Port Sunlight.
P/O Ronald Walter Winfield, 21, Clacton.
Sgt Alfred Frederick Sidney Day, 20, Barking.
Sgt Gordon Frederick Kilsby, 21, Streatham. Reichswald Forest War
   Cemetery.
Sgt Eric William Geraghty, 23, Ashford (Middlesex).

25 June, Gelsenkirchen.
ED831 WS/H. Four crew buried at Amsterdam New Eastern Cemetery.
Sq/Ldr Alan Murray Hobbs DFC, 25, Christchurch, New Zealand.
F/O John Hamilton Sams, second pilot, 27, Leatherhead.
Sgt Fred William Sanderson, 30, Ryelands. Amsterdam New Eastern
   Cemetery.
Sgt Kenneth George Mott, 20, London. Schellinkhout Protestant
   Churchyard.
Sgt Charles Parnell King, Harderwijk General Cemetery.
Sgt Edward Charles Bishop, 30, husband of Ivy Kate, Kingsworthy.
Sgt Walter Clive Rowlands, 20, Newtown (Montgomery).
F/Sgt William Slater, 21, West Hallam. Amersfoot General Cemetery.

EE125, 106 Squadron.
F/O James Bell DFM, rear gunner, 23, Taynuilt. Runnymede.

3 July, Cologne.
ED689 WS/K. Six crew commemorated at Runnymede.

F/Lt John Alfred Wakeford DFC, 22, Torquay.
Sgt Thomas Geoffrey Porter, second pilot, 21, West Kirby (Cheshire).
Sgt John Elwyn Owen.
F/O Jonah Bruce Reeves, Durhamville, New York.
Sgt Harold Joseph Hawkridge, 20, Leeds.
Sgt Alec Frederick Backler, 22, Burnage. Rheinberg War Cemetery.
Sgt Harry Leonard Wilson, 22, husband of Phyllis Margaret, Oxford.
W/O2 George Francis Dohany, Canada. Rheinberg War Cemetery.

15 July, Reggio nell' Emilia.
JA679 WS/P.
Sgt Edward William Edwards, flight engineer, 21, Guisborough. Ravenna
   War Cemetery.

29 July, Hamburg.
JA692 WS/D. Crew buried at Hamburg Cemetery.
F/Lt Charles William Fox.
F/Sgt John David Dodds, 20, Brigg.
P/O William Henry Hodson, 24, Hednesford.
Sgt John Piper, 20, Walsall.
Sgt Thomas Norman Robinson, 20, Leicester.
Sgt Stanley Ernest Russell, 22, Bristol.
F/Sgt Charles Frederick Sargent, husband of Vera.
F/O Anthony Alexander Rossie, navigator.

2 August, Hamburg.
ED493 WS/A. Three crew commemorated at Runnymede.
P/O David Mackenzie, 21, Helmsdale. Bergen-op-Zoom War Cemetery.
Sgt Robert Hugh Jones.
P/O Thomas McKean McCall, 22, Muirkirk. Bergen-op-Zoom War
   Cemetery.
Sgt Robert Reid, 24, Falkirk. Den Burgh General Cemetery, Texel.
Sgt George Arthur Filleul. Bergen-op-Zoom War Cemetary.
Sgt Leslie Francis Gilkes, Siparia, Trinidad.
Sgt William Miller Welsh, 27, Tweedmouth.

7 August, Bardney.
W4133 WS/Z/S. Two crew buried at Newport Cemetery, Lincoln.
Sgt John Bernard Davis, 21, Bexleyheath. Woolwich Cemetery.
Sgt John Donald Lofthouse, 23, Preston. New Hall Lane Cemetery,
   Preston.
Sgt Peter Clifford Wilfred Wyatt, 21, Ealing.

Sgt Stanley Robertson, 19, Warrington. Warrington Cemetery.
Sgt James Henry Stevens, 21, Hackney. City of London and Tower Hamlets Cemetery.
Sgt Eric Taylor. Pelton Cemetery.
F/Sgt Frank Meres, Rockdale, New South Wales.

11 August, Nürnburg.
ED654 WS/W.
Sgt Percy Lynam, mid-upper gunner, 24, Swanwick. Ripley Cemetery.

31 August, Mönchengladbach.
ED551 WS/M. Crew commemorated at Runnymede.
W/O Gilbert Eric Hall, 23, husband of Beatrice Irene, Appleton.
Sgt Leon John George Field, 26, Hildenborough.
Sgt William David Evans, Carmarthen.
P/O Clarence Howard Anderson, second navigator, 28, husband of Edith, Calgary, Alberta.
Sgt Edward Colbert, 27, Atherton.
Sgt Oliver John Overington.
Sgt Robert Alexander Chorley, 27, husband of Joan, Catford.
Sgt Henry Gordon Williams, 31, Eltham.

5 September, Mannheim.
R5744 WS/E. Crew buried at Dürnbach War Cemetery.
Sgt Reginald Arthur Knight, 23, husband of Maisie, Carshalton.
Sgt Thomas William Bradford, 31, husband of Lilian Georgina, Waltham Cross.
Sgt George Alexander Munro, 24, Calgary, Alberta.
Sgt John William Noble, 21, Mansfield.
Sgt David Gordon Connor, 20, Workington.
Sgt Chester Andith Davis.
Sgt Robert Gilchrist Nelson, 22, Glasgow.

ED666 WS/G. Crew buried at Dürnbach War Cemetery.
P/O Thomas Henry Gill, 25, husband of Mollie Irene, Birmingham.
Sgt Matthew McPherson, 21, Glasgow.
Sgt Raymond Victor Gough, Cheltenham.
F/Sgt Bernard Peter Devine, 22.
Sgt William Alexander Morton.
Sgt Kevin McDonagh, 23, Limerick.
Sgt Robert McKee, 23, Bolton.

22 September, Hannover.
R5700 WS/N. Crew buried at Hannover War Cemetery.
P/O Edward Jeptha Crabtree, 21, Surrey Hills, Victoria.
Sgt Malcolm John Macritchie.
Sgt George Alastair Sales, 20, Wadhurst.
W/O2 Nelson Albert Noble, Toronto, Ontario.
Sgt V Hurst-Gee, 21, Bradford.
Sgt Dennis Everest, 21, Ontario.
Sgt Victor James Lander, 23, husband of Lillian, Oldham.

23 September, Mannheim.
JA852 WS/L. Crew buried at Rheinberg War Cemetery.
P/O Robert Charles Ord, 28, husband of Ruth Ellen, South Gosforth.
Sgt George Palmer.
F/O Edward Raymond Davies, 21, Swansea.
Sgt Thomas Elliot Brydon Graham, 32, husband of Gladys, Edgware.
Sgt John Wilson, 22, Pelton.
Sgt Rowland Arthur Williams.
Sgt Gordon Charles Fowler, 21, West End, Queensland.

29 September, Bochum.
ED648 WS/D.
Sgt Kenneth Norman Taylor, flight engineer. St Mary's Churchyard, Manby.
P/O Kenneth Herbert Beames, bomb aimer, 32, husband of Kathleen, Bristol. Runnymede.

3 October, Kassel.
ED654 WS/W.
Sgt Angus Earle Leslie, mid-upper gunner, 23, husband of Kathleen, Romford. West Ham Cemetery.

7 October, Stuttgart.
ED836 WS/C. Six crew buried at Dürnbach War Cemetery.
1 Lt Eric George Roberts PH, USAAF, 23, Merchantville, Camden County, New Jersey.
Sgt Percy Shaw, 39.
F/O Frank George Arliss, 27, Retford.
(P/O W Chadwick POW)
Sgt Arthur Bailey, 23, St Helens.
Sgt Thomas Henry Tibbles.

Sgt Robert John Darby, 20, Herne Bay.

JA869 WS/H. Crew buried at Dürnbach War Cemetery.
P/O Arthur Mair, 22, Perivale.
Sgt James Stonehouse, 23, Willington.
Sgt Derrick John Edwin Adams, 19, Lee.
Sgt Thomas John Pounder, 20, Bradford.
F/Sgt Frank Harry Dennis, 27, West Croydon.
Sgt Leslie Felix Collins, 23, husband of Millicent, Scunthorpe.
F/Sgt William Alexander Robertson.

18 October, Hannover.
ED499 WS/X. Six crew buried at Hannover War Cemetery.
F/O Howard James Gould, 22, Maryfield, Saskatchewan.
Sgt John William Grain, 19, Doncaster. Runnymede.
Sgt Oswald William Douglas Hodges, 22, South Croydon.
F/O Stanley David Smith.
Sgt Norman Beer.
P/O Leon Abraham Titof, 19, Flin Flon, Manitoba.
Sgt Stanley George Barlegs, 21, husband of Joan Barbara, Bromley.

22 October, Kassel.
EE188 WS/B.
Sgt Gilbert George Provis, mid-upper gunner, 27, Ystrad. Rhondda
    (Treorchy) Cemetery.

18 November, Berlin.
ED871 WS/Z.
Sgt Leonard Stanley Harris, rear gunner, 20. Runnymede.

DV284 WS/G. Crew buried at Berlin War Cemetery.
P/O Gordon Alan Graham, Canada.
P/O John Graham McComb, second pilot, Belfast.
Sgt Walter George Statham.
F/O Duncan Macdonald, 34, husband of Jane, Glasgow.
Sgt Ronald McKenzie Innes.
Sgt Arthur Fenwick Williamson, 20, Tynemouth.
F/Sgt Hector Ferdinand Altus, 33, Wilkawatt, South Australia.
Sgt Kenneth Mellor, 21, Lower Hopton.

22 November, Berlin.
JB304 GT/Z, 156 Squadron.

W/O John Alfred Cronin Lovis* DFC, rear gunner, 22. Runnymede.

23 November, Berlin.
JB284 OL/C, 83 Squadron. Crew buried at Berlin War Cemetery.
F/Lt John Percival Crebbin* DFC, 23.

ED656 WS/V. Scamblesby after Berlin.
P/O Norman John Robinson, 26, Carbury, Co Kildare. Holy Trinity
    Churchyard, Derrinturn.
F/O Charles Godfrey Hinton, second pilot, 25, Cheltenham. Cheltenham
    Cemetery.
Sgt Robert George Taylor, flight engineer. Cambridge City Cemetery.
F/Sgt Thomas Rhodes Davis, navigator, 20, Streatham. St Nicholas
    Churchyard, Withernsea.
F/Sgt Bertram John Pitman, bomb aimer, 21, husband of Vera May, South
    Norwood. St Nicholas Churchyard, Sandford Orcas.
Sgt Walter Espley Jones, w/op, 23, Saughall Massie. Flaybrick Hill
    Cemetery, Birkenhead.

26 November, Berlin.
JB459 OL/T, 83 Squadron.
F/O Victor William Joseph Nunn, navigator. Dürnbach War Cemetery.

JB592 ZN/W, 106 Squadron.
F/O Harry George Stuffin, rear gunner, 22, Scunthorpe. Dürnbach War
    Cemetery.

2 December, Berlin.
DV332 WS/D. Crew buried at Berlin War Cemetery.
F/Lt Robert Frederick Wells.
Sgt Douglas John Nuttman.
P/O Allan Uriah Duncan, 25, Above Rocks, Jamaica.
F/Sgt Kenneth Garnett, 23, Churwell.
F/Sgt Frank Smith, 23, Leigh.
Sgt William Ellis Gough.
Stephen Vincent Moss, 22, husband of Vera Maud, Burton-on-Trent.

DV334 WS/C. Gamston after Berlin.
P/O Kenneth Edgar Warwick, 20, Ascot. St Mary's Churchyard, Winkfield.
Sgt Robert William Davison, 29, husband of Audrey, Forest Hall.
    Longbenton Cemetery.

F/Sgt John Graham, 23, Carlisle. Upperby Cemetery, Carlisle.

F/Sgt Thomas Butterfield, 27, Leeds. St Mary's Churchyard, Middleton.

Sgt Derrick Ivor Thomas Munn, 22, Hereford. St Mary's Churchyard, Much Cowarne.

Sgt Richard Emrys Jones, 22, husband of Edith, Wallasey. Rake Lane Cemetery, Wallasey.

(F/Lt L B Owen survived)

3 December, Leipzig.

ED920, 630 Squadron.

P/O John Syme, pilot, 26, Adelaide, South Australia. Runnymede.

Sgt Eric Hubbert, navigator, 21, Swinton. Runnymede.

F/O John Christopher Doherty, bomb aimer, 22, Carshalton Beeches. Berlin War Cemetery.

Sgt James Heron, rear gunner, 22, Gateshead. Berlin War Cemetery.

16 December, Berlin.

EE188 WS/B. Crew buried at Reichswald Forest War Cemetery.

F/O Ian Campbell Bennett Black, 21, Aberdeen.

Sgt Edward Lionel Button.

F/O George Edward McTaggart, Vancouver, British Columbia.

F/Sgt George Brothers, 29, husband of Alice, Liverpool.

Sgt Albert Elvin Baumann, 22, Portslade.

Sgt Norman Ellis Adams, 21, Norwich.

Sgt Douglas Travell Gordon, 26, St Helens.

DV293 WS/Y. Crew buried at Berlin War Cemetery.

P/O Richard Anthony Bayldon, 20, Hove.

Sgt Francis Sidney Cope, 21, Cheam.

F/O Bernard Otter, 31, husband of Gwendolen Jessie, Gainsborough.

Sgt John Kendal Widdop.

Sgt Edward Egan.

Sgt Raymond John Baroni, Glendale, California.

Sgt Arnold Richardson, Sheffield.

JB119 OF/F, 97 Squadron.

P/O John Towler Pratt DFM, flight engineer, Clitheroe. Clitheroe Cemetery.

F/O William Alfred Colson DFM, bomb aimer, 28, husband of Florence Amelia. Willesden New Cemetery.

JA963 OF/Q, 97 Squadron.

F/Lt David James Brill, pilot, 22, Corsham. Runnymede.

Sgt Harry Chappell, w/op, 23, Southey. Berlin War Cemetery.

P/O Gordon James Little, mid-upper gunner, 21, Canada. Berlin War Cemetery.

F/Sgt Ernest John Battle, rear gunner, 22, Rose Bay, New South Wales. Berlin War Cemetery.

20 December, Frankfurt.

ED700 WS/O

F/Sgt Vincent Cooke Lindsay Knox, rear gunner, 19, Victoria, British Columbia. Runnymede.

1944

2 January, Berlin.

JA711 WS/A. Crew buried at Hannover War Cemetary.

F/O Geoffrey Ward, 23, Dewsbury.

Sgt Jack Sutton.

Sgt Eric Douglas Keene.

F/Sgt George Lloyd James.

Sgt George Frederick Kenneth Bedwell, 24, husband of Joan Louisa, Saxmundham.

Sgt Norman Frederick Dixon, 19, Old Balderton.

W/O2 Willard Lawrence Doran, 21, Edmonton, Alberta.

14 January, Brunswick.

ED721 WS/S. Five crew buried at Hannover War Cemetery.

F/O Edward James Argent, 20, St Margaret's, Middlesex.

(Sgt W Lyons POW)

F/O Frederick Edward Forshew, 23, Strood.

(Sgt H T Jolliffe POW)

Sgt George Fradley.

F/Sgt Alfred Kenneth Trevena, 23, Hawthorn, Victoria.

W/O2 David Alexander Powley.

27 January, Berlin.

LL745 WS/M. Four crew buried at Dürnbach War Cemetary.

F/Lt Stanley James, 19, Harrow.

P/O George Robert Tomlinson, 21, Clitheroe.

F/Sgt Austin William Archer.

(F/Sgt A Howie POW)

Sgt Ronald Ernest Burke, 22, Andover.

(Sgt M W Chivers POW)

(F/Sgt H Croxson POW)

19 February, Leipzig.
W5010 WS/L. Crew buried at Berlin War Cemetery.
F/Sgt Denis Percy John Denny Froud, 22, Leyton.
Sgt Fred Harman.
Sgt David Brynmor Carlick, 21, Treharris.
F/Sgt Leonard Thomas Fairclough, 20, Adlington.
Sgt Wilfred Henry Shirley, 19, Langley.
Sgt Stanley Lewis Jones.
F/Sgt Robert Lloyd Biers, 19, Cochrane, Ontario.

20 February, Stuttgart.
ED654 WS/W. Crew buried at Dürnbach War Cemetery.
P/O William John Chambers, 23, Ilford.
Sgt William Edward Haywood, 20, Richmond (Surrey).
W/O James Braithwaite Mandall, 26, Rosgill.
Technical Sgt James John Hannon USAAF, Bronx, New York City.
Sgt Illtyd Melville Mulcuck, 23, husband of Madge, Cilfynydd.
Sgt Arthur Llewellyn Steward, 19, Northwold.
F/Sgt James John Campbell, 21, Naracoorte, South Australia.

LM447 WS/K. Crew commemorated at Runnymede.
P/O Patrick Eric Norman Nice, 23, Streatham.
Sgt Peter James Vincent Pitcher, 20, Leicester.
F/Sgt David Isadore Cohen.
Sgt Felix Fitzsimmons.
Sgt James Tomlinson, 21, Hull.
Sgt Albert Chappell, 19, Cadishead.
Sgt Frederick Samuel Coote, 23, Attleborough (Warwickshire).

24 February, Schweinfurt.
LM433 WS/H. Crew buried at Dürnbach War Cemetery.
P/O George James Denson.
Sgt Colin Barry Todd, 19, Colchester.
Sgt John Marcel Charlier, Ben Rhydding.
Sgt David Waldie Marshall.
Sgt Herbert Alfred Masters, 23, Bournemouth.
Sgt Stephan August Loftson, 20, Lundar, Manitoba.
Sgt Leonard Edward Parker, 19, Selly Oak.

15 March, Stuttgart

HK540 WS/H. Five crew buried at Dürnbach War Cemetery.
(Sq/Ldr Backwell-Smith POW)
(Sgt N V Sirman POW)
F/O Herbert Keith Sheasby, 31, husband of Marjorie Eileen, Shirley.
P/O Douglas Raymond Eley, Victoria BC.
Sgt Ronald West, 21, Nottingham.
Sgt Brian Glover, 19, Didsbury.
F/Sgt Eric Alfred Birrell, 21, Mount Gambier, South Australia.

JB361 OF/B, 97 Squadron.
F/Lt William Alexander Meyer DFC, pilot, 34, London. Dürnbach War
   Cemetery.

22 March, Frankfurt.
LM422 WS/N. Crew buried at Rheinburg War Cemetery.
P/O Angus James Jubb, 26, Hexham, Victoria.
Sgt Sidney Lascelles Fereday.
Sgt John Noel Carter, 21, Port Isaac.
F/O Richard Charles Collins, Canada.
F/Sgt Allan Clyde Johns, 21, Broken Hill, New South Wales.
Sgt Richard Whalley, 28, husband of Elsie, Blackpool.
Sgt Frank Bolton, 19, Liverpool.

LM430 WS/B. Seven crew buried at Brussels Town Cemetery.
F/O Albert Edward Manning, 28, husband of Lilian, Ipswich.
Sgt William Frederick Burkitt, 22, Hornsey.
F/O James White Hearn, 30, Bonnyrigg.
W/O Peter Warywoda, Canada.
(F/Sgt G T M Caines POW)
Sgt John Joseph Zammit.
F/Sgt Arthur Finch.
Gp/Capt Norman Charles Pleasance, station CO, passenger.

28 March, Horncastle.
LM432 WS/O.
P/O Kenneth Leslie Porter, pilot, 20, Worcester Park. Sutton and Cheam
   Cemetery.

29 March, after escape from Stalag Luft III, Sagan.
Buried at Poznan Old Garrison Cemetery.
Sq/Ldr Thomas Gresham Kirby-Green, pilot, 9 and 40 Squadrons.
F/Lt Leslie George Bull DFC, pilot, 9 and 109 Squadrons.

30 March, Nürnburg.
W5006 WS/X. Six crew buried at Hannover War Cemetery.
F/O James Gordon Richmond Ling, 23, Newmins.
Sgt Leonard Moss, 19, Manchester.
(Sgt H Laws POW)
F/Sgt Thomas Santola Fletcher.
Sgt Edgar Alexander Gauld, 23, Aberdeen.
Sgt Edward James Rush, 22, husband of Hazel Jean, Calgary, Alberta.
Sgt Italo Prada.

ED502 WS/V.
Sgt Bernard Thomas Utting, mid-upper gunner, 22, Hempton. Fakenham
    Cemetery.

10 April, Tours.
DV198 WS/U. Six crew buried at Nantes Communal Cemetery.
W/O Colin Albert Peak, 21, Tursmore, South Australia.
Sgt Eric Warnford Kindred, 27, Rainworth.
Sgt Thomas William Varey, 33, husband of Doris May, Hurst (Berkshire).
F/O John Enoch Wilkes, Barrington, Rhode Island. US Military Cemetery,
    St-Laurent-du-Mer.
Sgt Vernon William George Torbett, 21, Hadley.
Sgt John Weir Nelson, 23, Lanark.
Sgt John Hogan, 22, Liverpool.

13 April, Breslau after escape from Stalag Luft III, Sagan.
F/Lt James Leslie Robert Long, pilot. Poznan Old Garrison Cemetery.

18 April, Juvisy.
LM361 WS/T. Four crew buried at Clichy Northern Cemetery.
Sgt Ronald Wilson, flight engineer.
F/Sgt Dennis Elvet Moss, navigator, 21, Willenhall.
Sgt Frank Heath, w/op, 22, Witley.
Sgt Dudley Clive Bates, rear gunner, 20, Brisbane, Queensland.

23 April, Brunswick.
ME724 WS/O.
F/Sgt David Henry Williams, navigator, 23. Reichswald Forest War
    Cemetery.
Sgt Ronald Hydes, mid-upper gunner. Hannover War Cemetery.
Sgt Stephen Grove, rear gunner, 19, Tredegar. Hannover War Cemetery.

25 April, Munich.
LM445 WS/O. Crew buried at Dürnbach War Cemetery.
Sq/Ldr Brian Montgomery Gilmour DFC, New Zealand.
F/Sgt Ernest Edward James Patmore, 23, Camberwell.
F/Lt Clifton Francis Benefield DFC, 25, Wanganui, New Zealand.
P/O Sidney Arthur Jeapes, 27, Edmonton.
F/O Arthur Hewitt Milward, 27, Monkseaton.
F/Lt Kenneth Charles Hoad DFC, 32, Eastbourne.
Sgt William Bingham, 22, Prescot.

27 April, Friedrichshafen.
JB676 MG/K, 7 Squadron.
F/Lt Leslie Dennis Goldingay* DFC, bomb aimer, Wallasey. Dürnbach
    War Cemetery.

3 May, Mailly-le-Camp.
LL787 WS/Y. Five crew buried at Normee Churchyard, Marne.
F/O James Frank Ineson, 22, husband of Monica, New Farnley.
P/O Leonard Charles Margetts, 29, husband of Frances Christine,
    Edinburgh.
P/O Hugh Fraser Mackenzie, 21, Spirit River, Alberta.
(F/O T L M Porteous, New Zealnd, POW)
Sgt Henry Robert Warren.
(Sgt H S Chappell evaded)
Sgt James Wilkinson.

10 May, Lille.
LM528 WS/D. Four crew buried at Hellemmes-Lille Cemetery.
P/O Hugh Donald Campbell, 23, husband of Jean Elizabeth, Gatton,
    Queensland.
Sgt Elliott Fullerton, 19, Leigh.
F/O Arthur Bennett, 25, Whalley.
F/O Albert Edward Tyne, 33, husband of Beatrice May, Penshurst, New
    South Wales, Forest-sur-Marque Communal Cemetery.
Sgt Jack William Logg Parker, 24, Leeds, Runnymede.
Sgt James Henry Butler, Forest-sur-Marque Communal Cemetery.
F/O Hubert Edward Botting, 33, husband of Mary Ann, Hove.

LM520 WS/X. Four crew buried at Forest-Sur-Marque Communal
    Cemetery.
P/O Alan Gregory Stafford, 22, Dunedin, New Zealand.

Sgt Henry Charles Dixey, 19, Kelowna, British Columbia.
Sgt Edward Bancroft Hudson, Enfield.
F/L Gilbert Bell DFC, Exeter. Runnymede.
Sgt Harold William Matthews, 22, Shoreham. Runnymede.
Sgt Donald Antony Cato, 19, Flixton (Lancashire). Runnymede.
F/Sgt Walter John White, 23, Cloncurry, Queensland.

11 May, Bourg Leopold.
ND951 WS/Z. Crew buried at Wilsele Churchyard, Leuven.
P/O Maurice Bunnagar, 20, Irby.
Sgt Russell Frederick Leggitt, 20, Lowestoft.
Sgt Arthur Ian Henderson, 20, Crosby.
F/O John Tudor Isfan, 27, Dysart, Saskatchewan.
Sgt John Albert Chambers.
Sgt Bernard Gordon Easterlow, 21, husband of Cynthia, Coventry.
Sgt Ronald George Thomas Watson, 20, Portsmouth.

21 May, Duisburg.
DV295 WS/T. Crew commemorated at Runnymede.
F/Sgt Raymond Summers Cornelius, 22, husband of Ellen.
Sgt Frederick Frank Violett, 19, Oxley.
F/Sgt James Leslie Gledhill, 23, husband of Margaret, Westminster.
Sgt Alexander Porter, 20, Carlisle.
Sgt Leslie Frank Chappell, 22, Wallesey.
Sgt Ralph James Hawksworth, 19, Sheffield.
Sgt Joseph Marshall, 24, husband of Maleta, Malton.

22 May, Brunswick.
LM519 WS/N. Crew buried at Reichswald Forest War Cemetery.
P/O Leslie Jack Baker, 22, Raynes Park.
P/O Eric James Brittain, 28, husband of Dorothy.
(Sgt W E Stephenson POW)
F/O Joseph McKee.
Sgt Richard William England.
Sgt George Gow, 20.
Sgt Norman Reginald Pike.

6 June, St-Pierre.
ND739 OF/Z, 97 Squadron.
F/O Henry William Edward Jeffery DFM, bomb aimer, 22, Southall.
  Runnymede.

7 June, Belvoir Castle after Argentan.
ME579 WS/A.
P/O Clifford Roy King, 23, husband of Kathleen, Boscombe. City of
London Cemetery.
Sgt Rubin Iain Hood. Newport Cemetery, Lincoln.
P/O James Morton Stevenson, 20, New York City. Stonefall Cemetery,
Harrogate.
Sgt Frank Norman Harder, 23, Southampton. South Stoneham Cemetery.
F/Sgt Edward Arthur Hannah, husband of Jean, Stowmarket. Runnymede.
Sgt William Frederick Smith, husband of Molly, Ontario. Stonefall
Cemetery, Harrogate.
(Sgt G Hasson, rear gunner, survived)

21 June, Scholven-Buer.
ME704 WS/B.
F/O Lorne Sinclair McMurchy, pilot, husband of Lucy, Calgary, Alberta.
Groesbeek Canadian War Cemetery.
Sgt Philip Bowen-Chennell, w/op. Ede Cemetery.
Sgt Donald Andrew Harvey Redshaw, rear gunner, 18, Lethbridge,
Alberta. Amersfoort Cemetery.

LM548 WS/C.
F/O Alfred Kidd, bomb aimer. Reichswald Forest War Cemetery.

24 June, Prouville.
ND948 WS/H. Crew buried at Yvrencheux Churchyard.
P/O Ronald Henry Craig, 20, Liverpool.
Sgt Cyril Edward Hansford, 19, Parkstone.
F/Sgt Gordon Ernest Freeman.
(F/Sgt K Hughes POW)
Sgt Arthur Rex Marwood, 22, Shap.
(F/O R R Nightingale POW)
Sgt Denis Victor George Smith.

LL853 WS/W. Crew buried at Coulonvillers Cemetery.
F/Sgt John Edward Halshaw, 21, Bacup.
Sgt David Arthur Keith Davison, 22, Southend.
P/O Herbert Blaydes, 28, husband of Marguerite Marie, St James,
Manitoba.
F/Sgt Norman Wells Brown.
W/O Richard William Agg DFM.
Sgt Stanley James Abbott.

(Sgt Henry Garratt POW)
(Sgt William Wilson, extra gunner, POW)

LL970 WS/Y. Five crew buried at Longuenesse Souvenir Cemetery, St Omer.
P/O Harold Oliver Rae, Canada.
Sgt Lawrence Albert Dolby, 24, Derby.
Sgt John Elias Jones, 23, Flint. Auxi-le-Château Cemetery.
F/Sgt Arthur Jack Lewis, 34, Laindon.
Sgt William Hubert Wells, 23, East Grinstead.
(Sgt D R Grant POW)
P/O Francis Lawrence Rey, 19, Victoria, British Columbia.

4 July, St Leu d'Esserant.
LL785 WS/F. Seven crew buried at Criel Communal Cemetery.
P/O Dennis William Ryan, 21, Edgware.
F/Lt James Victor Patrick, 23, second pilot, husband of Ruth Margaret, New Zealand.
Sgt Harold Peter Frank Eveleigh, 19, Broadstairs.
F/Sgt Ian Archibald Buchanan, 32, Oswestry.
F/Sgt Victor Henry Grayson, 21, Cheam.
Sgt Ronald James Atkin, 22, Skegness. Marissel National Cemetery, Oise.
F/Sgt Stanley Edward William Marshall, 20, Fulham.
Sgt James Thomas Theaker, 31, husband of Barbara, Leeds.

7 July, St Leu d'Esserant.
JB116 WS/T. Four crew buried at Millebosc Communal Cemetery.
(P/O G A Langford POW)
(Sgt C G Fenn POW)
F/Sgt John Llewellyn Wright.
(F/Sgt S M Mitchell POW)
Sgt Israel Feldman, 22, Southall.
P/O James Wright, 19, Toronto, Ontario.
F/O Geoffrey Thomas Baseden, 38, husband of Vera Lucy, Blackheath.

JA957 WS/D. Six crew buried at Ecquevilly Communal Cemetery, Yvelines.
F/O Peter Douglas Blackham.
(Sgt J D Massie evaded)
F/O John Wenger, 26, Regina, Saskatchewan.
F/O Douglas Elphick, 25, Catharines, Ontario.

F/O George Albert White, 27, Markham, Ontario.
Sgt Victor Clement Arthur Stokes, 20, Smethwick.
P/O James Martin Hickey, 31, husband of Jean, Peterborough, Ontario.

JA690 WS/M.
Sgt James Thomas Price, 21, wireless operator, Hugglescote. Beaumont-les-Nonaines Communal Cemetery, Oise.

13 July, Culmont-Chalindrey.
LM221 WS/K. Crew buried at Cour L'Eveque Churchyard.
F/O William Alfred Martin Hallett, 21, Fort Vermilion, Alberta.
Sgt Allan Fleming Grieve, 19, Kirkaldy.
F/O John Frederick Armstrong, 21, Victoria, British Columbia.
F/Sgt Donald George Wentworth Brown, 24, Lane Cove, New South Wales.
Sgt Frank Everett Shaw, 21, Norwich.
F/Sgt Allen Douglas Tagget, 26, husband of Ethel Mildred.
F/Sgt Malcolm Henry Payne, 22, Karoonda, South Australia.

19 July, Revigny-sur-Ornain.
ME833 WS/Z. Five crew buried at Somsois Churchyard.
P/O Leslie John Wood.
Sgt Michael Terence Gordon.
(F/Sgt N Oates, POW)
Sgt Leslie Richard Lutwyche, 21, Birmingham. Chatelraould St Louvent Churchyard.
Sgt David George Mumford, 21, Plymouth.
Sgt Neil Hannah.
P/O Joseph Edward Shuster, 21, Toronto, Ontario.

21 July, Courtrai.
PD205 WS/H. Six crew buried at Wevelgem Communal Cemetery.
F/O Graham Robert Garlick, 20, Wembley Park.
Sgt Frank William Mills, 30, husband of Florence May, Ponder's End.
F/Sgt Kenneth Charles Stuart, 30, husband of Helen Rafferty, Glasgow.
P/O John Howard Morriss. Adagem Canadian War Cemetery.
Sgt Douglas Walter Dagger, 21, West Dulwich.
F/Sgt Roy Haywood Barnes, 20, Long Melford.
Sgt Thomas Woodman Elliott, 21, Newcastle-upon-Tyne.

27 July, Givors.
ND856 OL/E, 83 Squadron.

F/Lt John Gilmour* DFM, navigator/H2S op, 24, Glasgow. Mazargues War Cemetery.

29 July, Stuttgart.
ME615 JO/V, 463 Squadron.
F/Lt Brian Moorhead* DFC, rear gunner, Choloy War Cemetery.

31 July, Rilly-la-Montagne.
LM453 WS/E. Crew buried at Clichy Northern Cemetery.
F/O Charles Edward Michael Worner.
Sgt William Edward Moseley, 19, Nottingham.
P/O Thomas James Peacore.
P/O Robert Francis McKinney, 20, Winnipeg, Manitoba.
F/Sgt William David Phillips, 20, Pencoed.
Sgt John Stodart Anderson, 19, Crossford (Lanarkshire).
Sgt John Kerfoot, 21, Batley, husband of Margaret.

8 August, Mare de Magne.
ND817 6O/S, 582 Squadron.
F/O Reginald William Blaydon* DFM, w/op, 29, Sutton (Cambridgeshire). St Vigor d'Ymonville Churchyard.

13 August, Brest.
ME757 WS/O. Six crew buried at Plougastel-Daoulas Communal Cemetery.
F/Lt Edward Harry Maxwell Relton, 34.
Sgt Frederick Walter Johnson, 23, East Ham.
F/Sgt Charles Herbert Edwards, 23, Gympie, Queensland.
F/Sgt John Keith Scott, 21, Beechmont, Queensland.
F/Sgt Cyril Thomas Scott, 28, husband of Caroline, Matraville, New South Wales.
F/Sgt Douglas William McConville, 27, Narrandera, New South Wales.
F/Sgt William Ronald Andrew, 22, Bell, Queensland. Hottot-les-Bagues War Cemetery, Calvados.

14 August, Brest.
PB146 WS/A.
Sgt Henry John Tollast, w/op, 18, Thames Ditton. Brookwood Military Cemetery.

17 August, Stettin Bay.

NE167, 97 Squadron.
W/Cdr Edward Leach Porter DFC and Bar, pilot, 33. Poznan Old Garrison
  Cemetery.

25 August, Darmstadt.
PB398 OF/M, 97 Squadron.
Sq/Ldr Stuart Martin Parkeshouse Parkes* DSO, pilot, 24, husband of
  Patricia, Moreton in the Marsh. Dürnbach War Cemetery.

23 September, Münster Aqueduct.
LL901 WS/V. Six crew buried at Holten General Cemetery.
F/Lt Charles Berrie Scott, 22, Glasgow.
Sgt Jack Edward Simkin, 23, Seaford.
F/Sgt Louis Arthur Harding.
(F/Sgt L W Langley POW)
Sgt Maurice Edward Hayward, 21, Ludgershall.
Sgt Frank Alfred Saunders, 30, husband of Ellen, West Kensington.
Sgt Leslie Joseph Hambly, 19, Millom.

LL914 WS/U. Three crew buried at Wierden General Cemetery.
F/O William Begg, 21, Lugar. Runnymede.
Sgt Eric Haskins, 34, Hoylake. Runnymede.
F/Sgt Harold Herbert Joseph Bromley, Farnham. Runnymede.
P/O Timothy Ambrose Harrington, Canada.
Sgt James Moreton. Runnymede.
Sgt Archibald Donald Jones.
Sgt Frederick Wilcock.

Ladbergen.
NF923 KC/M, 617 Squadron.
F/Lt Geoffrey Stevenson Stout DFC, pilot, 23, Whitehaven. Lochem New
  General Cemetery.

19 October, Nürnburg.
LM715 WS/O. Crew buried at Dürnbach War Cemetery.
F/O Richard Davies.
Sgt Edward Morgan Penry Rice, 21, Swansea.
Sgt Harold Victor Ward, 20, Kirk Ireton.
F/Sgt Clifford Dudley Richards, 21, Llanelli.
F/Sgt Ernest Newman.
F/Sgt Robert Marr, 23, North Berwick.
Sgt Leonard Phillips, 19, Skewen.

11 November.

PB450 OF/D, 97 Squadron. Crew commemorated at Runnymede.

F/Lt John Seymour Runnacles*, pilot, 31, husband of Dorothy Beatrice, Sproughton. Runnymede.

21 December, Bardney after Pölitz.

PD213 WS/F.

Sgt Edward Arthur White, flight engineer, 19, Rotherham. St Leonard's Old Churchyard, Thrybergh.

F/Sgt Victor Sinclair Willis, bomb aimer, 23, Bradfield (Yorkshire). St Nicholas's Churchyard, Bradfield.

1945

1 January, Bardney.

NG252 WS/R. Three crew buried at Stonefall Cemetery, Harrogate.

F/O Clifford Sinclair Newton, Rosewood, Michigan.

Sgt Colin Booth, 31, husband of Dora, Brighouse. Brighouse Cemetery.

P/O Percy Grant, 30, husband of Constance, Streatham. London Road Cemetery, Mitcham.

(P/O R C Flynn injured)

Sgt Lawrence Gerard Kelly, 23, Oldham. Greenacres Cemetery, Oldham.

F/Sgt Edgar Harvey Cooper, 21, Washago, Ontario.

P/O Robert Slade Stevens, 21, husband of Margaret Jean, Canada.

Ladbergen.

NG223 WS/D. Four crew buried at Reichswald Forest War Cemetery.

F/O Peter William Reaks.

Sgt Thomas Scott, 19, Selkirk.

(F/Sgt F Alton POW)

P/O Edward Percy Bates, 31, Neston.

F/Sgt Stanley William Guy Currigan, 23, Dagenham.

(Sgt V Peace POW)

(Sgt G Bamforth POW)

PD377 WS/U.

F/Sgt George Thompson VC, w/op, 24, Glencraig, died 23 January. Brussels Town Cemetery.

Sgt Ernest John Potts, mid-upper gunner, 30, husband of Bessie, Newport (Monmouthshire), died 2 January.

12 January, Bergen.

NG257 WS/N. Crew commemorated at Runnymede.
F/O Ernest Cyril Redfern DFC, 22, husband of Frances, Salford.
F/Sgt John Walter Williams, 20, Trimdon.
Sgt Ronald William Riverston Cooper, 22, Welling.
F/O Owen Percy Hull.
Sgt Lewis George Roberts, 23, husband of Lydia Jean, Ilsington.
Sgt Walter Brand, 28, Sheffield.
Sgt Dennis Winch, 20, Grantham.

14 January, Leuna.
NN722 WS/Q. Six crew buried at Choloy War Cemetery, Meurthe-et-Moselle.
F/O Keith Alan Cook, 21, North Ballarat, Victoria.
Sgt Howard Taylor, 19, Bridlington.
F/Sgt Robert Watt, 28, Johnstone.
F/Sgt Bruce Cowper MacKnight, 20, Cremorne, New South Wales.
F/Sgt Maurice James McNamara, 32, Melbourne, Victoria.
F/Sgt John Erskine Brown MacLean, 21, Toowoomba, Queensland.
F/Sgt Michael John Kerrigan, 27, South Hurstville, New South Wales, POW, died 22 March. Berlin 1939–1945 War Cemetery.

14 February, Altenbeken.
NF937 WS/E. Crew buried at Rheinburg War Cemetery.
F/Lt John Joseph Dunne DFC, 22, East Brighton, Victoria.
Sgt Horace John Ockerby.
P/O Maurice Joseph Thain.
F/O Cuthbert Lawson Philpott.
F/Sgt James William Knight.
P/O John Thomas Rose, Canada.
F/Sgt John Frederick Jordan, 29, husband of Rose May, Birmingham.

7 April, Wantage after Molbis.
HK788 WS/E. Crew buried at Botley Cemetery, Oxford.
F/O Alfred Edward Jeffs, 29, husband of Bessie Margaret, Birmingham.
Sgt Clarence Victor Higgins, 23, husband of Irene, Birmingham.
F/Sgt Kenneth Charles Mousley, 36, husband of Miriam Grace, Streatham.
W/O2 Hugh Alexander Fisher, 24, Dauphin, Manitoba.
F/Sgt Campbell McIntosh McMillan, 20, husband of Betty, Kettlethorpe.
F/Sgt Willy Thomas, 20, Cleckheaton.
F/Sgt Gordon John Symonds, 20, Wantage.

8 April, Lutzkendorf.

NG235 WS/H. Six crew buried at Berlin War Cemetery.

F/O Bernard Selby Woolstencroft, 21, Newport, Victoria.

Sgt William Charles Lewis.

F/Sgt Lindsay Arthur Bailey, 29, husband of Valma Eileen, Coogee, New South Wales.

F/O Christopher Paul Wyeth Warren, 20, Shawford.

F/Sgt Leslie Robinson.

Sgt Geoffrey Terence Greenwood, 20, Bradford.

(Sgt E Williams POW)

20 April, Windlesham.

Stirling LJ930, 190 Squadron.

W/Cmdr Richard Henry Bunker DSO, DFC and Bar, pilot, 25, husband of Stella. Brookwood Military Cemetery.

Bibliography and Sources

Operations Record Book, Combat Reports and Squadron Archive, No. 9
Squadron.
RAF Bomber Command Losses of the Second World War, vols 1 to 6. W
R Chorley 1992 ff.
The Bomber Command War Diaries. Martin Middlebrook and Chris
Everitt 1985.
The Luftwaffe War Diaries. Cajus Becker 1964.
Despatch on War Operations. Sir Arthur T Harris 1995.
Evaders' and other records from the Public Record Office and the National
Archives.
Commonwealth War Graves Commission.
How the RAF Works. A H Narracott 1941.
Pilot's and Flight Engineer's Notes – Lancaster. Air Ministry 1944.
RAF Operational Diary, Operation Paravane. Squadron Leader E S
Harman.
9 Squadron. T Mason 1965.
A WAAF in Bomber Command. Pip Beck 1989.
313 Days to Christmas. Alan Mackay 1998.
Moonless Night. B A 'Jimmy' James 1983.
The Third Son as Night Bomber. Mike Dee 2002.
Lancaster Valour. Clayton Moore 1995.
Before the Dawn. Jim Brookbank 1984.
We Sat Alone. Fred Whitfield and Tony Eaton 1998.
T.A.B.S. (9 Squadron Association) magazines, 1981 ff.
Wellington at War. Chaz Bowyer 1982.
Luck and a Lancaster. Harry Yates DFC 1999.
Lancaster to Berlin. Walter Thompson DFC & Bar 1985.
The Brave Die Never. Jean Barclay 1993.
'No. 9 Squadron Diary', *Aviation News*. Bill Chorley.
'The Battle of Heligoland Bight', *FlyPast Magazine*. John Foreman and
Christopher P Shores.
The Lancaster Story. Peter Jacobs 2002.
A Hell of a Bomb. Stephen Flower 2002.
Aviation, an Illustrated History. Christopher Chant 1978.
Battle of Britain. Len Deighton 1980.
Sledgehammers for Tintacks. Steve Darley 2002.

Die deutschen Ubootbunker und Bunkerwerften. Sönke Neitzel.

Quand les Alliés bombardaient la France. Eddy Florentin.

The Mare's Nest. David Irvine 1964.

Into Thin Air. Nigel Press 2001.

The Air War in Europe. Ronald H Bailey 1981.

617 Squadron, the Dambusters at War. Tom Bennett 1986.

Avro Lancaster, the definitive record. Harry Holmes 1997.

Tirpitz, *hunting the beast*. John Sweetman 2000.

British Aircraft of World War II. John Frayn Turner 1975.

VCs of the Air. John Frayn Turner 1993.

British Bombers of World War Two, vol 1. Moyes.

The Dambusters. Paul Brickhill 1951.

The Lancaster at War, vols 1, 2, 3 & 5. Mike Garbett & Brian Goulding 1971 ff.

The Great Escape. Paul Brickhill 1952.

Countdown to Victory. Karen Farrington 1995.

The Air War in Europe. Ronald H Bailey 1981.

The War in the Air. Gavin Lyall 1968.

www.rafcommands.com

www.raf.mod.uk

www.467463raafsquadrons.com

www.armyairforces.com

and various RAF, RCAF, USAAF and WW2 history websites.

INDEX